FINANCIAL
INSTITUTION
STAFFING

FINANCIAL INSTITUTION STAFFING

Analyzing and Modeling Staff
Levels in a Competitive and
Consolidating Industry

KENT S. BELASCO
Executive Vice President
Chief Information Officer
First Midwest Bank, N.A.
Itasca, Illinois

McGraw-Hill

New York San Francisco Washington, D.C. Auckland Bogotá
Caracas Lisbon London Madrid Mexico City Milan
Montreal New Delhi San Juan Singapore
Sydney Tokyo Toronto

332.1068
B42f

Library of Congress Cataloging-in-Publication Data

Belasco, Kent S.
 Financial institution staffing
 analyzing & modeling staffing levels in a competitive and consolidating industry
 / Kent S. Belasco.
   p.   cm.
 Includes index.
 ISBN 0-7863-1106-1
 1. Banks and banking—Personal management.   2. Bank employees.
 3. Bank employees—Effect of technological innovations on.   4. Financial institutions—
 Employees.   I. Title.
 HG1615.5.B45   1997
 332.1'068'3—dc21   97-9645

McGraw-Hill

*A Division of The **McGraw·Hill** Companies*

1 2 3 4 5 6 7 8 9 0   DOC/DOC   9 0 2 1 0 9 8 7

ISBN 0-7863-1106-1

The sponsoring editor for this book was Jim Keefe, the managing editor was Kevin Thornton, the editing supervisor was Donna Namorato, and the production supervisor was Suzanne W. B. Rapcavage. It was set in Palatino by Judy Brown.

Printed and bound by R. R. Donnelley & Sons Company.

This publication is designed to provide accurate and authoritative information in regard to the subject matter covered. It is sold with the understanding that neither the author or the publisher is engaged in rendering legal, accounting, or other professional service. If legal advice or other expert assistance is required, the services of a competent professional person should be sought.

  —*From a Declaration of Principles jointly adopted by a Committee*
  of the American Bar Association and a Committee of Publishers.

McGraw-Hill books are available at special quantity discounts to use as premiums and sales promotions, or for use in corporate training programs. For more information, please write to the Director of Special Sales, McGraw-Hill, 11 West 19th Street, New York, NY 10011. Or contact your local bookstore.

 This book is printed on recycled, acid-free paper containing a minimum of 50% recycled de-inked fiber.

This book is dedicated to all managers who know and understand the challenges of effectively managing our most important asset, employees.

Special acknowledgments are given to pioneers of management science, such as Frederick Taylor, who provided an ample foundation for understanding the dynamics of productivity and efficiency and whose theories continue to play a role today.

CONTENTS

Chapter 1

Staffing the Teller Area   1

Chapter 2

Commercial Lender and Support Staffing   43

Chapter 3

Staffing the Personal Banking and Support Area   159

LIST OF FIGURES

Peter Drucker once said, "The single greatest challenge facing managers in the west today is to raise the productivity of knowledge and service workers. Productivity will dominate management thinking for many decades." This powerful statement emphasizes the on-going management need to understand and optimize the deployment of our most expensive asset, human resources.

Financial Institution Staffing is about managing staff size and scientifically analyzing both work processes and productivity. As Drucker points out, this need is not going away even with the changes occurring as a result of information technology. Because of the speed with which work processes can change, managers must understand more than ever the dynamics involved in determining and maintaining optimal staff size to promote efficient and profitable operations.

The staffing models and procedures contained in this book are designed to aid managers in understanding, analyzing, and maintaining optimal levels of staff to promote efficiency, to quickly predict staff levels in the case of acquisitions, and to leverage the opportunities available from the deployment of information technology. When new technology is installed, work processes are not always totally replaced, they change. When this occurs, management's challenge is to quickly assess the impact that this has on staff levels. This can only be accomplished through an understanding of the work process and the ability to access the tools to scientifically determine the staffing complement needed to perform the job. This is of paramount importance because the addition of technology adds to the cost of performing the job. If no consideration is provided for, the changes in work processes occurring as a result of this will be likely to present no change in the staff complement, and therefore the efficiency of the department will decline because more will be spent to do the same job. This constant balancing act is a "must" exercise for any manager today. Scientifically analyzing optimal staffing levels provides the methodology and tools to ensure that the "right" staff level is used especially when changes to the work process occur.

With the constant growth of information technology, business managers are continually confronted with a myriad of options for performing the tasks and work processes they are paid to manage. In some cases, information technology can change or even eliminate manual processes. It does not, however, change the output. This almost always remains the same. Nevertheless, technology is a fact of life and is purchased, installed, and used regularly in the world today. In most cases, the computers we use today don't necessarily eliminate the work process, they change it. It is up to the manager to staff the function in conjunction with the technology by changing the behavior to capitalize on the power brought about by the technology.

Unfortunately, this is no simple task considering the speed with which technology is changing. The ability to quickly assess staffing complements for labor-intensive functions using scientifically derived models, as contained in this publication, provide managers with not only a powerful tool, but also an understanding of the elements that go into its makeup. This is a necessity for management today. Human involvement in the work process will remain, only the amount of staff deployed will change. In this regard, the need for scientific analysis of the work process and the ability to consistently monitor staff levels will only grow in importance. Managers must still manage but now they must manage a work process that has changed as a result of technology.

In short, in the banking world people (staff) are not going away. More than ever the need to optimize the level of staff becomes an even greater challenge because a new element of cost has been added—the cost of technology. In the past, the predominant resource relied upon was the human resource to perform the work. Managing how effectively and efficiently humans performed work was a challenge of management in the last 1800s. Today, this challenge has doubled. Managers must now balance the management of human and technical resources, both of which have a substantial price tag on the operating expense of the bank.

In some regards, the proliferation of information technology has created a false sense of comfort that the technology will automatically optimize the amount of human intervention required. As a result, scientific analysis of the work process is often forgotten. More than ever the need to model staff levels and understand the dynamics of the work process are a must for the business world today. The true challenge of managers today will be to leverage the power of the technology on the work processes they manage and balance the combined efforts of human and technical resources to achieve the greatest level of efficiency and productivity in the work place.

Kent Belasco

INTRODUCTION

Staffing has long been a challenge to management seeking to achieve efficiencies within the organization. Although a fundamental issue, it wasn't until the financial industry was deregulated that staffing became a topic of vital necessity, requiring consideration, planning, and analysis of its impact to the organization. When this occurred, banks became increasingly competitive amongst themselves, but more importantly, they became competitive with nonbanking organizations now offering financial services. Attention shifted to pricing products with the onset of analyzing the costs of providing products and services to the client. These are issues not unknown in the highly competitive manufacturing environment. Now, financial institutions have begun to behave more and more like retail outlets, and rightfully so.

With the considerable increase in competition, it became very obvious that financial institutions could not easily compete on price (rates) alone. As a result, banks have attempted to differentiate themselves on the level of service, quality of service, and attention provided, as well as other ways to attract and retain customers. Among the primary elements which must be considered when products and services are delivered, is the cost to produce one dollar of revenue. This "efficiency ratio" has become a measure of how efficient the bank is in generating revenue based upon the cost of the resources put to bear on generating such revenue. This measure has steadily grown in importance and visibility over the recent years, and now is used to compare one bank to the other in overall performance. This ratio is calculated based upon total revenue to noninterest expense and is expressed as a percent. Noninterest expense, or operating expense, is the overhead and costs of running a business, the largest element of which is salaries.

Salaries are the costs of the employees staffed to perform the various duties of the bank to ultimately provide products and services to customers. The purpose of this book is to emphasize not only the importance of staffing on the overall success of the bank, but also to provide a methodology for analyzing and optimizing staffing throughout the bank in various areas. Today, financial institutions are constantly challenged by both nonbank and bank competitors. Furthermore, consolidations continue to abound. Several years ago 12,000 independent banks existed in the United States. This number is projected to decrease dramatically by the turn of the century. As banks consolidate to increase market share, expand distribution points, or simply to raise share price, staffing will always be a consideration. Given the impact of the consolidated organization on the bank's financial picture, attention must be placed on the economies generated from ongoing consolidations. Economies cannot and will not be achieved until and unless staffing levels are optimized and achieved in an organized, efficient way, to ensure success. The recommendations and models developed in this book are designed to aid bank managers in planning optimum staffing levels, but also to identify, through models, what staff levels may be required in the consolidated environment.

The role of information technology is still in the process of being understood. All would agree that technology is the future and will continue to develop; however, how it is used and how it changes the behaviors and processes which occur in a financial institution is yet to be fully grasped. The goal of information technology is to empower or enable staff employees to garner more information from which to make decisions, and/or to aid them in executing their duties more efficiently. In the latter case, information technology should create an ability to increase the level of productivity of the staff member, so that he or she can handle increased volumes of work. It remains to be seen where information technology will lead the financial industry. In manufacturing, the computer has drastically altered the design of new plants, which are now built taking into consideration the robotics and other automation required, changing the physical layout from those of the past. This evolution has occurred over time and has been instrumental in producing more goods while at the same time improving quality. The auto industry is a good example. In banking however, automation has yet to evolve to that level although the growth of microcomputer technology (hardware and software) is paving the way for more self-activated technologies such as interactive ATMs and automatic loan machines.

The changes that are occurring in this technological, consolidating environment are causing financial institutions to become ever more conscious of the level of efficiency from which products and services are sold. Because technology carries a considerable price tag, and because human workers are expensive, especially when one weighs the cost of competitive benefit structure, the need for emphasizing and monitoring the efficiency ratio is an absolute must. Efficiency ratios in industries such as manufacturing are considerably less than those of financial institutions. The goal of banks is to learn from this and change. How effective the bank is at delivering products and services, and producing income at less cost, will make the difference between the survivors and the losers in the financial industry.

Consolidations will reduce the financial workforce, as will technology. But by how much, and at what level? These questions must still be posed and answered if the financial institution is to be a viable player in the industry. Staffing, and understanding how to scientifically determine optimum levels of staffing, will be crucial to anyone planning mergers and acquisitions as well as for those simply planning to improve their efficiency ratios. This, in conjunction with the incorporation and integration of information technology, is the challenge for at least the next several years and beyond. Staffing levels will be important until truly "self-activated" financial centers become the norm. Even if this comes to pass, the dynamics of standards, volumes, and other staffing elements will be key elements in optimizing costs.

## CHAPTER 1

Staffing the Teller Area

The teller area of a bank is generally the first service point and sales contact point for bank clients. In most cases, the impression and service the teller provides to customers affects their relationship with the bank. Therefore, the teller line usually receives exposure at the CEO level.

When customers enter the bank to transact business, they usually go to the teller line, a personal banker, or a commercial or real estate lender. In the past, the majority of clients entering the bank went to tellers since it was the only means of depositing money, cashing checks, and receiving cash. Today these numbers have been reduced due to the advent of strategically placed automatic teller machines (ATMs). Although arguments continue over whether ATMs have truly reduced teller traffic significantly or not, the fact remains they have had some impact. Since a number of people refuse to use ATMs and prefer the face-to-face contact of a live teller, teller lines remain part of the architecture of banks and an area of considerable attention as a sales and service point. Customers who seek face-to-face contact still expect the competence, consistency, speed, and accuracy of an ATM.

Because of these needs, the bank must not only offer teller services but do so in a way that does not require excessive numbers of employees. In other words, the bank must determine the optimal number of tellers required to meet the volume of traffic and adequately handle the transactions. The approach suggested is to evaluate staffing levels of the teller line scientifically—that is, by determining standards, traffic patterns, and measures.

The scientific analysis of teller staffing levels is not a new concept. Many outside consulting firms offer software packages that analyze transaction volumes and ultimately tell the user how many tellers to staff, by hour. These can be purchased individually or in addition to outside consulting assistance. These systems are generally very good, although they can be expensive and, in some cases, fairly complex. In addition, a teller staffing model does not always explain how teller staffing is developed. This chapter will provide the background for understanding the elements of teller staffing and how to quickly and efficiently build an effective model, designed in-house, using Lotus 1, 2, 3. The model will provide the necessary information for determining optimum teller staffing levels.

METHODOLOGY

The analysis of teller staffing levels involves the interview process, profile development, data gathering, model development, and reports.

Interviews

The first step in determining the elements of staffing is to find out what tellers do. The interviewer confers with a selected number of tellers and develops an outline of functions, issues, and concerns. This forms the basis for the development of a teller profile, which is the foundation of the staffing model.

The interviewer should select a representative number of tellers to confer with at each location. If more than one branch or location is involved, interviews should be conducted at each location, as some of the additional duties may differ. Unlike the other sales areas in this book, tellers spend the majority of their time—as much as 75 percent—handling window transactions, but it is still important to find out what other miscellaneous functions they perform.

During the interview phase, it is important to determine not the amount of time devoted to each function but rather what functions actually occur. For tellers, the interview should focus on two basic types of duties: transactions and nonwindow functions. The teller should be questioned as to the most common types of transactions handled at the window. For most organizations this will fall into a common list: cashing checks, depositing checks, withdrawing savings, making loan payments, issuing travelers' checks, money orders, and cashier's checks, making savings cash-back deposits, and paying utilities bills. But some organizations have special windows or handle a significant volume of bank-specific transactions that must be accounted for. In any event, an effort must be made to compile a list of the types of transactions typically taken at the window.

Once transaction types are recorded, the interviewer must determine the other duties the tellers perform, which generally do not involve customer contact. Virtually all tellers in all financial institutions perform nonwindow duties, beginning with cash drawer setup and ending with cash drawer balancing at the end of the day.

These functions will vary depending on the needs of the organization and its particular location. They may include counting coin and currency or strapping food coupons. In any event, they must be identified and accounted for, so the interviewer should speak with each teller and list the other functions performed on a regular basis. It is important to capture only regular activities, as opposed to those performed when traffic is slow.

Profile Development

The profile development phase funnels the information determined during the interviews into broad outputs or outcomes.

The outputs relate primarily to the key functions or attributes that define a teller's role. Essentially, these are the key volume indicators.

In the case of tellers, the primary output or key volume indicator is the number of transactions handled. Since most tellers spend at least 75 percent of their time at windows, the work actually performed is the processing of customer transactions. This type of output is considered valuable in that the total amount of time required for handling transactions relates directly to the volume taken.

Fixed outputs also exist, involving functions or tasks performed that do not relate to volume. The time required for completing these tasks is generally the same day after day, without concern for actual business volume. One such fixed output that relates to tellers is "other duties;" duties performed regularly unrelated to handling transactions. Included in this group are teller cash drawer setup and balancing, which are performed daily regardless of transaction traffic. Other duties that may be included are counting coin and currency, general receptionist duties, filing, vault-related duties, and so forth. It is important to identify the other duties performed by tellers.

Aside from "other duties," other fixed time commitments affect overall staffing. These include lunches, breaks, meetings, and other general administrative functions. These items can be lumped into two broad categories: personal and administrative.

The teller profile will consist of fixed activities, (personal, administrative, and other duties) and variable activities (window transactions handled).

In other words, these activities account for 100 percent of a teller's time. It is by these activities that time is accounted for and the role of a teller defined. While the personal, administrative, and other duties are not necessarily unique to tellers, the variable duties are.

The teller profile results from the raw data gleaned during the interview process. The breakdown of each activity is also important, although not reflected. During the next stage, the breakdown will be used to obtain detailed information within the broad activities. Figure 1 is an expanded version of these activities.

F I G U R E 1

Teller Profile

1. Fixed activities
   A. Personal
      - Lunches
      - Breaks
      - Other
   B. Administrative
      - Meetings (staff)
      - Telephone calls
   C. Other activities
      - Setup/balancing
      - Coin/currency counting
      - Vault duties
      - Filing
      - Receptionist duties

2. Variable activities
   A. Window transactions
      - Cashing checks
      - Depositing checks
      - Withdrawing savings
      - Depositing savings
      - Recording loan payments
      - Issuing travelers' checks
      - Issuing money orders/cashier's checks
      - Making savings cashback deposits
      - Transacting utility payments

Data Gathering

The teller profile will form the foundation for gathering information about the activities involved. In order to truly understand teller staffing, it is necessary to determine specific data. In most cases, this means determining times and volumes relating to the teller activities.

Using the teller profile as a guide, a teller survey document can be developed similar to that contained in Appendix Exhibit A. The survey document is a questionnaire that asks for information about the fixed and variable activities found in the teller profile. Each teller from the particular bank and/or location should complete the form. In Exhibit A, Sections I through IV merely ask for an estimate or best guess as to the amount of time (minutes) required per item and its frequency. It is important to instruct the respondents to be as accurate as possible without resorting to a stopwatch. All individuals must complete the survey and return it at a designated time to a designated individual. A lack of attention to this could result in a poor response and sketchy information.

Section III of the survey may require more attention than the others. The activities recorded in this section are those determined from the interviews. It is not necessary that each teller perform these activities, but it *is* important to capture all regularly occurring weekly activities. The survey itself, when filled out by the tellers, will indicate who actually performs the duty. Again, instruct the tellers to be as accurate as possible in determining the time required to perform these functions and how often they perform the function each week.

Before circulating the survey, select a time period for its completion that is a typical, normal time in consumer patterns; avoid selecting a holiday period or heavy vacation time. The goal is to obtain a snapshot of what typically occurs to avoid distorting the information.

Although Sections I through IV can be completed in one sitting, Sections V and VI cannot. These production sheets or data-gathering documents must be completed over a period of time and require special handling. Although gathering time information is important, volumes are a necessary ingredient in any staffing analysis. In the case of tellers, this involves the volume of transactions handled through the window. This information can be obtained either manually or automatically through the mainframe computer reports.

Window Transactions

Some mainframe systems capture teller transaction data as they are entered into the teller system, but few segregate the type of transaction actually taking place. This is unfortunate, because different transactions vary in the amount of time they require for completion. Most mainframe systems provide the raw volume of transactions handled, hour by hour, throughout the day. This information is still very valuable and will be used later in the actual model.

If the bank's system does not automatically capture teller transaction volume, it will be necessary to gather this information manually, using the production sheet in Section V, Exhibit A. Even if the bank's system captures raw teller transaction volumes, this manual approach will still be required to isolate and determine the types of transactions occurring.

The first step in analyzing teller transaction volumes is to gain an understanding of the types of transactions occurring. This is accomplished by implementing the production form indicated in the appendix (Exhibit A, Section V) and doing the following:

1. From the data determined in the interviews, record the most common types of teller transactions taken through the window. Since the production sheet should be limited to one page, this is a finite number. If the types of transactions recorded account for 90 to 95 percent of all transactions, the remaining 5 percent can be lumped into an "other" category.

2. Circulate the production sheet to all tellers (including head tellers) at all locations. Provide enough copies of each sheet to cover a 10-day period (two weeks). This should be submitted with the full teller survey (Exhibit A).

3. Instruct all tellers in its usage. Advise them to record the heading information (name, location, date) first. This is very important because some days are much heavier in transaction volumes than others. Explain to the tellers that a new sheet should be completed each day and a tally mark should be recorded for each transaction handled to correspond to the type of transaction and the hour interval in which it occurs. Figure 2 is an example of a completed production form.

FIGURE 2

Teller Daily Production Form

Transaction Type	7:00–8:00	8:00–9:00	9:00–10:00	10:00–11:00	11:00–12:00	12:00–1:00	1:00–2:00	2:00–3:00	3:00–4:00	4:00–5:00	5:00–6:00	6:00–7:00	TOTAL
Cashing checks		卌	卌 卌	卌 卌	卌	=	卌	卌	卌				
Depositing checks	≡												
Savings withdrawals		=		卌	卌	=							
Loan payments							–	–					
Travelers' checks													
Money orders, cashier's checks													
Savings cashback withdrawals													
Utility payments													
Other													
TOTAL													

4. Have all tellers bundle their production forms for the two weeks and turn them into a central collector, usually the head teller or manager. The collector should pass them on to the analyst of the data.
5. The analyst must accumulate the data so that the aggregate volume by hour and by day is totaled for all tellers by location.

At this stage, the analyst has both actual volume data *and* a breakdown of transaction types. The actual volumes can be input into the model if transaction data are not available on the system. The next step is to determine the weighted average time required to handle each transaction.

Since a number of different transactions occur, each requiring a different amount of time for handling, it is desirable to determine a weighted average time which can be used for any transaction. Calculating this information makes it much easier to perform a staffing analysis periodically in the future, because only the raw volume of transactions will be required, not a breakdown by type, since the weighted average time can be applied to any transaction.

At the close of the two-week period, the tellers should have submitted not only the teller production form but also the full survey document (Exhibit A, Sections I–VI). These will provide the necessary data to determine the weighted average time per transaction.

Weighted Average Transaction Time   Determining a weighted average transaction time is a matter of relating the percentage frequency of occurrence of each transaction type to its average time (in minutes) for completion. The total of the factors determined yields the weighted average time per transaction.

Since more than one teller is involved, the first step is to determine the average transaction time, in minutes, for each transaction type listed in the survey (Section IV). Because no actual time study was performed, the average of all teller responses will provide a sufficiently accurate estimate of the time required for each type. Figure 3 shows how this is determined. This sort of spreadsheet organization aids in determining the raw average time per transaction from whence the weighted average will come.

From the average for each transaction, the weighted average can be calculated using the volumes from the teller production form, as shown in Figure 4. The process indicated weights the average transaction time by the percentage of time the transaction takes in relation to the total transactions. This produces a weight factor that, when totaled, shows an overall weighted average transaction time. In this example, 1.78 minutes is the time required, on average, to handle any transaction (regardless of how long it actually takes).

Once the bank knows the weighted average transaction time, it can determine optional staffing levels without having to capture detailed transaction volumes by type. All that is needed now is the raw volume of transactions handled throughout the day. Since many mainframes already captured this data, regular staffing analyses may be conducted more often with much less manual data captured. If the bank's system does not capture the data, a manual count of transactions handled is still much easier than the original analysis, as performed in Figure 2.

Actually, all that is needed is a modified teller production form that requires only transaction volumes by hour, not by type. An example of this modified form is shown in Figure 5. This type of manual capture is not difficult, nor is it disruptive to productivity, so it can be used regularly.

The weighted average transaction time, determined in Figure 4, becomes the variable factor that will be applied in the model. (This will be explained more fully in the next section of this chapter.) Once the weighted average transaction time is determined, it can be used over and over again. Unless a significant change is made to the teller system (for example, an upgrade to newer teller equipment) or the mix in types of transactions taken changes drastically, there is no need to repeat the analysis. To be safe, however, it is recommended that the mix of transactions, time per transaction, and weighted average analysis be conducted every 8 to 12 months even if no change in procedure is made.

FIGURE 3

Average Transaction Times

Transaction Type	Teller #1	Teller #2	Teller #3	Teller #4	Teller #5	Average
			Minutes per Transaction			
Cashing checks	.85	.95	1.10	1.00	1.00	.98
Depositing checks	1.50	1.25	2.00	1.75	1.50	1.60
Savings withdrawals	1.75	2.00	2.00	2.00	1.85	1.92
Loan payments	1.25	1.00	1.00	.95	1.00	1.04
Travelers' checks	7.50	8.00	8.50	7.75	7.00	7.75
Money orders/ cashier's checks	3.00	3.50	4.00	3.50	3.50	3.50
Savings cashback deposits	4.00	4.25	3.75	3.95	3.70	3.93
Utility payments	1.00	1.00	1.25	1.30	1.25	1.16
Other	3.50	3.00	4.25	5.00	4.75	4.10

FIGURE 4

Weighted Average Transaction Time Calculation

Transaction Type	Total Volume Handled	Percent of Total Transactions		Average Minutes per Transaction		Weight Factor
Cashing checks	7,800	19.5%	×	.98	=	.19
Depositing checks	17,320	43.3	×	1.60	=	.69
Savings withdrawals	1,280	3.2	×	1.92	=	.06
Loan payments	5,920	14.8	×	1.04	=	.15
Travelers' checks	120	.3	×	7.75	=	.02
Money orders/ cashier's checks	1,160	2.9	×	3.50	=	.10
Savings cashback deposits	1,400	3.5	×	3.93	=	.14
Utility payments	1,080	2.7	×	1.16	=	.03
Other	3,920	9.8	×	4.10	=	.40
Total	40,000	100.0%				

Weighted average minutes per transaction   =   1.78

F I G U R E   5

Modified Teller Production Form

Hour of Day	Transaction Handled	Total
7 – 8		
8 – 9		
9 – 10		
10 – 11		
11 – 12		
12 – 1		
1 – 2		
2 – 3		
3 – 4		
4 – 5		
5 – 6		
6 – 7		
Total		

Window transactions are the key volume indicator that define a teller's job. They are also the only activity that varies by volume taken. The next categories relate to the fixed activities in the teller profile, which will also be used in the model. Fixed activities include personal activities, administrative activities, and other duties.

Personal Activities

All employees of the bank devote time during the day to personal activities. For the most part these relate to lunches and breaks. The data are determined from the teller survey document (Exhibit A, Section I).

Lunches and breaks are considered fixed activities because they occur regularly (every day) for a fixed amount of time. Based upon the data in the interview, this amount of time is calculated as in Figure 6.

F I G U R E 6

Personal Time Spent per Teller

Frequency per Month		Average Total Minutes		Minutes per Hour		Average Hours per Teller per Month
19.8	×	60	÷	60	=	19.8

As indicated, all information is computed on a monthly basis. The first figure in the calculation, 19.8, is the average number of days in a month. This is determined using the actual policy of the financial institution and includes such factors as holidays, vacation days, and personal days.

This should be determined individually by each bank according to its own policy, using the format in Figure 7, which calculates the actual working hours per month by teller. The actual

F I G U R E 7

Monthly Working Hours per Teller

1. Number of weeks per year	52	
2. Number of days per week	× 5	
Working days per year		260
3. Less: Holidays per year	10	
Personal days per year	2	
Vacation days per year (avg.)	10	
Days not worked per year		− 22
4. Number of total hours per day (standard day)		× 8.5
5. Total actual working hours per year		= 2,023
6. Number of months per year		÷ 12
7. Total actual monthly working hours per teller		= 168.6

total indicated, 168.6 hours, when divided by 8.5 hours per day, results in a frequency per month of 19.8. Although Figure 7 is typical, any of the numbers supplied can be changed to conform to the individual needs of the bank. For example, line 4 may be changed to eight hours if the bank's typical workday is from 8 AM to 4 PM. These adjustments will keep the results of the staffing model accurate from the perspective of the bank using it.

Although the format of Figure 7 will be used throughout this book, it is important to note that the teller area may have different working hours and days in the month—for example, drive-up hours, Saturday morning, and possibly late hours on Friday. Although these may differ, a typical teller usually works a standard, five-day workweek and a standard eight-hour day (or its equivalent). The variables in Figure 7 are not likely to change, except possibly for holidays, personal days, and vacation days.

The last step is to convert the average hours per month devoted to personal activities to a percentage of total monthly hours. This is determined by the following formula:

19.8 hours per month ÷ 168.6 total monthly hours × 100 = 11.7%

So 11.7 percent of the total available monthly hours are devoted to personal activities. All fixed activities are converted to a percentage of monthly available hours. This will become more evident when the model is actually used.

Administrative Activities

The second set of fixed activities, administrative, is again typical for most bank employees. Although these activities vary by bank, they generally encompass meetings and telephone calls made or received. In other words, they are regularly occurring activities that typically do not relate directly to or are an interruption of the primary output of handling window transactions. Many staffing analyses do not account for these items, but if a telephone is available calls will be taken and will be made which will interrupt the flow of the primary output. These calls must be accounted for.

Once again, the teller survey will provide this information. In Section II of Exhibit A, each teller estimates the average minutes spent in meetings and their frequency per month. These should be regularly occurring meetings only, not impromptu ones. An average should be taken of all teller responses for this category (as will be shown in Figure 9).

The most common administrative interruptions besides meetings are telephone calls. To calculate the average amount of time devoted to phone calls, some volume information must be captured.

From the teller survey, an approximate amount of time per type of call should be estimated. Types of calls are outbound, inbound, and call transfers (see Section II of Exhibit A). These estimates should then be averaged for all tellers responding to the survey. Each teller should also complete the call tally form (Section VI), which captures the number of inbound, outbound, and transfer calls handled each day over a two-week period. An overall average will be determined from these data.

Once all teller call tallies are submitted, an average should be calculated for all tellers in the study. Simply add up the number of calls, by category, for all tellers and divide by the number of tellers in the population. From this typical daily pattern of phone calls, calculate the average number of calls taken per day, by category, as in Figure 8. Using the average time estimates provided in the survey, determine the total time in minutes per day devoted to handling telephone calls. Since 19.8 working days per month per teller are available, calculate the total number of hours devoted to this activity, as shown in Figure 8.

The average time spent in meetings and on phone calls must now be combined to determine the percentage of total monthly hours devoted to administrative duties. Figure 9 shows that, on average, 5.6 percent of a teller's monthly hours are devoted to administrative duties.

At this stage, a pattern should begin to emerge. Combining the percentage of time devoted to personal and administrative activities yields 17.3 percent (11.7 percent personal + 5.6 percent administrative = 17.3 percent). Since the total time is 100 percent, only 82.7 percent of the teller's time now remains for handling the primary function, window transactions. In other words, staffing

F I G U R E   8

Average Daily Calls by Teller and Type

Type of Call	Average per Teller per Day		Average Minutes per Call		Total Minutes Spent Handling Calls
Inbound	10	×	1.50	=	15
Outbound	5	×	2.00	=	10
Transfer	10	×	.20	=	2
Total	25				27 min.

Working Days per Month		Average Minutes per Day for Calls		Number of Minutes per Hour		Average Hours per Teller per Month
19.8	×	27	÷	60	=	8.9

must be forecast based on tellers who do not devote 100 percent of their time to handling window transactions.

To attempt to predict staff levels without taking into account these other activities would distort the overall staff needs. A side benefit to this is that the bank may realize that considerably more time may be spent in meetings or handling calls than management realized. Both of these are easy to control. Meetings can be limited or even eliminated; telephone(s) could be removed from the teller area. In either case, analysis could lead to greater control of time devoted to the primary output of handling teller transactions.

Other Duties
The final fixed activity area covers all other miscellaneous activities performed by tellers. These are primarily duties performed regularly by tellers but not necessarily by each teller individually.

Section III of Exhibit A is the standard vehicle for capturing information about other duties. From the initial interviews, a complete list of types of other duties performed should be recorded on the teller survey form. Each teller can then estimate his

FIGURE 9
Administrative Duties

1. Meetings

Frequency per Month		Average Minutes per Meeting		Number of Minutes per Month		Average Hours per Month
1	×	30	÷	60	=	.5

2. Telephone Calls

Working Days per Month		Average Minutes per Day for Calls		Number of Minutes per Hour		Average Hours per Month
19.8	×	27	÷	60	=	8.9

Total hours per month for administrative duties	=	9.4
Percentage of total monthly hours per teller = 9.4 ÷ 168.6 hours	=	5.6%

or her average time and frequency for the activity. Unlike the other fixed categories, for other duties it is necessary to accumulate the total raw time spent on all back-office functions. An average will be calculated only when this total is developed.

As indicated in Figure 10, each teller's time spent is a weekly total, determined by multiplying the average time per activity by its weekly frequency (from the teller survey). This provides an effective analysis of how time is spent within the department on other functions. Note that not all tellers perform the same functions. In fact, the only ones likely to be similar are teller drawer setup and balancing. Other duties as defined here are regularly performed tasks. Miscellaneous activities performed as needed are not included.

The next step is to establish an average amount of time per teller devoted to back-office duties and convert this to a percentage of total monthly teller hours, as in the other figures. Using the result from Figure 10 (45 hours total per week), determine an

F I G U R E   10

Aggregate Time Spent on Other Duties
(Hours per Week)

Duties	Teller #1	Teller #2	Teller #3	Total
1. Drawer setup	1.25	1.25	1.25	3.75
2. Balancing	2.5	2.75	2.5	7.25
3. Filing	—	5.0	2.0	7.00
4. Coin/currency counting	3.0	1.0	—	4.00
5. Vault duties	8.0	—	—	8.00
6. Other	2.0	7.0	6.0	15.00
Total other hours				45.00

average (mean) number of hours per teller by dividing this number by the number of full-time equivalent (FTE) tellers on staff. If five tellers are on the payroll, the result is nine weekly hours per teller (45 hours ÷ 5 FTE = 9 weekly hours).

To be consistent, this should be translated into the average number of hours spent on back-office duties per month, per teller. This is determined to be 39 hours, calculated as follows:

$$\begin{array}{r} 9 \text{ weekly hours per teller for "other duties"} \\ \times \quad 52 \text{ weeks per year} \\ \hline 468 \text{ annual hours per teller (other duties)} \\ \div \quad 12 \text{ months per year} \\ \hline = \quad 39 \text{ monthly hours per teller for other duties} \end{array}$$

The 39 monthly hours per teller (on average) should then be restated as a percentage of total monthly hours available. The reasons for this will become much clearer when the actual staffing model is developed in the next section of this chapter. Convert other duties to a percentage of total monthly hours by dividing 39 monthly hours per teller by 168.6 monthly hours per FTE and multiplying by 100. The result is 23.1 percent.

The monthly hours per teller for other duties will vary by location and institution. The figure of 39 hours is used merely as an example.

Model Development

The model development is a standardized mechanism that can be used to predict optimal staffing levels. The approach recommended in this book is a model that uses Lotus 1, 2, 3. To predict teller staffing effectively and efficiently, it is necessary to have a reporting mechanism that can evaluate the data input using parameters unique to the financial institution. The model used here is pictured in Figure 11.

Bank management can easily build this model using Lotus 1, 2, 3 and following the instructions contained in this section. Once built and preserved on a diskette, the staffing model can be used over and over again to analyze teller staffing levels.

Creating the Model

Anyone reasonably proficient in Lotus 1, 2, 3 software can build the model relatively quickly. This book assumes that the developer can copy the basic structure (headings, captions, input brackets, model borders, and cosmetics) as displayed in Figure 11. Beyond this, the actual calculations, formulas, and linkages necessary for the staffing analysis are provided.

Once the basic model is developed, the next step is to understand what information and/or formulas are to be contained in its various cells. Numbers 1 through 33, placed in various sections of the report, represent locations where either an input item is required (name or value) or a formula will be recorded. The numbers in the following explanation correspond to the numbers in Figure 11.

Keep in mind that the Lotus equivalent formula must be input into the cell for each particular category. The item numbers here and in Figure 11 must be replaced with the actual cell numbers in a Lotus 1, 2, 3 spreadsheet. Lotus cell numbers are in the form of A1, B2, C3, D4, and so forth, and will be at the point where the formula or the space between brackets is to be input.

F I G U R E 11

Teller Staffing Model

```
BANK:        [ 1 ]      TELLER STAFFING MODEL           PERIOD:      [ 5 ]
BRANCH:      [ 2 ]                                      LOBBY:       [ 6 ]
LOCATION:    [ 3 ]                                      DRIVE-UP:    [ 7 ]
             [ 4 ]                                      WALK-UP:     [ 8 ]
```

A. DATA REQUIRED

```
             1. AVERAGE NUMBER TOTAL HOURS PER FTE, PER DAY:        [  9 ]
             2. DESIRED TELLER UTILIZATION PERCENT:                 [ 10 ]
             3. TELLER TRANSACTION VOLUMES:
```

	7-8	8-9	9-10	10-11	11-12	12-1	1-2	2-3	3-4	4-5	5-6	6-7	TOTAL
MONDAY	[ ]	[ ]	[ ]	[ ]	[ ]	[ ]	[ ]	[ ]	[ ]	[ ]	[ ]	[ ]	
TUESDAY	[ ]	[ ]	[ ]	[ ]	[ ]	[ ]	[ ]	[ ]	[ ]	[ ]	[ ]	[ ]	
WEDNESDAY	[ ]	[ ]	[ ]	[ ]	[ ]	[ ]	[ ]	[ ]	[ ]	[ ]	[ ]	[ ]	
THURSDAY	[ ]	[ ]	[ ]	[ ]	[ ]	[ ]	[ ]	[ ]	[ ]	[ ]	[ ]	[ ]	
FRIDAY	[ ]	[ ]	[ ]	[ ]	[ ]	[ ]	[ ]	[ ]	[ ]	[ ]	[ ]	[ ]	
SATURDAY	[ ]	[ ]	[ ]	[ ]	[ ]	[ ]	[ ]	[ ]	[ ]	[ ]	[ ]	[ ]	
SUNDAY	[ ]	[ ]	[ ]	[ ]	[ ]	[ ]	[ ]	[ ]	[ ]	[ ]	[ ]	[ ]	
TOTAL	12												12A

```
======================================================================================
B. FIXED ACTIVITY HOURS:         ||  C. VARIABLE ACTIVITY HOURS:
                                 ||
                                 ||                           WEIGHTED AVERAGE
                                 ||                           HOURS PER TRANSACTION
PERSONNEL:          [ 13 ]       ||
ADMINISTRATION:     [ 14 ]       ||   WINDOW TRANSACTIONS:     [  16                    ]
OTHER DUTIES:       [ 15 ]       ||
                    ------       ||
TOTAL               15A          ||
                    ======       ||
======================================================================================
```

D. STAFFING ANALYSIS (FTE):

	7-8	8-9	9-10	10-11	11-12	12-1	1-2	2-3	3-4	4-5	5-6	6-7	AVERAGE
MONDAY	17												18
TUESDAY													
WEDNESDAY													
THURSDAY													
FRIDAY													
SATURDAY													
SUNDAY													
AVERAGE	0	ERR	ERR	ERR	ERR	ERR	ERR	ERR	ERR	ERR	ERR	ERR	0

```
======================================================================================
E. STAFFING SUMMARY:
```

	MONTHLY HOURS REQUIRED	FTE REQUIRED	PERCENT TO TOTAL
WINDOW TRANSACTIONS:	19	20	29
PERSONNEL:	21	22	30
ADMINISTRATION:	23	24	31
OTHER DUTIES:	25	26	32
TOTAL:	27	28	33

1. Bank: Within the brackets the bank name should be recorded for identification. The developer should leave enough space between the brackets for this purpose.

2. Branch: Within the brackets the name of the branch being evaluated is recorded.

3. and 4. Location: The exact address of the branch or facility being evaluated is recorded.

5. Period: This is the time period over which the analysis was conducted. It is typically two, three, or four weeks. The actual display can be written as follows:

$$9/01/91 - 9/31/91$$

6., 7., and 8. Lobby, drive-up, and walk-up: Record an *x* within the brackets of the appropriate service delivery type being analyzed. A staffing analysis could be performed for each separate service delivery type at the bank location.

Section A: Data Required

9. Average number of total hours per FTE teller per day: This begins the "data required" section. Record the total number of hours in a typical working day for a teller. This is the total raw hours, from the time the teller starts to the time the teller ends work. In other words, this is the bank's workday. Lunches and breaks are *not* excluded from this count. For example, 8:30 AM to 5:00 PM = 8.5 hours; 9:00 AM to 5:00 PM = 8.0 hours; and so forth.

10. Desired utilization percentage: Within these brackets, record a percentage (1 to 100) to indicate how fully the bank wants each teller to be at his or her window station. The higher the percentage, the fewer the gaps in time between customer transactions. At 100 percent, it would be management's desire to have a continual stream of customers seeing the teller one after another. In reality, of course, it is unknown how many transactions will occur in a given hour. If 100 percent is used, the total number of tellers required to handle a given volume will decrease because they will be fully utilized. A lesser percentage indicates that the bank desires to decrease lines or line time by having more tellers available. This could create gaps in customer transactions among tellers.

11. Teller transaction volume: Record the actual average monthly transaction volumes (as whole numbers). These are the number of transactions taken monthly, as an average of the period of time surveyed. This aggregate number of transactions handled by *all* tellers at that location, averaged by the number of weeks sampled, is taken directly from the modified teller production form (Figure 5) or from a mainframe report, if available. As an example, if four weeks were sampled and 10 tellers were involved at a particular location, for each Monday all 10 tellers' transaction sheets would be added together. This total would be added to the other three Mondays in the analysis time period and recorded in the brackets to correspond to the hours and days involved.

11A. Total transactions, by day: This is a summation of each day (combined with the other three or four Mondays in the month) to determine the total Monday business. The formula is:

(Each hour internal coded together)

12. Total transaction volume: This is the total monthly volume by hour. It is merely the sum of the average transactions, by hour, for Monday through Sunday.

This portion of the model does not contain brackets because it can be summed automatically via formula. For each hour, input the "sum" formula:

@sum(cellXX..cell XX)

This standard Lotus 1, 2, 3 formula should be used for each hour of the day. For simplicity and clarity in reporting, it is a whole number, not a decimal.

12A. Total monthly volume: This represents the grand total transactions for all tellers, hours, and days. The same formula is used as in item 12.

Section B: Fixed Activity Hours
13. Personal: This section of the model is also a variable item that requires the input of a number. Personal activities are located in category B, fixed hours per FTE. This represents the percentage of time devoted to lunches, breaks, and any other nonwork-re-

lated activities. The average time from the teller survey is translated into a percentage of the total monthly hours available for work. This percentage is input and calculated as follows:

Frequency of lunches/ breaks per month		Average minutes per occurrence		Average hours per FTE per month		Total monthly hours available		Hours devoted to personal activities
19.8	×	60/60	=	19.8	×	168.6	=	11.7%

In this example, 11.7 percent would be input into the brackets.

Bracketed items can be changed at any time by the individual using the model. Personal activity hours will vary if the bank's policies change with respect to lunches and breaks.

14. Administrative: Like personal activities, this line is variable. Administrative activities can change over time, depending on need or changes of management. Administrative duties are also translated into a percentage of monthly available hours, based on the raw data supplied in the initial teller survey. From the information contained in the profile development section of this chapter, an overall percentage can be determined as in Figure 9.

In this example, 5.6 percent should be input into the brackets.

15. Other duties: The last category under fixed activities is the final block of time regularly devoted to nonwindow activities. The total hours for other duties are determined as in Figure 10 and ultimately translated into a percentage of total monthly hours. In this example, input 23.1 percent.

Section C: Variable Activity Hours

16. Window transactions: For tellers, only one activity is truly variable. Only window transactions require a teller's time based upon the volume of transactions handled. This section calls for a factor that will be applied to the actual monthly volumes in section A of the model to determine the total window time required, on average. Figure 4 provides the format used to calculate a weighted average time per transaction, as determined from the teller survey. The formula for weighted average minutes per transaction is:

Weighted average minutes per transaction		Number of minutes per hour		Weighted average hours per transaction
1.78	÷	60	=	.0297

Input .0297 hours within the brackets.

Section D: Staffing Analysis   It is important to note that all the figures used through item 16 are subject to change. The actual figures used are for illustrative purposes only and will vary by financial institution, based on the results of the teller survey. The remaining sections of the model (items 17 through 33) cannot change. They reflect the information entered into sections A, B, and C of the model. In section D, formulas are entered to display the results of the staffing analysis.

17. Staffing analysis: This section parallels section A, the transaction volume section, but translates the volumes into the number of FTE required per hour, per day, on average. These are the actual staffing requirements, based on the volume results of the organization. Items 17 and 18 outline FTE requirements at the window only. Fixed activities (personal, administrative, and other duties) are factored into the total staffing requirements in items 19, 20, and 21. The staffing analysis (by day and hour) uses the weighted average hours per transaction (item 16) to produce the required FTE at the windows. Because of this, the section can also provide assistance in scheduling tellers.

Formulas must be built in the model to calculate this information. Although the formulas conform to the proper format in Lotus 1, 2, 3, the identifying numbers must be replaced by actual cell numbers.

By hour, daily staffing requirements are:

$$
\left(
\begin{array}{c}
\text{Monthly} \\
\text{transaction} \\
\text{volume}
\end{array}
\times
\begin{array}{c}
12\ \text{months} \\
\text{per year}
\end{array}
\right)
\div
\begin{array}{c}
52\ \text{weeks} \\
\text{per year}
\end{array}
\times
\begin{array}{c}
\text{Weighted average} \\
\text{hours per} \\
\text{transaction}
\end{array}
$$

$$
\div
\left(
\begin{array}{c}
\text{Time per} \\
\text{interval} \\
\text{(usually 1 hour)}
\end{array}
\times
\begin{array}{c}
\text{Desired} \\
\text{utilization} \\
\text{percentage}
\end{array}
\right)
=
\begin{array}{c}
\text{FTE tellers required} \\
\text{on average for that} \\
\text{day and item}
\end{array}
$$

Or, from the model:

$$((\#11 \times 12 \text{ months})/52 \times \#16)/(1 \times \#10)$$

Input this formula in every cell under both day and hour in the staffing analysis section so that all spaces are filled with formulas except for the "total" line. The result will be an FTE requirement for every hour of every day throughout the week. This will indicate the number of tellers needed to staff the teller windows, on average, for each day.

An individual proficient in Lotus 1, 2, 3 can format each formula in a way that will allow ease of copying for the entire staffing analysis section.

18. Average staffing analysis: The average provides an arithmetic mean that indicates the daily average FTE needs for any given day of the week for each particular hour. This figure is a baseline for the number of tellers required to handle window transactions. The formula is:

$$\left(\left(\left(\begin{array}{c}\text{Monthly}\\\text{total}\\\text{volume}\\\text{p/day}\end{array} \times \begin{array}{c}12\\\text{months}\end{array}\right) \div \begin{array}{c}52\\\text{weeks}\\\text{per}\\\text{year}\end{array} \times \begin{array}{c}\text{Weighted}\\\text{average}\\\text{hours per}\\\text{transaction}\end{array}\right) \div \left(1 \times \begin{array}{c}\text{Desired}\\\text{utilization}\\\%\end{array}\right)\right) \div$$

$$\frac{10 \text{ peak}}{\text{intervals}} = \text{Average}$$

Or, from the model:

$$(((\#11A \times 12 \text{ months})/52 \text{ weeks} \times \#16)) /$$
$$(1 \times \#10))/10 \text{ intervals}$$

Section E: Staffing Summary   Section E recaps the monthly hours required for the branch by each category (window transactions, personal, administrative, and other duties). In addition, it provides a percentage breakdown (percent to total) to show the concentration of hours in one segment over another. Finally, the monthly hours are translated into full-time equivalents and totaled to show the optimal staffing level needed for the particular location to perform teller activities. Management should compare its current staffing level to this to determine if there is an opportunity to reduce or a need to increase staff.

19. Window transactions, monthly hours required: This line calls for a monthly total number of hours needed to perform window transactions. Take the monthly average transaction volume totals and multiply by the weighted average hours per transaction factor (item 16). This will provide the total raw hours required to handle window transactions. The formula for calculating this amount is:

$$\begin{array}{c}\text{Total}\\\text{monthly}\\\text{volume}\end{array} \times \begin{array}{c}\text{Weighted}\\\text{average hours}\\\text{required per}\\\text{transaction}\end{array} \div \left(\begin{array}{c}1 \times\\\text{Utilization}\%\end{array}\right) = \begin{array}{c}\text{Total}\\\text{window hours}\\\text{required}\end{array}$$

Or, from the model:

$$((\#12A \times \#16)/(1 \times \#10))$$

20. Window transactions, FTE required: The monthly raw hours required can now be translated into full-time equivalents. What is the complement of staff required to handle the monthly volume of transactions taken? Determine this by analyzing how many actual hours are available to accommodate variable transaction volume. First learn how many hours per month are devoted to the fixed activities of personal, administrative, and other activities and thus unavailable for the handling of window transactions. To calculate accurately the FTE required, use the following formula:

$$\begin{array}{c}\text{Total}\\\text{window}\\\text{hours}\\\text{required}\\(\text{from }\#19)\end{array} \div \begin{array}{c}\text{Number}\\\text{of monthly}\\\text{available}\\\text{hours per}\\\text{teller}\end{array} \times \frac{238 \text{ days}}{12 \text{ months}} = \begin{array}{c}\text{FTE required}\\\text{for window}\\\text{transactions}\end{array}$$

Or, from the model:

$$(\#19/(\#9 \times 238/12))$$

21. Personal activities, monthly hours required: The number of hours recorded in this section is also determined by an arithmetic formula. It represents the total number of hours per month devoted to the personal activities previously defined. This amount must be extrapolated from the FTEs required for window transactions, using the formula:

$$\left(\left(\begin{array}{c}\text{Total}\\\text{monthly}\\\text{transaction}\\\text{volume}\end{array}\times\begin{array}{c}\text{Weighted}\\\text{average}\\\text{hours per}\\\text{transaction}\end{array}\div\left(\begin{array}{c}\text{Hours per}\\\text{interval}\end{array}\times\begin{array}{c}\text{Desired}\\\text{utilization}\\\text{percentage}\end{array}\right)\right)\div\right.$$

$$\left.\left(\left(\begin{array}{c}\text{Average}\\\text{hours per}\\\text{FTE}\end{array}\times\dfrac{238}{12\ \text{months}}\right)\times\left(\begin{array}{c}1-\text{total}\\\text{activity}\,\%\end{array}\right)\right)\right)\times$$

$$\left(\begin{array}{c}\text{Average}\\\text{hours per}\\\text{FTE}\end{array}\times\dfrac{238}{12\ \text{months}}\right)\times\begin{array}{c}\text{Personal}\\\text{activity}\,\%\end{array}$$

Or, from the model:

$$((\#12\times\#16\,/\,(1\times\#10))\,/\,((\#9\times238\,/\,12)\times(1\text{--}\#15A)))\times(\#9\times238\,/\,12)\times\#13$$

Since only a percentage (usually 60 to 75 percent) is devoted to window transactions, the formula accounts for the other 25 to 40 percent.

22. Personal activities, FTE required: Simply translate the monthly hours into the number of full-time equivalents, using the formula:

$$\begin{array}{c}\text{Total monthly}\\\text{personal hours}\\\text{required}\end{array}\div\begin{array}{c}\text{Number of monthly}\\\text{available hours}\\\text{per teller}\end{array}=\begin{array}{c}\text{FTE required}\\\text{for personal}\\\text{activities}\end{array}$$

Or, from the model:

$$(\#21\,/\,(\#9\times238\,/\,12))$$

23. Administrative activities, monthly hours required: Like personal activities, this is determined by formula. The total monthly hours devoted to regular administrative assignments and functions are extrapolated from the original hours required for window transactions, as in the following formula:

$$\left(\left(\begin{array}{c}\text{Total}\\\text{monthly}\\\text{transaction}\\\text{volume}\end{array}\times\begin{array}{c}\text{Weighted}\\\text{average}\\\text{hours per}\\\text{transaction}\end{array}\div\left(\begin{array}{c}\text{Hours per}\\\text{interval}\end{array}\times\begin{array}{c}\text{Desired}\\\text{utilization}\\\text{percentage}\end{array}\right)\right)\div\right.$$

$$\left(\left(\begin{array}{c}\text{Monthly}\\\text{hours}\\\text{available}\\\text{per teller}\end{array}\times\left(\begin{array}{c}1-\text{Fixed}\\\text{hours total}\\\text{percentage}\end{array}\right)\right)\times\begin{array}{c}\text{Monthly}\\\text{hours}\\\text{available}\\\text{per teller}\end{array}\times\begin{array}{c}\text{Fixed}\\\text{hours}\\\text{admin.}\\\text{activity}\\\text{percentage}\end{array}=\begin{array}{c}\text{Admin.}\\\text{activities,}\\\text{monthly}\\\text{hours}\\\text{required}\end{array}\right.$$

Or, from the model:

$$((\#12\times\#16\,/\,(1\times\#10))\,/\,((\#9\times238\,/\,12)\times(1{-}\#15A)))\times(\#9\times238\,/\,12)\times\#14$$

24. Administrative activities, FTE required: The total monthly administrative hours are translated into the number of FTE required via the following formula:

$$\begin{array}{c}\text{Total monthly}\\\text{admin. hours}\\\text{required}\end{array}\div\begin{array}{c}\text{Number of}\\\text{monthly hours}\\\text{available}\\\text{per teller}\end{array}=\begin{array}{c}\text{FTE required}\\\text{for admin.}\\\text{activities}\end{array}$$

Or, from the model:

$$(\#23\,/\,(\#9\times238\,/\,12))$$

25. Other duties, monthly hours required: This category involves regularly performed activities that do not relate directly to the main function of a teller—window transactions. Other duties were determined as a fixed percentage of a teller's time, using the formula:

$$\left(\left(\begin{array}{c}\text{Total}\\\text{monthly}\\\text{transaction}\\\text{volume}\end{array}\times\begin{array}{c}\text{Weighted}\\\text{average}\\\text{hours per}\\\text{transaction}\end{array}\div\left(\begin{array}{c}\text{Hours per}\\\text{interval}\end{array}\times\begin{array}{c}\text{Desired}\\\text{utilization}\\\text{percentage}\end{array}\right)\right)\div\right.$$

$$\left(\left(\begin{array}{c}\text{Monthly}\\\text{hours}\\\text{available}\\\text{per teller}\end{array}\times\left(\begin{array}{c}1-\text{Fixed}\\\text{hours total}\\\text{percentage}\end{array}\right)\right)\times\begin{array}{c}\text{Monthly}\\\text{hours}\\\text{available}\\\text{per teller}\end{array}\times\begin{array}{c}\text{Fixed}\\\text{hours}\\\text{other duties}\\\text{activity}\\\text{percentage}\end{array}=\begin{array}{c}\text{Other}\\\text{duties,}\\\text{monthly}\\\text{hours}\\\text{required}\end{array}\right.$$

Or, from the model:

$$((\#12\times\#16\,/\,(1\times\#10))\,/\,((\#9\times238\,/\,12)\times(1\text{–}\#15A)))\times(\#9\times238\,/\,12)\times\#15$$

26. Other duties, FTE required: The total monthly other duties are translated into the number of FTE required, as in the following formula:

$$\begin{array}{ccc}\text{Total monthly} & \text{Number of} & \text{FTE required}\\\text{other duties} \div & \text{monthly hours} = & \text{for other}\\\text{hours required} & \text{available per teller} & \text{duties}\end{array}$$

Or, from the model:

$$(\#25\,/\,(\#9\times52\,/\,12))$$

27. Total monthly hours required: This line is the sum of the monthly hours required for all four categories (window transactions, personal, administrative, and other duties). The formula is:

$$\begin{array}{ccccc}\text{Window} & \text{Personal} & \text{Administrative} & \text{Other} & \text{Total}\\\text{transactions} & \text{activity} & \text{activity} & \text{duties} & \text{monthly}\\\text{monthly} + & \text{monthly} + & \text{monthly} + & \text{monthly} = & \text{hours}\\\text{hours} & \text{hours} & \text{hours} & \text{hours} & \text{required}\end{array}$$

Or, from the model:

$$@\text{SUM}(\#19..\#25)$$

28. Total FTE required: This is the same approach as for total monthly hours. It is the sum of the FTE requirements for each category, as in the following formula:

$$\begin{array}{ccccc}\text{Window} & \text{Personal} & \text{Admin.} & \text{Other duties} & \text{Total FTE}\\\text{transaction} + & \text{activity} + & \text{activity} + & \text{activity} = & \text{tellers}\\\text{FTE} & \text{FTE} & \text{FTE} & \text{FTE} & \text{required}\end{array}$$

This is the bottom-line result and the purpose for the entire model. Based upon all previous information input and formulas developed, this tells the bank what the optimal staff level should be for the location. It should be compared to the actual FTE tellers on staff to determine if there are any shortages or overages in staff.

29. Percentage to total hours, window transactions: Using the monthly hours required from the model (items 19, 21, 23, and 25), determine a percentage of the total hours required for each category. The results for items 29 through 33 provide a quick analysis of the mix of activities and time spent. The formula is as follows:

$$\left(\begin{array}{c}\text{Monthly} \\ \text{window} \\ \text{transaction} \\ \text{hours required}\end{array} \div \begin{array}{c}\text{Total} \\ \text{monthly} \\ \text{hours} \\ \text{required}\end{array}\right) \times 100 = \begin{array}{c}\text{Percentage of} \\ \text{total hours} \\ \text{devoted to window} \\ \text{transactions}\end{array}$$

Or, from the model:

$$(\#19 / \#27) \times 100$$

30. Percentage to total hours, personal activities:

$$\left(\begin{array}{c}\text{Monthly} \\ \text{personal} \\ \text{activity hours} \\ \text{required}\end{array} \div \begin{array}{c}\text{Total} \\ \text{monthly} \\ \text{hours} \\ \text{required}\end{array}\right) \times 100 = \begin{array}{c}\text{Percentage of} \\ \text{total hours} \\ \text{devoted to} \\ \text{personal activities}\end{array}$$

Or, from the model:

$$(\#21 / \#27) \times 100$$

31. Percentage to total hours, administrative activities:

$$\left(\begin{array}{c}\text{Monthly} \\ \text{admin.} \\ \text{hours} \\ \text{required}\end{array} \div \begin{array}{c}\text{Total} \\ \text{monthly} \\ \text{hours} \\ \text{required}\end{array}\right) \times 100 = \begin{array}{c}\text{Percentage of} \\ \text{total hours} \\ \text{devoted to} \\ \text{admin. activities}\end{array}$$

Or, from the model:

$$(\#23 / \#27) \times 100$$

32. Percentage to total hours, other duties:

$$\left(\begin{array}{c} \text{Monthly} \\ \text{other duties,} \\ \text{hours} \\ \text{required} \end{array} \div \begin{array}{c} \text{Total} \\ \text{monthly} \\ \text{hours} \\ \text{required} \end{array} \right) \times 100 = \begin{array}{c} \text{Percentage of} \\ \text{total hours} \\ \text{devoted to} \\ \text{other duties} \end{array}$$

Or, from the model:

$$(\#25\,/\,\#27)\times100$$

33. Total percentage: This is the sum of the individual percentages calculated for items 29, 30, 31, and 32. The formula is:

$$\begin{array}{c} \text{Window} \\ \text{transactions} \\ \text{percentage} \\ \text{to total} \end{array} + \begin{array}{c} \text{Personal} \\ \text{activities} \\ \text{percentage} \\ \text{to total} \end{array} + \begin{array}{c} \text{Admin.} \\ \text{activities} \\ \text{percentage} \\ \text{to total} \end{array} + \begin{array}{c} \text{Other duties} \\ \text{activities} \\ \text{percentage} \\ \text{to total} \end{array} = 100\%$$

Or, from the model:

$$@SUM(\#29..\#32)$$

At this point, the creation of the teller staffing model is complete. Be sure to save it and create at least two backup copies. Although the developer can customize the model as desired, it may be prudent to copy it as displayed in Figure 11, an exact representation of how it would be viewed on a PC or in a report.

The next section discusses the actual running of the model and the procedures required to produce the desired analysis.

Running the Model

Once the model is complete, running it involves inputting the variable information unique to the organization (items 1 through 16 in Figure 11). For the most part, the information supplied is from the teller survey form. To recap, the following section explains the information that must be supplied in the model.

Headings Brackets are provided to supply the bank name, branch, and location for identification purposes. The period of time covered should also be documented in the appropriate space.

Finally, place an x in one of the delivery types listed: lobby, drive-up, or walk-up window.

Data Required   The first two items relate to general questions not found in the teller survey. The remaining volume data are determined from the teller production sheets.

   1. Average number total hours per FTE, per day: This refers to the actual hours from start to end of the teller's day, including lunches and breaks. It is the standard number of hours required for bank policy. For example, if the tellers' hours are from 8:30 AM to 5:00 PM, the total hours are 8.5.

   2. Desired utilization percentage: The utilization percentage (1 through 100) indicates the level at which tellers are devoted to handling window traffic. At 100 percent tellers are handling customers one after another, with no gaps in traffic flow. The lower the percentage the more time exists between customers, and therefore, the more tellers are available and not fully utilized. Care must be taken when selecting an actual percentage. On one hand, 100 percent is not desirable, as this may cause overwork, extended lines, and possibly poor service. On the other hand, targeting the utilization percentage too low would be an inefficient use of personnel. The optimum selection is one that is challenging yet allows enough gap time so customers are serviced on a timely basis. Record a value of 1 to 100 in this section.

   3. Teller transaction volumes: These are the actual total (aggregate) teller transaction volumes taken over the past month (four weeks). All tellers' volumes are combined for each hour interval and day of the week. The information is taken from the teller daily production form of the teller survey. A specific value must be input in each bracket in this section of the model.

Fixed Hours   The fixed hours are designated percentages that correspond to the three areas of regularly occurring activities. These activities do not relate to the key volume indicator (window transactions), but rather to the other demands on time for the average teller.

   1. Personal: Lunches, breaks, and other miscellaneous personal time spent away from the job are accounted for in this category. The information is determined from the teller survey and calculated using the format in the data-gathering section of this chapter. The model calls for a percentage to be input into the designated section.

2. Administrative: This represents the fixed time devoted to meetings, handling phone calls, and other administrative tasks. Again, input a percentage.

3. Other duties: This set of activities involves all other functions that are performed regularly by tellers. It is also a percentage.

Variable Hours   The last area requiring input is the most important. Input the number of hours required to handle a single transaction on a weighted average basis. The appropriate response for this space will likely be a decimal. For example, a factor of 15 minutes would equal .25 hours, and a full hour would be 1.00. Translate the data into hours so the model can run properly.

Once these fields are all input, the model is complete and the actual analysis/result is performed instantly. Figure 12 is a completed example of the model, using fictitious data for discussion.

ANALYSIS, MEASUREMENT, AND USE

The previous sections defined the elements of the model and the process of determining the appropriate data to use. This last section discusses the usage and benefits of the staffing analysis and approach.

Whenever the model is run, some form of analysis must follow to draw conclusions from the data presented. This begins with an understanding of the current teller staffing levels for the particular location. A comparison is made between the actual level and the staffing level determined in the model to reveal whether or not the location is under-, over-, or appropriately staffed. Using the data in Figure 12, the analysis is best outlined in a report similar to Figure 13. From this report, further data can be determined that will indicate the financial impact the result has on the organization.

In Figure 13, it appears an opportunity exists; that is, an overstaffed situation of 3.5 FTE tellers has been determined. Reducing the staff at the designated locations by the number indi-

FIGURE 12

Completed Teller Staffing Model

BANK:	[ ]	TELLER STAFFING MODEL	PERIOD:	[ ]
BRANCH:	[ ]		LOBBY:	[ ]
LOCATION:	[ ]		DRIVE-UP:	[ ]
	[ ]		WALK-UP:	[ ]

A. DATA REQUIRED

1. AVERAGE NUMBER TOTAL HOURS PER FTE, PER DAY: [8.5]
2. DESIRED TELLER UTILIZATION PERCENT: [100.0%]
3. TELLER TRANSACTION VOLUMES:

	7–8	8–9	9–10	10–11	11–12	12–1	1–2	2–3	3–4	4–5	5–6	6–7	TOTAL
MONDAY	[ ]	[ ]	[275]	[274]	[267]	[256]	[207]	[178]	[218]	[235]	[154]	[ ]	2,064
TUESDAY	[ ]	[ ]	[215]	[201]	[192]	[229]	[196]	[176]	[214]	[234]	[111]	[ ]	1,768
WEDNESDAY	[ ]	[ ]	[167]	[184]	[257]	[219]	[186]	[183]	[170]	[173]	[179]	[ ]	1,718
THURSDAY	[ ]	[ ]	[198]	[205]	[219]	[223]	[153]	[181]	[178]	[228]	[177]	[ ]	1,762
FRIDAY	[ ]	[ ]	[258]	[260]	[237]	[226]	[246]	[239]	[267]	[264]	[220]	[63]	2,280
SATURDAY	[ ]	[ ]	[203]	[207]	[225]	[165]	[ ]	[ ]	[ ]	[ ]	[ ]	[ ]	800
SUNDAY	[ ]	[ ]	[ ]	[ ]	[ ]	[ ]	[ ]	[ ]	[ ]	[ ]	[ ]	[ ]	0
TOTAL	0	0	1,316	1,331	1,397	1,318	988	957	1,047	1,134	841	63	10,392

B. FIXED ACTIVITY HOURS: ‖   C. VARIABLE ACTIVITY HOURS:

			WEIGHTED AVERAGE
			HOURS PER TRANSACTION
PERSONNEL:	[5.0%]		
ADMINISTRATION:	[10.0%]	WINDOW TRANSACTIONS:	[0.030]
OTHER DUTIES:	[5.0%]		
TOTAL	20.0%		

D. STAFFING ANALYSIS (FTE):

	7–8	8–9	9–10	10–11	11–12	12–1	1–2	2–3	3–4	4–5	5–6	6–7	AVERAGE
MONDAY	0.00	0.00	0.42	0.41	0.40	0.39	0.31	0.27	0.33	0.36	0.23	0.00	0.26
TUESDAY	0.00	0.00	0.33	0.30	0.29	0.35	0.30	0.27	0.32	0.35	0.17	0.00	0.22
WEDNESDAY	0.00	0.00	0.25	0.28	0.39	0.33	0.28	0.28	0.26	0.26	0.27	0.00	0.22
THURSDAY	0.00	0.00	.030	0.31	0.33	0.34	0.23	0.27	0.27	0.34	0.27	0.00	0.22
FRIDAY	0.00	0.00	0.39	0.39	0.36	0.34	0.37	0.36	0.40	0.40	0.33	0.10	0.29
SATURDAY	0.00	0.00	0.31	0.31	0.34	0.25	0.00	0.00	0.00	0.00	0.00	0.00	0.10
SUNDAY	0.00	0.00	0.00	0.00	0.00	0.00	0.00	0.00	0.00	0.00	0.00	0.00	0.00
AVERAGE	0.00	0.00	0.28	0.29	0.30	0.28	0.21	0.21	0.23	0.25	0.18	0.01	0.19

E. STAFFING SUMMARY:

	MONTHLY HOURS REQUIRED	FTE REQUIRED	PERCENT TO TOTAL
WINDOW TRANSACTIONS:	311.7	1.849	80.0%
PERSONNEL:	19.48	0.115	5.0%
ADMINISTRATION:	38.97	0.231	10.0%
OTHER DUTIES:	19.48	0.115	5.0%
TOTAL:	389.7	2.311	100.0%

F I G U R E 13

Teller Staffing Comparison

| As of date _____ | | | |
Teller Location	Actual Staff Level	Required Staff Level	Over (Under) Staffed
Main lobby	5.0	3.5	1.5
Main drive-up	3.0	2.0	1.0
Branch #1 lobby	3.0	3.0	–
Branch #1 drive-up	2.0	2.0	–
Branch #2 drive-up	3.0	2.0	1.0
Total	16.0	12.5	3.5

cated would translate into a monetary benefit correspondent to the salary plus benefits paid to the tellers who would be eliminated. This is a fairly obvious conclusion to draw from the data presented. If data gathering and model building were done properly, the results are reliable.

When performing this type of analysis, round any fractional FTE totals down to the nearest whole number. In Figure 13, the 3.5 FTE staff overage would actually round to 3.0 FTE. This is a more realistic approach than attempting to trim to part-time hours to account for the fraction.

What would happen if the analysis revealed that the locations were understaffed? These are entirely likely results, and the answer lies in a detailed analysis of the elements in the model relative to the teller profile.

If the teller location is shown to be understaffed, most bankers would not immediately go out and hire someone on the spot. Budgets must be considered, requisitions approved, and managers convinced that increasing the staff is fully justified. If this approach is followed, the model itself should be justification enough and can be accepted at face value. Still, the decision to add to staff is always a difficult one. The likely result of this scenario is that further questions will be posed, focusing on what can be done to avoid hiring additional people. Without a detailed staffing model, it is difficult to provide appropriate answers. With the model, however, very specific ideas for maintaining efficiency without adding to staff can be tested, with tangible results.

To accomplish this, the teller manager should display the model on a PC, including all data previously input. The next step is to evaluate each of the fixed and variable teller profile categories. Since the values contained on these lines have a direct impact on the staffing levels determined by the model, any adjustment of these values would produce a different result. In other words, if personal activities were reduced from 11.7 percent of a teller's day to 5 percent, the immediate result would be less staff required than the original numbers indicated (see Figure 14). The benefit of using the staffing model on-line is that the banker can perform various "what-if" scenarios with immediate feedback. This will guide the individual to determine the best approach to take.

In Figure 14, if personal activity were reduced to 5 percent, we might find that the location is no longer understaffed and no additional tellers need be hired. But can this be done? The action required would be to virtually eliminate lunches, which is not a feasible solution to the problem. This leaves administrative, other duties, and window transaction time, all of which are appropriate candidates for analysis.

If either the administrative or other duties percentage were reduced, no additional personnel would be required. For example, to reduce administrative activities, refer to the initial teller survey form (Appendix Exhibit A). This document shows exactly how much time is spent on various administrative activities (meetings, phone calls, etc.). From this, determine what activities might be eliminated or redirected. If a considerable amount of time is spent in staff meetings every week, this is easy to control. The manager can simply reduce the frequency of meetings and / or reduce the length of each meeting.

So the first step in using the model is to set up hypothetical situations by adjusting the fixed activities percentages. If this provides the desired FTE staff level, the manager knows what areas (activities) to focus on. When various activities and tasks are eliminated, the hypothetical percentages become the standard for future measurement.

F I G U R E 14

Modified Teller Staffing Model

```
BANK:        [First National  ]      TELLER STAFFING MODEL      PERIOD:    [June 1991 ]
BRANCH:      [Main            ]                                 LOBBY:     [ X        ]
LOCATION:    [Center St.      ]                                 DRIVE-UP:  [          ]
             [Chicago, IL     ]                                 WALK-UP:   [          ]
```

A. DATA REQUIRED

```
            1. AVERAGE NUMBER TOTAL HOURS PER FTE, PER DAY:        [  8.5   ]
            2. DESIRED TELLER UTILIZATION PERCENT:                 [100.0%]
            3. TELLER TRANSACTION VOLUMES:
```

	7–8	8–9	9–10	10–11	11–12	12–1	1–2	2–3	3–4	4–5	5–6	6–7	TOTAL
MONDAY	[ ]	[ ]	[ ]	[275]	[274]	[267]	[256]	[207]	[178]	[218]	[235]	[154]	[ ]	2,064
TUESDAY	[ ]	[ ]	[ ]	[215]	[201]	[192]	[229]	[196]	[176]	[214]	[234]	[111]	[ ]	1,768
WEDNESDAY	[ ]	[ ]	[ ]	[167]	[184]	[257]	[219]	[186]	[183]	[170]	[173]	[119]	[ ]	1,658
THURSDAY	[ ]	[ ]	[ ]	[198]	[205]	[219]	[223]	[153]	[181]	[178]	[228]	[177]	[ ]	1,762
FRIDAY	[ ]	[ ]	[ ]	[258]	[260]	[237]	[226]	[246]	[239]	[267]	[264]	[220]	[63]	2,280
SATURDAY	[ ]	[ ]	[ ]	[203]	[207]	[225]	[165]	[ ]	[ ]	[ ]	[ ]	[ ]	[ ]	800
SUNDAY	[ ]	[ ]	[ ]	[ ]	[ ]	[ ]	[ ]	[ ]	[ ]	[ ]	[ ]	[ ]	[ ]	0
TOTAL	0	0	1,316	1,331	1,397	1,318	988	957	1,047	1,134	781	63	10,332

```
B. FIXED ACTIVITY HOURS:            ||  C. VARIABLE ACTIVITY HOURS:
                                    ||
                                    ||                          WEIGHTED AVERAGE
                                    ||                          HOURS PER TRANSACTION
PERSONNEL:        [  5.0%  ]        ||
ADMINISTRATION:   [ 10.0%  ]        ||     WINDOW TRANSACTIONS:      [  0.030              ]
OTHER DUTIES:     [  5.0%  ]        ||
                  ---------         ||
TOTAL              20.0%            ||
                  ======           ||
```

D. STAFFING ANALYSIS (FTE):

	7–8	8–9	9–10	10–11	11–12	12–1	1–2	2–3	3–4	4–5	5–6	6–7	AVERAGE
MONDAY	0.00	0.00	0.41	0.41	0.40	0.38	0.31	0.27	0.33	0.35	0.23	0.00	0.26
TUESDAY	0.00	0.00	0.32	0.30	0.29	0.34	0.29	0.26	0.32	0.35	0.17	0.00	0.22
WEDNESDAY	0.00	0.00	0.25	0.28	0.38	0.33	0.28	0.27	0.25	0.26	0.18	0.00	0.21
THURSDAY	0.00	0.00	0.30	0.31	0.33	0.33	0.23	0.27	0.27	0.34	0.27	0.00	0.22
FRIDAY	0.00	0.00	0.39	0.39	0.35	0.34	0.37	0.36	0.40	0.40	0.33	0.09	0.28
SATURDAY	0.00	0.00	0.30	0.31	0.34	0.25	0.00	0.00	0.00	0.00	0.00	0.00	0.10
SUNDAY	0.00	0.00	0.00	0.00	0.00	0.00	0.00	0.00	0.00	0.00	0.00	0.00	0.00
AVERAGE	0.00	0.00	0.28	0.28	0.30	0.28	0.21	0.20	0.22	0.24	0.17	0.01	0.18

E. STAFFING SUMMARY:

	MONTHLY HOURS REQUIRED	FTE REQUIRED	PERCENT TO TOTAL
WINDOW TRANSACTIONS:	309.96	1.84	80.0%
PERSONNEL:	19.37	0.11	5.0%
ADMINISTRATION:	38.75	0.23	10.0%
OTHER DUTIES:	19.37	0.11	5.0%
TOTAL:	387.45	2.30	100.0%

The weighted average time required to handle each transaction should not be overlooked. Although this factor is produced from teller estimates, volumes, and the weighted average calculation approach used earlier in the chapter, it can still be changed. Several methodologies can be employed to improve the rate per transaction. Evaluating these opportunities begins with a review of the teller survey form. The time estimates by transaction, the volume of transactions by type, and their relative percentage to the total will highlight which transaction types to attend to. If a particular transaction occurs frequently, it may behoove the manager to evaluate the steps involved in handling that transaction. A simplified flowchart, similar to that in Figure 15, will highlight the procedure and reveal activities or tasks that are unnecessary or may be bottlenecks. Analysis of these activities and appropriate brainstorming may allow the manager to eliminate some of the steps involved.

In Figure 14, several opportunities are available:

1. If the teller system is old, requiring myriad entry requirements, or if response time is slow due to substandard networking and loops, considerable time may be lost during each transaction. To improve this situation, evaluate the network communications equipment in terms of controllers, modem speeds, line capacity, and so forth. Any data communication specialist (from the bank's in-house data processing department or a service bureau) can provide this analysis. The results may indicate a need to upgrade equipment, which will improve the response time of the system. This will ultimately reduce the overall weighted average time per transaction.

   Of course, the bank may not want to spend money on upgraded equipment. This is always a dilemma, but if the improved performance and response time allow a reduction in staff or preclude hiring an additional teller, the savings of the teller salary plus benefits may offset the cost of the new equipment. Remember that the savings obtained from holding down staff size occur year after year, not just the first year.

F I G U R E 15

Flowchart for Check-Cashing Transactions

2. Another opportunity may simply be to improve the procedures used. If tellers have to walk a long distance to find a CRT to check a customer's balance and account, this can be a great time waster. The goal is to waste as little time as possible during the transaction. Strategically placed CRTs can eliminate this problem.

3. The evaluation of signatures is always time-consuming, especially if the signature card must be retrieved from a control file. This takes time away from the window not only to find the card but also to review the signature. Microfiche can improve this, as duplicate copies of the fiche can be made accessible to tellers. Still, time is required to find them.

Part of the solution may be establishing dollar limits that require the review of a signature card. For example, checks below $1,000 may not warrant a signature review.

Finally, signatures can now be digitized so they can be placed on the teller terminal screen for review. Search time is thus drastically reduced, and tellers no longer have to leave their station. Many systems are available today to make this process a reality.

These are but a few opportunities for reducing the overall average time per window transaction. The model can help managers determine scientifically the optimal staffing level for the bank and the best ways to achieve it. The result is the development of standards for fixed and variable activities, which should be used, location by location, to assess the average level of staffing for the teller departments.

This book provides a uniform methodology for assessing teller staffing levels, but it does not mandate actual times that go into making up the standards. The major drawback of many approaches is that they generalize too much. Some banks rely on a ratio of number of accounts to number of tellers based upon national or regional averages. The estimates produced from these will always be suspect because they do not take into account the different systems used by banks, different procedures, different policies, and different mixes of transaction types. For this reason, the model approach offered in this book tailors the results to the individual bank, leading to far greater accuracy than the broad generalizations made from other methods.

Finally, once the analysis has been completed and the bank is comfortable with the results, the fixed and variable activities items should become the standard for the bank. They should be used for evaluating staffing levels periodically. Running the model every six months or so will provide management with a level of comfort throughout the year and an opportunity to make adjustments should staff levels begin to creep up.

SUMMARY

The focus of this chapter has been on developing a staffing model for the analysis of teller staffing levels in the bank or branch.

This book provides readers with the tools necessary to build an effective staffing model that can be used over and over again. The methodology begins with an interview process using a teller survey form. This provides the foundation for the development of the information that is used in the model.

A teller profile is developed that indicates the fixed and variable activities accounting for 100 percent of a teller's time. These include fixed activities (personal, administrative, and other duties) and variable activities (window transactions). The variable activity is generally regarded as the key volume indicator—that is, it is the primary reason the teller position exists. Fixed activities do not relate to the volume of transactions handled but do occur on a regular basis.

Data are gathered next for each area of the teller profile. This information is used to develop the actual standards used in the model to determine the optimum staff level of tellers required, given the volume of customer transactions.

Finally, the model is developed. The chapter provides specific details, with examples, of how to construct the staffing model using Lotus 1, 2, 3. Actual Lotus formulas are provided and a step-by-step approach is discussed.

When the model is used, analysis must follow to determine what action should be taken. A flowchart is recommended to determine what areas may be trimmed to improve the overall standard, thus having a positive impact on staffing. This provides the direct control over the staffing levels required and allows managers the opportunity to diagnose and take action to control staff levels for the future. In this sense, the model can be used to run "what-if" scenarios to help management achieve the desired results.

The model should be run at six-month intervals. This will provide appropriate checkpoints, preventing staff overruns by allowing timely analysis for action.

## CHAPTER 2

Commercial Lender and Support Staffing

One of the most difficult areas for developing a staffing analysis and model is the commercial loan department. Commercial loans has historically been the corporate sales department for banks, the one that solicits clients from the business community. For this reason, the sales environment has seldom come under scrutiny with respect to the optimum number of employees needed. Unlike production-based departments, the volume of work for commercial loans is not very clear. For a teller or production area, the daily workload (volume) is expected to occur on a regular basis. In the sales environment, especially commercial, this is not a given—in fact, the staff actually creates its own workflow through its sales efforts. Determining how many commercial loan officers are needed becomes very obscure, since it is unknown what the workload will become.

As a result, banks tend to staff commercial loan officers based on the revenue they may conceivably bring in, without taking into account the other aspects of the job. Adding commercial lenders to staff is certainly more involved than adding tellers. Commercial lending officers are at a premium and usually command salaries in the middle to the high end of the officer ranges. In short, they are costly FTEs. How many officers does it take to generate a given volume of business? What does it cost the bank in premium salaries and benefits to meet its sales goals? This salary cost must be subtracted from the revenue gained to determine a true picture of commercial lending's profitability.

Managing sales becomes even more complex. One officer may generate much more business than another. This inconsistency gives rise to the beliefs that sales personnel cannot be measured like production personnel and that sales itself is an art, not a science, and therefore cannot be reduced to standard staffing formulas.

This chapter will dispel that myth and provide a means to evaluate scientifically the commercial loan staffing needs of any bank. The eternal question is how many commercial lenders are necessary to manage a given number of accounts. However, lenders must not only manage and service existing accounts but also bring in new business and, finally, monitor and control accounts to prevent losses to the bank. Historically, a financial institution either is sales-intensive or focuses on servicing; an emphasis on one will cause the other area to suffer. The goal ultimately is to determine the appropriate mix of attention on the three primary areas: sales, servicing, and control.

It is up to the bank to determine what standards will produce the desired results. As with the teller utilization percentage discussed in the previous chapter, if the bank requires commercial lenders to spend a large percentage of their time servicing customers, meeting its sales goals may require more staff. You can't have both high sales volumes and few employees. It is simply not possible to spend 75 percent of one's time on new business development and 75 percent on servicing and maintaining relationships. Something will give, resulting in higher delinquencies and subsequently more losses, a high rate of customers leaving the bank, and/or failure to meet sales goals and forecasts.

The consequences of a poor mix in commercial lending are severe. The bank can lose market share and overall profitability. The first step in solving the problem is to gain an understanding of the elements of commercial lending. The next is to determine the proper mix of sales, servicing, and control. It is then possible to determine scientifically the necessary complement of FTEs to meet the standards of the bank. Staffing commercial personnel in light of these standards will allow the financial institution to maintain a cost-effective sales presence without losing customers due to inadequate servicing.

The rest of this chapter is devoted to determining what the actual standards should be and what the baseline is today for sales, servicing, control, and other activities. Analyzing the information and activities involved within each of the four categories will afford management the opportunity for continued staff control.

This chapter discusses the other key commercial loan positions and provides a methodology for determining optimum staffing levels for these positions as well. Four categories of staffing analysis are discussed: commercial loan officers, administrative assistants/secretaries, loan operations and support personnel, and credit analysts.

The model will array the FTE staff needs for each position. The bank may learn that some functions should be performed by credit analysts, administrative assistants, or loan operations clerks rather than by loan officers. Channeling tasks to other, more appropriate positions decreases overall costs, since these staffers are not paid as much as lending officers. For example, having credit analysts perform all financial analyses on potential customers and loan committee write-ups may preclude the need to hire a new loan officer. The difference in salary between the officer and the credit analyst is a true savings to the bank.

The analysis, measurement, and usage section of this chapter outlines various ways of determining actual activities performed, along with ways to channel these activities to more appropriate personnel at lower cost.

METHODOLOGY

The specific methodology used is similar to that of the teller analysis. However, because of the variety of activities and types of personnel required, the study becomes more complex. In general, the analysis of commercial loan staffing levels involves the interview process, survey development and implementation, data gathering, and model development.

Interviews

During the interview process, the manager meets with staff personnel on a one-on-one basis to learn what functions they perform. If one were starting from scratch, the interview process would determine the raw data that would be used in a commercial loan survey document. Since the purpose of this book is to provide the methodology, this portion of it has already been done. The usual activities of each position in a typical commercial loan department are already documented in a standard commercial loan survey form, which will be discussed later in the chapter.

Interviewing personnel about what they do will assist greatly in the development of commercial loan profiles. It is not important to learn how much time is required for each function. Ideally, the functions actually performed should be organized in a flowchart fashion for later review. This is highly recommended if enough time is available. The detail provided by the flowchart will prove invaluable when staffing levels are fully analyzed to determine opportunity areas.

Profile Development

The profile development stage is the foundation of the staffing analysis. Without a firm understanding of how commercial loan staff members spend their time, a reliable analysis cannot be performed. Understanding the time spent by the commercial staff leads to the development of a core profile of commercial lenders and supporting commercial loan staff (administrative assistants/secretaries, loan support personnel, and credit analysts). The profile defines the major categories of activities or key volume indicators for each position.

Every position in a bank (or any company) can be defined by the output it produces. In fact, the output produced may be incorporated into the job title. For example, the loan officers' key volume indicator is making loans, since that is how they spend most of their working hours. If analysis reveals that a loan officer is devoting less than half of his or her time to making loans, an argument could be made that this individual is not a loan officer. This conclusion will be highlighted in the analysis section of the chapter.

Ultimately, all tasks and activities performed by a loan representative can be allocated to the key volume indicator to account for all time utilized during a given day. All day-to-day duties will fit into one of the activity categories contained in the commercial loan profile. This will determine the staffing levels required. According to research and analysis, the typical commercial loan officer and representatives perform seven types of activity: business development, administrative, personal, new loans, renewed loans, maintenance/monitoring, and handling past-due loans.

All the tasks performed by loan officers can be assigned to one of these seven categories. Identifying the key volume indicators and their purpose requires further breakdown of the seven core categories into fixed and variable activities. For commercial lenders, activities are split as follows:

1. Fixed activities:
   - Business development
   - Administrative
   - Personal
2. Variable activities
   - New loans
   - Renewed loans
   - Maintenance/monitoring
   - Past-due loans

Fixed activities are performed on a regular basis, without deviation, for a standard amount of time. For example, lunches and breaks are taken daily for a fixed or predictable period of time (e.g., 60 minutes), so they do not vary with volume. In short, fixed activities occur with a high degree of regularity, regardless of the volume of work received.

If the position is a commercial loan officer, the key volume indicator must be the number of loans handled. So, the variable activities must relate specifically to the volume of loans in some fashion. As previously indicated for commercial loan officers, variable activities relate to the volume of loans in the categories of new and renewed loans, the maintenance of existing loans, and the handling of past due loans. In essence, the volume of loans handled relates directly to these variable categories. In other words, if no new loans were taken in during a given period of time, no time would be devoted to handling new loans. However, time would still be devoted to fixed activities since these do not vary with volume. Generally speaking, for an additional position there is usually only one key volume indicator, although there can be a number of variable activities associated with the key volume indicator—as is the case with commercial loan personnel.

The actual profile was completed based upon interviews and other research of commercial loan activities. Appendix Exhibits B through E contain the surveys necessary to gather information for commercial loan officers, administrative assistants/secretaries, loan operations and support personnel, and credit analysts.

The profile of these four positions are similar, except that business development and past-due handling are generally the sole domain of the commercial lender. The staffing analysis in this chapter is a complete departmental analysis. Each position is analyzed separately to develop the appropriate standards for the model. This step is detailed more fully in the data-gathering section of the chapter. The profile for each position conforms to the chart in Figure 16.

Finally, when the model has been completed, run, and analyzed, the profile can be translated into four abbreviated categories: sales (encompassing business development and new loans), servicing (maintenance/monitoring and renewed loans), control (past-due loans), and other (administrative and personal activities).

Ultimately, the percentage of time devoted to each category will indicate the degree of success or difficulty experienced. This will be fully analyzed in the section on analysis, measurement, and usage.

F I G U R E 16

Commercial Loan Profiles, by Position

Profile	Commercial Lender	Secretary/ Admin. Assistant	Loan Operations Support	Credit Analyst
1. Fixed activities				
■ Business development	x	–	–	–
■ Administrative	x	x	x	x
■ Personal	x	x	x	x
2. Variable activities				
■ New loans	x	x	x	x
■ Renewed loans	x	x	x	x
■ Maintenance/monitoring	x	x	x	–
■ Past due	x	–	–	–

Data Gathering

Specific information must be obtained from each of the positions within the commercial loan department. This is accomplished by using the survey documents contained in Exhibits B through E circulated according to job title.

The survey documents should be circulated to the commercial loan positions with instructions that they be returned in two weeks. The data-gathering period should be a typical time. Selecting a two-week period that is close to a major holiday or in which unusual activity will occur would distort the results and may cause the model to calculate staffing levels based on peak periods.

The survey documents contain two major sections. One section seeks an estimate of time and frequency for the items covered in the survey. This portion can be completed in one sitting. It is important to instruct the individuals completing it to provide an average estimate; in other words, the typical time it takes on average to complete the particular task.

The second section requires completion over the two-week period. These production sheets, which capture volume information over a period of time, merely require tally marks to record volume and do not require much time. It is important, however, that the respondents be as accurate as possible when recording the information, because it will be used to develop the standards used in the model to predict appropriate staffing levels.

The sections of this chapter explain how this information is gathered and translated into a standard. The model is very flexible; it will calculate the amount of FTE required for each position based on the information input in the model. The information input is the result of the data-gathering stage and can become the standard for the financial institution. Once standards are developed, the model can be run over and over again for different time periods and locations, with only the volume changing.

Commercial Loan Officers
The analysis of commercial loan officers, like the others, requires an estimate of time required, frequency of occurrence, and volume information captured using production sheets. As with the teller analysis, the time estimates can be averaged for all responding commercial loan officers, or senior management can use one document and arrive at a consensus regarding its expectations. In some ways, the latter may be more accurate.

During the research for this book, some bank presidents claimed they knew exactly how much time should be spent during an average customer call or on the financial analysis of a customer. Letting senior management establish these factors is forcing a standard.

Since little has been written about establishing standards for commercial lenders, this is up to the lender, which makes for wide fluctuations in commercial loan officer productivity. The standard development approach discussed in this book will even out productivity and expectations among all commercial loan officers, not just one or two.

As in the first chapter, the model calculates information based upon the total monthly hours per employee. It is necessary to use a standard format for computing this figure. Figure 17 shows the format for this calculation.

The net result of 168.6 monthly hours is used throughout this chapter, although in reality it may vary from bank to bank accord-

F I G U R E   17

Total Monthly Available Hours Calculation

	52	Weeks per year
×	5	Working days per week
	260	Gross working days per year
−	10	Holidays per year
−	2	Personal days per FTE per year
−	10	Average valuation days per FTE per year
=	238	Net working days per year
×	8.5	Total available hours per day
=	2,023	Total hours per year
÷	12	Number of months per year
=	168.6	Total monthly available hours per FTE per month

ing to its personnel policy regarding holidays, personal days, and vacation days. The format in Figure 17 can be modified to accommodate the specific policies of the financial institution.

The standards used for each profile activity for commercial loan representatives are developed from the data obtained in the commercial loan officer survey document (Exhibit B). The time estimates and frequency section of the survey document can be completed by consensus of senior management, or the survey can be circulated among all commercial loan officers. Regardless of the approach taken, at the close of the two-week data-gathering period the survey document information should be averaged so that there is one set for the entire commercial lending division. This will form the basis for calculating the actual standards.

Business Development   Business development includes prospecting, strategy, and referral base development—the activities performed to attract and develop potential customers and a customer base. Since business development is not volume-driven but relates to a specified amount of time regularly devoted to developing new business, it falls under the fixed activities category of the commercial lender profile. A percentage of time devoted to this activity will be determined for the model. To determine the percentage of time devoted to the function per officer, evaluate the three primary functions associated with business development:

- Prospect contact/communication
- Strategy and planning
- Referral base development

Again, once the information is obtained from the lenders or senior lender group from the survey, it can be averaged and input in the analysis to arrive at a standard. For prospect contact/communication, use either an average number or the volume of calls required or expected. This information is obtained from the survey's commercial loan tally sheet, in the survey shown in Figure 18.

This production sheet must be filled out for two consecutive weeks. It reveals the volume and frequency of commercial loan officer calls for both prospects and new customers. The lender merely records a tally mark in the appropriate box as contact is made each day. From these production sheets, the average number of calls per officer per month can be determined. How much time, on average, is spent with each call is taken from the survey document (item 4). It too can be averaged for all lenders or based on a specific expectation standard.

The information obtained in the tally sheet is translated into the table in Figure 19, which shows the average or expected hours per officer spent on prospect contacts.

All volumes are reflected in terms of monthly occurrences, so the information gathered over the two-week period must be converted into a monthly average. This is accomplished by using the following formula:

1. Total each category for all lenders (both weeks).
2. Divide by two to obtain the average weekly volume.
3. Divide this by the number of loan officers responding to determine the average weekly volume per officer.
4. Multiply this amount by 52 weeks per year.
5. Finally, divide this result by 12 months per year to yield the average monthly volume per officer.

Commercial Loan Tally Sheet

Day	Interval Calls Received/Made	Category	In-Person Meeting with Client		Telephone Calls		Correspondence (letters)
			At customer Location	In Bank	Inbound	Outbound	
Monday		Existing customer					
		Potential customer					
Tuesday		Existing customer					
		Potential customer					
Wednesday		Existing customer					
		Potential customer					
Thursday		Existing customer					
		Potential customer					
Friday		Existing customer					
		Potential customer					
Saturday		Existing customer					
		Potential customer					
Total		Existing customer					
		Potential customer					

F I G U R E 19

Prospect Contact/Communication

Function	Monthly Occurrence per Officer	Average Minutes per Item		Minutes per Item		Average Hours per Officer per Month
1. Call to prospect at prospect location	4.6	×	49	÷	60	=	3.76
2. Prospect visit to bank	13.1	×	32	÷	60	=	6.99
3. Inbound phone call from prospect	21.4	×	9	÷	60	=	3.21
4. Outbound phone call to prospect	26.8	×	13	÷	60	=	5.81
5. Correspondence to prospect	.8	×	19	÷	60	=	.26
Total hours						=	20.03

The average minutes are simply an arithmetic mean taken from the survey estimates provided. The result, 20.03 hours per month per loan officer, is the average amount of time spent on prospect contact/communication. The numbers used in Figure 19 and throughout this chapter are not representative of the banking industry. They are used for example only.

The next part of business development involves the amount of time spent on strategy and planning—that is, analyzing the approach to be used to attract certain customers or devising a game plan for bringing in new accounts. This is simply the amount of raw time spent per week engaged in this activity. In Figure 20, the data are translated into the total amount of hours devoted to this activity per month per officer. In this example, each officer devotes an average of 8.66 hours per month to strategy and planning.

The last part of business development is referral base development. Contained within this category are such items as com-

F I G U R E 20

Strategy and Planning

Function	Avg. Minutes/ Officer/ Week		Minutes/ Hour		Weeks/ Year		Month/ Year		Avg. Hours/ Officer/ Month
1. Prospect relationship management	60	÷	60	×	52	÷	12	=	4.33
2. Potential market development	60	÷	60	×	52	÷	12	=	4.33
Total monthly hours								=	8.66

munity activities and entertainment (golf outings, picnics, and the like). The average time spent on these activities is taken from the survey or assigned as an expected amount of time. It is translated into monthly hours per officer, as shown in Figure 21.

Now that all areas of business development have been calculated, the total amount of time devoted to business development per officer can be determined. The total monthly hours for the three categories should be combined and translated into a

F I G U R E 21

Referral Base Development

Function	Avg. Minutes/ Officer/ Week		Minutes/ Hour		Weeks/ Year		Month/ Year		Avg. Hours/ Officer/ Month
1. Community activities	165	÷	60	×	52	÷	12	=.	11.92
2. Entertainment	50	÷	60	×	52	÷	12	=	3.61
Total monthly hours								=	15.53

percentage of total monthly hours. Since the staffing model uses percentages and business development is considered a fixed activity, it must be reduced to a percentage of total monthly hours, as shown in Figure 22.

An average of 26.2 percent of the total available monthly hours per loan officer is devoted to the fixed activity of business development. This amount will be used as an input variable in the model.

Administrative   Administrative activities involve the following standard activities:

- Internal phone calls made and received.
- Meetings.
- Special projects.

Administrative activities are so titled because they relate to the day-to-day administration of the function of a commercial loan officer. In general, they involve activities or time commitments that occur regularly regardless of loan volume. It is extremely important that administrative activities not be ignored in the staffing analysis. It is a fact of life that they occur and take up time.

F I G U R E 22

Business Development

Category		Total Monthly Hours
1. Prospect contact/communication		20.03
2. Strategy and planning		8.66
3. Referral base development		15.53
Total monthly hours		44.22
Total available hours	÷	168.60
Percentage of total available hours	=	26.23%

Like business development, administrative activities are considered fixed in that they occur regardless of loan volume. In the data-gathering stage, the goal is to arrive at an average standard or expected level of time devoted to this area, expressed as a percentage of the total monthly available hours of a commercial lender. To arrive at this percentage, gather information from the commercial loan officer survey in Exhibit B. This survey provides the questions and responses that will form the basis for the analysis.

Again, two approaches can be used in gathering this data. The first is to circulate it to all lenders and have each fill it out in accordance with his or her own impressions. In the second, the senior lending management of the bank can meet as a group and complete one survey reflecting their consensus of the bank's expectations. The latter approach is preferred, since senior management will have certain expectations on how much time should be devoted to business development, administrative activities, and the like.

Unlike other bank positions, commercial loan officers are relatively free to devote their time to pursuing loans and deposits. Unfortunately, without specific expectations it can be quite difficult to predict staff levels, because different lenders operate at different levels of productivity. Developing standards for activities not only determines specific staffing levels but also provides guidance to lenders as to what is expected. This leads to more uniformity in production and quality and thus to better results.

To begin to gather the information, tally the volume of internal phone calls, the first administrative area. This is an average of how many internal (within the bank) phone calls are made and received that require time but are not directly related to the primary function of customer contact. These calls involve internal bank communication—perhaps contact with human resources, notifying individuals of new policies and changes, or general communications. The category also includes calls made to other departments toward resolving customer issues or general issues.

Tally the number of internal calls made and received over a two-week period of time, using the same tally sheet previously used for business development (see Figure 18 and Exhibit B). Each commercial lender should complete two sheets, one for each week. Once the data are received, calculate the average number of calls made and received by each lender each month. This can be done easily using the following formula:

1. Calculate a raw total volume of calls made and received for all lenders over the two-week period.

2. The total volume by the number of working days in the period (usually 10 days). This will produce a daily average for the bank.

3. Divide the daily bank total by the number of commercial officers responding to produce a daily average volume per commercial officer.

4. Multiply this volume by 52 weeks per year to determine the annual volume per officer, then divide this total by 12. This yields the average monthly volume of internal calls made and received per commercial officer per month.

After this information is determined, complete the standard calculation as in Figure 23. The other variable in this formula, average minutes per call, is taken directly from the survey as an average for all lenders or as a consensus of senior lenders. The

F I G U R E 23

Internal Phone Calls Made and Received

Average Number of Calls per Officer per Month		Average Minutes per Call		Minutes per Hour		Average Hours per Officer per Month
43.6	×	5	÷	60	=	3.64

result of this calculation, 3.64 hours per lender, indicates the average time per officer per month devoted to making and receiving internal phone calls.

The next category, meetings, follows the same basic approach. In most financial institutions, the types of meetings loan officers attend on a regular basis fall into the following categories:

- Sales meetings
- Officer meetings
- Loan committee meetings
- Training seminars

The survey requests two responses per type of meeting: average minutes per meeting and average frequency of occurrence. Meetings cannot be overlooked, because they take up a lot of time. The average minutes per meeting and frequency per month are used to arrive at the average number of hours per month commercial loan officers spend on meetings. See Figure 24 for an example.

The final part of administrative activities is special projects, a broad category that encompasses all tasks that are not part of the commercial loan officer's day-to-day routine. The title "special

F I G U R E 24

Meetings

Meeting Type	Frequency per Month		Average Minutes per Meeting		Minutes per Hour		Average Hours per Officer per Month
1. Sales	2	×	90	÷	60	=	3.00
2. Officer	2	×	75	÷	60	=	2.50
3. Loan committee	2	×	30	÷	60	=	1.00
4. Training	.2	×	480	÷	60	=	1.60
Total hours per officer per month						=	8.10

projects" implies isolated or nonrecurring activities, but it is still important to gather the amount of time devoted to handling these projects on an ongoing basis. In other words, a particular special project may be nonrecurring, but the assignment of special projects may be a regular occurrence.

Special projects can be anything, but they usually involve preparing special reports, documents, or analyses at the request of senior management or a parent company. As in the previous activities, the commercial loan survey is used to determine the average number of monthly hours devoted to handling these special projects. The survey asks respondents to estimate the monthly time spent on these tasks. Once this information is averaged for all lenders, it can be displayed as in Figure 25.

It is entirely possible that no time may be devoted to special projects. Or senior management may wish to respond to this category by saying that no special projects will be assigned to commercial lenders.

This completes the administrative section of the profile. Since the model calls for one figure or value, it is necessary to translate the time spent in this section into a percentage of total monthly available hours per loan officer. This recap is provided in Figure 26, which indicates that, on average, 10.5 percent of the total monthly available hours per officer is taken up by administrative activities. This percentage will be used in the model as another fixed factor occurring on a regular basis.

FIGURE 25

Meeting Time Spent

Function	Average Hours per Officer per Month
1. Bank projects	2
2. Parent company projects	4
Total average monthly hours per loan officer	6

Administrative Time Spent

Category	Total Average Monthly Hours
1. Internal phone calls made/received	3.64
2. Meetings	8.10
3. Special projects	6.00
Total monthly hours per officer	17.74
Total monthly available hours per officer ÷	168.6
Percentage of Total monthly hours available per officer =	10.5%

Personal Personal activities are those devoted to nonbusiness functions or activities that occur during the workday but do not relate to the business of banking. For the most part, they involve lunches and breaks. These fixed activities require a portion of the monthly available hours per loan officer and must be accounted for.

As in the other categories, the starting point is the commercial loan officer survey document. Once completed by all lenders, the survey will show how much time (in minutes) these activities require and how frequently they occur. Since the survey asks for average minutes per occurrence, it must be restated in terms of monthly frequency.

Occurrences per day	1
Days per week	× 5
Occurrences per week	5
Weeks per year	× 52
Occurrences per year	260
Months per year	÷ 12
Occurrences per month	21.7

In this scenario, daily lunches and breaks equal 21.7 occurrences per month. Once this is determined, and an average time

F I G U R E 27

Personal Activities

Category	Frequency per Loan Officer per Month		Average Minutes per Occurrence		Minutes per Hour		Average Hours per Officer per Month
Lunches	21.7	×	60	÷	60	=	21.7
Breaks	21.7	×	10	÷	60	=	3.62
Total monthly hours per loan officer						=	25.3
Total monthly available hours per loan officer						÷	168.6
Percentage to Total monthly available hours per officer						=	15.0%

per occurrence is obtained, the total monthly hours required can be calculated, as in Figure 27. The percentage to total available hours per loan officer will be the factor used in the model as the fixed percentage of time devoted to personal activities.

This concludes the fixed categories of activities that must be accounted for in the staffing analysis for commercial lenders. A summary of the percentages for these fixed activities is shown in Figure 28. In this example, 51.7 percent of a commercial loan officer's time is devoted to these fixed activities before he or she even deals with the actual loan volumes, which are termed variable. Although these numbers are only examples, they illustrate

F I G U R E 28

Summary of Fixed Activities

Activity	Percentage of Total Available Monthly Hours per Officer
Business development	26.2%
Administrative	10.5
Personal	15.0
Total fixed activities	51.7%

how much time can be pulled away from the key volume indicator activities of making loans, maintaining/servicing loans, and handling past-due loans. Most financial institutions would find some very interesting results if they conducted this survey. What to do about these figures will be explored more fully in the analysis and measurement section of this chapter.

New/Renewed Loans   New loan handling begins the variable category of the commercial loan officer profile. This is truly the key volume indicator, as it has a direct relationship to the volume of loans made and customers on the books. New and renewed loans are products of the business development effort. As new loans and/or accounts are opened, a number of specific, key functions are triggered at the commercial lender position: review and evaluation, financial statement analysis, credit analysis, loan structuring, and approval.

New and renewed loans require other loan administration functions, such as credit file development, document printing and filing, and collateral file development. These functions are typically performed by note cage and/or loan operations personnel and are, therefore, included in the analysis of those positions.

Within each category, a number of detailed activities are involved in handling new and renewed loans. Although the detailed activities are the same for each loan type, different amounts of time will be devoted to them. A new loan is often a new customer, so all detailed activities will typically be performed. A renewed loan usually involves an existing customer, so the detailed steps may require considerably less time, and some may be skipped altogether. The detailed activity steps for the five broad categories are as follows:

1. Review and evaluation:
   - Initial interview and analysis of request.
   - Review of client business history.
   - Review of banking relationships.
2. Financial statement analysis:
   - Review and analysis.

3. Credit analysis:
   - Review of borrower's strengths, weaknesses, and character.
   - Collateral evaluation.
   - Review of management.
4. Loan structuring:
   - Pricing the loan.
   - Developing repayment terms.
   - Collateral adequacy review.
5. Approval:
   - Presentation to supervisor.
   - Renegotiation/agreement.
   - Commitment letter.

Activities like loan committee write-ups, loan committee presentation, and financial statement spreads are also required in this process, but since they can be performed by credit analysts they are included in the credit analyst survey document. If the financial institution is relatively small and has no credit analysts, loan officers should fill out this survey document as well as their own.

Variable activities require a time commitment factor for each new or renewed loan made, as opposed to fixed activities' percentage of total monthly hours available. This factor is based on the results of the commercial loan officer survey document. The resulting average time per new or renewed loan is the cumulative amount of time spent on each task within the five broad categories, expressed as hours required per unit sold. In Figure 29, this time factor is 4.02 hours.

Variable activities are not translated into percentages because the time spent on them varies with volume. If more volume is received, more overall time will be spent. If no volume is received, no time will be spent.

The time required per new loan initially is called the baseline time if it is an average of all commercial lenders' input via the commercial loan survey document. This also can become a standard if it is established by senior management as the expected or

F I G U R E   29

Average Time Required per New Loan

	Average Minutes	Total Minutes
1. Review and evaluation		
▪ Initial interview and analysis	52	
▪ Review of business history	22	
▪ Review of banking relationship	12	86
2. Financial statement analysis		
▪ Review and analysis	14	14
3. Credit analysis		
▪ Review of borrower's strengths	24	
▪ Collateral evaluation	16	
▪ Review of management	12	52
4. Loan structuring		
▪ Pricing the loan	8	
▪ Developing repayment terms	8	
▪ Collateral adequacy review	8	24
5. Approval		
▪ Presentation to supervisor	15	
▪ Renegotiation/agreement	26	
▪ Commitment letter	24	65
Total minutes		241
Total hours per loans (241 ÷ 60 minutes per hour)		4.02

normal time required per loan or the baseline is factored based on an analysis of the elements that go into the hourly rate, resulting in a standard.

For purposes of the model, the time required per new loan need not be translated into a percentage. The scenario can be repeated for renewed loans, with some reductions in time spent, and possibly even elimination of one or two activities because a renewed loan is based on an existing loan relationship, it will not require as much analytical time as a new customer relationship.

The goal of determining these time factors is to arrive at an hourly time factor that is representative of the time currently being spent (baseline) on new and/or renewed loans or to establish a desired time factor for handling such items.

The commercial loan officer survey is the vehicle for determining these data. When it is completed, whether by consensus of senior management or as an average for the bank, the hourly rates must be compared to reality. When a commercial lender or senior management member completes the survey with time estimates, he or she is indicating that this is the typical time the given activity should take. The reality, however, is that the actual time spent per new or renewed loan is usually much less, because lenders and managers tend to streamline where possible and actually increase output to meet the volume received.

In order to arrive at this true hourly rate, the surveyed average of 4.02 hours must be reanalyzed in comparison with the other variable activities and restated to take into account how much lending officer time is available to work on variable activities after all the fixed activities are factored out. (This analysis will be illustrated in Figure 39.)

Maintenance and Monitoring Maintenance and monitoring encompasses all ongoing activities related to servicing existing customers. The major categories within this section are customer communications and relationships, loan administration, and monitoring.

As a variable category, maintenance and monitoring are vital to the overall success of a commercial bank. The amount of time spent on existing customers can significantly impact overall customer satisfaction and their decision whether to remain with the bank or not. Timely attention to existing relationships and loans allows commercial lenders to remain fully up to date with a given relationship, so they can learn early if a customer is having financial difficulties and may require further assistance to prevent a potential loss to the bank.

If a financial institution's major focus is on new business development and making new loans, maintenance and monitoring can suffer greatly. While new business might increase, a high customer attrition rate might also result. The following specific areas are involved in this category for most commercial lenders.

1. Customer communications and relationships:
   - Outside call on a customer at the customer's location.
   - Meeting with the customer in the bank.
   - Inbound phone call received from the customer (problems, research, questions, etc.).
   - Outbound phone call made to the customer.
   - Written correspondence to the customer.

2. Loan administration:
   - Overdraft report handling.

3. Monitoring:
   - Field audits.
   - Financial statement analysis.
   - Review/monitor compliance with loan agreement.
   - Periodic review of loan documentation.
   - Review of customer account balances.
   - Collateral control review.

This discussion of loan administration includes only one activity, overdraft report handling. There are many other activities associated with loan administration, such as payment handling, advances/draws, and statement handling, but they are typically more in the realm of the note cage, loan operations, or administrative assistants. As such, they are included in the surveys of those individuals.

The amount of time spent on these activities is again determined through the usage of the commercial lender survey in Exhibit B, under maintenance and monitoring. The survey's time estimates can be gathered from all lenders and averaged, or produced by consensus of senior management. The commercial loan tally sheet will also be used to determine the average volume of calls made to customers. (The tally sheet was last used for the business development fixed activity.)

Once all of the raw data are obtained from the survey, the hourly factor can be developed. Maintenance and monitoring is a variable set of activities, related specifically to the number of customer relationships on the books. The goal is to determine the amount of time devoted to each existing customer relationship per month. To do this it is necessary to associate the volume of calls and other activities to the volume of existing commercial customers in the bank.

Actually, the final hourly factor will be associated with the number of customer relationships, not the number of loans, because calls and other maintenance tasks are generally related to a customer rather than a loan. One customer may have several loans, and bank personnel will call to discuss the full relationship, not just one loan.

To arrive at the factors (baseline) that will be used in the model, first obtain the number of commercial customers for the bank. Once this is determined, the calculations in Figure 30 can be performed. The total volume for the two-week period is taken from the survey's tally form. The frequency per customer per month is derived from the calculation.

It is important to note that since maintenance activities occur daily, a time factor must be determined per customer to determine the staffing requirements necessary to provide this service. In other words, how much time, on average, is required to provide service to each customer? First, the bank must know how many commercial customer relationships it has. In Figure 30, the factor of .66 hours per customer per month indicates that each customer requires approximately 39 minutes of contact (by phone or visit) each month, or 7.9 hours annually. This may seem like a lot of time, but when you factor in outside calls and the fact that this is an average it becomes more realistic.

The remaining two parts of maintenance, loan administration and monitoring, are also associated with how much time is devoted on average to each customer. When the model is fully developed, to determine optimum staffing needs this section will use an hourly factor that is multiplied by the number of customer relationships on file, not by loan volume. The number of commercial customers must be known to arrive at a factor that represents the amount of time spent per customer. This is in contrast to new

F I G U R E 30

Customer Communications

Activity	Frequency per Customer per Month	Average Minutes per Loan	Minutes per Item	Average Hours per Customer per Month
1. Outside call to customer location	.12	× 75	÷ 60 =	.15
2. Meeting with customer in bank	.34	× 30	÷ 60 =	.17
3. Inbound call	.58	× 13	÷ 60 =	.13
4. Outbound call	.74	× 13	÷ 60 =	.16
5. Written correspondence	.32	× 16	÷ 60 =	.05
Total			=	.66

Total Vol. for 2-Wk. Period	Weeks	Total Vol./Year	Months/ Year	# of Customers on File	Freq./ Customer/ Month
100	× 26	= 2,600	÷ 12	÷ 1,805	= .12

and renewed loans, for which the model uses actual loan volume as opposed to customers.

The next subcategory of maintenance is loan administration. For commercial loan officers loan administration is not intensive, since the bulk of these activities are performed by administrative assistants or note cage clerks. However, loan officers are typically responsible for evaluating overdraft reports to determine whether the checks should be paid or returned and the fee assessed or waived. The time devoted to this is determined from the survey and the time factor is determined in relation to time spent per customer, as shown in Figure 31.

The remaining sections of loan administration are found in the survey documents for administrative assistants and loan operation clerks. If the commercial division of the financial institu-

F I G U R E 31

Loan Administration

Activity	Frequency per Customer per Month		Average Minutes per Report		Minutes per Hour		Average Hours per Customer per Month
Overdraft report handled	.18	×	2	÷	60	=	.01

Report Frequency per Month		Number of Officers		Number of Customers on File		Frequency per Customer per Month
21	×	15	÷	1805	=	.18

tion is very small, it may be necessary for commercial loan officers to fill out those surveys if they handle some of these activities themselves.

The last subcategory of maintenance and monitoring also relates specifically to customers. Monitoring involves the various analytical functions performed to maintain a comfort level with the progress of a customer relationship. It can include activities such as field audits for asset-based loans, which require timely inventory and/or receivable monitoring. Other activities are performed at periodic intervals to monitor the continuing strength of commercial customers and assess whether problems or financial difficulties are brewing.

Since monitoring activities must be associated specifically with customers, not loans, determining the hourly factor to be used in the model follows the same approach as before. Figure 32 analyzes these activities.

In most cases the items included in Figure 32 occur annually for each customer, making the calculation of the factor simple. In other cases—for example, the collateral review—reviewing quarterly or three times per year may be necessary.

Monitoring

Activity	Frequency per Customer per Month	Average Minutes per Activity	Minutes per Hour	Average Hours per Customer per Month
1. Fixed audits	.09	× 98	÷ 60	= .15
2. Financial statement analysis	.09	× 23	÷ 60	= .04
3. Review/monitor of loan agreement compliance	.09	× 13	÷ 60	= .02
4. Loan documentation review	.09	× 10	÷ 60	= .02
5. Review of account balances	.09	× 8	÷ 60	= .02
6. Collateral control review	.25	× 8	÷ 60	= .04
Total hours				= .29

Frequency per Customer per Year		Months per Year		Frequency per Customer per Month
1	÷	12	=	.09
3	÷	12	=	.25

Some types of loans require more intensive monitoring than others. With asset-based or agricultural credits, field audits may be completed quarterly or even monthly. This can add to the time required to process a new loan, as more documentation may be required. To account for these differences, three approaches can be taken.

1. Many financial institutions are segregated by division. That is, separate lending divisions are available to handle specific types of credit, such as asset-based, commercial, agribusiness, and real estate construction

loans. In this case, when completing the commercial loan officer survey keep all divisions separate and perform a separate staffing analysis for each.

2. Keep all surveys separate, but develop a weighted average analysis; that is, weight the different types of loans by their volume so that only one set of factors is used for the staffing model. Figure 33 is an example of how this might be accomplished.

The 4.33 hours shown in Figure 33 indicates that based on the portfolio mix, this is the weighted average amount of time required per new loan. In other words, to determine optimum staff size the analyst could use an hourly factor of 4.33 without having to perform four separate analyses.

The same approach would be used for the maintenance category. However, instead of the number of notes in the portfolio, the volume of customer relationships is used, as shown in Figure 34.

Like the previous example, Figure 34 provides a weighted average factor that can be applied to all

---

F I G U R E 33

Weighted Average Analysis (New Loans)

Type of Loan	Portfolio Volume of Notes	Percentage to Total Volume		Hourly Factor per New Loan		Weighted Average Hourly Factor
1. Asset-based	1,000	17.2%	×	5.0	=	.86
2. Commercial	3,500	60.3	×	4.0	=	2.41
3. Agribusiness	800	13.8	×	5.5	=	.76
4. Real estate construction	500	8.7	×	3.5	=	.30
Total	5,800	100.0%				
Total weighted average hours per loan					=	4.33

F I G U R E 34

Weighted Average Analysis (Maintenance)

Type of Loan	Portfolio Number of Customers	Percentage to Total Volume		Hourly Factor per New Loan		Weighted Average Hourly Factor
1. Asset-based	300	15.5%	×	1.08	=	.168
2. Commercial	1,200	61.9	×	.96	=	.595
3. Agribusiness	280	14.4	×	1.25	=	.180
4. Real estate construction	160	8.2	×	1.15	=	.095
Total	1,940	100.0%				
Total weighted average hours per customer					=	1.038

customers to avoid making four separate analyses by loan type.

3. The last approach is simply to average (mean) the results from the survey and combine them into one analysis. This would work best for banks with small commercial loan departments where each lender handles a smattering of different types of credit. Since no specific concentration of loan types or segregation of loan divisions exists, an average would be representative.

These three options can be used as well for the other commercial department surveys (for administrative assistants, loan operations, personnel, and credit analysts).

Now that all subcategories have been determined for the maintenance activity category, a recap can be computed reflecting the total average hours required per month per customer. Figure 35 illustrates this recap.

The .96 hour from Figure 35 will be the actual hourly factor used in the staffing model. The only difference between this factor

F I G U R E 35

Summary Hours per Customer

Category	Average Hours per Customer per Month
1. Customer communication	.66
2. Loan administration	.01
3. Monitoring	.29
Total maintenance hours per customer per month	.96

and the one used for new and renewed loans is that for maintenance it will be applied against the number of commercial customers, whereas for new and renewed loans it will be applied
against actual loan volume (notes booked). The sample financial
institution spends .96 hour, or 57 minutes, on average for each
commercial customer relationship per month. Again, this is a
variable category, since the total time required and staff needed
will fluctuate with the number of customers on the books.

Past-Due Handling   The final variable activity category is past-
due handling, or control, which takes in all activities related to the
collection and monitoring of delinquent commercial customer
loans. Commercial loan delinquency is handled at the individual
commercial lender level, as opposed to the central collection
department used for consumer loans (installment and credit
cards). It becomes another variable activity category involved in
the determination of commercial loan officer staffing levels.

Past-due handling consists of telephone calls to customers,
written correspondence to customers, and meetings with customers. Within each subcategory, loan delinquencies are broken
down into the following stages:

- 15–29 days delinquent.
- 30–59 days delinquent.

- 60–89 days delinquent.
- 90+ days delinquent.

In other words, a specific activity is performed on each delinquent account at a given delinquency level throughout the month. The performance of this function has a direct impact on the bottom-line loan losses of the bank. It is important not only that this be a part of the commercial loan officer profile but that appropriate time be devoted to this function to minimize the bank's loan losses.

The commercial loan officer survey requests information as to the amount of time, on average, devoted each of the three primary activities by delinquency stage. It is also necessary to know the number of attempts being made for each activity per month. The key to success in this category is consistency in performing the tasks.

Based on the data obtained in the commercial loan officer survey, determination of the total hourly factor for usage in the model begins as in Figure 36, which shows the average hours spent on delinquent commercial loans by delinquency stage. This breaks down how often the three activities are performed on delinquent loans each month. To perform this analysis, the bank must know the number of delinquent commercial notes by delinquency stage. Ideally, this should be an average of at least six months to one year of data to make the breakdown more representative.

Most financial institutions have good records of delinquency volume over a period of time. After this information is retrieved, it should be averaged, arrayed by delinquency stage, and totaled. Then a percentage to the total is assigned for each stage, as in Figure 37. This will form the basis for arriving at a single hourly factor for handling any stage of delinquent loan. The average number of delinquent loans reflects the average volume over the past 6 to 12 months.

The last phase of this process is to arrive at a weighted average hourly rate for the amount of time spent on a delinquent commercial loan regardless of delinquency stage. The result is the variable factor that will be included in the model. The determina-

F I G U R E 36

Average Hours per Loan per Stage

	Frequency per Delinquent Loan per Month		Average Minutes per Task		Minutes per Hour		Average Hours per Delinquent Loan per Month
1. 15–29 Days							
Phone calls	2	×	5	÷	60	=	.167
Written correspondence	1	×	5	÷	60	=	.083
Meetings	0	×	0	÷	60	=	00
Total hours							.25
2. 30–59 Days							
Phone calls	5	×	8	÷	60	=	.67
Written correspondence	3	×	10	÷	60	=	.50
Meetings	2	×	17	÷	60	=	.57
Total hours							1.74
3. 60–89 Days							
Phone calls	3	×	9	÷	60	=	.45
Written correspondence	2	×	15	÷	60	=	.50
Meetings	2	×	25	÷	60	=	.84
Total hours							1.79
4. 90+ Days							
Phone calls	3	×	11	÷	60	=	.55
Written correspondence	3	×	19	÷	60	=	.95
Meetings	3	×	33	÷	60	=	1.65
Total hours							3.15

tion of this amount uses the data from Figures 36 and 37, and the actual calculation is illustrated in Figure 38.

The factor of 1.2 hours per delinquent loan per month is a weighted average that takes into account the historical experience of the bank with respect to delinquent handlings. This is the final variable factor for commercial lenders.

F I G U R E 37

Average Delinquent Accounts by Stage

Delinquency Stage	Average Number of Delinquent Loans	Percentage to Total Delinquent Loans
15–29 days	25	51.6%
30–59 days	12	25.8
60–89 days	3	6.5
90+ days	8	16.1
Total	48	100.0%

F I G U R E 38

Weighted Average Hours per Delinquent Account per Month

Delinquency Stage	Average Hours per Delinquent Loan per Month		Percentage to Total Delinquent Loans		Weighted Average Factor per Delinquent Loan per Month
15–29 days	.25	×	51.6%	=	.129
30–59 days	1.74	×	25.8	=	.449
60–89 days	1.79	×	6.5	=	.116
90+ days	3.15	×	16.1	=	.507
Weighted average hours per delinquent loan per month				=	1.20

Recap: Commercial Lenders   Now that the full profile activities have been developed for commercial lenders, the items must be translated into the proper format for the model. The first step is to develop a chart of all data determined thus far, illustrated in Figure 39.

Technically, the information in Figure 39 could be included in the model. However, the fixed hourly factors should be restated to represent what is actually occurring. The 4.02 hours required

F I G U R E 39

Commercial Lender Profile Summary

1. Fixed	Percentage of Officer Time
■ Business development	26.5%
■ Administrative	10.5
■ Personal	15.0

2. Variable	Hourly Factor
■ New loans	4.02
■ Renewed loans	3.00
■ Maintenance	.95
■ Past dues	1.20

per new loan is not utilized fully, since a commercial lender usually does not have the full day available for variable activities, due to the amount of time already used up in the fixed activities. In Figure 39, more than half the loan officer's time is committed to fixed activities. This leaves only 48.3 percent of the lender's day to handle variable activities. Since 168.6 monthly hours are available per officer (Figure 17), only 81.4 hours per month are available to handle the volume of new / renewed loans, maintenance, and past dues.

Since a given volume of loans is actually booked during a given month, a true hourly factor for fixed activities can be calculated as the baseline. This requires some volume information, which will ultimately be needed anyway for the model. The information required is the average monthly volume for new loans made, renewed loans made, total past-due loans (all stages of delinquency), and number of commercial loan customers on file. This can be an average over the last three months.

It is also necessary to obtain the number of commercial lenders (FTE) on staff. From these data, the amount of time devoted to fixed activities can be determined as in Figure 40. This analysis calculates exactly how many hours are committed to fixed activities, up front, before variable tasks are even considered.

F I G U R E 40

Total Departmental Fixed Hours Committed

1. Total monthly hours available per lender   168.6
2. Total number of lenders on staff   ×   4
3. Total departmental hours available per month   674.4

Fixed Activity	Percentage of Time Devoted		Total Departmental Hours Available		Total Departmental Fixed Hours Committed
Business development	26.2%	×	674.4	=	176.7
Administrative	10.5	×	674.4	=	70.8
Personal	15.0	×	674.4	=	101.2
Total					348.7

Of the original monthly hours available, only 325.7 remain for variable activities (674.4 – 348.7). This number is used in Figure 41 to calculate the baseline hourly factor. The numbers in the calculated factor column come from Figure 39. The hours remaining come from Figure 40.

The actual variable hourly factors now appear quite different from in the original analysis.

Variable Activity	Standard Hours	Actual Hours
1. New loans	4.02	1.74
2. Renewed loans	3.00	1.30
3. Maintenance	.96	.42
4. Past dues	1.20	.52

The wide variance between the standard and the actual suggests that the department may be understaffed. Based on the volume of work completed, much less time is spent per loan or customer than the lenders or senior management are saying they should spend. If the reverse were true, the department would likely be overstaffed. If the standard variable hourly factors were equal or close to the actual, staffing would appear to be adequate.

F I G U R E 41

Variable Activity Hourly Factors

Variable Activity	Average Monthly Volume		Calculated Factor		Total Hours Required	Percentage of Total Hours
New loans	40	×	4.02	=	160.8	21.4%
Renewed loans	33	×	3.00	=	99.0	13.2
Maintenance	452	×	.96	=	433.9	57.8
Past dues	48	×	1.20	=	57.6	7.6
Total					751.3	100.0%

Variable Activity	Percentage of Total Hours		Hours Remaining Available for Variable Activities		Average Monthly Volume		Actual Variable Activity Hourly Factor
New loans	21.4%	×	325.7	÷	40	=	1.74
Renewed loans	13.2	×	325.7	÷	33	=	1.30
Maintenance	57.8	×	325.7	÷	452	=	.42
Past dues	7.6	×	325.7	÷	48	=	.52

But how does one tell how much a department is over- or understaffed? This is accomplished by inputting the factors determined into the staffing model, as shown in Figure 42. Fixed and variable factors are reflected only for commercial lenders to illustrate their placement. From these data, the model will calculate the total FTE staffing levels for the commercial lending division. The steps for building the model and the various formulas is explained later in this chapter, but first the basic profile data must be developed for administrative assistants/secretaries, loan operations and support personnel, and credit analysts.

Administrative Assistants/Secretaries

Administrative assistants and secretaries perform very valuable roles in the day-to-day handling of commercial loans. An accurate staffing analysis for commercial loans could not be accomplished without considering this group. The administrative assistant/sec-

F I G U R E 42

Commercial Loan Staffing Model

BANK: [   ]   COMMERCIAL BANKER STAFFING MODEL   DATE: [   ]
LOCATION: [   ]
BRANCH: [   ]

DATA REQUIRED
  # NEW LOANS THIS MONTH   [   ] AVG. # TOTAL HOURS PER FTE PER DAY: [   ]
  # RENEWALS THIS MONTH: [   ] NUMBER LOANS PAST DUE THIS MONTH: [   ]
                                  AVERAGE NUMBER OF LOAN ACCOUNTS ON FILE: [   ]

A. FIXED HOURS (PER FTE):

	% OF TOTAL MONTHLY HOURS			
	COMMERCIAL LENDER	ADMINISTRATIVE ASSISTANT	LOAN SUPPORT	CREDIT ANALYST
BUSINESS DEVELOPMENT:	[26.50%]	[ ]	[ ]	[ ]
ADMINISTRATION:	[10.50%]	[ ]	[ ]	[ ]
	[ ]	[ ]	[ ]	[ ]
PERSONAL TIME:	[15.00%]	[ ]	[ ]	[ ]
TOTAL:	57.00%	0.00%	0.00%	0.00%

B. VARIABLE HOURS:

	STANDARD HOURS REQUIRED PER ITEM			
	COMMERCIAL LENDER	ADMINISTRATIVE ASSISTANT	LOAN SUPPORT	CREDIT ANALYST
NEW LOANS:	[4.02]	[ ]	[ ]	[ ]
RENEWAL LOANS:	[3.00]	[ ]	[ ]	[ ]
MAINTEN. MONITOR:	[0.95]	[ ]	[ ]	[ ]
PAST DUE:	[1.20]	[ ]	[ ]	[ ]

C. DISTRIBUTION OF FTEs BY POSITION:

	FULL-TIME EQUIVALENTS REQUIRED				
	COMMERCIAL LENDER	ADMINISTRATIVE ASSISTANT	LOAN SUPPORT	CREDIT ANALYST	TOTAL FTE STAFF
NEW LOANS:	[ ]	[ ]	[ ]	[ ]	[ ]
RENEWAL LOANS:	[ ]	[ ]	[ ]	[ ]	[ ]
MAINTENANCE:	[ ]	[ ]	[ ]	[ ]	[ ]
PAST DUES:	[ ]	[ ]	[ ]	[ ]	[ ]
BUSINESS DEVELOPMENT:	[ ]	[ ]	[ ]	[ ]	[ ]
ADMINISTRATIVE:	[ ]	[ ]	[ ]	[ ]	[ ]
PERSONAL:	[ ]	[ ]	[ ]	[ ]	[ ]
TOTAL FTE:	[ ]	[ ]	[ ]	[ ]	[ ]

retarial function has basically the same profile elements as a commercial lender, with a few exceptions:

1. Fixed activities:
   - Administrative
   - Personal
2. Variable activities
   - New loans
   - Renewed loans
   - Maintenance

Business development and past-due handling activities generally are not part of the administrative assistant's role. In addition, the subcategories within the fixed and variable categories will differ from those of commercial lenders based upon what is performed by this group.

The methodology used to gather such data is no different from that used for commercial lenders. The administrative assistant/secretarial survey document is shown in Appendix Exhibit C. The survey asks for time estimates that can be provided in a single sitting. Tally sheets should be completed over a two-week period. The overall hour factors and percentage of time variables will be determined from these documents.

Administrative Administrative activities for administrative assistants/secretaries are quite different from those for commercial lenders, but they are nevertheless vital to the success of the operation. Administrative subcategories are typing, handling phone calls, and general administrative duties.

Administrative activities, as a fixed profile category, are those activities that occur without regard to loan volume or portfolio size. The first subcategory, typing, covers only internally generated documents and miscellaneous reports that are of a general nature and not specific to commercial loans. The amount of time devoted to general typing is obtained from the completed survey (Exhibit C). The time estimates obtained from a pool of administrative assistants and secretaries should be averaged to produce a relatively realistic time estimate for any type of memo or report.

The next step is to determine the average amount of typing required per secretary per month. This is obtained from the activity tally sheet, shown in Figure 43.

This tally sheet should be completed by each administrative assistant/secretary over a two-week period (10 production tally sheets). Once they are received, the calculation for administrative typing can be determined, as shown in Figure 44.

Figure 44 shows how much time, on average, is devoted to miscellaneous typing basically unrelated to commercial loans. The average hours will be fixed as a percentage of total monthly hours.

The next subcategory, general administrative activities, involves office functions that do not relate specifically to the production of commercial loans. As in general typing, an average volume of these types of activities is needed. This is obtained from the same tally production sheet used in Figure 43. The specific activities being evaluated are appointments scheduled, meetings scheduled, and other duties.

As with typing, the idea is to arrive at an average amount of time spent per administrative assistant per month on these tasks. This will further define the fixed percentage of time devoted to administrative tasks overall. The actual volumes and time estimates from the survey are put into the formula in Figure 45 to obtain the hours spent on these activities.

The last subcategory of administrative activities is handling general telephone calls (not customer communications). This category involves internal calls made and/or received, calls routed to someone else, and messages taken.

Telephone information is captured in the administrative assistant/secretary document survey using a different tally form than for the other duties, as shown in Figure 46.

Over a two-week period, each administrative assistant/secretary should simply record a tally mark for each call type received or made under the appropriate heading.

Other headings are included on this tally sheet because it will also be used to capture other types of call volumes. Since the production tally sheet can be used for an entire week, two of these

F I G U R E 43

Activity Tally Sheet

Volume Category	Tally	Total
Customer correspondence		
Call reports		
Internal memos		
Miscellaneous reports		
Items filed in the credit file		
Payments handled		
Correspondence/call reports filed		
Advances/draws handled		
Statement updates handled		
Appointments scheduled		
Meetings scheduled		
Other _____		
Other _____		
Other _____		

General Typing

Subcategory	Total Dept. Vol.		Weeks to Annualize		Months/Year		No. of Admin. Asst.		Avg. Vol. Produced/Admin. Asst./Month		Avg. Minutes/Item		Minutes/Hour		Avg. Hours/Admin. Asst./Month
Internal memos	36.5	×	26	÷	12	÷	4	=	19.8	×	8	÷	60	=	2.64
Misc. reports	73.3	×	26	÷	12	÷	4	=	39.7	×	11	÷	60	=	7.28
Total typing hours per administrative assistant per month															9.92

General Administration

Subcategory	Total Dept. Vol.		Weeks to Annualize		Months/Year		No. of Admin. Asst.		Avg. Vol. Produced/Admin. Asst./Month		Avg. Minutes/Item		Minutes/Hour		Avg. Hours/Admin. Asst./Month
Appts. sched.	19.50	×	26	÷	12	÷	4	=	10.56	×	5	÷	60	=	.88
Meetings sched.	14.95	×	26	÷	12	÷	4	=	8.10	×	2	÷	60	=	.27
Other duties	13.85	×	26	÷	12	÷	4	=	7.50	×	8	÷	60	=	1.00
Total general administrative hours per administrative assistant per month															2.15

F I G U R E 46

Telephone Call Tally Form

DAY	Inbound Calls Received from Customer	Outbound Calls Made to Customers	Internal Calls Made/ Received	Calls Taken and Rerouted	Messages Taken
Monday					
Tuesday					
Wednesday					
Thursday					
Friday					
Saturday					
Total					

forms cover the survey period. Once all forms have been accumulated, they should be totaled for the entire group or department of administrative assistants/secretaries. The hourly factor can then be determined for phone call handling, in accordance with Figure 47. This indicates, on average, how much fixed time is devoted to handling miscellaneous phone call volume. Remember, the phone calls recorded in this area are general in nature and do not relate to loan customer communications.

This completes the administrative category for administrative assistants/secretaries. From the previous calculations, the hourly factors must be summarized and restated in terms of a percentage to total monthly hours for each administrative assistant/secretary. The summary is outlined in Figure 48, which

F I G U R E 47

General Telephone Call Volume

Subcategory	Total Dept. Vol.		Weeks to Annualize		Months/Year		No. of Admin. Asst.		Avg. Vol. Produced/Admin. Asst./Month		Avg. Minutes/Item		Minutes/Hour		Avg. Hours/Admin. Asst./Month
Interval calls received/made	365.5	×	26	÷	12	÷	4	=	198	×	4	÷	60	=	13.20
Calls routed to another	415.4	×	26	÷	12	÷	4	=	225	×	2	÷	60	=	7.50
Messages taken	886.15	×	26	÷	12	÷	4	=	480	×	.50	÷	60	=	4.00
															24.70

Total telephone call hours per administrative assistant per month

F I G U R E   48

Administrative Activities

Category	Average Hours per Administrative Assistant/ Secretary per Month
1. General typing	9.92
2. General administration	2.15
3. General telephone handling	24.70
Total hours	36.77
Total monthly hours available	÷168.6
Percentage of time spent on administrative activities per administrative assistant/ secretary per month	21.8%

shows that 21.8 percent of an administrative assistant's time is spent on these administrative activities each month. This leaves approximately 78.2 percent of the assistant's time for customer-related activities and other fixed activities.

Personal   The only other fixed activity category associated with administrative assistants/secretaries is that of personal activities: lunches or other personal time occurring on a daily basis. The administrative assistant/secretarial document survey form provides a time estimate for these activities, and an average (mean) is calculated for all administrative assistants/secretaries. Once this has been obtained, the total monthly hours per administrative assistant/secretary can be determined as shown in Figure 49. The frequency per month derives from 52 weeks per year multiplied by 5 days per week, divided by 12 months per year.

This completes the fixed activities for administrative assistants/secretaries. To recap, 37.9 percent of an administrative assistant/secretary's time is devoted to administrative activities performed on a regular basis regardless of the amount of commercial loan volume. The next section begins the variable categories, which are affected by loan volume.

Personal Activities

Category	Frequency per Month	Average Minutes per Occurrence	Minutes per Hour	Average hours per Admin. Asst. per Month
1. Lunches	21.7 ×	60 ÷	60 =	21.7
2. Breaks	21.7 ×	15 ÷	60 =	5.4
Total hours				27.1
Total monthly hours available			÷	168.6
Percentage of time spent on personal activities				16.1%

New/Renewed Loans   New and renewed loans are variable activities that relate specifically to the key volume indicators of commercial loan volume or portfolio size of customers. No volume, no activity.

The category of new / renewed loans refers to activities performed by administrative assistants/secretaries that relate directly to the handling of new and renewed loans. In contrast to commercial lenders, for administrative assistants the tasks performed in booking new and renewed loans consist of typing and loan administration.

Within each of these subcategories, a number of specific tasks are performed.

1. Typing.
   - Loan committee write-ups.
   - Commitment letters.
   - Financial statements/credit analyses.
   - Notes/documents.
2. Loan administration.
   - Credit files built and filed.

As before, the information used to determine the hourly factors is obtained in the administrative assistant/secretary survey form (Exhibit C). A time estimate, in minutes, for handling the

F I G U R E 50

New/Renewed Loans: Typing

Subcategory	Average Minutes per Loan	
	New	Renewed
Loan committee write-ups	93	93
Commitment letters	9	9
Financial statements/credit analyses	14	14
Notes/documents	_7_	_7_
Total minutes	123	123
Minutes per hour	÷60	÷60
Total hours per loan	2.05	2.05

tasks of new and renewed loans is requested. This time estimate should be an average (mean) for all administrative assistants/secretaries in the department. Once it has been obtained, the hourly factor per administrative assistant/secretary is calculated in Figure 50.

From an administrative assistant/secretarial perspective, loan administration involves building and filing a credit file. The credit file organizes data, correspondence, financial statements, analysis, and so forth for each customer. A new credit file must be developed for each new customer added to the bank's clientele.

The credit file is usually the responsibility of the commercial loan officer, but someone must initially set one up and then physically file it for safekeeping. This is generally done by administrative assistants/secretaries, but it can also be done by loan operations or loan support individuals. In any case, it is driven by the number of new or renewed customers developed, making it a variable activity.

The time required for loan administration is an average of the time estimates provided from the administrative assistant/secretary survey. Based on the information obtained, an analysis of time is prepared as in Figure 51. As might be expected, for renewed loans a new credit file is not built because there is

F I G U R E 51

New/Renewed Loans: Loan Administration

	Time Estimates (minutes)	
Subcategory	New	Renewed
Credit files developed and filed	43	15
Minutes per hour	÷60	60
Hours per loan	.72	.25

already a custodial relationship and an existing file. Some data
will need to be added, but renewed loans take less administrative
time than new ones.

This completes the new/renewed loan section for administrative assistants/secretaries. Since only one hourly factor will be
used for new and renewed loans, a recap of the hourly factors for
this category is shown in Figure 52.

Maintenance   The last variable activity category for administrative assistants/secretaries is maintenance. As with commercial
lenders, maintenance relates directly to activities involving existing commercial loan customers. Since the total time involved
relates specifically to the number of commercial loan customers
on file, one must know the average portfolio size (commercial

F I G U R E 52

New/Renewed Loans: Recap

	Hourly Rate per Loan	
Subcategory	New	Renewed
Typing	2.05	2.05
Loan administration	.72	.25
Total hours required per loan	2.77	2.30

customer count) to develop the hourly factors used in the staffing analysis.

Maintenance for administrative assistants/secretaries consists of three broad subcategories: typing, telephone, and loan administration. These subcategories are similar to those in the administrative and new/renewed loan activity sections, but they differ in the tasks they contain.

1. Typing:
   - Customer correspondence.
   - Call reports.
2. Telephone:
   - Inbound phone calls received from commercial customer.
   - Outbound phone calls made to commercial loan customer.
3. Loan administration:
   - Correspondence/call report filing (credit file).
   - Payment handling.
   - Advances/draws handled.
   - Statements handled.
   - Miscellaneous customer documents filed.
   - Other.

Some of the tasks under loan administration may be performed by a loan operations/support clerk, so they are also included in the loan operations/support group analysis.

The necessary time estimate data for maintenance are obtained through the administrative assistant/secretary survey. The two production tally sheets shown in Figures 43 and 46 will again be used. These relate to telephone call, typing, and loan administration task volumes. Both production forms represent two weeks of volume and should be held until completed.

Beginning with the subcategory of typing, once the production tally sheet is retrieved for the entire staff an hourly factor can be developed. All maintenance items must be associated with the number of commercial loan customers in the portfolio, not with the volume of loans as in the new/renewed loan category. Figure 53 provides the calculation for typing.

F I G U R E   53

Maintenance Activity: Typing

Activity	Frequency/ Customer/ Month		Average Minutes/ Item		Minute/ Hour		Average Hours/ Customer/ Month
Customer correspondence	.38	×	7	÷	60	=	.05
Call reports	.07	×	11	÷	60	=	.02
Total hours per customer per month						=	.07

Activity	Total Dept. Vol.		Annualized		Min./ Year		# of Customers (Portfolio)		Freq./ Customer/ Month
Customer correspondence	316.5	×	26	÷	12	÷	1,805	=	.38
Call reports	58.3	×	26	÷	12	÷	1,805	=	.07

In Figure 53, .07 hour (4.2 minutes) is devoted to each customer on file per month (on average) for typing.

The next category, telephone calls, is similarly calculated. To capture this volume, use the telephone call tally production sheet (Figure 46). Now the focus is on calls to and from commercial customers directly. Each production sheet contains a full week of data, so only two sheets need be submitted. Once this information is retrieved, the aggregate base volume should be determined for the entire staff of administrative assistants/secretaries. Then the hourly factor can be determined as in Figure 54.

The last subcategory, loan administration, accounts for the remaining maintenance time. Loan administration refers to ongoing servicing of existing customers. Although there are specific tasks in the survey form, an "other" subcategory is available for servicing requirements unique to the bank. As before, the data are taken from the activity production tally sheet (Figure 43). All amounts must be tallied for all administrative assistants/secretar-

F I G U R E 54

Maintenance Activity: Telephone Calls

Activity	Freq./ Customer/ Month		Avg. Min./ Item		Min./ Hour		Avg. Hrs./ Customer/ Month
Inbound phone calls from customers	.74	×	4	÷	60	=	.05
Outbound phone calls to customers	.14	×	6	÷	60	=	.014
Total hours per customer per month						=	.064

	Total Dept. Vol.		Annualized		Min./ Year		No. of Customers (Portfolio)		Freq./ Customer/ Month
Inbound	616.5	×	26	÷	12	÷	1,805	=	.74
Outbound	116.6	×	26	÷	12	÷	1,805	=	.14

ies in the aggregate to develop the hourly factor for the subcategory, as shown in Figure 55.

Figure 55 shows that .30 hour, or approximately 18 minutes per customer per month, are devoted to loan administration type functions.

The three subcategories of telephone calls, typing, and loan administration are summarized to arrive at the single hourly factor devoted to the maintenance function, which will be instrumental in the staffing model. The summary in Figure 56 shows that .434 hour is devoted to servicing and maintaining customers on a monthly basis.

This completes the last category of the profile for administrative assistants/secretaries. The final portion of this analysis is to recap the information learned and translate it into usable factors and percentages for the staffing model.

Recap: Administrative Assistants/Secretaries   The recap is the final portion of analyzing the administrative assistant/secretarial

F I G U R E 55

Maintenance Activity: Loan Administration

Activity	Freq./ Customer/ Month		Avg. Min./ Item		Min./ Hour		Avg. Hrs./ Customer/ Month
Correspondence/ call report filing	.05	×	8	÷	60	=	.01
Payment handling	.50	×	5	÷	60	=	.05
Advances/draws	.15	×	15	÷	60	=	.04
Statements	.30	×	5	÷	60	=	.03
Misc. items filed	.25	×	8	÷	60	=	.04
Other	.50	×	15	÷	60	=	.13
Total hours per customer per month						=	.30

Activity	Total Dept. Vol.		Annualized		Month/ Year		No. of Customers (Portfolio)		Freq./ Customer/ Month
Correspondence/ call report	41.7	×	26	÷	12	÷	1,805	=	.05
Payments	416.5	×	26	÷	12	÷	1,805	=	.50
Advances/draws	12.5	×	26	÷	12	÷	1,805	=	.15
Statements	249.9	×	26	÷	12	÷	1,805	=	.30
Misc. filing	208.3	×	26	÷	12	÷	1,805	=	.25
Other	416.5	×	26	÷	12	÷	1,805	=	.50

function and accounting for all activities and time related to commercial loans. Based on the information captured in the preceding sections, a recap table can be prepared as in Figure 57 for the administrative assistant/secretarial function.

As in the commercial lender analysis, the variable activities represent the amount of time estimated by administrative assistants and secretaries for various tasks, not necessarily how long they actually spend on these tasks. Analysis will reveal whether there is a significant difference between the two figures. If substantially fewer hours are actually spent than are estimated for

F I G U R E 56

Maintenance Summary

Category	Hourly Factor per Customer
1. Typing	.07
2. Telephone calls	.064
3. Loan administration	.30
Total hours per customer per month	.434

F I G U R E 57

Administrative Assistant/Secretary Profile Recap

1. Fixed activities	Percentage of Time Available
■ Administrative	21.8%
■ Personal	16.1
2. Variable activities	**Hourly Factor**
■ New loans	2.77
■ Renewed loans	2.30
■ Maintenance	.434

variable activities, the department may be understaffed. This can translate into errors, inefficiencies, and ultimately unhappy customers, resulting in significant erosion of the commercial loan effort.

The analysis focuses solely on the variable activities. Since fixed activities do not relate to loan volume or customer portfolio size, the percentage of time devoted to them will remain constant no matter how many loans are received. Figure 57 shows that 37.9 percent of an administrative assistant's/secretary's time is committed already, regardless of how much loan volume is received.

This leaves only 62.1 percent of the assistant's time for variable activities. If a high enough volume of new/renewed loans is received and completed, something must give. The time spent per new or renewed loan may be considerably less than the factor indicated in Figure 57, and the department is probably understaffed. If much more time is spent per new or renewed loan than Figure 57 suggests, the department is probably overstaffed.

The next step is to learn the amount of time already committed to fixed activities, which will also reveal the hours remaining for other duties. This analysis is shown in Figure 58.

From a departmental standpoint, only 408.8 monthly total hours are available for variable activities. Figure 59 shows the actual hourly factors for variable activities. The calculated hourly factor comes from Figure 57 and the hours remaining come from Figure 58.

In contrast to the commercial lenders example, Figure 59 shows that more time is actually being devoted to the variable

F I G U R E 58

Total Departmental Fixed and Variable Hours

1. Total monthly hours available per administrative assistant/secretary — 168.6
2. Total number of administrative assistants/secretaries on staff — × 4
3. Total departmental hours available per month — 674.4

Fixed Activity	Percentage of Time Devoted		Total Departmental Hours Available		Total Departmental Fixed Hours Committed
Administration	21.8%	×	674.4	=	147.02
Personal	16.1	×	674.4	=	108.6
Total fixed hours				=	265.6
Total variable hours available (674.4 − 265.6 = 408.8)				=	408.8

F I G U R E   59

Actual Variable Activity Hourly Factors

Variable Activity	Average Monthly Volume		Calculated Hourly Factor		Total Hours Required	Percentage of Total Hours
New loans	40	×	2.77	=	110.8	28.9%
Renewed loans	33	×	2.30	=	75.9	19.8
Maintenance	452	×	.434	=	196.2	51.3
Total					382.9	100.0%

Variable Activity	Percentage of Total Hours		Hours Remaining for Various Activities		Average Monthly Volume		Actual Variable Activity Hourly Factor
New loans	28.9%	×	408.8	÷	40	=	2.95
Renewed loans	19.8	×	408.8	÷	33	=	2.95
Maintenance	51.3	×	408.8	÷	452	=	.46

tasks than the survey indicated. This indicates that the bank may be overstaffed on administrative assistants/secretaries, since more time is being taken than is actually needed.

Variable Activity	Standard Hours	Actual Hours
1. New loans	2.77	2.95
2. Renewed loans	2.30	2.45
3. Maintenance	.43	.46

To determine actual staffing requirements, use the staffing model shown in Figure 60. The standard amounts were used for the variable factors (for example, 2.77 hours per new loan). This figure produces a staff number level less than what exists today. The difference between the calculated result and the existing FTE staff level indicates the number of FTE by which the bank is overstaffed and ultimately the opportunity available.

It is recommended that standard amounts be used in the model. They also become the norm to use in the model repeatedly

F I G U R E 60

Staffing Model for Administrative Assistants/Secretaries

```
BANK:           [          ]   COMMERCIAL BANKER STAFFING MODEL      DATE:    [          ]
LOCATION:       [          ]
BRANCH:         [          ]
```

```
DATA REQUIRED
  # NEW LOANS THIS MONTH     [        ] AVG. # TOTAL HOURS PER FTE PER DAY:          [        ]
  # RENEWALS THIS MONTH:     [        ] NUMBER LOANS PAST DUE THIS MONTH:           [        ]
                                        AVERAGE NUMBER OF LOAN ACCOUNTS ON FILE:  [        ]
```

A. FIXED HOURS (PER FTE):

	% OF TOTAL MONTHLY HOURS			
	COMMERCIAL LENDER	ADMINISTRATIVE ASSISTANT	LOAN SUPPORT	CREDIT ANALYST
BUSINESS DEVELOPMENT:	[ ]	[ ]	[ ]	[ ]
ADMINISTRATION:	[ ]	[21.80%]	[ ]	[ ]
PERSONAL TIME:	[ ]	[16.10%]	[ ]	[ ]
TOTAL:	0.00%	37.90%	0.00%	0.00%

B. VARIABLE HOURS:

	STANDARD HOURS REQUIRED PER ITEM			
	COMMERCIAL LENDER	ADMINISTRATIVE ASSISTANT	LOAN SUPPORT	CREDIT ANALYST
NEW LOANS:	[ ]	[ ]	[ ]	[ ]
RENEWAL LOANS:	[ ]	[2.77]	[ ]	[ ]
MAINTEN. MONITOR:	[ ]	[2.30]	[ ]	[ ]
PAST DUE:	[ ]	[0.43]	[ ]	[ ]

C. DISTRIBUTION OF FTEs BY POSITION:

	FULL-TIME EQUIVALENTS REQUIRED				
	COMMERCIAL LENDER	ADMINISTRATIVE ASSISTANT	LOAN SUPPORT	CREDIT ANALYST	TOTAL FTE STAFF
NEW LOANS:	[ ]	[ ]	[ ]	[ ]	[ ]
RENEWAL LOANS:	[ ]	[ ]	[ ]	[ ]	[ ]
MAINTENANCE:	[ ]	[ ]	[ ]	[ ]	[ ]
PAST DUES:	[ ]	[ ]	[ ]	[ ]	[ ]
BUSINESS DEVELOPMENT:	[ ]	[ ]	[ ]	[ ]	[ ]
ADMINISTRATIVE:	[ ]	[ ]	[ ]	[ ]	[ ]
PERSONAL:	[ ]	[ ]	[ ]	[ ]	[ ]
TOTAL FTE:	[ ]	[ ]	[ ]	[ ]	[ ]

as a gauge for staffing levels in the future. This provides the true benefit of the model—consistency in staffing. By using these standards, the bank can maintain staff levels at consistent levels in direct relation to volume and, of course, fixed activities.

Administrative assistants/secretaries do not perform all support activities for commercial loans. Much of the support is performed by back-office personnel in the note cage and loan operations. The next section outlines the specific activities relative to loan support.

Loan Operations and Support Personnel

Loan operations and support is the behind-the-scenes group that performs a variety of clerical activities vital to the process of making commercial loans. Most commercial banks could not operate without individuals who can perform these various duties and activities. However, very small banks may not have separate loan operations and support areas. Many of their tasks and functions may be absorbed by administrative assistants/secretaries and partially by loan officers themselves. This is not the norm, however, so the focus of this section will be on loan operations and support as a group supporting the commercial loan function in the bank.

Loan support personnel have the same basic activity (output) profile as administrative assistants/secretaries and commercial loan officers. Fixed activities include administrative and personal, while variable activities include new loans, renewed loans, and maintenance.

The fixed activities are standard for most bank positions (although the subcategories may differ). The variable activities relate directly to the key volume indicators of new loans made and customers on file. Since this is support for commercial loans, the variable activities relate directly to the business of making and retaining loan relationships. The subtasks, however, differ from those of commercial loan officers and administrative assistants. The next sections explain in detail each of the fixed and variable activities.

Administrative   Administrative activities for loan support personnel may vary by bank, but at a minimum they consist of handling telephone calls, meetings, and general administrative duties. Administrative activities are part of the fixed category, activities that do not relate directly to the processing of commercial loans but to the ongoing, day-to-day activities standard to the position. The time spent in this category will remain constant regardless of loan volume.

The first administrative subcategory is handling telephone calls. Under administrative activities, only phone calls made and received internally are generic in nature and therefore relate to the position rather than to loan volumes. The types of phone activity involved are internal calls made and received, calls taken and rerouted, and messages taken.

Each of the three requires little time, but collectively throughout the course of a day the time commitment can add up. To capture this information, a standard survey form is used (Exhibit D). The survey contains two parts, as in the previous positions; one for time/frequency estimates and another for volume information. The survey document should be circulated to all loan operation and support personnel. The volume required data will be completed over a two-week period; the time and frequency estimates can be completed in one sitting.

In the survey, the information for telephone call handling is obtained under the administrative section. The volume of phone calls is obtained from the loan operation and support loan tally form, shown in Figure 61. One sheet contains an entire week of data (Monday through Saturday), so two sheets should be submitted. The loan clerk merely records a tally mark for each call under the appropriate heading.

Only the last three columns of the tally form apply to administrative phone volume. To determine the average administrative telephone volume per month per clerk, total all tally sheets for the loan support personnel. Then the calculations in Figure 62 will produce the desired time spent.

F I G U R E   61

Telephone Call Tally Form

DAY	Inbound Calls Received from Customer	Outbound Calls Made to Customers	Internal Calls Made/ Received	Calls Taken and Rerouted	Messages Taken
Monday					
Tuesday					
Wednesday					
Thursday					
Friday					
Saturday					
Total					

The analysis in Figure 62 yields the average monthly hours spent on general telephone handling per loan operations / support clerk. This call volume is general in nature and is more departmentally oriented than customer oriented. This is one of the more often overlooked areas of staffing analysis.

The next subcategory of administrative activities is meetings. Although meetings are not typically intensive for loan support personnel, it is important to account for them. These meetings are general in nature, and most likely departmental staff meetings. Meetings *must* occur regularly to be included in the calculation for administrative activities. To determine the amount of time devoted to meetings per loan operations clerk, Figure 63 uses the data obtained from Exhibit D.

General Telephone Volume

Subcategory	Vol./Month		Weeks to Annualize		Months/Year		No. of Loan Support on Staff		Avg. Vol. Produced/ Loan Clerk/ Month		Avg. Minutes/ Item		Minutes/ Hour		Avg. Hours/ Loan Support Clerk/ Month
Internal calls received/made	96.2	×	26	÷	12	÷	5	=	41.67	×	4	÷	60	=	2.78
Calls routed to another	50	×	26	÷	12	÷	5	=	21.67	×	2	÷	60	=	.72
Messages taken	100	×	26	÷	12	÷	5	=	43.33	×	.50	÷	60	=	.36
														=	3.86

Total phone hours per loan support clerk per month

F I G U R E   63

Meeting Time Spent

	Frequency/ Month	Avg. Minutes/ Meeting	Minutes/ Hour	Avg. Hours/ Loan Support Clerk/ Month
Meetings	1 ×	45 ÷	60 =	.75

The last subcategory of administrative activities is "other" general administrative activities. These are unique tasks performed by the loan operations clerks that are departmentally related—that is, performed regardless of commercial loan activity. This category may include report development, report distribution, and a few other items. Other miscellaneous tasks should relate to the production of a specific output (a report, document, or piece of correspondence). General administrative activities are captured and calculated as shown in Figure 64.

Once all administrative information is obtained, the time factors must be totaled and translated into a percentage of total available hours. This will reveal the fixed percentage of time required for the administrative activities for the particular function. Figure 65 shows its analysis and calculations based on the information captured thus far.

In Figure 65, an average of 9.2 percent of the total available time per month is devoted to administrative tasks that do not relate to commercial loan volume. This leaves 90.8 percent of a loan support clerk's time available for other duties. The only other fixed category that will absorb some of the available time is that of personal activities.

Personal Activities   As with all other departments, personal activities refer to lunches and breaks, occur on a regular basis, and do not relate to commercial loan volume or portfolio size. The loan operations and support survey asks for time estimates for lunches and breaks. These time estimates are analyzed and translated into

FIGURE 64

General Administrative Tasks

Subcategory	Total Vol./ Month		Weeks to Annualize		Months/ Year		No. of Loan Support Clerks on Staff		Avg. Vol. Produced/ Loan Clerk/ Month		Avg. Minutes/ Item		Minutes/ Hour		Avg. Hours/ Loan Support Clerk/ Month
Reports dev.	5	×	26	÷	12	÷	5	=	13	×	50	÷	60	=	10.83
Reports distrib.	23	×	26	÷	12	÷	5	=	9.9	×	10	÷	60	=	1.65
Total general admin strative task hours per loan support clerk per month														=	12.48

F I G U R E 65

Administrative Percentage to Available Hours

Subcategories		Average Hours per Loan Support Clerk per Month
1. Telephone call handling		3.86
2. Meetings		.75
3. General administrative tasks		12.48
Total monthly hours per loan support clerk		17.09
Available hours per loan clerk per month	÷	186.6
Fixed percentage of time per clerk for administrative activities per month	=	9.2%

F I G U R E 66

Personal Activities: Percentage to Available Hours

Category	Frequency per Month	Average Minutes per Occurrence	Minutes per Hour	Average Hours per Loan Support Clerk per Month
1. Lunches	21.7 ×	60 ÷	60 =	21.7
2. Breaks	21.7 ×	15 ÷	60 =	5.4
Total hours			=	27.1
Total monthly hours available			÷	168.6
Percentage of time spent on personal activities, per clerk			=	16.1%

a percentage of available time, as shown in Figure 66. The frequency per month derives from 52 weeks per year multiplied by 5 days a week, divided by 12 months.

This completes the fixed activity categories for loan operations and support clerks. The percentage of available time devoted to these activities is 25.3 percent (9.2 percent for administrative plus 16.1 percent for personal). This leaves 74.7 percent of the loan support clerk's day for activities specifically related to loan volume and/or portfolio size. The remaining activities associated with loan support personnel (handling new/renewed loans and maintenance) are variable and occur in direct proportion to the volume of loans and/or commercial loan portfolio size (number of customers).

New and Renewed Loans Work performed by loan operations/support personnel in the category of new and renewed loans involves back-office functions that are seldom vested in the commercial loan officers themselves. For the most part, loan operation and support personnel are dedicated to loan administration aspects of opening new loans rather than to the additional tasks of typing, as with the administrative assistants. Within the subcategory of loan administration, the specific tasks they perform are:

1. Documentation.
2. Note booking.
3. Filing notes/documents.
4. Developing collateral file.
5. Developing credit file.
6. Disbursing funds.
7. Producing credit reports.

The loan operation/support personnel survey (Exhibit D) asks for time estimates (in minutes), which will provide the basis for determining the hourly factor used for new and renewed loans. The purpose of this analysis is to determine the average amount of time required per new/renewed loan for loan administrative tasks. Since this is a variable activity, only an hourly factor is determined, not a percentage of total monthly hours. The total amount of time devoted to these activities relates directly to the amount of loans opened.

Once the survey is completed, an average time per subcategory and task can be determined per loan, as is illustrated in

F I G U R E 67

New and Renewed Loan Handling

		Average Minutes per Loan	
Subcategory		**New**	**Renewed**
1. Documentation		20	20
2. Note booking		10	10
3. Note/document filing		5	5
4. Collateral file development		10	10
5. Credit file development		15	15
6. Funds disbursed		10	10
7. Credit reports produced		<u>10</u>	<u>10</u>
Total minutes		80	80
Minutes per hour	÷	<u>60</u>	÷ <u>60</u>
Average hours per loan		1.33	1.33

Figure 67. The result in this example is that, on average, each new and renewed loan will require approximately 1.33 hours of loan operations/support clerk's time.

An argument can be made that some note types will require more work—on documentation, for example—than other types. To account for this difference, the analyst must determine whether the notes requiring more time occur on a regular basis with a predictable degree of frequency. If so, simply averaging all time estimates will produce an accurate blend of time to apply to the staffing analysis. This assumes, of course, that these types of loans will continue to occur in the future.

Another way to account for this is to calculate a weighted average amount of time per task, based on the mix of loans made. To do this it is necessary to review the types of loans made over the past three to six months. Using these data, the bank can perform the weighted average analysis in Figure 68. The volume of loans used in this figure is an average over three to six months.

Once the weighted average analysis is completed for each task within the new/renewed loan category, it can be applied to

F I G U R E 68

Weighted Average Analysis:
New/Renewed Loans

Loan Category	Volume of Loans Made/ Month	Percent to Total		Document Action Time/Hour		Weighted Avg.Time Factor/ Loan Type
1. Term loans	200	30.7%	×	20	=	6.14
2. Real estate construction	100	15.4	×	30	=	4.62
3. Agribusiness	50	7.7	×	25	=	1.93
4. Asset-based	300	46.2	×	40	=	18.48
	650	100.0%				
Weighted average time required per loan					=	31.17

any type of loan. The weighted average will be representative for any type of loan made by the bank, unless the mix changes significantly.

Maintenance   The final variable category is maintenance, the ongoing servicing of existing customer relationships. For loan operations and support personnel, maintenance consists of three broad subcategories: customer communications, loan administration, and monitoring. Within these subcategories, various tasks are involved in the process of maintaining existing relationships.

1. Customer communications.
   - Inbound phone calls received from customers.
   - Outbound phone calls made to customers.
   - In-person meetings with customers.
2. Loan administration.
   - Loan closing/releases.
   - Payment handling.
   - Payoff handling.

- Document receipt and filing.
- Advances/draws handling.
- Statement handling.
- Filing customer correspondence and call report.
- Overdraft report handling.

3. Monitoring.
   - Loan documentation review.
   - Collateral review.
   - Review/monitoring of compliance with loan agreement.
   - Review of customer balances.

In order to quantify this information and obtain time estimates, the loan operation/support survey (Exhibit D) is used. Once all data have been returned and averaged, the analysis can be completed. Since maintenance is a variable activity it will result in an hourly factor to be applied to the volume of commercial loan customers.

The first subcategory, customer communications, involves direct conversations with existing customers over the phone or in person. Although the time estimates per contact are estimated in the survey, the actual volume must be determined. This is accomplished using the call tally form in Exhibit D (the same form used previously for administrative activities in Figure 61). Tally marks are recorded for each call received and made and each in-person visit. Since the tally form represents a full week, only two sheets are needed to cover the survey period. Based on the totals from this survey, an hourly factor per customer can be determined, as in Figure 69.

The next subcategory, loan administration, involves the various servicing activities for commercial customers. These functions also must be quantified in terms of volume per month. Time estimates are determined and averaged in the survey, but the actual volumes are determined from another tally document, shown in Figure 70. The tally document requires tally marks for the occurrence of each item and must be completed over a two-week period. The tally document includes not just loan admini-

F I G U R E 69

Customer Communications

Activity	Frequency/ Customer/ Month	Average Minutes/ Call	Minutes/ Hour	Average Hours/ Customer/ Month
1. Inbound phone call from customer	1.17 ×	10 ÷	60	= .20
2. Outbound phone call to customer	.06 ×	5 ÷	60	= .01
3. In-person meeting with customer	.25 ×	10 ÷	60	= .04
Total hours per customer per month			=	.25

Activity	Total Departmental Volume	Annualized	Months/ Year	No. of Customers (Portfolio)/ Month	Freq./ Customer/ Month
1. Inbound phone call from customer	974.7 ×	26 ÷	12 ÷	1,805	= 1.17
2. Outbound phone call to customer	50 ×	26 ÷	12 ÷	1,805	= .06
3. In-person meeting	208.3 ×	26 ÷	12 ÷	1,805	= .25

stration, but monitoring tasks as well. The latter will be discussed shortly.

Once the data have been collected for this category, a departmental total must be determined. Using this total and factoring in the amount of commercial loan customers on file, determine an hourly factor per customer per month, as shown in Figure 71. In this example, .078 hour (approximately 4.68 minutes) is devoted

F I G U R E   70

Loan Administration/Monitoring Volume Tally Report

Volume Category	Tally	Total
Documents prepared/printed		
Notes filed		
Documents filed		
Collateral files developed		
Credit files opened		
Funds disbursed (checks issued)		
Credit reports produced		
Loan closings/releases		
Payments handled		
Payoffs/paydowns handled		
Advances/draws handled		
Statements handled		
Correspondence, call reports, etc. filed		
Overdraft reports handled		
Documentation, collateral, compliance, or balance review		
Number of times reports disbursed and distributed		
Number of reports developed		
Other _____		

F I G U R E 71

Loan Administration Activities

Task	Freq./ Customer/ Month		Avg. Minutes/ Item		Minutes/ Hour		Avg. Hours/ Customer/ Month
Loan closing/ releases	.02	×	10	÷	60	=	.003
Payment handling	.31	×	10	÷	60	=	.05
Payoff handling	.03	×	10	÷	60	=	.005
Document receipt/filing	.02	×	5	÷	60	=	.002
Advances/draws	.03	×	10	÷	60	=	.005
Statement handling	.08	×	8	÷	60	=	.01
Filing customer correspondence	.02	×	5	÷	60	=	.002
Overdraft report handling	.01	×	5	÷	60	=	.001
Total hours per customer per month						=	.078

Task	Total Dept. Volume		Annual- ized		Months/ Year		No. of Customers on File		Freq./ Customer/ Month
Loan closing/ releases	16.7	×	26	÷	12	÷	1,805	=	.02
Payment handling	258.3	×	26	÷	12	÷	1,805	=	.31
Payoff handling	25.0	×	26	÷	12	÷	1,805	=	.03
Document receipt/filing	16.7	×	26	÷	12	÷	1,805	=	.02
Advances/ draws	25.0	×	26	÷	12	÷	1,805	=	.03
Statement handling	66.7	×	26	÷	12	÷	1,805	=	.08
Filing customer correspondence	16.7	×	26	÷	12	÷	1,805	=	.02
Overdraft report handling	8.3	×	26	÷	12	÷	1,805	=	.01

to each customer, on average, each month. Therefore, the total loan administration maintenance time will fluctuate directly with the volume of customers.

The final subcategory under maintenance is monitoring. For loan support personnel, monitoring involves periodic checks on loan adherence to policy, compliance, or general control monitoring. Although in most cases monitoring activities are performed directly by the commercial loan officer, some of the regular policing required is more easily controlled by the loan support clerk.

For loan support personnel, monitoring tasks consist of loan documentation review, collateral review, review/monitoring of compliance to loan agreements, and review of customer balances.

As with the loan administration subcategory, these items are directly related to the number of customers on file. To determine the average time involved in performing these tasks, use the loan operation and support survey (Exhibit D). The first segment of data, the time estimates involved for each task, is an average (mean) for all loan support personnel at the bank location.

The second portion of this analysis is determined from the volume tally report (Figure 70). The tally form must be completed over a two-week period and a total volume count taken for each of the four monitoring tasks. The information is then used in Figure 72 to calculate the hourly factor per customer on file. In this example, slightly more time is spent on monitoring activities than on loan administration activities.

This completes the maintenance activities profile for loan operations and support personnel. The three subcategories are summarized as in Figure 73 to arrive at a single hourly factor for the staffing model. In this example, .43 hour, or 25.8 minutes, reflects the servicing time per loan customer.

Recap: Loan Operations and Support Personnel   The recap section is necessary to restate and organize the percentages and time factors into the format that will be used in the staffing model. A recap table should show both fixed and variable activities and factors, as in Figure 74.

F I G U R E 72

Loan Monitoring Activities

Task	Freq./ Customer/ Month		Avg. Minutes/ Item		Minutes/ Hour		Avg. Hours/ Customer/ Month
Loan documentation review	.09	×	10	÷	60	=	.02
Collateral review	.25	×	8	÷	60	=	.04
Review/ monitoring of compliance to loan agreement	.09	×	13	÷	60	=	.02
Review of customer balance	.09	×	8	÷	60	=	.02
Average hours per customers per month						=	.10

Task	Total Dept. Vol.		Annualized		Months/ Year		No. of Customers on File		Freq./ Customer/ Month
Loan documentation review	75	×	26	÷	12	÷	1,805	=	.09
Collateral review	208.3	×	26	÷	12	÷	1,805	=	.25
Review/ monitoring of compliance to loan agreement	75	×	26	÷	12	÷	1,805	=	.09
Review of customer balance	75	×	26	÷	12	÷	1,805	=	.09

The fixed activity percentages from Figure 74 will be used as is in the staffing model. These are time requirements and will not change with fluctuations in volume. In this example, about one-

F I G U R E 73

Maintenance Activities Summary

Subcategory	Hourly Factor
1. Customer communications	.25
2. Loan administration	.078
3. Monitoring	.10
Total maintenance hours per customer per month	.43

F I G U R E 74

Loan Operations/Support Profile Summary

1. Fixed activities	Percentage of Time Required
■ Administrative	9.2%
■ Personal	16.1%

2. Variable Activities	Hourly Factor
■ New loans	1.33
■ Renewed loans	1.33
■ Maintenance	.43

quarter (25.3 percent) of a loan support person's time is used to perform fixed activities. This leaves approximately three-quarters (74.7 percent) of the clerk's day to devote to the key volume indicators of new/renewed loans and loan customers on file. Thus, only three-quarters of an FTE is available to perform the variable tasks.

Before the variable hourly factors can be used in the model, they must be analyzed to determine whether the time factor stated is truly devoted to each loan or customer. The first step is to determine the total available hours for the variable activities.

F I G U R E 75

Total Departmental Fixed and Variable Hours

1. Total monthly hours available per loan support clerk		=	168.6
2. Total number of loan support clerks on staff		=	× 5
3. Total departmental hours available per month		=	843.0

Fixed Activity	Percentage of Time Devoted	Total Departmental Hours Available	Total Departmental Fixed Hours Committed
1. Administrative	9.2%	× 843	= 77.6
2. Personal	16.1	× 843	= 135.7
Total fixed hours committed			= 213.32
Total hours available for variable activities (843 − 213.32 = 629.7)			= 629.7

Although it has been determined that approximately 75 percent of a clerk's time is devoted to these tasks, the aggregate departmental hours available must be calculated, as shown in Figure 75. The *actual* variable hourly factors can be determined for the categories of new/renewed loans and maintenance. Since a portion of the loan support clerk's day is already expended in fixed activities, only a specific percentage of the total available hours remains.

If a specific volume of new and renewed loans is completed during the month and the size of the loan portfolio (customers) is known, the remaining time available can be assigned to this volume to produce actual time factors. The comparison of these actual and standard factors will determine not only whether the department is over- or understaffed but also the factors for future use. The completion of this analysis is shown in Figure 76.

In Figure 76, more time is actually devoted to new/renewed loans and maintaining customers than the surveys indicated.

F I G U R E   76

Actual Variable Activity Hourly Factors

Variable Activity	Average Monthly Volume		Calculated Hourly Factor		Total Hours Required	Percentage of Total Hours
New loans	40	×	1.33	=	53.2	18.3%
Renewed loans	33	×	1.33	=	43.9	15.1
Maintenance	452	×	.43	=	194.4	66.6
					291.5	100.0%

Variable Activity	Percentage of Total Hours		Hours Remaining for Variable Activities		Monthly Volume		Actual Variable Activity Hourly Factor
New loans	18.3%	×	629.7	÷	40	=	2.88
Renewed loans	15.1%	×	629.7	÷	33	=	2.88
Maintenance	66.6%	×	629.7	÷	452	=	.93

Variable Activities	Standard Hours	Actual Hours
New loans	1.33	2.88
Renewed loans	1.33	2.88
Maintenance	.43	.93

This indicates that the department may be slightly overstaffed. More time than necessary is being devoted to the existing volume, thereby inflating the hourly factors. For the staffing model the standard factors should be used, since they will reveal the overall staffing requirements. Figure 77 is a sample of the staffing model that incorporates the profile and factors determined for loan operations/support personnel.

At this point, virtually 90 percent of all the activities and tasks that comprise the commercial loan function have been accounted for. The last area to evaluate is the credit analysis function.

F I G U R E 77

Staffing Model for Loan Operations/Support Personnel

```
BANK:            [       ]    COMMERCIAL BANKER STAFFING MODEL        DATE:     [        ]
LOCATION:        [       ]
BRANCH:          [       ]


DATA REQUIRED
   # NEW LOANS THIS MONTH    [        ] AVG. # TOTAL HOURS PER FTE PER DAY:          [        ]
   # RENEWALS THIS MONTH:    [        ] NUMBER LOANS PAST DUE THIS MONTH:            [        ]
                                        AVERAGE NUMBER OF LOAN ACCOUNTS ON FILE:   [        ]
```

A. FIXED HOURS (PER FTE):

	% OF TOTAL MONTHLY HOURS COMMERCIAL LENDER	ADMINISTRATIVE ASSISTANT	LOAN SUPPORT	CREDIT ANALYST
BUSINESS DEVELOPMENT:	[ ]	[ ]	[ ]	[ ]
ADMINISTRATION:	[ ]	[ ]	[9.20%]	[ ]
	[ ]	[ ]	[ ]	[ ]
PERSONAL TIME:	[ ]	[ ]	[16.10%]	[ ]
TOTAL:	0.00%	0.00%	25.30%	0.00%

B. VARIABLE HOURS:

	STANDARD HOURS REQUIRED PER ITEM COMMERCIAL LENDER	ADMINISTRATIVE ASSISTANT	LOAN SUPPORT	CREDIT ANALYST
NEW LOANS:	[ ]	[ ]	[1.33]	[ ]
RENEWAL LOANS:	[ ]	[ ]	[1.33]	[ ]
MAINTEN. MONITOR:	[ ]	[ ]	[0.43]	[ ]
PAST DUE:	[ ]	[ ]	[ ]	[ ]

C. DISTRIBUTION OF FTEs BY POSITION:

FULL-TIME EQUIVALENTS REQUIRED

	COMMERCIAL LENDER	ADMINISTRATIVE ASSISTANT	LOAN SUPPORT	CREDIT ANALYST	TOTAL FTE STAFF
NEW LOANS:	[ ]	[ ]	[ ]	[ ]	[ ]
RENEWAL LOANS:	[ ]	[ ]	[ ]	[ ]	[ ]
MAINTENANCE:	[ ]	[ ]	[ ]	[ ]	[ ]
PAST DUES:	[ ]	[ ]	[ ]	[ ]	[ ]
BUSINESS DEVELOPMENT:	[ ]	[ ]	[ ]	[ ]	[ ]
ADMINISTRATIVE:	[ ]	[ ]	[ ]	[ ]	[ ]
PERSONAL:	[ ]	[ ]	[ ]	[ ]	[ ]
TOTAL FTE:	[ ]	[ ]	[ ]	[ ]	[ ]

Credit Analysts

Credit and financial analyses ultimately enable a commercial lender to render decisions about potential loans. The tasks performed in this area are vital. Depending on the size of the bank, they are performed either by a commercial lender or by a separate staff of credit analysts.

Credit analysts are usually commercial lender trainees—individuals just out of school who are preparing to become commercial lenders. The benefits of having a lender training program are many. One of the most important is that while employees are learning they can be performing a worthwhile function. This can reduce the time commercial lenders spend on these tasks, giving them more time to devote to business development and customer relations. In addition to this, credit analysts perform their tasks at a much lower salary cost than seasoned lenders. In time, credit analysts may rotate through lending divisions and eventually become junior commercial loan officers.

The functions and tasks that can be performed by credit analysts are similar to those in the commercial loan officer profile, but some of the detailed tasks within each subcategory differ.

1. Fixed activities:
   a. Business development
      - Customer contact
      - Strategy and planning
   b. Administrative
      - Meetings
      - Phone calls
      - Special projects
   c. Personal
      - Lunches and breaks
2. Variable activities
   a. New and renewed loans
      - Financial statement analysis
      - Credit analysis
      - Approval

    b. Maintenance
- Customer communications
- Monitoring

Of course, not all banks employ credit analysts. Sometimes these duties are performed by others, usually commercial lenders. If the financial institution does not staff credit analysts, the commercial lenders should fill out the credit analyst survey as well as their own.

Analyzing the credit analyst staffing needs of a bank involves the use of a standard survey document (Exhibit E) structured very much the same as the others. Time estimates are required, as well as some volume-related information that should be completed over a two-week period. All time estimates should be averaged for all credit analysts, and volumes should simply be totaled. These procedures are explained in detail within each category of the fixed and variable profile categories.

Business Development   Business development is much the same for credit analysts as for commercial lenders. The only exception is that credit analysts generally do not initiate it. They may merely accompany seasoned commercial lenders to learn the ropes in terms of making calls to potential bank clients.

Business development is typically a fixed activity category because it is an ongoing function that does not directly depend upon new/renewed loans or customers on file. In fact, the business development time of credit analysts should occur on a regular, ongoing basis as part of their training to become commercial lenders. The specific subcategories and tasks associated with business development are as follows:

1. Contact with potential customers:
   - Outside meetings at customers' locations.
   - Phone calls to potential customers.
2. Strategy and planning:
   - Market development.
   - Customer relationship development.

The credit analyst survey captures the data needed to analyze the percentages of available time these activities require. In the first instance, potential customer contact, both the time estimate involved in each call (averaged for all credit analysts) and the volume of calls made are required.

The call volume is obtained from the standard call tally form, Figure 78 (Exhibit E), which requires completion over a two-week period and should be totaled for all credit analysts. One sheet contains an entire week of data, so only two sheets are needed. Tally marks should be recorded for the appropriate categories in the "potential customer" row. These are individuals who are not yet customers but may become so. Once the data are accumulated they can be organized as in Figure 79 to determine the average time spent.

The next subcategory, strategy and planning, is the time devoted to the tasks of market development and customer relationship development. A credit analyst may spend a designated amount of time each month with a commercial lender to learn the process of market development and prospect planning. Again, in order for this to be a fixed activity it must occur on a regular basis. Since credit analysts are always in training, the time here may simply be a standard or targeted amount of time in which senior management desires them to be part of the planning process, from an educational perspective. The actual time estimates are taken as an average for all credit analysts from the credit analyst survey and calculated as in Figure 80.

Once average time spent on strategy and planning is determined, the percentage of time available for business development can be calculated. Credit analysts, like other personnel, have a finite number of monthly hours available to them. The factor used to determine the percentage of hours available is 168.6. Figure 81 shows that business development, as a fixed activity, requires approximately 6.6 percent of the available hours of each credit analyst. This percentage will be used in the overall staffing analysis.

Administrative   Administrative functions of credit analysts are not unlike those of the other personnel within the commercial lending department. These are administrative tasks that would

FIGURE 78

Call Tally Form

Day	Interval Calls Received/Made	Category	In-Person Meeting with Client		Telephone Calls		Correspondence (letters)
			At customer Location	In Bank	Inbound	Outbound	
Monday		Existing customer					
		Potential customer					
Tuesday		Existing customer					
		Potential customer					
Wednesday		Existing customer					
		Potential customer					
Thursday		Existing customer					
		Potential customer					
Friday		Existing customer					
		Potential customer					
Saturday		Existing customer					
		Potential customer					
Total		Existing customer					
		Potential customer					

F I G U R E 79

Potential Customer Contact

Subcategory	Total Dept. Vol.		Weeks to Annualize		Months/ Year		No. of Credit Analysts on Staff		Avg. Vol. Produced/ Credit Analyst/ Month		Avg. Minutes/ Item		Minutes/ Hour		Avg. Hours/ Credit Analyst/ Month
Outside meetings w/potential customers	6	×	26	÷	12	÷	3	=	4.3	×	50	÷	60	=	3.58
Phone calls to potential customers	25	×	26	÷	12	÷	3	=	18.1	×	5	÷	60	=	1.51
Total contact hours per credit analyst per month														=	5.09

F I G U R E 80

Strategy and Planning

Subcategory	Average Time Spent/ Analyst/Month
1. Market development	4
2. Customer relationship development	2
Total hours per month per credit analyst	6

F I G U R E 81

Business Development: Percentage of Available Hours

Subcategory	Hours Available/Credit Analyst/Month
1. Potential customer contact	5.09
2. Strategy and planning	6
Total business development hours per analyst per month	11.09
Total available hours per month	÷ 168.6
Percentage of available time devoted to business development per credit analyst	6.6%

occur regardless of the volume of commercial loan business entering the department. For credit analysts, the subcategories of administrative activities are as follows:

1. Meetings:
   - Sales meetings
   - Officer meetings
   - Loan committee meetings
   - Departmental meetings
   - Training/seminars

F I G U R E 82

Meeting Time Spent

Meeting Type	Avg. # of Times Held/Month		Avg. Minutes/ Session		Minutes/ Hour		Avg. Hours/Credit Analyst/ Month
Sales	1	×	45	÷	60	=	.75
Officer	N/A	×	–	÷	60	=	–
Loan committee	2	×	90	÷	60	=	1.50
Departmental	1	×	30	÷	60	=	.50
Training/ seminars	4	×	120	÷	60	=	2.00
Total hours per credit analyst per month						=	4.75

2. Special projects
3. Communications:
   - Internal phone calls made
   - Internal phone calls received

The first subcategory, meetings, accounts for all time that is regularly devoted to various types of meetings. From the credit analyst survey, the length of each meeting and frequency per month held can be averaged, as shown in Figure 82.

Since management may want credit analysts to spend a specific amount of time per month in formal training, seminars and training are included in the meeting category. Other meetings are discretionary, based upon management's desire for the credit analyst to participate. This is all part of the training process.

The next subcategory under administrative activities is special projects. Credit analysts are likely candidates to be involved with special projects that may relate to specific loan reports, analyses, and other such documents. Again, this is discretionary. Management may choose to require credit analysts to work on special projects or not. The time estimate, taken directly from the

F I G U R E 83

Special Projects/Analyses

	Avg. Minutes/ Analyst/Month		Minutes/Hour		Avg. Hours/ Analyst/Month
Special projects	60	÷	60	=	1̲

survey, is an average for all credit analysts on staff. It is analyzed as in Figure 83.

The last subcategory under administrative activities is communications. The key activity within this category is internal telephone calls made and received. Whether these calls have a direct bearing on commercial loan customers or not, they occur on a regular basis. As long as phones are available, calls will be made and received, and the time involved must be accounted for.

The credit analyst survey provides the average time estimate per call. To capture volume data, use the credit analyst telephone survey document shown previously (Figure 78), but total only the first column, "Internal calls received/made." Since this document provides for a full week of data on one sheet, only two sheets are required. The volume of calls recorded should be totaled for all credit analysts in the aggregate. This and the respective time estimates are used to calculate the overall time factor devoted to communications, as illustrated in Figure 84.

This completes the administrative segment of the credit analyst profile. Since this is a fixed activity category, it must be stated as a percentage of total available hours per credit analyst. Because there are a number of subcategories under administrative activities, Figure 85 recaps the time commitments and restates them in a percentage of available hours. The result, 5.6 percent of total monthly available hours, will be used in the overall credit analyst staffing model.

Personal   The final fixed activity is the personal activity category. This accounts for lunches and breaks and must ultimately

128

F I G U R E 84

Communications

Subcategory	Total Dept. Vol.		Weeks to Annualize		Months/ Year		No. of Credit Analysts on Staff		Avg. Vol. Handled/ Credit Analyst/ Month		Avg. Minutes/ Item		Minutes/ Hour		Avg. Hours/ Credit Analyst/ Month
Internal calls made/received	100	×	26	÷	12	÷	3	=	72	×	3	÷	60	=	3.6
Total internal call hours per credit analyst per month														=	3.6

Administrative Activities Summary

Subcategory		Average Hours Required per Credit Analyst per Month
1. Meetings		4.75
2. Special projects/analyses		1.00
3. Communications		3.60
Total monthly hours per analyst		9.35
Total available monthly hours per analyst	÷	168.6
Percentage of total available hours per credit analyst per month	=	5.6%

be stated as a percentage of available hours. As always, the credit analyst survey documents the time spent on lunches and breaks per credit analyst. Since these occur daily, the frequency per month is assumed to be 21.6 (5 days per week times 52 weeks per year divided by 12 months per year). Based on these assumptions, the hours are calculated as in Figure 86.

Personal Activities

Frequency/ Month		Avg. Minutes for Lunches/Breaks		Minutes/ Hour		Avg. Hours/ Officer/Month
21.7	×	75	÷	60	=	27.1
Average available hours per credit analyst per month					÷	168.6
Percentage of available hours per credit analyst per month					=	16.1%

In this example, approximately 28.3 percent in total is required for fixed activities (6.6 percent for business development
plus 5.6 percent for administrative plus 16.1 percent for personal
activities). This leaves approximately 71.7 percent of a full-time
equivalent to devote to the actual volume of commercial loans put
on the books and to maintenance/monitoring activities. From a
staffing standpoint, a little less than three-quarters of an FTE is
available for the variable activities. This is the reason for isolating
the fixed percentages of time committed. In reality, one FTE is
never one FTE; it is only a fraction of one FTE, due to the fixed
activities.

The next sections outline the variable activities for credit
analysts, which are directly related to loan volume and portfolio
size (number of customers).

New/Renewed Loans   Although credit analysts do not have the
authority to make or renew loans, they are an integral part of the
analytical process of commercial loans. In all new and renewal
relationships, the bank must conduct various financial and credit
analyses in order to make an informed decision about the particular loan. Credit analysts are ideally suited to perform such analyses, since it is something they must learn to become effective
decision makers.

Performing these analyses not only educates credit analysts
but also fulfills a necessary function at a lesser cost than if commercial lenders conducted them. If the financial institution does
not employ credit analysts, the commercial lender will have to
make the analyses. This is certainly acceptable, but the cost of
performing such analyses will then increase.

For new/renewed loans, the subcategories involved are financial statement analysis, credit analysis, and approval. Within
each, a number of specific tasks or activities are performed.

1. Financial statement analysis:
   - Financial statement spread.
   - Ratio analysis.
2. Credit analysis:

- Analysis of local and economic conditions.
- Industry analysis.
- Form of organization analysis.
- Review of credit reports and strengths/weaknesses.
- Financial statement/cashflow report development (as needed).

3. Approval:
- Loan committee write-up.

When these activities are conducted by credit analysts, commercial lenders are freed up for more customer contact/relationship handling. Since new and renewed loans are variable activities, they relate directly to the actual volume of new and renewed loans made. A time factor (hourly) must be determined and applied to the volume of commercial loans made and renewed to determine the optimal amount of full-time equivalent credit analysts required. This will be reflected in the form of an hourly factor, not a percentage of monthly available hours as with the fixed activities.

The credit analyst survey (Exhibit E) will provide time estimates for each of the activities previously listed. These time estimates must be averaged for all credit analysts and the results recorded, as in Figure 87. In this example, more than two hours of analytical work are needed, on average, per new or renewed loan to enable management to render a decision. These standard factors will be used in the overall staffing analysis model.

As with commercial lenders, it may be more desirable and more accurate to assign these time factors based on consensus of senior lending management. The factor used becomes the expectation (in the experience of senior management), and the staffing level determined reflects this expectation.

Maintenance   The final variable category for credit analysis is maintenance and monitoring. As with commercial lenders, the process of maintaining accounts is a function of direct customer contact and regular, ongoing analysis of existing loan relationships. Credit analysts typically work with a seasoned commercial

F I G U R E 87

New/Renewed Loans

	Average Minutes per Item	
	New	Renewed
1. Financial statement analysis		
■ Financial statement spread	23	20
■ Ratio analysis	14	13
2. Credit analysis		
■ Analysis of economic and local conditions	10	9
■ Industry analysis	6	5
■ Form of organization evaluation	11	0
■ Review of credit reports and strengths/weaknesses	8	6
■ Financial statement/cashflow report development	30	30
3. Approval		
■ Loan committee write-up	60	60
Total minutes per loan	162	143
Minutes per hour	÷ 60	÷ 60
Hourly factor per loan	2.70	2.38

lender in this function. Periodic visits to customer locations are necessary to maintaining relationships and afford on-the-job training for credit analysts. The maintenance category for credit analysts consists of the following subcategories and related activities:

1. Customer communications
   - Outside calls or (meetings with) existing customers at their locations.
   - Call report development.
2. Monitoring
   - Financial statement spreads.

The data necessary to analyze these activities are contained in the credit analyst survey document. Estimates are first required of the amount of time (average per customer for all credit analysts) spent on customer calls and call report development. The volume of calls made is obtained from the credit analyst call tally (Figure 78). The same form is used for this category as for business development and administrative activities. Since the call tally form contains one week of data, two are required to complete the survey.

Credit analysts are also likely to prepare call reports as part of their training to relieve commercial lenders of the task. Call report volume is obtained directly from the last column of the credit analyst call tally document. In order to determine the hourly rate factor for the staffing model, the volume information and time estimate data are analyzed as in Figure 88.

In this example, .02 hours, or 1.2 minutes, are spent per customer per month. Thus, 14.4 minutes are spent per customer

F I G U R E 88

Maintenance: Customer Communications

Subcategory	Freq./ Customer/ Month		Avg. Min./ Call		Min./ Hour		Avg. Hours/ Customer/ Month
Meetings at customers' site	.01	×	60	÷	60	=	.01
Call reports developed	.01	×	30	÷	60	=	.01
Total hours per customer per month						=	.02

	Total Departmental Volume		Weeks to Annualize		Min./ Year		No. of Customers/ Month		Freq./ Customer/ Month
Meetings at customers' sites	4	×	26	÷	12	÷	1,805	=	.01
Call reports developed	4	×	26	÷	12	÷	1,805	=	.01

per year. This may not sound like a lot of time, but since credit analysts do not call on every customer, the true amount of time per customer is actually higher.

The final subcategory within the maintenance category is monitoring. For credit analysts, monitoring refers to the ongoing, periodic financial review of existing customer relationships. Credit analysts do not typically perform the actual review, but they are instrumental in preparing the information for review, in the form of financial statement spreads. In most financial institutions, existing commercial relationships require periodic (quarterly or annual) financial statements to monitor the financial strength of customers. When statements are received, they must be spread in the format the bank uses for analysis. This is one of the key roles performed by credit analysts.

The data needed to determine the time devoted to this activity are again taken from the credit analyst survey form. Both the average minutes required to spread a financial statement and the frequency with which statements are received per customer are required. The latter number will be based upon bank policy. If the bank requires quarterly statements, this line should read 4; if semiannual, 2; and if annual 1. This will enable management to determine the approximate volume of statement spreads.

The actual time factors for use in the staffing model are determined as in Figure 89. Here .12 hours, or 7.2 minutes, are allocated to each customer on file per month, for a total annual time factor of 86.4 minutes, or 1.44 hours per year. Roughly an hour and a half per customer per year is devoted to spreading financial statements in preparation for the financial review by a commercial lender.

Customer communications and maintenance must be combined to form the complete hourly factor for the variable category of maintenance. This summary is illustrated in Figure 90.

Recap: Credit Analysts   Now that all percentages and factors have been determined for each category under credit analysis, a recap table can be prepared as in Figure 91.

F I G U R E   89

Maintenance: Monitoring

Frequency/ Customer/ Month		Avg. Minutes/ Spread		Minutes/Hour		Avg. Hours/ Customer/ Month
.34	×	20	÷	60	=	.12
Total hours per customer per month					=	.12

Frequency per Customer		Months per Year		Frequency per Customer per Month
4	÷	12	=	.34

F I G U R E   90

Maintenance Activities Summary

Subcategory	Hourly Factor per Customer on File
1. Customer communications	.02
2. Monitoring	.12
Total hours per customer per month	.14

It appears from the recap that a total of 28.3 percent of the credit analyst's time is devoted to fixed or regularly occurring activities. This leaves approximately 71.7 percent of the available time to devote to the variable activities related to loan volume.

To use these factors in the staffing model, one must refine the hourly factors based on time available after the fixed activities. Once determined, fixed activity percentages are a given. Since they exist regardless of volume, those percentages in Figure 91 will be used as is in the staffing model.

F I G U R E 91

Credit Analyst Profile Summary

1. Fixed activities	Percentage of Available Time Required
▪ Business development	6.6%
▪ Administrative	5.6%
▪ Personal	16.1%

2. Variable activities	Hourly Factor
▪ New loans	2.70
▪ Renewed loans	2.38
▪ Maintenance	.14

The hourly factors for variable activities are another matter. The variable factors represent either what the staff members say is required or what management expects. In this sense, they can be considered a sort of imposed standard. If, however, only 71.7 percent of an analyst's time is available after the fixed activities, it may be that more or less time is devoted to the individual variable factors than was determined in the standard.

To illustrate this point, calculate an actual hourly factor for each item in this section, beginning with an analysis of the actual hours available per month for the department to devote to variable activities. An example of this analysis is shown in Figure 92.

In this example, only 363.17 hours are available for variable activities. If a specified volume of loans were completed, it would reveal the actual (or more realistic) time factor involved in these functions. To complete this analysis, average the monthly volume of new and renewed loans over the past three to four months. Figure 93 suggests that more time is actually being taken per loan than the surveys stated. The calculated hourly factors here are taken from Figure 91.

F I G U R E 92

Total Departmental Fixed and Variable Hours

1. Total monthly hours available per credit analyst			168.6
2. Total number of credit analysts on staff			× 3
3. Total departmental hours available per month			= 505.8

Fixed Activities	Percentage of Time Devoted		Total Departmental Hours Available		Total Departmental Fixed Hours Committed
Business development	6.6%	×	505.8	=	33.38
Administrative	5.6	×	505.8	=	28.32
Personal	16.0	×	505.8	=	80.93
Total fixed hours committed				=	142.63
Total hours available for variable activities (505.8 − 142.63 = 363.17)				=	363.17

Figure 93 indicates that excess time is available and that the department may be overstaffed.

Variable Activity	Standard Hours	Actual Hours
New loans	2.70	3.92
Renewed loans	2.38	3.45
Maintenance	.14	.20

The credit analysts are saying that each variable activity should take only the standard amount of time determined. But in reality it is taking much more time. The logical conclusion is that the credit analysts are filling in time for excess time available. For purposes of the staffing model, the standard factors should be used, as illustrated in Figure 94.

This completes the analysis of all functions / positions related to the commercial loan department. Based on the previous analysis, the information learned will be used to build the staffing model. The next section of this chapter outlines how to develop and use the commercial loan staffing model.

F I G U R E 93

Actual Variable Activity Hourly Factors

Variable Activity	Average Monthly Volume		Calculated Hourly Factor		Total Hours Required	Percentage of Total Hours		Hours Remaining for Variable Activities		Monthly Volume		Other Variable Activity Hourly Factor
New loans	40	×	2.70	=	108	43.2%	×	363.17	÷	40	=	3.92
Renewed loans	33	×	2.38	=	78.5	31.4	×	363.17	÷	33	=	3.45
Maintenance	452	×	.14	=	63.3	25.4	×	363.17	÷	452	=	.20
					249.8	100.0%						

F I G U R E 94

Credit Analyst Staffing Model

```
BANK:          [        ]    COMMERCIAL BANKER STAFFING MODEL      DATE:    [        ]
LOCATION:      [        ]
BRANCH:        [        ]
```

DATA REQUIRED

# NEW LOANS THIS MONTH	[ ]	AVG. # TOTAL HOURS PER FTE PER DAY: [ ]
# RENEWALS THIS MONTH:	[ ]	NUMBER LOANS PAST DUE THIS MONTH: [ ]
		AVERAGE NUMBER OF LOAN ACCOUNTS ON FILE: [ ]

A. FIXED HOURS (PER FTE):

% OF TOTAL MONTHLY HOURS

	COMMERCIAL LENDER	ADMINISTRATIVE ASSISTANT	LOAN SUPPORT	CREDIT ANALYST
BUSINESS DEVELOPMENT:	[ ]	[ ]	[ ]	[6.60%]
ADMINISTRATION:	[ ]	[ ]	[ ]	[5.60%]
PERSONAL TIME:	[ ]	[ ]	[ ]	[16.00%]
TOTAL:	0.00%	0.00%	0.00%	28.20%

B. VARIABLE HOURS:

STANDARD HOURS REQUIRED PER ITEM

	COMMERCIAL LENDER	ADMINISTRATIVE ASSISTANT	LOAN SUPPORT	CREDIT ANALYST
NEW LOANS:	[ ]	[ ]	[ ]	[2.70]
RENEWAL LOANS:	[ ]	[ ]	[ ]	[2.38]
MAINTEN. MONITOR:	[ ]	[ ]	[ ]	[0.14]
PAST DUE:	[ ]	[ ]	[ ]	[ ]

C. DISTRIBUTION OF FTEs BY POSITION:

FULL-TIME EQUIVALENTS REQUIRED

	COMMERCIAL LENDER	ADMINISTRATIVE ASSISTANT	LOAN SUPPORT	CREDIT ANALYST	TOTAL FTE STAFF
NEW LOANS:	[ ]	[ ]	[ ]	[ ]	[ ]
RENEWAL LOANS:	[ ]	[ ]	[ ]	[ ]	[ ]
MAINTENANCE:	[ ]	[ ]	[ ]	[ ]	[ ]
PAST DUES:	[ ]	[ ]	[ ]	[ ]	[ ]
BUSINESS DEVELOPMENT:	[ ]	[ ]	[ ]	[ ]	[ ]
ADMINISTRATIVE:	[ ]	[ ]	[ ]	[ ]	[ ]
PERSONAL:	[ ]	[ ]	[ ]	[ ]	[ ]
TOTAL FTE:	[ ]	[ ]	[ ]	[ ]	[ ]

Model Development and Reports

The commercial loan department staffing model is the standard format used to determine optimum staffing levels. Once created, the model can be used over and over again to determine or simply monitor staffing requirements. This section of the chapter outlines both the steps required to create the model and how to run it. A final section analyzes the results.

Creating the Model

The staffing model was developed using Lotus 1, 2, 3, version 2.01. An exact duplicate of Figure 95 can be created in any bank using the Lotus spreadsheet software. As noted in Figure 95, each bracket or blank space is coded by a number. This section provides exact instructions for building the model, including formulas and number codes.

The individual responsible for creating the model should first develop its structure or format. This is its appearance—headings, titles, brackets, boundary lines, and so on. Figure 95 should be copied so that it fits on an 8-1/2" x 11" sheet of paper. The spacing and positioning of headings, brackets, and so forth should copy the example as closely as possible.

The developer should then review the explanations corresponding to the code numbers in the model. In some cases, nothing needs to be added at this time; in other cases, a formula is required. A narrative formula explains the components of the formula, and a formula in the language of Lotus 1, 2, 3 follows.

Since the cell addresses are uncertain, the code numbers in Figure 95 will be used in place of cell addresses. When the developer inputs the appropriate formula, he or she must translate the code number into the proper cell format on the spreadsheet.

1. Bank: Record the name of the bank for which the analysis is being conducted. To indicate that an input is required, brackets set off the cell in which the input will be made. The cell (within the brackets) should be large enough to accommodate a bank's name or abbreviated name.

2. Location: Record the address or location of the bank. Again, brackets indicate that an input is required.

F I G U R E 95

Commercial Loan Staffing Model

```
BANK:              [   1   ]    COMMERCIAL BANKER STAFFING MODEL      DATE:      [   4   ]
LOCATION:          [   2   ]
BRANCH:            [   3   ]
```

DATA REQUIRED

# NEW LOANS THIS MONTH	[5]	AVG. # TOTAL HOURS PER FTE PER DAY: [7]
# RENEWALS THIS MONTH:	[6]	NUMBER LOANS PAST DUE THIS MONTH: [8]
		AVERAGE NUMBER OF LOAN ACCOUNTS ON FILE: [9]

A. FIXED HOURS (PER FTE):

% OF TOTAL MONTHLY HOURS

	COMMERCIAL LENDER	ADMINISTRATIVE ASSISTANT	LOAN SUPPORT	CREDIT ANALYST
BUSINESS DEVELOPMENT:	[10A]	[10B]	[10C]	[10D]
ADMINISTRATION:	[11A]	[11B]	[11C]	[11D]
	[ ]	[ ]	[ ]	[ ]
PERSONAL TIME:	[12A]	[12B]	[12C]	[12D]
TOTAL:	13A	13B	13C	13D

B. VARIABLE HOURS:

STANDARD HOURS REQUIRED PER ITEM

	COMMERCIAL LENDER	ADMINISTRATIVE ASSISTANT	LOAN SUPPORT	CREDIT ANALYST
NEW LOANS:	[14A]	[14B]	[14C]	[14D]
RENEWAL LOANS:	[15A]	[15B]	[15C]	[15D]
MAINTEN. MONITOR:	[16A]	[16B]	[16C]	[16D]
PAST DUE:	[17A]	[17B]	[17C]	[17D]

C. DISTRIBUTION OF FTEs BY POSITION:

FULL-TIME EQUIVALENTS REQUIRED

	COMMERCIAL LENDER	ADMINISTRATIVE ASSISTANT	LOAN SUPPORT	CREDIT ANALYST	TOTAL FTE STAFF
NEW LOANS:	18A	18B	18C	18D	26
RENEWAL LOANS:	19A	19B	19C	19D	27
MAINTENANCE:	20A	20B	20C	20D	28
PAST DUES:	21A	21B	21C	21D	29
BUSINESS DEVELOPMENT:	22A	22B	22C	22D	30
ADMINISTRATIVE:	23A	23B	23C	23D	31
PERSONAL:	24A	24B	24C	24D	32
TOTAL FTE:	25A	25B	25C	25D	33

3. Branch: Record the particular name of a branch, if desired.
4. Date: Record the date for which the analysis was conducted. Enough space should be created in the cell (between the brackets) for a month and year, since the model is based on monthly data (e.g., November 1991).
5. Number of new loans this month: This begins the "data required" section of the model. Each caption has corresponding brackets indicating that a value must be input. Allow enough space in the cell, within the brackets, to accommodate at least six to seven characters. This particular item calls for the number of loans made this month.
6. Number of renewed loans this month: As with new loans, space must be created to record the volume of renewed loans made this month.
7. Average number total hours per FTE, per day: Space should be made available to record the average hours worked per day.
8. Number of loans past due this month: Create space for a specific number of loans made this month.
9. Average number of loan accounts on file: Create enough space to accommodate a raw number.

Section A: Fixed Hours (per FTE)
10A–12D. Business development, administration, and personal time: This begins the fixed activity section of the model. Format each bracketed cell so a percentage will appear. Only one decimal should be used; the percentage will be rounded to the nearest tenth. The same size brackets should be developed for each position and each cell formatted to reflect a percentage once the raw data are input.
13A–13D. Total: For items 13A through 13D no brackets are required, because no input will be allowed into the cell. The number will be determined by formula.

Each code number is a total of the percentages recorded in lines 10, 11, and 12. The formulas are as follows:

13A   @sum(10A..12A)
13B   @sum(10B..12B)

13C   @sum(10C..12C)
13D   @sum(10D..12D)

Section B: Variable Hours

14A–17D. New loans, renewal loans, maintenance/monitoring, and past due: This is the variable activity section of the report. Space must be made available under each position for each activity. Brackets should set off each cell, indicating that an input is required. Allow enough space within each cell to accommodate at least six to eight characters. No totals are required for this section, so no formulas are used.

Section C: Distribution of FTEs by Position

18A–18D. New loans: This last section of the model is the most important. This analytical section calculates the FTE requirements by activity and position, using built-in formulas. No brackets are used, since this is *not* an input section. Every cell in section C (cells 18A–33) contains a formula. The formulas used produce the results of the staffing analysis. For new loans, the narrative formula used for each of the four positions (commercial lender, administrative assistant, loan support, and credit analyst) is as follows:

$$\left(\begin{matrix} \text{New} \\ \text{loans} \end{matrix} \times \begin{matrix} \text{Hours per} \\ \text{new loan} \end{matrix} \right) \div \left(\left(\begin{matrix} \text{Average} \\ \text{total hours} \\ \text{per FTE} \\ \text{per day} \end{matrix} \times \begin{matrix} \text{Number of} \\ \text{working days} \\ \text{per year} \end{matrix} \right) \div 12 \right)$$

The Lotus formulas are as follows:

18A   (5*14A)/((7*240)/12)
18B   (5*14B)/((7*240)/12)
18C   (5*14C)/((7*240)/12)
18D   (5*14D)/((7*240)/12)
*   (52 weeks × 5 days per week – 10 holidays –
        10 vacation days)

19A–19D. Renewal loans: The narrative formula for calculating optimum staffing levels is:

$$\left(\begin{array}{c}\text{Number of} \\ \text{renewals} \\ \text{this month}\end{array} \times \begin{array}{c}\text{Hourly} \\ \text{rate per} \\ \text{renewed loan}\end{array}\right) \div \left(\left(\begin{array}{c}\text{Average} \\ \text{total hours} \\ \text{per FTE} \\ \text{per day}\end{array} \times \begin{array}{c}\text{Working} \\ \text{days} \\ \text{per year}\end{array}\right) \div 12\right)$$

The Lotus 1, 2, 3 formulas are:

19A   (6*15A)/((7*240)/12)
19B   (6*15B)/((7*240)/12)
19C   (6*15C)/((7*240)/12)
19D   (6*15D)/((7*240)/12)

20A–20D. Maintenance: The narrative formula for calculating optimum staffing levels is:

$$\left(\begin{array}{c}\text{Number of} \\ \text{customers} \\ \text{on file}\end{array} \times \begin{array}{c}\text{Maintenance} \\ \text{hourly factor}\end{array}\right) \div \left(\left(\begin{array}{c}\text{Average} \\ \text{total hours} \\ \text{per FTE} \\ \text{per day}\end{array} \times \begin{array}{c}\text{Working} \\ \text{days} \\ \text{per year}\end{array}\right) \div 12\right)$$

The Lotus 1, 2, 3 formulas are:

20A   (9*16A)/((7*240)/12)
20B   (9*16B)/((7*240)/12)
20C   (9*16C)/((7*240)/12)
20D   (9*16D)/((7*240)/12)

21A–21D. Past dues: The narrative formula for calculating optimum staffing levels is:

$$\left(\begin{array}{c}\text{Number of} \\ \text{loans past due} \\ \text{this month}\end{array} \times \begin{array}{c}\text{Past-due} \\ \text{hourly factor}\end{array}\right) \div \left(\left(\begin{array}{c}\text{Average} \\ \text{total hours} \\ \text{per FTE} \\ \text{per day}\end{array} \times 240\right) \div 12\right)$$

The Lotus 1, 2, 3 formulas are:

21A   (8*17A)/((7*240)/12)
21B   (8*17B)/((7*240)/12)
21C   (8*17C)/((7*240)/12)
21D   (8*17D)/((7*240)/12)

22A–22D. Business development: The narrative formula for calculating optimum staffing levels is:

$$\left(\left(\begin{pmatrix} \text{Sum of} \\ \text{new/} \\ \text{renewed} \\ \text{loans} \end{pmatrix} + \text{Maintenance} + \begin{pmatrix} \text{Past-} \\ \text{due} \\ \text{FTEs} \end{pmatrix}\right) \times \left(\begin{pmatrix} \text{Average} \\ \text{hours} \\ \text{per FTE} \end{pmatrix} \begin{array}{c} \text{Working} \\ \times \quad \text{days} \\ \text{per year} \end{array} \div 12\right)\right)$$

$$\div \left(\left(\begin{pmatrix} \text{Average} \\ \text{hours} \times 240 \\ \text{per FTE} \end{pmatrix} \div 12\right) - \left(\begin{pmatrix} \text{Average} \\ \text{hours} \times 240 \\ \text{per FTE} \end{pmatrix} \div 12 \times \begin{array}{c} \text{Total} \\ \text{fixed} \\ \text{activity} \\ \text{percentage} \end{array}\right)\right)$$

$$\times \left(\left(\left(\begin{pmatrix} \text{Average} \\ \text{hours} \times 240 \\ \text{per FTE} \end{pmatrix} \div 12\right) \times \begin{pmatrix} \text{Business} \\ \text{development} \\ \text{percentage} \end{pmatrix} \div \left(\begin{pmatrix} \text{Average} \\ \text{hours} \times 240 \\ \text{per day} \end{pmatrix} \div 12\right)\right)\right)$$

The Lotus 1, 2, 3 formulas are:

22A   ((@sum(18A..21A)*((7*240)/12))/(((7*240)/12)-(((7*240)/12)*13A)))*((((7*240)/12)*10A)/((7*240)/12))

22B   ((@sum(18B..21B)*((7*240)/12))/(((7*240)/12)-(((7*240)/12)*13B)))*((((7*240)/12)*10B)/((7*240)/12))

22C   ((@sum(18C..21C)*((7*240)/12))/(((7*240)/12)-(((7*240)/12)*13C)))*((((7*240)/12)*10C)/((7*240)/12))

22D   ((@sum(18D..21D)*((7*240)/12))/(((7*240)/12)-(((7*240)/12)*13D)))*((((7*240)/12)*10D)/((7*240)/12))

23A–23D. Administrative: The narrative formula for calculating optimum staffing levels is:

$$\left(\left(\begin{pmatrix} \text{Sum of} \\ \text{new/renewals} \\ \text{maintenance} \\ \text{\& past due} \end{pmatrix} \times \begin{pmatrix} \text{Average} \\ \text{hours} \times \text{Working} \\ \text{per FTE} \quad \text{days} \end{pmatrix} \div 12\right)\right)$$

$$\div \left(\left(\begin{pmatrix} \text{Average} \\ \text{hours} \times 240 \\ \text{per FTE} \end{pmatrix} \div 12\right) - \left(\begin{pmatrix} \text{Average} \\ \text{hours} \times 240 \\ \text{per FTE} \end{pmatrix} \div 12 \times \begin{array}{c} \text{Total} \\ \text{fixed} \\ \text{activity} \\ \text{percentage} \end{array}\right)\right)$$

$$\times \left(\left(\left(\begin{array}{c} \text{Average} \\ \text{hours} \\ \text{per FTE} \end{array} \times 240 \right) \div 12 \right) \times \begin{array}{c} \text{Administrative} \\ \text{percentage} \end{array} \div \left(\begin{array}{c} \text{Average} \\ \text{hours} \\ \text{per day} \end{array} \times 240 \right) \div 12 \right)$$

The Lotus 1, 2, 3 formulas are:

23A ((@sum(18A..21A)*((7*240)/12))/(((7*240)/12)-
(((7*240)/12)*13A)))*((((7*240)/12)*11A/((7*240)/12))

23B ((@sum(18B..21B)*((7*240)/12))/(((7*240)/12)-
(((7*240)/12)*13B)))*((((7*240)/12)*11B/((7*240)/12))

23C ((@sum(18C..21C)*((7*240)/12))/(((7*240)/12)-
(((7*240)/12)*13C)))*((((7*240)/12)*11C/((7*240)/12))

23D ((@sum(18D..21D)*((7*240)/12))/(((7*240)/12)-
(((7*240)/12)*13D)))*((((7*240)/12)*11D/((7*240)/12))

24A–24D. Personal: The narrative formula for calculating optimum staffing levels is:

$$\left(\left(\left(\begin{array}{c} \text{Sum of new/} \\ \text{renewals} \\ \text{maintenance} \\ \text{\& past due} \end{array} \right) \times \left(\begin{array}{c} \text{Average} \\ \text{hours} \times \begin{array}{c} \text{Working} \\ \text{days} \end{array} \\ \text{per FTE} \end{array} \right) \div 12 \right) \right.$$

$$\div \left(\left(\left(\begin{array}{c} \text{Average} \\ \text{hours} \\ \text{per FTE} \end{array} \times 240 \right) \div 12 \right) - \left(\left(\begin{array}{c} \text{Average} \\ \text{hours} \\ \text{per FTE} \end{array} \times 240 \right) \div 12 \right) \times \begin{array}{c} \text{Total} \\ \text{fixed} \\ \text{activity} \\ \text{percentage} \end{array} \right)$$

$$\times \left(\left(\left(\begin{array}{c} \text{Average} \\ \text{hours} \\ \text{per FTE} \end{array} \times 240 \right) \div 12 \right) \times \begin{array}{c} \text{Personal} \\ \text{percentage} \end{array} \div \left(\begin{array}{c} \text{Average} \\ \text{hours} \\ \text{per day} \end{array} \times 240 \right) \div 12 \right)$$

The Lotus 1, 2, 3 formulas are:

24A ((@sum(11A..21A)*((7*240)/12))/(((7*240)/12)-
(((7*240)/12)*13A)))*((((7*240)/12)*12A/((7*240)/12))

24B ((@sum(11B..21B)*((7*240)/12))/(((7*240)/12)-
(((7*240)/12)*13B)))*((((7*240)/12)*12B/((7*240)/12))

24C $((@sum(11C..21C)*((7*240)/12))/(((7*240)/12)-$
$(((7*240)/12)*13C)))*((((7*240)/12)*12C)/((7*240)/12))$

24D $((@sum(11D..21D)*((7*240)/12))/(((7*240)/12)-$
$(((7*240)/12)*13D)))*((((7*240)/12)*12D)/((7*240)/12))$

25A–25D. Total FTE: This is a total column of full-time equivalents for each position. The narrative formula is:

$$\left(\begin{array}{c}\text{New}\\\text{loan}\\\text{FTE}\end{array} + \begin{array}{c}\text{Renewal}\\\text{loan}\\\text{FTE}\end{array} + \begin{array}{c}\text{Main-}\\\text{tenance}\\\text{FTE}\end{array} + \begin{array}{c}\text{Past-}\\\text{due}\\\text{FTE}\end{array} + \begin{array}{c}\text{Business}\\\text{develop-}\\\text{ment}\\\text{FTE}\end{array} + \begin{array}{c}\text{Adminis-}\\\text{trative}\\\text{FTE}\end{array} + \begin{array}{c}\text{Personal}\\\text{FTE}\end{array}\right)$$

The Lotus 1, 2, 3 formulas are:

25A	@sum(18A..24A)
25B	@sum(18B..24B)
25C	@sum(18C..24C)
25D	@sum(18D..24D)

26–32. Total FTE staff: This section totals the FTE requirements for the bank by activity. It displays the number of people who should be devoted to the particular activity for all positions in the aggregate for commercial loans. The narrative formula for each activity is as follows:

$$\left(\begin{array}{c}\text{Commercial}\\\text{lender}\\\text{FTE}\end{array} + \begin{array}{c}\text{Administrative}\\\text{assistant}\\\text{FTE}\end{array} + \begin{array}{c}\text{Loan}\\\text{support}\\\text{FTE}\end{array} + \begin{array}{c}\text{Credit}\\\text{analyst}\\\text{FTE}\end{array}\right)$$

The Lotus 1, 2, 3 formulas are as follows:

26	@sum(18A..18D)
27	@sum(19A..19D)
28	@sum(20A..20D)
29	@sum(21A..21D)
30	@sum(22A..22D)
31	@sum(23A..23D)
32	@sum(24A..24D)

33. FTE grand total: This represents the total number of FTEs required by the bank for the commercial loan function. The narrative formula for this total of the individual FTE requirements for all commercial loan functions is as follows:

$$\left(\begin{array}{c}\text{Total} \\ \text{new} \\ \text{loan} \\ \text{FTEs}\end{array} + \begin{array}{c}\text{Total} \\ \text{renewal} \\ \text{loan} \\ \text{FTEs}\end{array} + \begin{array}{c}\text{Total} \\ \text{main-} \\ \text{tenance} \\ \text{FTEs}\end{array} + \begin{array}{c}\text{Total} \\ \text{past-} \\ \text{due} \\ \text{FTEs}\end{array} + \begin{array}{c}\text{Total} \\ \text{business} \\ \text{develop-} \\ \text{ment} \\ \text{FTEs}\end{array} + \begin{array}{c}\text{Total} \\ \text{adminis-} \\ \text{trative} \\ \text{FTEs}\end{array} + \begin{array}{c}\text{Total} \\ \text{personnel} \\ \text{FTEs}\end{array}\right)$$

The Lotus 1, 2, 3 formula is:

@sum(26..32)

Running the Model

Now that the model has been created on Lotus 1, 2, 3, the next task is to input the actual data into the model to develop the staffing analysis. For an explanation of what data are required and where it should be placed on the model, refer to Figure 95. The following discussion of code numbers explains the origin of the information required.

1. Bank: The name of the bank should be typed in for identification. It can be abbreviated to fit within the brackets.

2. Location: This is the address or street name where the bank is located. (It can also be a city.)

3. Branch: If multiple branches are being evaluated, a branch name, number, or identifier can be input in this section.

4. Date: Record the date or time period for which the report is run. This is typically the month and year (e.g., November 1991), since the report is usually run monthly. If the report is run as a monthly average for a quarter, record the name of the quarter (e.g., 4th Quarter 1991).

5. Number of new loans this month: Input the specific number of new commercial loans made this month. This can either be the actual number for the month or the average amount of new loans made per month. The best approach is to average the amount of new loans made over a period of three to six months. The resulting staff needed will thus be based on current trends, not on one particular and possibly atypical month.

6. Number of renewed loans this month: The input required for this section is the same as for new loans. Take the monthly average of renewal loans over a period of time.

7. Average total hours per FTE per day: Input the total working hours per commercial loan staff member per day. This represents the total raw hours (including lunches and breaks) that an employee is at work from start to finish. Use the standard published bank hours (its specified starting and ending hours for employees each day). For example, if the official hours are 8:30 AM to 5:00 PM, input 8.5 hours. Take into account only hours indicated by payroll policy, not extra hours worked.

8. Number of loans past due this month: Input the total number of loans past due for the particular month. This is a total of all delinquency stages (15–29, 30–59, 60–89, and 90+ days). Include only past-due loans that are still the responsibility of the commercial lending officer, not past-due loans that have been charged off, moved to a workout area, or referred to an agency or attorney. Again, a monthly average over a period of time is probably the most accurate approach.

9. Average number of customer accounts on file: Input the number of commercial customers on file, not the number of individual notes. One customer may have many loan relationships, so the number of customer accounts will be less than the number of notes on file. This, too, can be an average monthly amount, determined over a period of time.

Fixed Hours (per FTE)
10A–10D. Business development: Since this is a fixed category, input only percentages within the brackets. Because this segment of the model is formatted on Lotus 1, 2, 3 as a percentage, enter it as a decimal (e.g., 70 percent is .70). The number is taken from the various analyses and recaps for each position, as explained earlier in the chapter. For example, Figure 22 shows that 26.23 percent of a commercial lender's time is devoted to business development. Input .2623 in the business development cell under commercial lender.

Use this approach to record percentages for each position, based on the analyses that determined these factors, as outlined in this chapter.

11A–12D. Administration and personal time: For each of these activities, the same approach is used as for business development. Since these are fixed categories, only percentages are used. All percentages are determined via the methodology discussed earlier in the chapter, using the surveys contained in the appendix.

13A–13D. Total: No input is required in these cells. Formulas within each cell will total the percentages for each position to reveal the total percentage of time devoted to fixed activities.

Variable Hours

14A–17D. New/renewed loans, maintenance, and past-due activities: For each activity category, an input is required within the bracketed fields. Variable activities require hourly factors as opposed to percentages. For each position, input the hourly factor determined from the analysis earlier in the chapter. For example, for commercial lenders, the factor for new loans is 4.02 hours, taken from Figure 39. These standards reflect management's opinion of the optimal time for each activity.

Distribution of FTEs by Position

18A–33. Full-time equivalents required: This last section of the model, the analysis section, requires no input. It contains the formulas for calculating optimal staffing levels by activity, by position. Based on the raw data input in items 5 through 17D, the FTE requirements will automatically be displayed within these cells.

This completes the necessary input for the commercial loan staffing model. It can be run monthly, quarterly, or as required. Once the data have been determined from the survey for sections A and B, the analyst can change volumes while using the same standards. The true benefit of the model is that it allows "what-if" analysis to determine the most effective approach to take.

ANALYSIS, MEASUREMENT, AND USAGE

Once the standards have been determined and the model actually run, the final phase of the process is to analyze the results and determine how to use them.

The model is designed to provide the user with the optimum number of full-time equivalents needed for the commercial loan department (all positions). Once this is determined, the next issue is how to manipulate the information to provide a direction on what steps the bank should take to maximize productivity. In the case of commercial loans, the percentage of time spent on each activity must be analyzed. The key activities and/or key volume indicators used in commercial loans—business development, administrative, personal, new loans, renewed loans, maintenance, and past-dues—must be arrayed in percentage order.

To analyze where the greatest concentrations of time are being spent in order to take constructive action, refer to section C of the model. The column to the right of the activities shows a percentage of total time devoted to each commercial loan function. From these data, array the activities in descending order, as shown in Figure 96.

In the example, the majority of time is devoted to maintenance (38 percent). This grouping of activities can be further condensed into the categories of sales (new loans and business development), servicing (renewed loans and maintenance), control (past-due loans), and other (personal and administrative activities).

Figure 96 can thus be restated as service (46 percent), sales (29 percent), other (22 percent), and control (3 percent). The respective percentages for sales and servicing may not be what management anticipated. In fact, they could be quite a surprise to management.

A pie chart can be developed to display the percentages of the total as slices. As shown in Figure 97, this is an effective way to demonstrate impact.

The next steps are based on the decisions made by management. It may be that not enough new loans are made and that the

F I G U R E 96

Ranking of Activities by Percentage of Total Time

Activity	Percent to Total
Maintenance	38%
New loans	18
Personal	12
Business development	11
Administrative	10
Renewed loans	8
Past dues	3
	100.0%

overall sales effort is perceived to be weak. Reviewing Figure 97 would support this hypothesis, indicating that most of the department's time is spent servicing customers.

Of course, this information could be skewed because it represents a total for the entire department. Some functions, particularly administrative assistants and loan support, are heavily geared toward maintenance. To compensate for this the user could reanalyze the FTEs determined in the model for commercial lenders only, dividing the FTEs calculated by the total FTEs to obtain a percentage to total, then ranking them in descending order. Now management can evaluate how commercial lenders are spending their time in terms of sales, servicing, and control.

If the result is similar to the initial analysis, specific actions can be taken to adjust the mix. In the first place, the input factors can be changed to determine what factors will yield the desired assignment of time. Changing the percentage of time for some fixed activities in the model while on the screen will cause the program to immediately calculate a new optimum FTE. By doing this management can determine the best mix of time.

Of course, it is one thing to adjust numbers on a model to produce a desired result and quite another to do it in reality. To ensure success, the adjustments made in the model must be im-

F I G U R E 97

Pie Chart of Time Spent on Commercial Loans

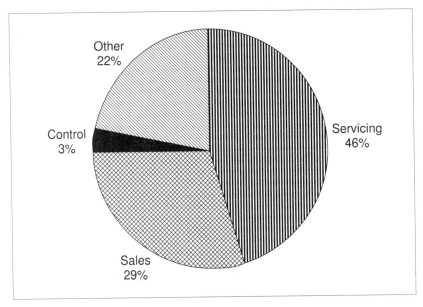

plemented in the real world. To illustrate this point, assume it is determined that 25 percent of a commercial lender's time is spent on administrative tasks, a fixed activity. Since management may wish to have commercial lending officers spend more of their time on sales, maintenance, and/or control (variable activities), the makeup of the 25 percent must be determined. If further analysis determines that commercial loan officers spend too much time in sales and/or officers' meetings, this can easily be controlled. By ordering a reduction in meetings, the bank can achieve a specific drop in the 25 percent fixed activity time. This, too, can be easily calculated. Simply refer back to the analysis that produced the 25 percent, plug in the new amounts of time to be spent in meetings, and recalculate. This will yield a new percentage that can be input into the model. The result will be more time available to officers to spend on sales, servicing, and control. Consequently, fewer commercial loan officers may be required.

By changing specifically controllable factors, management can dramatically alter the number of FTEs required and mix of time. The most controllable area to analyze is the fixed activity section (business development, administrative, and personal activities). Since these activities all occur regularly without concern for the volume of loans generated, they can easily be changed by a mandate that *only* designated times be spent on each area and no more.

This can be quite a learning experience for management. When the data are originally gathered and a pie chart constructed, the bank may be shocked to learn how much time officers spend on administrative duties (meetings). Since commercial loan officers are generally paid at a premium, it is doubtful that bank management will want to tie up these expensive resources in unproductive meetings.

Variable activities also have opportunities for change, albeit with more analysis. Variable activities (new loans, renewals, maintenance, and past dues) are directly affected by volume.

Once the hourly time factor is determined for each activity (based on survey data) how can it be arbitrarily changed? Management can change hourly factors only by analyzing, in detail, the steps involved in the actual tasks that comprise them. In other words, if the analysis says that 4.02 hours are required per new loan, how can this be reduced to 3.50 or even 3.00 hours? The user should attempt to flowchart the tasks leading toward completion of a new loan. Once the flowchart is complete, assign specific time estimates to each task, the aggregate of which will equal 4.02 hours per new loan. At this point, evaluate each step or task and department.

- Can the time required to complete this task be reduced?
- Can the task be automated and eliminated from the flow-chart of manual tasks?
- Is the task needed at all?

It is not unusual for a manager to find that some of the tasks being performed are no longer necessary. As banking continues to become more automated at a rapid pace, systems designed to eliminate manual tasks are put in place, but sometimes the tasks remain. Furthermore, people react differently to automation. Sometimes competent employees are reluctant to give up a tried and true function simply because they don't believe in the system; they feel they can do it just as fast, or because they were not told to stop doing it. At this point, management must step in to resolve these issues. Performing these types of analyses can indeed lead to changes in the specific hourly factors assigned to the variable tasks, although the most obvious changes will come from the fixed activities.

In the process of evaluating variable tasks (flowcharting) another important observation must be made. If the analyst cannot determine a way to eliminate a time-consuming task through automation or somehow, he or she should take into account who performs it. If a task is being performed by a commercial lender that could be done by another person (loan support, credit analyst, or secretary), an opportunity exists to move the function to another, less costly employee, thereby lowering the unit cost to perform the task. The unit costs for tasks performed by lending officers are higher than for any other position in commercial loans, so by moving tasks to less costly employees, the bank may find a need for more staff support but fewer loan officers. This would provide a true savings to the bank and an efficient means of having appropriate tasks performed.

Finally, it is very important to analyze the results in the model on the basis of percentage to total time for sales, servicing, control, and other. This is particularly important for commercial lenders, since the bulk of their time may be spent on sales but not on maintenance. Many new customers may be brought in, but will they be retained? If there is an intensive sales effort for new business, what about past dues? An inadequate monitoring program could lead to severe credit problems and subsequent losses.

What is the answer? The best approach is for management to determine the optimum time mix for commercial lenders. Other fixed and variable activities can be adjusted to achieve the desired mix. This can then be communicated to the staff and put into action. An optimum time dispersion might be:

- Sales   45%
- Servicing   30%
- Control   5%
- Other   20%

Note that a total of 80 percent of commercial lenders' time is devoted to sales, servicing, and control—standard lending functions. As a rule of thumb, at least three-quarters of an individual's time should be devoted to the key volume indicators that define his or her position. One might question employees' salaries if they are spending less than 75 percent of their time on core functions.

SUMMARY

The purpose of this chapter has been to develop and explain a commercial loan staffing tool and analysis. To assess optimum commercial loan staffing levels, a model must be developed that can perform a quick, accurate, and efficient analysis based upon data input and parameters established. The initial phase of developing a staffing analysis is to interview all employees within the department. These interviews will provide the basis for determining the functions performed within the department and various positions. From the information obtained, a profile is developed that consolidates the large amount of data learned into a core set of activities for each position. The profile, a determination of the output and/or key volume indicators of the positions, defines the positions. For commercial lending, the profile activities are:

- New loans
- Renewals
- Customer maintenance
- Past-due handling
- Business development
- Administrative
- Personal

These are common to all positions within commercial loans:

- Commercial lenders.
- Administrative assistants / secretaries.
- Loan operations and support personnel.
- Credit analysts.

The seven activities that constitute the profile can be segregated into fixed and variable activities. Fixed activities are those that occur regularly, day after day, without regard to loan or customer volume. Variable activities are directly affected by loan and / or customer volume.

Each activity within the fixed and variable groups is analyzed to determine a standard for the particular bank. Surveys completed by the commercial lending department forms the basis for the parameters that will be input into the staffing model.

The staffing model is built using Lotus 1, 2, 3 and is designed to provide immediate response. Specific steps, formulas, and procedures are provided to recreate the actual model discussed in the chapter. The model is run using volume and other required data. For the most effective results, use monthly volume averages over a period of time, to provide results based on trends.

Once all data have been input and run, analyze the results by determining the percentage of time devoted to each activity within the commercial loan profile. The seven profile activities are then summarized into four broad categories: sales, servicing, control, and other.

A pie chart is useful in illustrating how time is spent among the four categories. Management can then manipulate percentages and other parameters to arrive at the desired mix of time spent on activities. This in turn can affect the amount of commercial staff needed to achieve the organization's goals.

Analysis of the results is most important, for at this stage the standards are determined that will be used in the model. Once these standards are identified, the model can be run repeatedly as a check on staffing levels or to determine staffing levels for the future.

Staffing the Personal Banking and Support Area

Besides commercial lending, the predominant sales force of financial institutions is in personal banking. Next to tellers, personal bankers are probably the most familiar point of contact for most customers of a bank. As distinct from the commercial side, personal bankers are generally retail salespeople responsible for the sale of the standard individual customer bank products. For the most part, this includes the sale and handling of loans, deposit products, nondeposit products, and services.

Within each category, the specific products are (in general):

1. Loans:
   - Installment loans.
   - Home equity loans.
   - Overdraft lines of credit.
   - Home improvement loans.
   - Student loans.
2. Deposit products:
   - Money market accounts.
   - Negotiable order of deposit (NOW) accounts.
   - Savings accounts.
   - Certificates of deposit (CDs).
   - Individual retirement accounts (IRAs).

3. Nondeposit products:
   - ATM cards.
   - Safe deposit boxes.
   - Credit cards.
4. Services:
   - Balancing/reconciling checking accounts.
   - Stop payments/releases.
   - Wire transfers.

This is a core list of products and services that are found at most organizations, rather than an exhaustive list. Typically, the personal banking division is responsible for the sale and handling of such products and services, with the assistance of two other positions in the personal banking department: secretaries and personal banking support. As in commercial loans, the retail sales staff must have support in order to concentrate, for the most part, on customer or potential customer contact. This chapter will discuss the entire retail sales division, including support personnel, to present a complete picture of the required staff members.

Many critics question whether a scientific approach to staffing analysis can work in the sales area, arguing that standards and measurements cannot be applied to a customer contact business as they can in back-office operational areas. Because of this attitude, many financial institutions may find themselves overstaffed and incurring more expenses than absolutely necessary. In addition, although personal bankers are not usually at the pay scale of commercial lenders, they may be officers and receive higher pay than most back-office personnel. So this would seem to be an area of intense focus for the justification of staff size, yet it typically is not. Back-office areas are easier areas to measure, and perhaps the reason for a lack of focus on the retail sales effort in terms of staffing is a lack of understanding how to do it.

This chapter will provide a sound methodology for the periodic analysis and determination of staffing requirements for the personal banking division. The basic approach is essentially the same as that used in the commercial lending analysis in Chapter 2. Following the specific methodology and steps provided in this chapter will enable financial institutions to understand the elements of staffing analyses for personal bankers. They will also learn how to develop an actual model, for ongoing use, which will provide actual staff size predictions based upon data input.

The primary benefit of this approach is that it allows management the opportunity to effectively predict staffing levels for new locations and periodically assess whether current staffing is at optimum levels. The latter will either assure management that costly payroll dollars for retail sales personnel are efficiently utilized or give them a plan of action to take.

METHODOLOGY

The initial phase of the personal banking staffing analysis is the preparatory work necessary to obtain the information and, more importantly, determine what measures have the greatest impact on the predictability of staffing levels. This section of the chapter provides the steps for analyzing personal banking staffing and the detailed parameters for building a software staffing model for ongoing use. The staffing analysis involves interviews, profile development, data gathering, model development, and running the model. Upon completion of this section the reader will have a good understanding of the process necessary for building a staffing model.

Interviews

The first step in developing any type of program or model must be communication with the individuals who do the work. Although the structure, format, and operation of the staffing model can be applied to any financial institution, the specific standards and parameters used must be unique to the organization because not all banks use the same computer system, procedures, or policies. In short, the time required to handle an installment loan will differ from bank to bank.

This is why the process outlined in this chapter (and book) work better than reliance on generalized statistics and standards. Broad analyses based on number of accounts and/or dollars of deposit per personal banker simply do not provide analytical precision. To provide an accurate analysis of personal banking staffing, the approach in this book provides the financial institution using it precision and exclusivity of measurement.

With this in mind, the interview process becomes extremely important. It is at this stage that a broad list of functions and duties are determined for the individuals who perform them. Since the personal banking division consists of personal bankers, secretaries, and support personnel, interviews must be conducted with at least every type of position within each group.

As an example, within the support personnel group there may be five employees. Three may perform the exact same function, and the remaining two completely different functions. At least one of the three individuals performing the same function must be interviewed, as well as each of the two who perform different functions. This will identify all tasks and duties.

During the interview process, it is not as important to categorize the data as simply to record it all. Analysis of data will occur later. To be effective, the interviewer should be patient and a good listener. Upon completion of all interviews, the data should be arranged by the three positions in personal banking (personal bankers, secretaries, and support personnel). This information forms the basis of measurement and subsequent staffing analysis.

Profile Development

If one were beginning from scratch, the data obtained from the interviews would be summarized into a limited number of core activities or outputs, known as the profile of the personal banking representative. Although the information obtained in interviews is always useful, the purpose of this book is to provide immediately usable data, so the profile of a personal banking representative has already been determined. This profile should not change even though the tasks and data that flow into each output may differ among financial institutions. This will become clearer in the data-gathering section of this chapter.

The profile will be the same for all three positions within personal banking. The difference is in the tasks that lead to the output, but the output itself will remain the same. For example, one of the profile outputs is "new products sold." Both personal bankers and support clerks perform tasks leading to the sale of the product. The personal banker may be involved with the sale, application completion, and closing, whereas the support clerk is involved in the input and filing of the completed product. But the output for both is products sold.

Prior research and analysis determined a set of key attributes for personal banking that are the primary predictors of staffing levels.

- New products sold.
- Customers seen (not sold).
- Maintenance.
- Business development.
- Administration.
- Personal.

These six areas form the basis for the staffing model and define the personal banking position. All tasks and duties performed by representatives in the personal banking division will be assigned to these six attributes.

As in the commercial staffing analysis, the six areas can be divided between fixed and variable items. Fixed activities are those tasks and duties performed regardless of incoming volume or traffic. Variable activities, on the other hand, are totally dependent on volume. If no customer traffic occurred and no new products were sold, no time would be used on these tasks. Fixed activities are business development, administrative, and personal activities. Variable activities are new products sold, customers seen (not sold), and maintenance. These items will be defined in the staffing model and standards will be developed for each, based on the data gathered.

The process of developing the profile is all-important. Without it, a true staffing analysis could not be performed. The profile is determined through analysis of what the personal banking function produces. The variable activities (new products sold, customers seen, and maintenance) are key volume indicators. In other words, they relate directly to volume and are outputs produced by a personal banking representative. They define the purpose of a personal banking representative. What do personal banking representatives do? Why are they there? Their primary duties are to sell products and maintain customer relationships. These are the key volume indicators that must be measured. The miscellaneous tasks that support these outputs simply become a part of them.

Other activities exist simply by the nature of the position, including administrative duties (meetings, phone calls, etc.), personal activities (lunches and breaks) and, for sales reps, business development. These activities are not truly outputs or key volume indicators, but they cannot be ignored, since they may take up as much as 25 percent of a personal banking representative's time. Management must have a way to analyze how much time is actually spent on these activities in order to control them. It is unfortunate that many staffing analyses ignore these data, leading to gross distortions in the staff levels required.

The next phase is to analyze the detailed tasks involved in the profile items and begin to develop parameters and standards for each.

Data Gathering

Now that a personal banking representative profile has been developed, the analyst must determine the tasks associated with each profile item and the specific time devoted to each. Using the data gathered during the interview process, outline the tasks associated with each profile item. These outlines will form the foundation for the development of a personal banking survey for capturing data. Although the profile data will not change, the tasks and functions associated with each profile item will differ by position. The survey approach is the primary methodology used to gather data.

These surveys are contained in Appendix Exhibits F, G, and H. They should be circulated to each employee in the personal banking division (one exhibit for each position), with instructions to complete them over a two-week period. In most cases the survey will require two types of data, time estimates and volumes. The time estimates are the employees' best estimate of the minutes required to perform the particular task. Once it is averaged among all employees in the position, the estimate becomes more realistic.

For volume information, tally marks for each occurrence are made on a production sheet. These documents are held over the two-week period, since it is important to capture this information as it occurs. Circulate the survey document during a period that is representative of a normal time; selecting the two weeks before or after a major holiday or other significant event could distort some of the volume data.

For purposes of the staffing model and determining standards for each of the profile items, it is necessary to know the monthly available work hours per employee. To be uniform in the application of a specific amount of available hours, use the formula in Figure 98 based on the human resource policies in effect at the financial institution. For the purposes of this chapter, 168.6 monthly available hours is uniformly applied.

F I G U R E 98

Total Monthly Available Hours Calculation

	52	week per year
×	5	working days per week
	260	working days per year
−	10	holidays per year
−	2	personal days per FTE per year
	10	average number of vacation days per FTE per year
=	238	net working days per year
×	8.5	total available hours per FTE per day
=	2,023	total hours per year
÷	12	months per year
=	168.6	total monthly available hours per FTE

Since three separate positions constitute the personal banking division, each will be separately discussed in this section to determine the standards to be used in the model. The three positions and their respective involvement in the profile activities are shown in Figure 99. As indicated, some positions are not involved with some profile activities. The next sections explain the detail of each position survey and the calculation of standards to be used in the model.

Personal Bankers

Personal bankers are typically the retail sales personnel of a financial institution. Next to tellers, they are the most predominant retail customer contact group. Personal bankers are usually officers of the bank, carrying a degree of lending authority to accommodate the sale of various products.

To determine the specific parameters and standards for the model, use the personal banker survey (Exhibit F). From the information obtained, analysis of each profile activity item can commence.

F I G U R E 99

Profile Activity Involvement by Position

	Personal Bankers	Secretaries	Support Staff
1. Fixed:			
Business development	X		
Administrative	X	X	X
Personal	X	X	X
2. Variable:			
New products sold	X	X	X
Customers seen (not sold)	X		
Maintenance	X	X	X

Business Development   Business development for personal bankers is the process of soliciting and drawing in new business. The initial interview is important to reveal differences among banks, but many financial institutions now have an organized sales/calling effort even at the retail level.

Business development is a fixed activity. That is, it occurs without regard to the amount of customer traffic or product sales volume. Usually an allotted period of time each week is fully devoted to the task of bringing in new business. Since the time commitment occurs regularly (each day and/or each week) with a high degree of predictability, the factor used in the model will be a percentage of total available hours. This means that a specified percentage of time per month is fully devoted to new business development.

The profile activity of business development consists of two broad categories, potential customer communications and strategy and planning.

Within each broad category, a number of specific tasks are involved.

1. Potential customer communications:
   - Phone calls received.
   - Phone calls made.
   - Telemarketing calls made.
   - Outside visits.
   - Correspondence/follow-up.
2. Strategy and planning:
   - Market development.

To capture the appropriate data to determine the standards for these activities, use the personal banker survey (Exhibit F in the Appendix). For potential customer communications, the survey requires estimates for the amount of time required per subtask. Once the surveys are returned, these items should be averaged for all personal bankers responding. The average will be used in calculating the standard.

It is also necessary to gather volume data. This is accomplished by using the call tally sheet in the survey (also illustrated

F I G U R E 100

Call Tally Sheet

Week of: _____
Name: _____

Day	Interval Calls Received/Made	Category	In-Person Meeting with Client		Telephone Calls		Tele-mar-keting Calls	Correspon-dence (letters)
			At Customer Location	In Bank	Inbound	Outbound		
Monday		Existing customer						
		Potential customer						
Tuesday		Existing customer						
		Potential customer						
Wednesday		Existing customer						
		Potential customer						
Thursday		Existing customer						
		Potential customer						
Friday		Existing customer						
		Potential customer						
Saturday		Existing customer						
		Potential customer						
Total		Existing customer						
		Potential customer						

in Figure 100) over a two-week period. Total the "potential customer" data for the entire group of personal bankers. The analysis of potential customer communications activities is illustrated in Figure 101. According to this calculation, approximately 15.26 hours per personal banker are devoted to potential customer communications. Since all of the subtasks within this category are in the control of the personal banker, the overall time devoted to them is considered fixed. In other words, none of the subtasks are driven by the volume of new products sold.

The other subtasks of business development relate to the amount of time spent on strategy and planning. Part of the business development process is strategizing and planning how new business will be brought into the bank. This may be done by management, or the personal bankers may participate in the process. If they are involved, their time must be accounted for on the personal banker survey form. The amount of time devoted to this activity is averaged for all personal bankers on staff and analyzed to determine the amount of time spent per personal banker, as in Figure 102.

This completes the business development segment of the personal banker profile. Since this is a fixed activity, it must be restated as a percentage of total available monthly hours. This is accomplished by first summarizing the data for the two subcategories (potential customer communications and strategy and development) and then determining this percentage as illustrated in Figure 103. This percentage will be used in the personal banking staffing model to determine the amount of time devoted to business development.

As indicated in Figure 103, 10.3 percent of a personal banker's time will be used for business development in the staffing model.

Administrative   Administrative tasks are also considered fixed activities in that they are not directly related to the core business of selling bank products. All positions have administrative duties that come with the territory. In some cases little can be done to avoid them, but other cases offer opportunities for streamlining when the staffing analyst understands the details of the activities

FIGURE 101

Potential Customer Communications

	Total Vol. (All Personal Bankers)		Weeks to Annualize		Months/Year		No. of Personal Bankers		Avg. Vol./Personal Banker/Month		Avg. Minutes/Item		Minutes/Hour		Avg. Hours/Personal Banker/Month
Phone calls received	115.4	×	26	÷	12	÷	10	=	25	×	3	÷	60	=	1.75
Phone calls made	92.3	×	26	÷	12	÷	10	=	20	×	5	÷	60	=	1.67
Telemarketing calls made	184.6	×	26	÷	12	÷	10	=	40	×	12	÷	60	=	8.00
Outside visits	13.8	×	26	÷	12	÷	10	=	3	×	60	÷	60	=	3.00
Correspondence sent	23.1	×	26	÷	12	÷	10	=	5	×	10	÷	60	=	.84
															15.26

Total potential customer communications hours per personal banker per month

FIGURE 102

Strategy and Planning

Activity	Average Minutes/Week		Weeks/Year		Minutes/Year		Minutes/Hour		Average Hours/Personal Banker/Month
Market development	30	×	52	÷	12	÷	60	=	2.17

F I G U R E 103

Business Development Summary

Subcategory	Average Hours per Personal Banker per Month
1. Potential customer communications	15.26
2. Strategy and planning	2.17
Total hours per month per personal banker	17.43
Number of available hours per personal banker per month	÷ 168.6
Percentage of total available hours for business development per personal banker per month	= 10.3%

involved. Whether certain activities can be eliminated is a subject for later discussion; for now, they must be accounted for.

For personal bankers, administrative activities consist of meetings, telephone contact, and miscellaneous duties. These broad categories can be further defined to include the following specific tasks:

1. Meetings:
   - Sales meetings.
   - Officer meetings.
   - Training / seminars.
2. Telephone contact:
   - Internal phone calls made.
   - Internal phone calls received.
3. Miscellaneous duties.

From using the personal banker survey (Exhibit F), information pertinent to these items can be determined for analysis. Beginning with meetings, an estimate is requested of the time per session as well as frequency per month. Only meetings that are held on a regular, ongoing basis are included, not impromptu meetings.

F I G U R E 104

Administrative: Meeting Time Spent

	Avg. Minutes/ Session	Freq./ Month	Minutes/ Hour	Avg. Hours/ Personal Banker/ Month
Sales meetings	60 ×	1 ÷	60 =	1.00
Officer meetings	45 ×	1 ÷	60 =	.75
Training/seminars	90 ×	.34 ÷	60 =	.51
Average hours per personal banker devoted to meetings per month				2.26

Once the surveys have been returned, both session time and frequency must be averaged by meeting type. This information is analyzed in Figure 104 to develop the monthly hourly requirement per personal banker.

Administrative telephone call volume relates to noncustomer calls—specifically, intrabank calls. Intrabank calls can occur for any reason, whether job-related or simply by virtue of the individual's having access to a phone. Regardless of the reasons, intrabank phone calls are made and received, thereby taking up some of the available time of a personal banker.

Although one can never predict the number of internal phone calls made and received, they occur regularly and therefore must be accounted for. The call tally sheet (Figure 100) is used to track this information over a two-week period. Tally marks are recorded for each internal call made and received. Once the survey document is completed, the raw total for all personal bankers should be analyzed as in Figure 105 for the amount of hours, on average, personal bankers devote to handling internal calls each month.

The last part of administrative tasks is miscellaneous duties. At times personal bankers may take on additional duties that do not directly relate to customer contact—for example, report development, special projects, or other such duties as assigned. If a

F I G U R E   105

Administrative: Telephone Contact

Activity	Total Dept. Volume		Weeks to Annualize		Months/ Year		No. of Personal Bankers		Avg. Calls/ Personal Banker/ Month		Avg. Minutes/ Call		Minutes/ Hour		Avg. Hours/ for Calls/ Personal Banker/ Month
Internal calls made/received	554	×	26	÷	12	÷	10	=	120	×	3	÷	60	=	6.00

F I G U R E   106

Administrative: Miscellaneous Duties

Activity	Total Time Spent by All Personal Bankers/ Month (minutes)		Minutes/Hour		No. of Personal Bankers on Staff		Avg. Hours/Personal Banker/Month
Miscellaneous duties	900	×	60	÷	10	=	1.50

personal banker performs other miscellaneous duties on a regular basis (every month), then this time must be accounted for. On the survey, the personal banker estimates the amount of time devoted to miscellaneous each month. This is something of a catchall, but it accounts for all time used. Since not every personal banker is involved in miscellaneous duties, an average (mean) is taken for all personal bankers to arrive at the hourly factor, as illustrated in Figure 106.

The 1.5 hours per personal banker per month blends this time period over the entire group. It becomes the factor for determining the overall administrative time dedicated to these fixed activities.

The administrative activities of the personal banker profile can now be summarized and translated into a percentage of total available hours. Again, this is a fixed activity because the total time spent will not vary with product sale volume or customer contact traffic. This summary will yield the factor for the administrative activity to be used in the personal banking staffing model, as displayed in Figure 107.

Personal Activities   Every position uses time for personal activities. Lunches and breaks are fixed activities within the personal

F I G U R E 107

Administrative Summary: Personal Bankers

Subcategories	
1. Meetings	2.26
2. Telephone contact	6.00
3. Miscellaneous duties	1.50
Total hours per personal banker per month	9.76
Number of available hours per personal banker per month	÷ 168.6
Percentage of total available hours for administrative activities per personal banker per month	5.79%

F I G U R E 108

Personal Activities

Activity	Avg. Minutes/ Item		Working Days/ Year		Months/ Year		Minutes/ Hour		Avg. Hours/ Personal Banker/ Month
Lunches	60	×	260	÷	12	÷	60	=	21.67
Breaks	15	×	260	÷	12	÷	60	=	5.42
Total monthly hours per personal banker								=	27.09
Number of available hours per personal banker per month									÷
Percentage of available hours spent on personal activities per month								=	16.1%

banker profile, since they do not relate at all to the job but do occur on a very regular basis (daily) and for designated periods of time.

The hourly factor and subsequent percentage of available hours that personal activities demand can be determined from the raw data in the personal banker survey. All responses can be averaged to determine the time spent on lunches and breaks, or a time period can be assigned that corresponds to bank policy. The data are then analyzed as in Figure 108 and translated into a percentage of total available hours. Working days per year are calculated as five times 52.

This is the last of the fixed activities associated with the personal banker profile. The next section discusses the variable activities related to product sales volume and customer traffic.

New Products Sold In general, personal bankers are staffed to sell a variety of products rather than specializing in the sale of one or two types (as might occur with commercial lenders). So the output or key volume indicator is new products sold, which encompasses the full range of products available to be sold by personal bankers.

New products sold is the first variable activity in the personal banker profile used to determine optimum staffing levels. The total time spent by the personal banker is directly proportional to the number of products sold. If 10 products were sold, the total time would be the number sold multiplied by the time factor per product sold. The number of total products sold is usually readily attainable, but what is the time factor per product sold? To determine this as a factor that can be applied to any product, a weighted average analysis must be performed.

The weighted average analysis considers the individual time required, per product, in relationship to its frequency of occurrence. The combination of these two items will yield a blended or weighted average time factor, which can be applied to any product, making it unnecessary to track individual product types for the future. The weighted average time factor per product (expressed in hours) is used in the personal banking staffing model for the variable activity of new products sold.

To determine this weighted average, data must be captured for use in the overall calculations. The standard vehicle for this is the personal banker survey (Exhibit F), which requests time estimates for each type of product sold. The estimates, expressed in minutes, represent the total time required of the personal banker from initial interview and discussion with the customer to completion of the transaction. In other words, the factor covers all time a personal banker spends opening the account, including credit checks, verifications, underwriting, analysis, disbursement of funds, and so on. This is important; failure to include all tasks associated with the product could distort the overall analysis.

The weighted average time factor does not, however, include back-office functions performed by secretaries and/or support personnel. These are accounted for under these individual positions. Since the personal banker survey is completed by *all* personal bankers, an average (mean) is taken for each product to even out any distortions and produce reasonably accurate time estimates.

The average volume of products sold can be determined either by existing reporting mechanisms or through manual tracking. The former is by far the better approach. Mainframe reports that track the amount of new loans booked, new deposit products sold, and nondeposit products sold can easily provide historical data to calculate trends for the time pattern of products sold.

If such mechanisms are not available, a manual tally sheet must track the amount of products sold, by personal banker, over a period of time. This type of report, illustrated in Figure 109, contains one week's results, so only two are needed. The goal is to determine the grand total volume of products sold, by product.

The average time estimates and volumes by product form the foundation for determining the weighted average time per product. Before this is done, however, the interviewers must determine the full array of products sold by personal banking. These products will be recorded in the survey form requiring time estimates.

The following list of standard products usually found in a personal banking department is representative of most financial institutions, but it is not exhaustive.

1. Loan products:
   - Installment loans.
   - Home equity loans.
   - Overdraft credit lines.
   - Home improvement loans.
   - Student loans.

2. Deposit products:
   - Demand deposit accounts.
   - Money market accounts.
   - NOW accounts.
   - Savings accounts.
   - Certificates of deposit.
   - Individual retirement accounts.

3. Nondeposit products:
   - ATM cards.
   - Safe deposit boxes.
   - Credit cards.

F I G U R E   109

New Products Sold Tally

Products Sold	Mon.	Tues.	Wed.	Thu.	Fri.	Sat.	Total
1. Loans							
▪ Installment							
▪ Home equity							
▪ Overdraft lines							
▪ Home improvement							
▪ Student loans							
2. Deposits							
▪ DDAs							
▪ Money market							
▪ NOWs							
▪ Savings							
▪ CDs							
▪ IRAs							
3. Nondeposit							
▪ ATMs							
▪ Safe deposits							
▪ Credit cards							
Total							

Each financial institution should tailor this list to its own products, although the approach will remain the same. Once the time estimate and volume have been derived from the survey, the weighted average time per product is determined as in Figure 110. In this example, the overall time per product sold is 19.27 minutes, or .33 hour per product sold. Since on average, based upon frequency, every product will use this factor, it is unnecessary to expand the staffing model to take into account every product sold.

F I G U R E 110

Weighted Average Time per Product

	Total Volume Sold	Percentage to Total Volume	Average Minutes per Product Sold	Time Factor per Product Sold
1. Loan products				
Installment	113	5.4%	52	2.81
Home equity	17	.8	91	.73
Overdraft lines	44	2.1	30	.63
Home improvement	5	.2	90	.18
Student	2	.1	45	.05
2. Deposit products				
DDAs	538	25.7	17	4.37
Money market	55	2.6	17	.44
NOW	50	2.4	17	.41
Savings	543	26.0	15	3.90
CDs	374	17.9	20	3.58
IRAs	46	2.2	30	.66
3. Nondeposit products				
ATMs	254	12.1	10	1.21
Safe deposits	20	.9	15	.14
Credit cards	30	1.6	10	.16
TOTAL	2,091	100.0%		
Weighted average time per product sold				19.27

Over a period of time and due to specific product marketing, the mix of products sold could change. This would not change the individual time required per product but it might change the percentage to total for products sold, affecting the weighted average time per product. For this reason, a new analysis of the products sold mix (as in Figure 110) should be done semiannually. This will update the weighted average factor to ensure that the most accurate data are used in the analysis at all times. This can be done by obtaining historical volumes, by product, from the mainframe database or by manual tracking.

Customers Seen (Not Sold)   In the world of retail sales, not every customer who walks in the door is sold a product. The walk-in customer may not be interested in what is offered or, in the case of a loan, may not qualify. But even discussions that do not result in a sale take up time that must be accounted for. The number of customers seen, as well as the number of customers to whom products are sold, must be tracked over a period of time. The survey requests an estimate of how much time, on average, is devoted to customers who do not purchase any product.

It is also necessary to track customer sale patterns by capturing, on an ongoing basis, the total number of customers seen and the number to whom a product was sold. This is done by using the production sheet shown in Figure 111.

To determine optimum staffing levels for personal bankers, this production tally should be used on a regular basis. The number of products sold can also be reported here, unless it is easily captured by the bank's mainframe system. If the financial institution uses a platform automation system, the volume of customers seen and sold can be automatically captured, precluding the need for a tally sheet.

The factor that will be used in the staffing model for how much time is required per customer not sold a product is determined from an average of the time estimates submitted by all personal bankers, as shown in Figure 112.

In this example, the variable factor is 15 minutes (.25 hour) per customer seen but not sold a product. Of course, one must

F I G U R E   111
Customers Seen/Sold Tally

Day	Customers Seen	Customers to Whom a Product Was Sold
Monday		
Tuesday		
Wednesday		
Thursday		
Friday		
Saturday		
TOTAL		

know the volume of customers seen and customers sold products in order to account for the time required for unsold customers.

Maintenance   Maintenance of customers by personal bankers involves providing services to these individuals as needed. Servicing customers involves a number of tasks organized into two main categories: customer communications and relations and

F I G U R E   112
Average Time Required per Unsold Customer

Total Time Estimates for All Personal Bankers (Minutes)		Number of Personal Bankers		Minutes per Hour		Hourly Factor per Customer not Sold
150	÷	10	÷	60	=	.25

services provided. Broken down, the activities involved are as follows.

1. Customer communications and relations:
   - Outbound phone calls to customers.
   - Inbound phone calls received from customers.
   - Written correspondence to customers.
   - Outside visits to customer locations.
   - In-bank meetings with customers.
2. Services provided:
   - Balancing/reconciling accounts.
   - Stop payment/release handling.
   - Wire transfers.
   - Loan payoffs.
   - Bank errors.
   - Other.

The services provided will vary by bank and could involve a number of services not listed here.

As with the other variable and fixed standards, the starting point is the personal banker survey. Beginning with customer communications and relations, time estimates are assigned by each personal banker to each type of customer contact. An average for all personal bankers is determined to arrive at a single average time required per contact.

The volume or frequency of occurrence for each item is determined over a two-week period of time using the call tally form (Figure 100). Each sheet contains a full week of data, so only two need be completed. A total volume should be determined for each activity for all personal bankers in the aggregate. The existing customer row is used to tally the call volume, since maintenance refers to maintaining existing relationships.

The results learned from the personal banker survey must be analyzed and associated with the volume of all customers on file to determine an average time factor required per customer per month. This is achieved by completing the analysis in Figure 113.

In this example, .21 hour (12.6 minutes) is devoted to each customer on average per month. In reality, however, many retail

Customer Communications and Relations Maintenance

Call Type	Frequency per Customer per Month		Average Minutes per Item		Minutes per Hour		Average Hours per Customer per Month
Outbound calls	.75	×	4	÷	60	=	.05
Inbound calls	.50	×	6	÷	60	=	.05
Written correspondence	.25	×	10	÷	60	=	.05
Outside meetings	.03	×	60	÷	60	=	.03
In-bank meetings	.05	×	30	÷	60	=	.03
Total hours per customer per month						=	.21

Call Type	Total Department Volume		Weeks to Annualize		Months per Year		Number of Customers on File		Frequency per Customer per Month
Outbound calls	1,384	×	26	÷	12	÷	4,000	=	.75
Inbound calls	923	×	26	÷	12	÷	4,000	=	.50
Written correspondence	461	×	26	÷	12	÷	4,000	=	.25
Outside meetings	55	×	26	÷	12	÷	4,000	=	.03
In-bank meetings	92	×	26	÷	12	÷	4,000	=	.05

customers have virtually no contact with personal bankers. Remember that this is an average, which is loaded to all customers on file. Once it is known how many customers are on file, it is easy to apply the hourly factor to this volume to determine, on average, how much time should be devoted to customer relations.

The second part of maintenance is services provided. The job description of personal bankers calls for performing specific services for customers as requested. The most common types of services offered are balancing/reconciling checking accounts, initiating and releasing stop payments, implementing wire transfers, making loan payoffs, and resolving bank errors.

Depending on the bank, more or fewer of these services may be performed by personal bankers. Some may be performed by secretarial and/or support personnel. This example, however, assumes that all such services are performed by personal bankers.

As with customer communications, it is necessary to determine a time factor that can be applied to customers to indicate the time devoted to these services based upon the size of the portfolio. The personal banker survey requests time estimates for each type of service performed. Once all personal bankers have recorded their estimates an average should be calculated for each service. This will be instrumental in calculating the overall time factor to be applied.

Volume data must also be captured relative to the amount of services actually performed. This is accomplished by using the services performed tally (Figure 114) over a two-week period. This document is also contained in the survey (Exhibit F). It is used daily to record the volume of services performed by each personal banker. One sheet will be needed for each of the 10 working days monitored.

Upon completion of these documents and the close of the two-week survey period, the information should be totaled for all personal bankers by service performed. This volume information and the average time estimates are used as in Figure 115 to calculate the hourly factor which will be used for services performed.

F I G U R E 114

Services Performed Tally Sheet

Service	Number of Times Performed	Total
Balancing/reconciling		
Stop payment/releases		
Wire transfers		
Loan payoffs		
Bank errors		
Other		
Other		
Other		
Other		
Other		

In this example, .12 hour (7.2 minutes) per customer per month is devoted to performing specific services for customers. As in customer contact, some customers rarely if ever require services. This indicates that a specific percentage of customers require services and/or communication much more frequently. The calculation takes this into account, deriving a factor that can be applied equally to all customers in the staffing analysis.

This completes the maintenance segment of the personal banker profile, except that the two subcategories of maintenance (customer communications and services performed) must be combined as shown in Figure 116. The resulting hourly factor will be used in the personal banking staffing model.

FIGURE 115

Maintenance: Services Performed

Service Type	Frequency per Customer per Month		Average Minutes per Item		Minutes per Hour		Average Hours per Customer per Month
Balancing	.10	×	30	÷	60	=	.05
Stop payments	.06	×	10	÷	60	=	.01
Wire transfers	.05	×	11	÷	60	=	.01
Loan payoffs	.02	×	15	÷	60	=	.01
Bank errors	.03	×	20	÷	60	=	.01
Other	.14	×	10	÷	60	=	.03

Total hourly factor per customer per month = .12

Service Type	Total Department Volume		Weeks to Annualize		Months per Year		Number of Customers on File		Frequency per Customer per Month
Balancing	185	×	26	÷	12	÷	4,000	=	.10
Stop payments	110	×	26	÷	12	÷	4,000	=	.06
Wire transfer	80	×	26	÷	12	÷	4,000	=	.05
Loan payoffs	35	×	26	÷	12	÷	4,000	=	.02
Bank errors	50	×	26	÷	12	÷	4,000	=	.03
Other	250	×	26	÷	12	÷	4,000	=	.14

F I G U R E   116

Maintenance Summary: Personal Bankers

Subcategory	Hourly Factor
1. Customer communications and relations	.21
2. Services performed	.12
Total maintenance hours per retail customer per month	.33

In this example, the total of .33 hour indicates that approximately 19.8 minutes are devoted to maintaining/servicing each customer per month. This is based upon the actual activity patterns submitted in the personal banker survey.

This ends the profile development for personal bankers. The next segment recaps the complete profile for use in the staffing model.

Recap: Personal Bankers   With the development of all information relative to the personal banker profile, the data should be summarized as in Figure 117.

The recap shows that almost one-third (32.2 percent) of a personal banker's day is already committed to fixed activities, leaving 67.8 percent for variable activities. With this in mind, the standard or expected hourly factors can be compared with what is actually occurring. A large difference between the factors would indicate under- or overstaffed conditions in the department.

To begin, evaluate the total monthly available hours in the department with the fixed activity time designations already committed. Since fixed activities do not vary with product sales volume, subtracting them can yield a true availability of hours for the key volume indicators of products sold and maintenance. This analysis is illustrated in Figure 118.

In reality, only 7.2 effective FTEs are available for the variable activities to be performed (1210.54 ÷ 168.6). A staffing analyses

F I G U R E   117

Personal Banker Summary

1. Fixed activities	Percentage of Available Time Required
■ Business development	10.3%
■ Administrative	5.8%
■ Personal	16.1%
2. Variable activities	**Hourly Factor**
■ New products sold	.33
■ Customers seen (not sold)	.25
■ Maintenance	.33

that did not take into account such fixed activities would result in a gross distortion, as 2.8 FTEs (475.46 ÷ 168.6) of the 10 FTEs on staff are committed to fixed activities.

F I G U R E   118

Total Departmental Fixed and Variable Hours

1. Total monthly hours available per personal banker   168.6
2. Total number of personal bankers on staff   × 10
3. Total departmental hours available per month   = 168.6

Fixed Activities	Percentage of Time Devoted		Total Departmental Hours Available		Total Departmental Fixed Hours Committed
Business development	6.6%	×	1,686	=	111.28
Administrative	5.6%	×	1,686	=	94.42
Personal	16.0%	×	1,686	=	269.76
Total fixed hours committed				=	475.46
Total hours available for variable activities (1,686 − 475.46 = 1,210.54)				=	1,210.54

Continuing the analysis, the actual variable activity hourly factors to be calculated represent the actual time required for each variable activity. The format includes *only* the remaining variable hours available, not the fixed hours committed. If this is the only time available to perform the activities, and a specific volume is completed, an actual hourly factor must result, as illustrated in Figure 119. The calculated hourly factor is from Figure 117. The hours remaining are from Figure 118.

From the information contained in Figure 119, a comparison can be made with the standards previously developed.

F I G U R E 119

Actual Variable Activity Hourly Factors

Variable Activity	Avg. Monthly Volume		Calculated Hourly Factor		Total Hours Required	Percentage of Total Hours
New products sold	200	×	.33	=	297	17.6%
Customers seen (not sold)	300	×	.25	=	75	4.4
Maintenance (customers on file)	4,000	×	.33	=	1,320	78.0
					1,692	100.0%

Variable Activity	Percentage of Total Loans		Hours Remaining for Various Activities		Monthly Volume		Actual Variable Activity Hourly Factor
New products sold	17.6%	×	1,210.54	÷	900	=	.24
Customers seen (not sold)	4.4	×	1,210.54	÷	300	=	.18
Maintenance (customers on file)	78.0	×	1,210.54	÷	4,000	=	.24

Variable Activities	Standard Hours	Actual Hours
New products sold	.33	.24
Customers seen (not sold)	.25	.18
Maintenance	.33	.24

As indicated, less time is actually spent in each variable activity than was determined via the survey. This could indicate an understaffed situation resulting in less time put into each product sold and customers serviced. This continued pattern could result in increased errors, inadequate analysis of customer background and credits, and subsequent problems for the financial institution.

At this point, the bank must evaluate both the actual and standard factors to determine whether the standard is the expectation of senior management. If it is, the standard should be used in the staffing model, which will likely show a need to hire more personal bankers. This information and staffing model results are fully outlined at the end of this chapter. An example of the placement of the profile data is shown in Figure 120.

Secretaries

Within the retail sales environment, secretaries are employed to assist personal bankers with the administrative and paperwork burden. This allows the personal bankers to devote as much time as possible to the sales efforts. For every position within the retail sales (personal banking) area, the standard profile will apply, but not all activity categories of the profile apply to the secretarial group.

The profile for a retail sales secretary consists of fixed activities (administrative and personal) and variable activities (new products sold and maintenance). Omitted are business development activities and the time required for customers seen but not sold a product, since secretaries are not generally involved in these activities.

The goals of quantifying secretaries' activities are to determine the fixed percentage of time already committed and identify the tasks and times associated with the key volume indicators of

F I G U R E 120

Personal Banker Staffing Model

```
BANK:        [      ]    PERSONAL BANKING STAFFING MODEL      DATE:    [      ]
LOCATION:    [      ]
BRANCH:      [      ]


DATA REQUIRED
  # CUST. SEEN THIS MONTH:   [      ]  AVG. # TOTAL HOURS PER FTE PER DAY:        [      ]
  # CUST. SOLD THIS MONTH:   [      ]  AVERAGE NUMBER OF RETAIL ACCOUNTS ON FILE: [      ]
  # PROD. SOLD THIS MONTH:   [      ]

==============================================================================================
A. FIXED HOURS (PER FTE):

                              % OF TOTAL MONTHLY HOURS
                            PERSONAL      RETAIL        RETAIL
                            BANKER        SECRETARY     SUPPORT
                            =========     =========     =========
BUSINESS DEVELOPMENT:      [ 10.30% ]    [        ]    [        ]
ADMINISTRATION:            [  5.80% ]    [        ]    [        ]
PERSONAL TIME:             [ 16.10% ]    [        ]    [        ]

TOTAL:                       32.20%        0.00%         0.00%
                            =========     =========     =========


==============================================================================================
B. VARIABLE HOURS:

                            STANDARD HOURS REQUIRED PER ITEM
                            PERSONAL      RETAIL        RETAIL
                            BANKER        SECRETARY     SUPPORT
                            =========     =========     =========
NEW PRODUCTS SOLD:         [ 0.33 ]      [        ]    [        ]
CUSTOMERS SEEN, NOT SOLD:  [ 0.25 ]      [        ]    [        ]
MAINTENANCE:               [ 0.33 ]      [        ]    [        ]


==============================================================================================
C. DISTRIBUTION OF FTEs BY POSITION:
                                        FULL-TIME EQUIVALENTS REQUIRED
                                                                          TOTAL
                            PERSONAL      RETAIL        RETAIL            FTE
                            BANKER        SECRETARY     SUPPORT           STAFF
                            =========     =========     =========         =========
NEW PRODUCTS SOLD:                                                        0.00
CUSTOMERS SEEN, NOT SOLD:                                                 0.00
MAINTENANCE:                                                             0.00
BUSINESS DEVELOPMENT:                                                     0.00
ADMINISTRATIVE:                                                          0.00
PERSONAL:                                                                0.00

TOTAL FTE:                   0.00          0.00          0.00              0.00
                            =========     =========     =========         =========
```

new products sold and maintaining existing customers. This information is determined from the secretarial survey (Exhibit G). Like all previous positions, secretaries must account for the activities performed as well as times and volumes. This will allow for the linking of these times with key volume indicators and ultimately with staffing standards that will aid in determining the optimal number of secretaries needed.

The following sections outline each appropriate activity category for retail secretaries and provide the calculation formats for determining standards.

Administrative   Fixed administrative activities for retail secretaries are general in nature. They refer to tasks performed that do not occur as a direct result of product sales volume but more as a consequence of routine business activity. Administrative subcategories consist of typing, telephone calls, and general administrative tasks. More specifically, the subcategories consist of the following.

1. Typing:
   ▪ Internal memos.
   ▪ Miscellaneous reports.
2. Telephone calls:
   ▪ Internal calls made / received.
   ▪ Calls routed to another.
   ▪ Messages taken.
3. General administrative:
   ▪ Appointments scheduled.
   ▪ Meetings scheduled.
   ▪ General filing.

This is not necessarily an exhaustive list, but it is representative. The initial interview process will reveal the types of tasks that are performed.

The secretarial survey should be distributed to all secretaries to be completed over a two-week period. For fixed administrative activities, time estimates must be determined for each of the tasks as an average for the group. Volumes related to the tasks and phone calls must be tallied over a two-week period.

F I G U R E 121

Secretarial Activity Tally

Activity	Number of Items Handled	Total
Internal memos		
Miscellaneous reports		
Appointments scheduled		
Meetings scheduled		
Commitment letters typed		
Account files developed		
Documents/notes filed		
Customer correspondence typed		
Call reports typed		
Correspondence/call reports filed		
Payments handled		
Statements handled		
Stop payments/releases		
Loan payoffs handled		
Bank errors resolved		
Other _____		

In the first subcategory, typing, the secretarial activity tally (Figure 121) is used to log the volume of activities performed. Since each sheet represents one day, 10 must be submitted per secretary. Many more activities are recorded than were indicated for administrative typing, because other volumes must be obtained for other profile activities as well. Therefore, the standard form is a multipurpose document that can be used to capture all volume-related duties.

F I G U R E 1 2 2

Administrative: Typing

Subcategory	Total Dept. Vol.		Weeks to Annualize		No. of Mos./ Year		No. of Secretaries		Avg. Vol./ Secretary/ Month		Avg. Minutes/ Item		Minutes/ Hour		Avg. Hours/ Secretary/ Month
Internal memos	30	×	26	÷	12	÷	3	=	21.7	×	8	÷	60	=	2.90
Miscellaneous reports	10	×	26	÷	12	÷	3	=	7.2	×	11	÷	60	=	1.32
														=	4.22

Total administrative typing hours per secretary per month

F I G U R E 123

Secretarial Call Tally Sheet

Day	Internal Calls Made/ Received	Calls Routed to Another	Messages Taken	Customer Calls		Total
				In- bound	Out- bound	
Monday						
Tuesday						
Wednesday						
Thursday						
Friday						
Saturday						
TOTAL						

Once the survey information is received, the amount of time (in hours) spent on administrative typing can be calculated as in Figure 122.

The next subcategory, telephones, uses a different tally sheet to capture volume, as shown in Figure 123 (and in Exhibit G). In this case a full week of volume can fit on one sheet, so only two need to be completed. Telephone contact within the fixed administrative category is generally not customer related. For the most part it is internal in nature. These phone calls are received and made from within the bank and do not involve direct customer contact.

Secretaries also take messages for others and route calls, performing a sort of receptionist function. Although the time per call may be insignificant, there is usually enough volume to make tracking it essential. The hours required to perform these duties must be calculated with the data obtained, as illustrated in Figure 124. In this example, calls routed and messages taken use up nearly three hours per month (1.26 + 1.54). This certainly must be accounted for to achieve any precision in staffing analysis.

F I G U R E 124

Administrative: Telephone Calls

Subcategory	Total Dept. Vol.		Weeks to Annualize		Months/Year		No. of Secretaries		Avg. Vol./Secretary/Month		Avg. Min./Item		Min./Hour		Avg. Hours/Secretary/Month
Internal calls made/received	150	×	26	÷	12	÷	3	=	108.3	×	2	÷	60	=	3.61
Calls routed	210	×	26	÷	12	÷	3	=	151.7	×	.5	÷	60	=	1.26
Messages taken	170	×	26	÷	12	÷	3	=	122.8	×	.75	÷	60	=	1.54
Total monthly hours per secretary														=	6.41

F I G U R E 125

General Administrative

Subcategory	Total Dept. Vol.		Weeks to Annualize		Months/Year		No. of Secretaries		Avg. Vol./Secretary/Month		Avg. Min./Item		Min./Hour		Avg. Hours/Secretary/Month
Appointments scheduled	90	×	26	÷	12	÷	3	=	65	×	2	÷	60	=	2.17
Meetings scheduled	30	×	26	÷	12	÷	3	=	21.7	×	5	÷	60	=	1.81
															3.98

	Avg. Min./Week		Weeks to Annualize		Mos./Year						Min./Hour		Min./Hour		Avg. Hours/Secretary/Month
General filing	60	×	52	÷	12	÷					60	÷	60	=	4.33
Total hours per secretary per month														=	8.31

The last part of fixed administrative tasks is general administrative functions, miscellaneous office duties required of secretaries. These typical secretarial duties occur regardless of product volume. General administrative tasks are scheduling appointments and meetings and general filing.

To determine the hourly factor associated with these standard secretarial duties, the time estimates in the survey must be averaged. A volume count of their occurrence is also needed. This is achieved by using the form in Figure 121; these functions are items 3 and 4 on the form. The only exception to this is general filing, which requires only an overall weekly time estimate to cover all types of general filing. This is far more accurate than attempting to determine volume by each individual item filed. The analysis and calculation of these data are shown in Figure 125.

Now that the fixed administrative activities have been calculated for secretaries, the data must be summarized and restated as a percentage of total available hours. Since this is a fixed set of activities, not dependent on volume, a standard amount of time dedicated to these tasks must be determined. The percentage developed will become the factor used in the staffing model to determine the optimum number of personnel required for administrative activities. Figure 126 shows the summary.

F I G U R E 126

Administrative Summary: Secretaries

Subcategory	Average Hourly Factor per Secretary per Month
Typing	4.22
Telephone calls	6.41
General administrative	8.31
Total monthly hours	= 18.94
Monthly available hours per secretary	+ 168.6
Percentage of available hours dedicated to administrative tasks per secretary per month	= 11.2%

In this example, 11.2 percent of a secretary's monthly available hours are already committed before personal activities are addressed.

Personal Activities   Personal activities, as in previous positions, involve time spent away from the job due to personal needs, primarily lunches and breaks.

Once the time estimates for lunches and breaks are received from all retail secretaries, an average can be taken. The user may wish to forgo this step if the personnel policy of the bank dictates the amount of time allowed per lunch and break. In this case the time factor is merely supplied.

As a fixed activity occurring on a regular basis and unrelated to sales volume, personal time must be reduced to a percentage of the secretary's monthly available hours. This percentage is used in the staffing model to help determine the optimum staffing level for retail secretaries. This analysis and calculation are illustrated in Figure 127. (The number of working days per year is 5 days times 52 weeks.)

This completes the fixed activities of retail secretaries. The next segments outline the variable, volume-related tasks they perform.

F I G U R E   127

Personal Activities

Activity	Avg. Minutes/ Occurrence		No. of Working Days/Year		Months/ Year		Minutes/ Hour		Avg. Hours/ Secretary/ Month
Lunches	60	×	260	÷	12	÷	60	=	21.67
Breaks	15	×	260	÷	12	÷	60	=	5.42
Total monthly hours per secretary								=	27.09
Number of available hours per secretary per month								÷	168.6
Percentage of available hours devoted to personal activities per secretary per month								=	16.1%

New Products Sold   In the case of personal bankers, new products sold is exactly what the name says. But retail secretaries do not sell products, nor do they hold meetings with customers or potential customers. Why then is this an activity assigned to retail secretaries to determine optimum staffing levels? The answer is that secretaries perform specific tasks associated with the sale of a new product. The tasks are variable and specifically relate to products sold, because they would not be performed if the products were not sold.

Because the specific tasks in this activity can vary by financial institution according to individual policies and procedures, the interview process is vital to analytical accuracy. Interviewing secretaries will highlight which specific tasks are performed that relate to the sale of new products. For the purposes of this chapter, the broad categories of typing and account administration are considered part of this process. The specific tasks may vary, but in general they include the following:

1. Typing:
   - Documents typed.
   - Commitment letters typed.
2. Account setup:
   - Account file development.
   - Documents and note applications filed.
   - Credit reports run.

Again, the source of the data used to determine the factors in the model is the secretarial survey. The time estimates obtained should be evaluated for all secretaries. Additionally, the amount of items completed for the particular subcategory must be obtained. Volume data are determined using the secretarial activity tally (Figure 121). All tasks for new products sold must be totaled over the two-week survey period. From this result, the hourly factor to be used in the staffing analysis for new products sold can be calculated as shown in Figure 128.

The goal in Figure 128 is to determine an hourly factor that can be applied to any product sold. Analyzing the volume of tasks (performed only as a result of new products sold) in relation to

F I G U R E 128

New Products Sold

Subcategory	Avg. Vol. of Tasks/ Product Sold		Avg. Minutes/ Items		Minutes/ Hour		Avg. Hours Required/ Product Sold
1. Typing							
■ Documents	1.2	×	5	÷	60	=	.10
■ Commitment letters	.8	×	5	÷	60	=	.04
2. Account setup							
■ Account file development	1.1	×	10	÷	60	=	.18
■ Documents filed	1.3	×	7	÷	60	=	.15
■ Credit reports	.7	×	12	÷	60	=	.14
Total average hourly factor for new products sold, per product						=	.61

Subcategory	Total Departmental Volume		No. of Products Sold in Two Weeks		Avg. Vol. of Tasks Required/ Product Sold
1. Typing					
■ Documents	450	÷	375	=	1.2
■ Commitment letters	300	÷	375	=	.8
2. Account setup					
■ Account file development	425	÷	375	=	1.1
■ Documents filed	500	÷	375	=	1.3
■ Credit reports	250	÷	375	=	.7

the amount of new products sold will yield an average amount of items per product. Totaling these amounts will provide a time factor per product sold.

To check the accuracy of this factor, take several surveys at various intervals throughout the year. The original factor can be compared with these, or an average can be taken. An even more accurate method is to use the survey (secretarial activity tally) to track item volume over the entire year. Then perform the calculation in Figure 128, but use the total number of products sold throughout the year to make the hourly factor more precise. Although a two-week survey can be sufficient for this analysis, it is recommended that item volumes be tracked as a regular part of the job. Not only will this provide ongoing accuracy in determining hourly factors and standards for the staffing model, but it will also add a degree of organization and discipline in managing secretarial resources.

Maintenance The last variable activity for retail secretaries is maintenance. Retail secretaries provide maintenance and servicing to existing customers both directly and indirectly. Direct servicing involves customer telephone communications; indirect servicing involves typing and other procedures performed in support of customers.

In general, maintenance refers to servicing existing customers on file with the bank. This can involve any number of activities and tasks but usually falls into the broad activity categories of typing, telephone contact, and account administration.

These three categories are common throughout the secretarial analysis, as they are a big part of a secretary's role in most office environments. These categories and concepts can be used in other areas of the banks to track secretaries' productivity and determine optimum staffing. For retail secretaries, however, the tasks within these broad categories consist of the following:

1. Typing:
   - Customer correspondence.
   - Call reports.
2. Telephone contact:
   - Inbound calls from customers.
   - Outbound calls made to customers.
3. Account administration:
   - Correspondence and call report filing.

- Payment handling.
- Statement handling.
- Stop payment/release handling.
- Loan payoffs.
- Bank error resolution.

Of course, tasks may vary by financial institution. Differences and/or additions can be determined through interviews with secretaries. But the tasks listed will be representative for this analysis.

As with new products sold, the variable hourly factor for maintenance is determined by a combination of time estimates and volumes, both of which are learned from the secretarial survey. Time estimates for each activity should be an average for the full secretarial staff; volumes should be a total for the secretarial staff over a two-week period. For telephone call volume, use the secretarial call tally (Figure 123). The two columns at the right of the report are for capturing these data. For item volumes, the standard secretarial activity tally (Figure 121) is again used. For the two-week period only two call tally sheets are submitted, whereas for the activity tally 10 sheets are required.

Once all surveys are returned, the final analysis and calculation can be performed as in Figure 129. Although the two-week survey period is generally sufficient to determine the hourly factors for the staffing model, this type of tracking is very beneficial on an ongoing basis. In this example, approximately .141 hour (8.5 minutes) is spent per customer per month on maintenance, on average.

This completes the calculation of profile activity factors for use in the model. The next phase is to summarize the data for comparison of standards determined to actual times.

Recap: Retail Secretaries   Figure 130 summarizes the factors determined thus far for the retail secretarial profile.

In this example, approximately 27.3 percent of the retail secretary's day is committed to fixed activities not directly related

F I G U R E   129

Maintenance

Subcategory	Freq./ Customer/ Month		Avg. Min./ Item		Min./ Hour		Avg. Hours/ Customer/ Month
1. Typing							
■ Customer correspondence	.08	×	7	÷	60	=	.009
■ Call reports	.03	×	10	÷	60	=	.005
2. Telephone							
■ Inbound	.08	×	4	÷	60	=	.005
■ Outbound	.02	×	2	÷	60	=	.001
3. Account administration							
■ Correspondence/call report filing	.03	×	3	÷	60	=	.002
■ Payment handling	.12	×	6	÷	60	=	.012
■ Statement handling	.43	×	5	÷	60	=	.036
■ Stops/releases	.08	×	8	÷	60	=	.011
■ Loan payoffs	.16	×	10	÷	60	=	.027
■ Bank errors	.13	×	15	÷	60	=	.033
Total hours per customer per month						=	.141

Subcategory	Total Dept. Vol.		Weeks to Annualize		Months/ Year		No. of Customers on File		Freq./ Customer/ Month
1. Typing									
■ Customer correspondence	150	×	26	÷	12	÷	4,000	=	.08
■ Call reports	60	×	26	÷	12	÷	4,000	=	.03
2. Telephone									
■ Inbound	150	×	26	÷	12	÷	4,000	=	.08
■ Outbound	30	×	26	÷	12	÷	4,000	=	.02
3. Account administration									
■ Correspondence/ call report filing	60	×	20	÷	12	÷	4,000	=	.03
■ Payment handling	222	×	26	÷	12	÷	4,000	=	.12
■ Statement handling	800	×	26	÷	12	÷	4,000	=	.43
■ Stops/releases	150	×	26	÷	12	÷	4,000	=	.08
■ Loan payoffs	300	×	26	÷	12	÷	4,000	=	.16
■ Bank errors	250	×	26	÷	12	÷	4,000	=	.13

Retail Secretaries Summary

1. Fixed activities	Percentage to Total Available Hours
■ Administrative	11.2%
■ Personal	16.1%
2. Variable activities	Hourly Factor
■ New products sold	.61
■ Maintenance	.14

to the sale of new products or maintenance of customers. As a result, 72.7 percent of the secretary's day remains available to devote directly to the tasks associated with the sale of new products. In this sense, a true FTE retail secretary is equivalent to 72.7 percent of an FTE for purposes of planning staff levels on the basis of volume.

Now that standards have been determined for each profile activity, check the time actually spent on products sold and customer maintenance. Since 27.3 percent of a retail secretary's time is committed to fixed activities, it can easily be determined how much time the entire staff of secretaries has available for other activities. This analysis is shown in Figure 131.

In the example, the 367.72 hours available for variable activities are the equivalent of 2.18 FTEs (367.72 ÷ 168.6). The other .82 FTE is devoted to fixed activities.

The remaining 367.72 hours available can now be associated with the actual volume of new products sold and customers on file to determine the actual time spent per variable item. This analysis is completed in Figure 132. The calculated hourly factor comes from Figure 130, and the hours remaining come from Figure 131.

From the data in Figure 132, a comparison can be made between the standard fixed hourly factors and the actual.

F I G U R E 131

Total Departmental Fixed and Variable Hours

1. Total monthly hours available per retail secretary   168.6
2. Total number of secretaries on staff   × 3
3. Total departmental hours available per month   = 505.8

Fixed Activity	Percentage of Time Spent		Total Departmental Hours Available		Total Departmental Fixed Hours Committed
1. Administrative	11.2%	×	505.8	=	56.65
2. Personal	16.1%	×	505.8	=	81.43
Total fixed hours committed				=	138.08
Total hours available for variable activities (505.8 − 138.08 = 367.72)				=	367.72

F I G U R E 132

Actual Variable Activity Hourly Factors

Variable Activity	Avg. Monthly Volume		Calculated Hourly Factor		Total Hours Required	Percentage of Total Hours
New products sold	900	×	.61	=	549	49.5%
Maintenance	4,000	×	.14	=	560	50.5
					1,109	100.0%

Variable Activity	Percentage of Total Loans		Hours Remaining for Variable Activities		Average Monthly Volume		Actual Variable Activity Hourly Factor
New products sold	49.5%	×	367.72	÷	900	=	.20
Maintenance	50.5%	×	367.72	÷	4,000	=	.05

Variable Activity	Standard Hours	Actual Hours
New products sold	.61	.20
Maintenance	.14	.05

The considerable variance between the two amounts may indicate that the department is substantially understaffed. Secretaries are rushing through the new products sold and customer maintenance duties. They may be completing the work, but mistakes and errors are probably occurring. This can lead to having to do things over as well as to customer dissatisfaction.

On the other hand, perhaps the original time estimates used to determine the standard were much higher than needed. To compensate for this, an average of the standard and actual factors could reveal a truly accurate standard that should be used in the staffing analysis. The average for new products sold would be .40 hours and for maintenance .10 hours. This would change the overall profile factors to be used in the staffing model, as shown in Figure 133.

This information would then be included in the staffing model, shown in Figure 134.

This completes the analysis of the retail secretarial position for the personal banking department.

F I G U R E 133

Modified Secretarial Summary

1. Fixed activities	Percentage of Total Available Hours
■ Administrative	11.2%
■ Personal	16.1%
2. Variable activities	**Hourly Factor**
■ New products sold	.40
■ Maintenance	.10

F I G U R E   134

Staffing Analysis for Retail Secretaries

```
BANK:          [        ]     PERSONAL BANKING STAFFING MODEL      DATE:    [        ]
LOCATION:      [        ]
BRANCH:        [        ]


DATA REQUIRED
  # CUST. SEEN THIS MONTH:   [        ] AVG. # TOTAL HOURS PER FTE PER DAY:        [        ]
  # CUST. SOLD THIS MONTH:   [        ] AVERAGE NUMBER OF RETAIL ACCOUNTS ON FILE: [        ]
  # PROD. SOLD THIS MONTH:                                                        [        ]
```

A. FIXED HOURS (PER FTE):

	% OF TOTAL MONTHLY HOURS		
	PERSONAL BANKER	RETAIL SECRETARY	RETAIL SUPPORT
BUSINESS DEVELOPMENT:	[ ]	[ ]	[ ]
ADMINISTRATION:	[ ]	[11.20%]	[ ]
PERSONAL TIME:	[ ]	[16.10%]	[ ]
TOTAL:	0.00%	27.30%	0.00%

B. VARIABLE HOURS:

	STANDARD HOURS REQUIRED PER ITEM		
	PERSONAL BANKER	RETAIL SECRETARY	RETAIL SUPPORT
NEW PRODUCTS SOLD:	[ ]	[0.40]	[ ]
CUSTOMERS SEEN, NOT SOLD:	[ ]	[ ]	[ ]
MAINTENANCE:	[ ]	[0.10]	[ ]

C. DISTRIBUTION OF FTEs BY POSITION:

	FULL-TIME EQUIVALENTS REQUIRED			
	PERSONAL BANKER	RETAIL SECRETARY	RETAIL SUPPORT	TOTAL FTE STAFF
NEW PRODUCTS SOLD:				0.00
CUSTOMERS SEEN, NOT SOLD:				0.00
MAINTENANCE:				0.00
BUSINESS DEVELOPMENT:				0.00
ADMINISTRATIVE:				0.00
PERSONAL:				0.00
TOTAL FTE:	0.00	0.00	0.00	0.00

Retail Support

The last position to be analyzed in the personal banking department is retail support clerk. This position is truly back-office. Clerks perform the functions necessary to ensure that products sold and customer account relationships are properly entered into the system and set up for review and retrieval. This group usually performs a number of functions related to the retail sales effort. Its goal is to quickly and efficiently perform the tasks that will set up customers' accounts on the system and allow personal bankers to devote their time to increasing sales.

If the financial institution uses a platform automation system, many of the support group's tasks may have been eliminated. Any remaining back-office duties could be absorbed by retail secretaries, and the position totally eliminated.

The profile of retail support clerks conforms very closely to that of retail secretaries, at least for the major fixed and variable activities. The broad activities associated with retail support are fixed (administrative and personal) and variable (new products sold and maintenance.) Omitted are business development activities and the customers seen (not sold) category, which are used exclusively by personal bankers.

This profile provides the means for analyzing the tasks performed in the retail support position. It allows the user to determine the optimum number of retail clerks needed to provide support to personal bankers. Specifically, the individual tasks associated with the broad profile categories are as follows.

1. Fixed activities

    a. Administrative:
       - Telephone calls.
       - Meetings.
       - General administrative tasks.

    b. Personal:
       - Lunches.
       - Breaks.

2. Variable activities

    a. New products sold:
       - Account setup.

b. Maintenance:
- Customer communications.
- Account administration.

More detailed tasks and subtasks are illustrated in the retail support clerk survey (Exhibit H). This document is the primary information source for the data that will be used in developing the measurement factors for the retail support staffing analysis. The survey should be completed over a two-week period.

Explanations for each category and subcategory of the retail support profile are contained in the next several sections of this chapter.

Administrative Activities   Administrative activities of retail support clerks are very similar to those of retail secretaries, with the exception of typing. They require the performance of a number of miscellaneous tasks that have virtually nothing to do with the volume of work produced. These tasks fall into the broad categories of telephone calls, meetings, and general administrative tasks. Within each of the broad categories, special tasks must be completed.

1. Telephone calls:
   - Internal calls made/received.
   - Calls routed to another.
   - Messages taken.
2. Meetings:
   - Departmental.
   - Training/seminars.
3. General administrative:
   - Reports developed.
   - Reports distributed.
   - Miscellaneous filing.

This is a representative list, not exhaustive. For the most part, the key tasks and elements have been defined. The interview process will reveal any differences among banks that should be tracked.

The first administrative activity, telephone calls, requires two types of data: time estimates and volumes. Time estimates per

F I G U R E   135

Retail Support Call Tally

Day	Internal Calls Made/ Received	Calls Routed to Another	Messages Taken	Customer Calls			Total
				In- bound	Out- bound	In- Person Visit	
Monday							
Tuesday							
Wednesday							
Thursday							
Friday							
Saturday							
TOTAL							

call are captured from the survey as an average for all retail support personnel on staff. Volume is captured using the retail support call tally form, shown in Figure 135. For volume information, a departmental total is used (as opposed to averages) for calculating staffing model standards and factors.

The survey information should be analyzed to reveal the time factor devoted to telephone calls for retail support personnel. As shown in Figure 136, a fair number of hours can be devoted to the handling of miscellaneous phone calls. If this time is not accounted for, staff recommendations can be distorted. Furthermore, clarifying how much time is involved in handling these calls enables management to see their impact on time. Management can take steps to control or eliminate telephone activity if it is perceived to be detrimental to the main task.

FIGURE 136

Administrative: Telephone Calls

Subcategory	Total Dept. Vol.		Weeks to Annualize		Months/ Year		No. of Support Clerks		Avg. Vol. / Clerk/ Month		Avg. Min./ Item		Min./ Hour		Avg. Hours/ Clerk/ Month
Internal calls made/ received	100	×	26	÷	12	÷	2	=	108.33	×	1.50	÷	60	=	2.71
Calls routed	150	×	26	÷	12	÷	2	=	162.5	×	.50	÷	60	=	1.35
Messages taken	50	×	26	÷	12	÷	2	=	54.2	×	.65	÷	60	=	.59
Total hours per retail support clerk per month														=	4.65

Administrative: Meeting Time Spent

Subcategory	Avg. Freq./ Month	Avg. Minutes/ Session	Minutes/ Hour	Avg. Hours Spent in Meetings/ Month
Departmental meetings	.5 ×	45 ÷	60 =	.38
Training/seminars	.17 ×	90 ÷	60 =	.26
Total hours per support clerk per month			=	.64

The next part of the administrative category is meetings. Although the support group is typically not as meeting-laden as some of the other positions, ongoing departmental-type meetings may occur. If meetings are impromptu or sporadic, they should not be accounted for. But if they occur regularly, the time taken away from other duties must be quantified. This quantification begins with the retail support survey, which requests both frequency of occurrence and average minutes. Once the surveys are returned and an average calculated for these two items, an analysis can be performed as in Figure 137.

Figure 137 includes training seminars, because support personnel are subject to additional training as time goes on to hone skills or learn new procedures. The goal here is to determine the optimum frequency of occurrence for such seminars. If the financial institution is committed to excellence, it probably has an organized training program that calls for the periodic education of staff personnel. This function takes time away from the job which must be accounted for.

The last area of administrative activities is general administrative duties. Under this category, various miscellaneous tasks occur in all given departments simply because that is the way it has always been. These activities may not relate at all to the personal banking business, but they must still be accounted for. It is important that the interview results be evaluated at this stage, because it is *only* through interviews that management will learn what additional functions are performed in this area. Tasks that do not relate directly to the volume of products sold or customers serviced or to the business of personal banking must be included in the general administrative category of fixed activities.

Once types of duties are determined, they should be recorded in the retail support activity tally document shown in Figure 138. The categories recorded can change based on the results of the interview process.

F I G U R E 138

Retail Support Activity Tally

Activity	Tally	Total
Reports developed		
Reports distributed		
Document developed		
Account/note input		
Account files developed		
Notes/documents filed		
Funds disbursed		
Credit reports produced		
Payments handled		
Loan/account closings		
Payoff handlings		
Document receipt and filing		
Customer correspondence filing		

F I G U R E 1 3 9

General Administrative Activities

Subcategory	Total Dept. Vol.		Weeks to Annualize		Months/ Year		No. of Support Clerks		Avg. Vol./ Clerk/ Month		Avg. Min./ Item		Min./ Hour		Avg. Hours/ Support Clerk/Month
Reports developed	20	×	26	÷	12	÷	2	=	21.67	×	20	÷	60	=	7.22
Reports distributed	40	×	26	÷	12	÷	2	=	43.33	×	15	÷	60	=	10.83
Total hours per support clerk per month														=	18.05

	Avg. Min./ Week		Weeks to Annualize		Mos./Year		Min./Hour		Avg. Hours/ Support Clerk/Month
Miscellaneous filing	90	×	52	÷	12	÷	60	=	6.50
Total monthly general administrative hours per support clerk								=	24.55

Only three items are used in this example: reports developed, reports distributed, and miscellaneous filing. Obviously, more tasks can be included, as the interview process will determine.

In the case of reports developed and distributed, a raw volume is needed. For miscellaneous filing, a time factor per week is required. This should account for the other miscellaneous duties typically performed by retail support clerks. Once a time average has been determined from the survey and a total volume from the activity tally, the average time committed to these activities must be calculated as shown in Figure 139.

This completes the administrative section of the retail support profile. Since three separate categories are involved, it is necessary to summarize the data as shown in Figure 140. Also, the resulting factor must be restated as a percentage of total monthly available hours per support clerk, since this is a fixed activity.

In this example, 17.7 percent of each support clerk's time is used up every month on administrative tasks, without regard to product sales volume. This leaves 82.3 percent of the clerk's time to devote to other tasks and activities.

Personal Activities Like all other activities, personal activities—lunches and breaks—must be accounted for. Time estimates are

F I G U R E 140

Administrative Summary: Support Clerks

Activity	Hours Required
1. Telephone calls	4.65
2. Meetings	.64
3. General administrative tasks	24.55
Total monthly hours per support clerk	29.84
Monthly available hours per support clerk	÷ 168.6
Percentage of monthly available hours per support clerk	= 17.7%

F I G U R E   141

Personal Activities

	Avg. Min./ Occurrence		No. of Working Days/Year		Months/ Year		Min./ Hour		Avg. Hours/ Support Clerk/ Month
Lunches	60	×	260	÷	12	÷	60	=	21.67
Breaks	15	×	260	÷	12	÷	60	=	5.42
Total monthly hours per support clerk								=	27.09
Number of available hours per support clerk per month								÷	168.6
Percentage of monthly available hours devoted to personal activities per support clerk								=	16.1%

required for the retail support survey. After the time spent is averaged, the monthly hours required can be calculated as in Figure 141. The number of working days per year is 5 days times 52 weeks.

From the raw data in the survey, the time estimates are converted to hours and then to a percentage of monthly available hours—in this case, 16.1 percent. A percentage is used because this is a fixed activity that occurs with a high degree of frequency on a regular basis.

This completes the fixed activities for retail support clerks. The next section will outline their variable activities.

New Products Sold   As new retail products are sold by personal bankers, a number of tasks must be completed to put the accounts on the books and make sure the necessary record-keeping has been attended to. Typically these tasks are performed by back-of-fice support personnel. For retail support clerks, the category of new products sold involves account setup, including the following tasks:

- Document development
- Account/note input
- Account file development
- Note/document filing
- Funds disbursement
- Credit report production

All these tasks are associated only with opening new accounts, not with handling existing accounts. Since retail support may perform more functions at different banks, the interview process will again be very helpful.

New products sold begins the variable section of the retail support profile. This means that the tasks performed are directly related to the volume of new products sold. If no new products are sold, no time is spent performing these tasks. Instead of an overall percentage to monthly hours available, only a time factor will be developed for variable activities, expressed in hours and applied to the volume of new products sold for the department.

Data gathering for this activity involves time estimates by task performed, recorded in the retail support survey and averaged for the full staff of retail support personnel. Volume information must be obtained for the tasks performed in order to link this with the volume of products sold. Since each product sold may have different requirements in terms of setup, the goal is to determine, on average, how much support time is required for any product sold. The combination of these two items will produce the overall factors used in the staffing model for new products sold.

The volume of tasks performed is determined from the retail support activity tally (Figure 138), the same document used to capture volume information for the fixed subcategory of general administration. Once these documents are completed over a two-week period, an overall total for the group will be used in the overall time factor calculation, as shown in Figure 142. It can be seen from this example that each new product sold requires approximately .75 hour, or 45 minutes, on average, for back-office tasks.

New Products Sold

Task	Avg. Volume of Tasks/ Product Sold		Avg. Min./ Item		Min./ Hour		Avg. Hours/ Product Sold
Document development	1.74	×	10	÷	60	=	.29
Account/note input	1.00	×	7	÷	60	=	.12
Account file development	.40	×	12	÷	60	=	.08
Note/document filing	1.74	×	5	÷	60	=	.15
Funds disbursement	.27	×	8	÷	60	=	.04
Credit report production	.40	×	10	÷	60	=	.07
Total available hourly factor for new products sold						=	.75

Task	Total Departmental Volume		No. of Products Sold in Two Weeks		Avg. Volume of Tasks/ Product Sold
Document development	650	÷	375	=	1.74
Account/note input	375	÷	375	=	1.00
Account/file development	150	÷	375	=	.40
Note/document filing	650	÷	375	=	1.74
Funds disbursement	100	÷	375	=	.27
Credit report production	150	÷	375	=	.40

Maintenance   The last area of the retail support profile is maintenance activities, which involve providing services to existing customers. These are tasks better suited to being performed by retail support clerks than personal bankers. The specific tasks performed by this group for existing customers fall into the categories of customer communications and account administration. Within these, the detailed tasks are usually as follows:

1. Customer communications:
   - Inbound phone calls from customers.
   - Outbound phone calls to customers.
   - In-person meetings with customers.

2. Account administration:
- Payment handling.
- Payoff handling.
- Document receipt / filing.
- Customer correspondence filing.

This list is not exhaustive, but it is representative. Depending on the individual bank, more tasks may be added based on the interview process.

To find the hourly factors associated with these variable activities, use the retail support survey to take a departmental average of all time estimates for customer communications and account administration. In addition to this, determine specific volumes over a two-week period from the retail support call tally (Figure 135) and the retail support activity tally (Figure 139). Both tally documents are also contained in the survey document. The number of retail customers on file will be needed to determine hourly factors per customer.

Retail support personnel are likely to have direct contact with customers via telephone or in person. They perform specific tasks directly related to a customer to maintain the account and relationship. Based on the time estimate averages and two-week volumes (all retail support clerks), the hourly factor, per customer, for retail support maintenance can be calculated as in Figure 143.

This completes the maintenance section and data gathering for the entire retail support profile.

Recap: Retail Support   The data obtained and information developed for the retail support group are summarized in Figure 144.

It is evident that a considerable portion of a retail support clerk's time—one-third in fact (17.7 plus 16.1 percent)—is devoted to fixed activities. This leaves only 66.2 percent of an FTE to accommodate the incoming volume of new products sold and servicing existing customers. In light of this, it is important to understand specifically how time is allocated to the key volume indicators of new products sold and customers serviced. The time factors determined for the variable activities represent how long the activity *should* take, not necessarily how long it takes currently.

F I G U R E   1 4 3

Maintenance Summary: Retail Support

Subcategory	Frequency/Customer/Month	Average Minutes/Item	Minutes/Hour	Average Hours/Customer/Month
Customer communications				
Inbound calls	.16 ×	2.5 ÷	60 =	.01
Outbound calls	.08 ×	1.75 ÷	60 =	.002
In-person visits	.03 ×	15 ÷	60 =	.01
Account administration				
Payment handling	.05 ×	10 ÷	60 =	.01
Loan/acct. closing	.03 ×	12 ÷	60 =	.01
Payoff handling	.02 ×	15 ÷	60 =	.01
Document receipt/filing	.07 ×	5 ÷	60 =	.01
Customer correspondence filing	.05 ×	5 ÷	60 =	.01
Total hours per customer per month				.072

Subcategory	Total Dept. Volume	Weeks to Annualize	Months/Year	No. of Customers on File	Frequency/Customer/Month
Customer communications					
Inbound calls	300 ×	26	12 ÷	4,000 =	.16
Outbound calls	150 ×	26	12 ÷	4,000 =	.08
In-person visits	50 ×	26	12 ÷	4,000 =	.03
Account administration					
Payment handling	90 ×	26	12 ÷	4,000 =	.05
Loan/acct. closing	60 ×	26	12 ÷	4,000 =	.03
Payoff handling	40 ×	26	12 ÷	4,000 =	.02
Document receipt/filing	120 ×	26	12 ÷	4,000 =	.07
Customer correspondence filing	100 ×	26	12 ÷	4,000 =	.05

F I G U R E   144

Retail Support Summary

1. Fixed activities	Percentage of Total Available Hours
■ Administrative	17.7%
■ Personal	16.1%
2. Variable activities	**Hourly Factor**
■ New products sold	.75
■ Maintenance	.072

To evaluate this, begin with the fixed activities. Since they occur regardless of volume, the percentage of time devoted to them will remain stable. This time is already committed and must be subtracted from the overall available time to yield the actual hours remaining for variable tasks. This analysis for retail support personnel is illustrated in Figure 145. Once this calculation is

F I G U R E   145

Total Departmental Fixed and Variable Hours

1. Total monthly hours available per retail support clerk   168.6
2. Total number of support clerks on staff   ×   2
3. Total departmental hours available per month   = 337.2

Fixed Activity	Percentage of Time Devoted		Total Departmental Hours Available		Total Departmental Hours Committed
Administrative	17.7%	×	337.20	=	59.68
Personal	16.1%	×	337.20	=	54.29
Total fixed hours committed				=	113.97
Total hours available for variable activities (337.20 − 113.97 = 223.23)				=	223.23

F I G U R E 146

Actual Variable Activity Hourly Factors

Variable Activity	Average Monthly Volume		Calculated Hourly Factor		Total Hours Required	Percentage of Total Hours		Hours Available for Variable Activities		Average Monthly Volume		Actual Variable Activity Hourly Factor
New products sold	900	×	.75	=	675	70.1%	×	223.23	÷	900	=	.174
Maintenance	4,000	×	.072	=	288	29.9%	×	223.23	÷	4,000	=	.017
					963	100.0%						

complete, the amount of time available for the variable functions must be further analyzed, as in Figure 146, to determine how much time actually is spent on each variable activity. In Figure 146, the calculated hourly factor comes from Figure 144 and the hours available from Figure 145.

From the data determined in Figure 146, a comparison must be made between the standard and actual time factors per variable activity.

Variable Activity	Standard Hours	Actual Hours
New products sold	.75	.174
Maintenance	.072	.017

The fairly large difference between the two could indicate that the department is understaffed and much less time is actually devoted to each new product sold and customer serviced than the survey determined was needed. Another possibility is that the time estimates offered by the support group were too conservative. To address these concerns, average the two factors. The result is .47 hour for new products sold and .05 hour for maintenance. This would change the overall profile for retail support personnel, as reflected in Figure 147.

The adjusted factors and complete profile data are reflected in the personal banking staffing model in Figure 148.

F I G U R E 147

Modified Support Summary

1. Fixed activities	Percentage of Total Available Hours
■ Administrative	17.7%
■ Personal	16.1%
2. Variable activities	Hourly Factor
■ New products sold	.47
■ Maintenance	.05

F I G U R E   148

Staffing Model for Retail Support

```
BANK:          [        ]      PERSONAL BANKING STAFFING MODEL        DATE:     [        ]
LOCATION:      [        ]
BRANCH:        [        ]


DATA REQUIRED
   # CUST. SEEN THIS MONTH:   [        ]  AVG. # TOTAL HOURS PER FTE PER DAY:           [        ]
   # CUST. SOLD THIS MONTH:   [        ]  AVERAGE NUMBER OF RETAIL ACCOUNTS ON FILE: [        ]
   # PROD. SOLD THIS MONTH:   [        ]
```

A. FIXED HOURS (PER FTE):

	% OF TOTAL MONTHLY HOURS		
	PERSONAL BANKER	RETAIL SECRETARY	RETAIL SUPPORT
BUSINESS DEVELOPMENT:	[ ]	[ ]	[ ]
ADMINISTRATION:	[ ]	[ ]	[17.70%]
PERSONAL TIME:	[ ]	[ ]	[16.10%]
TOTAL:	0.00%	0.00%	33.80%

B. VARIABLE HOURS:

	STANDARD HOURS REQUIRED PER ITEM		
	PERSONAL BANKER	RETAIL SECRETARY	RETAIL SUPPORT
NEW PRODUCTS SOLD:	[ ]	[ ]	[0.47]
CUSTOMERS SEEN, NOT SOLD:	[ ]	[ ]	[ ]
MAINTENANCE:	[ ]	[ ]	[0.05]

C. DISTRIBUTION OF FTEs BY POSITION:

	FULL-TIME EQUIVALENTS REQUIRED			
	PERSONAL BANKER	RETAIL SECRETARY	RETAIL SUPPORT	TOTAL FTE STAFF
NEW PRODUCTS SOLD:				0.00
CUSTOMERS SEEN, NOT SOLD:				0.00
MAINTENANCE:				0.00
BUSINESS DEVELOPMENT:				0.00
ADMINISTRATIVE:				0.00
PERSONAL:				0.00
TOTAL FTE:	0.00	0.00	0.00	0.00

Although the data shown in this and previous sections are typical for these positions, the numbers will differ for each individual financial institution. The purpose of the examples is to demonstrate the methodology. Although the core profile activities should not vary by financial institution, some of the tasks within the activity categories may change.

This completes the development of the information for all positions within the personal banking division for use in the staffing model. The next section outlines the creation and execution of the personal banking staffing model.

Model Development and Reports

The staffing model discussed in this book is an analytical tool that management can use to determine optimum staffing levels within the personal banking division. From the data determined in the data-gathering section of this chapter, the model will provide actual FTE levels for each of the three positions within the personal banking division: personal bankers, retail secretaries, and retail support.

This section of the chapter outlines the steps necessary to create the model and explains how to run it. All formulas required to create the model as pictured in the exhibits are included.

Creating the Model

The model was developed using Lotus 1, 2, 3, version 2.01. An exact duplicate of Figure 149 can be created in any bank using the Lotus spreadsheet software. This section provides exact instructions for building the model, including the formulas necessary to calculate optimum staffing levels. As shown in Figure 149, each bracket or cell is coded by a number. The following explanation for each number code includes a specific formula (if required) to calculate the actual data.

Before beginning, the individual responsible for creating the model should develop the format of the model. This is the physical appearance recording all headings, titles, brackets, and boundary lines. The spacing and positioning of heading, brack-

F I G U R E 149

Personal Banking Staffing Model

```
BANK:              [   1   ]      PERSONAL BANKING STAFFING MODEL        DATE:    [   4   ]
LOCATION:          [   2   ]
BRANCH:            [   3   ]


DATA REQUIRED
  # CUST. SEEN THIS MONTH:    [   5   ]  AVG. # TOTAL HOURS PER FTE PER DAY:       [   8   ]
  # CUST. SOLD THIS MONTH:    [   6   ]  AVERAGE NUMBER OF RETAIL ACCOUNTS ON FILE: [   9   ]
  # PROD. SOLD THIS MONTH:    [   7   ]
===========================================================================================
A. FIXED HOURS (PER FTE):

                                % OF TOTAL MONTHLY HOURS
                              PERSONAL        RETAIL           RETAIL
                               BANKER        SECRETARY         SUPPORT
                              ========       =========        =========
BUSINESS DEVELOPMENT:        [   10A   ]    [   10B   ]      [   10C   ]
ADMINISTRATION:              [   11A   ]    [   11B   ]      [   11C   ]
PERSONAL TIME:               [   12A   ]    [   12B   ]      [   12C   ]

TOTAL:                           13A            13B              13C
                              ========       =========        =========



===========================================================================================
B. VARIABLE HOURS:

                              STANDARD HOURS REQUIRED PER ITEM
                              PERSONAL        RETAIL           RETAIL
                               BANKER        SECRETARY         SUPPORT
                              ========       =========        =========
NEW PRODUCTS SOLD:           [   14A   ]    [   14B   ]      [   14C   ]
CUSTOMERS SEEN, NOT SOLD:    [   15A   ]    [   15B   ]      [   15C   ]
MAINTENANCE:                 [   16A   ]    [   16B   ]      [   16C   ]



===========================================================================================
C. DISTRIBUTION OF FTEs BY POSITION:
                                        FULL-TIME EQUIVALENTS REQUIRED
                                                                            TOTAL
                              PERSONAL        RETAIL           RETAIL        FTE
                               BANKER        SECRETARY         SUPPORT       STAFF
                              ========       =========        =========    =========
NEW PRODUCTS SOLD:              17A            17B              17C           24
CUSTOMERS SEEN, NOT SOLD:       18A            18B              18C           25
MAINTENANCE:                    19A            19B              19C           26
BUSINESS DEVELOPMENT:           20A            20B              20C           27
ADMINISTRATIVE:                 21A            21B              21C           28
PERSONAL:                       22A            22B              22C           29

TOTAL FTE:                      23A            23B              23C           30
                              ========       =========        =========    =========
```

ets, and so forth should be copied as close to the example as possible. This should be relatively simple for a seasoned Lotus 1, 2, 3 user. Figure 149 should be copied so that it fits on an 8 1/2" x 11" sheet of paper.

The developer can then review the explanations corresponding to the code numbers in the model. In some cases, nothing will need to be added at this time; in other cases, a formula is required. Narrative formulas are provided to explain the components of the Lotus 1, 2, 3 formulas. Since it is uncertain what the cell addresses will be, the code numbers in Figure 149 will be used in their place. When the developer inputs the appropriate formula, he or she must translate the code number into the proper cell format on the spreadsheet.

1. Bank: This is space created to input the name of the financial institution for which the analysis is being performed. When building the model, bracket cells in which data will be input. This will highlight those areas requiring information. Enough space should be left for the name of the bank or its abbreviation.

2. Location: Input the location of the bank. This could be a city or street name. The setup requirements are the same as for bank name.

3. Branch: This completes the identifier cells. The same size requirements and brackets should be used as before.

4. Date: The date filed should contain enough space to record a month and year or a period of time such as "Fourth Quarter 1991."

5–9. Data required (number of customers seen this month, number of customers sold this month, number of products sold this month, average number of total hours per FTE per day, and average number of retail accounts on file): These fields contain the volume, or given data the model will run on. For each item brackets should be placed around cells, providing room for at least six to nine characters to be input. The brackets indicate that these fields require an input. The actual cells, within the brackets, should be unprotected to allow the user to input data unimpeded.

Section A: Fixed Hours (per FTE)

10A–12C. Percentage of total monthly hours for business development, administration, and personal time: Brackets must be set up around each cell, for each position, to allow for input of a percentage. Enough space per cell should be available for at least seven characters. Each cell should be formatted for percents, with two decimals, so the percent sign will appear as the data are input. Finally, all cells should be unprotected.

13A–13C. Total—Percentage of total monthly hours (by position): These are the first of the automatic calculation fields that require no input. The total is automatically calculated by formula and reflected in the total section. No brackets are needed around these areas. The narrative formula is:

$$\left(\begin{array}{c} \text{Business} \\ \text{development} \\ \text{percentage} \end{array} + \begin{array}{c} \text{Administration} \\ \text{percentage} \end{array} + \begin{array}{c} \text{Personal} \\ \text{time} \\ \text{percentage} \end{array} \right)$$

Lotus formula:

13A @sum(10A..12A)
13B @sum(10B..12B)
13C @sum(10C..12C)

After the formulas are input, these fields should be protected to prevent overwriting.

Section B: Variable Hours

14A–16C. Standard hours required per item (for new products sold; customers seen, not sold; and maintenance): Each of these fields requires an input, so brackets should surround the cells as in Figure 149. Within the brackets, space should be allowed for at least six characters. The cells should be formatted for two decimals and unprotected to allow for data input.

Section C: Distribution of FTEs by Position

17A–17C. Full-time equivalents required (new products sold): In all of section C (17A-30), no input is required. Only formulas are input. This begins the actual determination of optimum staffing levels by position and by activity for the personal banking division.

For this first group, new products sold, the formulas will reveal the number of FTEs needed to handle the activities. The narrative formula is:

$$\left(\begin{array}{c} \text{Number} \\ \text{of products} \\ \text{sold this} \\ \text{month} \end{array} \times \begin{array}{c} \text{Standard} \\ \text{hours per} \\ \text{new product} \\ \text{sold} \end{array} \right) \div \left(\left(\begin{array}{c} \text{Average} \\ \text{numberof} \\ \text{total hours} \\ \text{per FTE} \end{array} \times \begin{array}{c} \text{Number of} \\ \text{working days} \\ \text{per year} \end{array} \right) \div 12 \right)$$

Lotus formulas:

    17A   (7*14A)/((8*240)/12)
    17B   (7*14B)/((8*240)/12)
    17C   (7*14C)/((8*240)/12)

Once the formulas are input, all fields should be protected, and at least six character fields should be formatted with two decimals.

18A–18C. Full-time equivalents required (customers seen, not sold): The narrative formula is:

$$\left(\left(\begin{array}{c} \text{Number of} \\ \text{customers} \\ \text{seen} \\ \text{this month} \end{array} - \begin{array}{c} \text{Number of} \\ \text{customers} \\ \text{sold} \\ \text{this month} \end{array} \right) \times \begin{array}{c} \text{Standard} \\ \text{hours per} \\ \text{customer} \\ \text{seen,} \\ \text{not sold} \end{array} \right) \div \left(\left(\begin{array}{c} \text{Average} \\ \text{total} \\ \text{hours} \\ \text{per FTE} \end{array} \times \begin{array}{c} \text{Number of} \\ \text{working} \\ \text{days} \\ \text{per year} \end{array} \right) \div 12 \right)$$

Lotus formulas:

    18A   ((5-6)*15A)/((8*240)/12)
    18B   ((5-6)*15B)/((8*240)/12)
    18C   ((5-6)*15C)/((8*240)/12)

19A–19C. Full-time equivalents required (maintenance): The narrative formula is:

$$\left(\begin{array}{c} \text{Average} \\ \text{number} \\ \text{of accounts} \\ \text{on file} \end{array} \times \begin{array}{c} \text{Standard} \\ \text{hoursper} \\ \text{customer} \\ \text{maintained} \end{array} \right) \div \left(\left(\begin{array}{c} \text{Average} \\ \text{total hours} \\ \text{per FTE} \end{array} \times \begin{array}{c} \text{Number of} \\ \text{working days} \\ \text{per year} \end{array} \right) \div 12 \right)$$

Lotus formulas:

19A   (9*16A)/((8*240)/12)
19B   (9*16B)/((8*240)/12)
19C   (9*16C)/((8*240)/12)

20A–20C. Full-time equivalents required (business development): The narrative formula is:

$$\left(\left(\begin{array}{c}\text{Sum} \\ \text{of new} \\ \text{products} \\ \text{sold}\end{array} + \begin{array}{c}\text{Customers} \\ \text{seen,} \\ \text{not sold}\end{array} + \begin{array}{c}\text{Mainte-} \\ \text{nance} \\ \text{FTEs}\end{array}\right) \times \left(\left(\begin{array}{c}\text{Average} \\ \text{hours} \\ \text{per FTE}\end{array} \times \begin{array}{c}240 \\ \text{working} \\ \text{days} \\ \text{per year}\end{array}\right) \div \begin{array}{c}12 \\ \text{months} \\ \text{per year}\end{array}\right)\right)$$

$$\div \left(\left(\left(\begin{array}{c}\text{Average} \\ \text{hours} \\ \text{per FTE}\end{array} \times 240\right) \div 12\right) - \left(\left(\begin{array}{c}\text{Average} \\ \text{hours} \\ \text{per FTE}\end{array} \times 240\right) \div 12 \times \begin{array}{c}\text{Total} \\ \text{fixed} \\ \text{activity} \\ \text{percentage}\end{array}\right)\right)$$

$$\times \left(\left(\left(\begin{array}{c}\text{Average} \\ \text{hours} \\ \text{per FTE}\end{array} \times 240\right) \div 12 \times \begin{array}{c}\text{Business} \\ \text{development} \\ \text{fixed} \\ \text{percentage}\end{array}\right) \div \left(\begin{array}{c}\text{Average} \\ \text{hours} \\ \text{per FTE}\end{array} \times 240\right) \div 12\right)$$

Lotus formulas:

20A   ((@sum(17A..19A)*((8*240)/12))/(((8*240)/12)-
       (((8*240)/12)*13A)))*((((8*240)/12)*10A)/((8*240)/12))
20B   ((@sum(17B..19B)*((8*240)/12))/(((8*240)/12)-
       (((8*240)/12)*13B)))*((((8*240)/12)*10B)/((8*240)/12))
20C   ((@sum(17C..19C)*((8*240)/12))/(((8*240)/12)-
       (((8*240)/12)*13C)))*((((8*240)/12)*10C)/((8*240)/12))

21A–21C. Full-time equivalents required (administrative): The narrative formula is:

$$\left(\left(\begin{array}{c}\text{Sum} \\ \text{of new} \\ \text{products} \\ \text{sold}\end{array} + \begin{array}{c}\text{Customers} \\ \text{seen,} \\ \text{not sold}\end{array} + \begin{array}{c}\text{Mainte-} \\ \text{nance} \\ \text{FTEs}\end{array}\right) \times \left(\left(\begin{array}{c}\text{Average} \\ \text{hours} \\ \text{per FTE}\end{array} \times \begin{array}{c}240 \\ \text{working} \\ \text{days} \\ \text{per year}\end{array}\right) \div \begin{array}{c}12 \\ \text{months} \\ \text{per year}\end{array}\right)\right)$$

$$\div \left(\left(\left(\left(\begin{array}{c}\text{Average}\\ \text{hours}\\ \text{per FTE}\end{array} \times 240\right) \div 12\right) - \left(\left(\begin{array}{c}\text{Average}\\ \text{hours}\\ \text{per FTE}\end{array} \times 240\right) \div 12\right) \times \begin{array}{c}\text{Total}\\ \text{fixed}\\ \text{activity}\\ \text{percentage}\end{array}\right)$$

$$\times \left(\left(\left(\left(\begin{array}{c}\text{Average}\\ \text{hours}\\ \text{per FTE}\end{array} \times 240\right) \div 12\right) \times \begin{array}{c}\text{Administrative}\\ \text{fixed}\\ \text{percentage}\end{array}\right) \div \left(\left(\begin{array}{c}\text{Average}\\ \text{hours}\\ \text{per FTE}\end{array} \times 240\right) \div 12\right)\right)$$

Lotus formulas:

21A ((@sum(17A..19A)*((8*240)/12))/(((8*240)/12)–
(((8*240)/12)*13A)))*((((8*240)/12)*11A)/((8*240)/12))

21B ((@sum(17B..19B)*((8*240)/12))/(((8*240)/12)–
(((8*240)/12)*13B)))*((((8*240)/12)*11B)/((8*240)/12))

21C ((@sum(17C..19C)*((8*240)/12))/(((8*240)/12)–
(((8*240)/12)*13C)))*((((8*240)/12)*11C)/((8*240)/12))

22A–22C. Full-time equivalents required (personal): The narrative formula is:

$$\left(\left(\begin{array}{c}\text{Sum}\\ \text{of new}\\ \text{products}\\ \text{sold}\end{array} + \begin{array}{c}\text{Customers}\\ \text{seen,}\\ \text{not sold}\end{array} + \begin{array}{c}\text{Mainte-}\\ \text{nance}\\ \text{FTEs}\end{array}\right) \times \left(\left(\begin{array}{c}\text{Average}\\ \text{hours}\\ \text{per FTE}\end{array} \times \begin{array}{c}240\\ \text{working}\\ \text{days}\\ \text{per year}\end{array}\right) \div \begin{array}{c}12\\ \text{months}\\ \text{per year}\end{array}\right)\right)$$

$$\div \left(\left(\left(\left(\begin{array}{c}\text{Average}\\ \text{hours}\\ \text{per FTE}\end{array} \times 240\right) \div 12\right) - \left(\left(\begin{array}{c}\text{Average}\\ \text{hours}\\ \text{per FTE}\end{array} \times 240\right) \div 12\right) \times \begin{array}{c}\text{Total}\\ \text{fixed}\\ \text{activity}\\ \text{percentage}\end{array}\right)$$

$$\times \left(\left(\left(\left(\begin{array}{c}\text{Average}\\ \text{hours}\\ \text{per FTE}\end{array} \times 240\right) \div 12\right) \times \begin{array}{c}\text{Personal}\\ \text{activity}\\ \text{percentage}\end{array}\right) \div \left(\left(\begin{array}{c}\text{Average}\\ \text{hours}\\ \text{per FTE}\end{array} \times 240\right) \div 12\right)\right)$$

Lotus formulas:

22A (((@sum(17A..19A)*((8*240)/12))/((((8*240)/12)–
        (((8*240)/12)*
        13A)))*(((((8*240)/12)*12A)/((8*240)/12))
22B (((@sum(17B..19B)*((8*240)/12))/((((8*240)/12)–
        (((8*240)/12)*
        13B)))*(((((8*240)/12)*12B)/((8*240)/12))
22C (((@sum(17C..19C)*((8*240)/12))/((((8*240)/12)–
        (((8*240)/12)*
        13C)))*(((((8*240)/12)*12C)/((8*240)/12))

23A–23C. Full-time equivalents required (total FTE): This is a summation, by position type, of the FTE requirements calculated by activity. The narrative formula for this calculation is:

$$\left(\begin{array}{c}\text{New}\\\text{products}\\\text{sold}\\\text{FTE}\end{array} + \begin{array}{c}\text{Customers}\\\text{seen,}\\\text{not sold}\\\text{FTE}\end{array} + \begin{array}{c}\text{Mainte-}\\\text{nance}\\\text{FTE}\end{array} + \begin{array}{c}\text{Business}\\\text{develop-}\\\text{ment}\\\text{FTE}\end{array} + \begin{array}{c}\text{Adminis-}\\\text{trative}\\\text{FTE}\end{array} + \begin{array}{c}\text{Personal}\\\text{FTE}\end{array}\right)$$

Lotus formulas:

23A   @sum(17A..22A)
23B   @sum(17B..22B)
23C   @sum(17C..22C)

24-29. Total FTE staff, by activity: This is a summation of the FTEs, by activity, for all personal banking positions. The narrative formula is:

$$\left(\begin{array}{c}\text{Personal}\\\text{banker FTE}\end{array} + \begin{array}{c}\text{Retail}\\\text{secretary FTE}\end{array} + \begin{array}{c}\text{Retail}\\\text{support FTE}\end{array}\right)$$

Lotus formulas:

24   (17A+17B+17C)
25   (18A+18B+17C)
26   (19A+19B+19C)
27   (20A+20B+20C)
28   (21A+21B+21C)
29   (22A+22B+22C)

30. FTE grand total: This is a summation of the total FTEs, by activity. The narrative formula is:

$$\left(\begin{array}{c} \text{Total} \\ \text{new} \\ \text{products} \\ \text{sold FTE} \end{array} + \begin{array}{c} \text{Total} \\ \text{customers} \\ \text{seen,} \\ \text{not sold} \\ \text{FTEs} \end{array} + \begin{array}{c} \text{Total} \\ \text{mainte-} \\ \text{nance} \\ \text{FTEs} \end{array} + \begin{array}{c} \text{Total} \\ \text{business} \\ \text{develop-} \\ \text{ment} \\ \text{FTEs} \end{array} + \begin{array}{c} \text{Total} \\ \text{adminis-} \\ \text{trative} \\ \text{FTEs} \end{array} + \begin{array}{c} \text{Total} \\ \text{personal} \\ \text{FTEs} \end{array} \right)$$

Lotus formula:

30   @sum(24..29)

Running the Model

Once the model is constructed, it is ready for the necessary input to the bracketed cells, which triggers the automatic calculations found in section C of the model.

This section explains the number codes found in the personal banking staffing analysis model (Figure 149). It discusses what is required in each area as well as what it means to the user.

1, 2, and 3. Bank, location, and branch: This provides the fields necessary to identify the bank, location, and branch of the entity being studied in the staffing model. This can be quite important if there are multiple branches or banks within the organization. The user simply types in the requested data within the brackets, abbreviating as necessary.

4. Date: The date is important from a historical basis. As each analysis is completed, the report produced is a permanent record of the staffing levels for a given time at a given volume level. This document may be retained for future comparisons.

The date field should be wide enough to allow the input of at least a month and year (e.g., June 1991) or a period of time, such as a monthly average over a quarter (e.g., 3rd Quarter 1991 Average).

5. Number of customers seen this month: This begins the key data necessary to trigger execution of the model. The data must first be captured from the personal banking staff via a production sheet that counts the total number of customers actually seen this month. If the bank uses a platform automation system, it can

F I G U R E 150

Customer Contact Tally Sheet

Day	Customers Seen	Customers Sold at Least One Product	Products Sold
Monday			
Tuesday			
Wednesday			
Thursday			
Friday			
Saturday			
TOTAL			

probably retrieve the data right from the system. If not, the data must be gathered monthly on a production sheet like the one in Figure 150.

This is an ongoing production sheet; that is, it will be used in perpetuity. This type of volume data is absolutely necessary to the determination of staffing levels. Since a full week of data is available per sheet, the supervisor or manager should develop a summary reporting mechanism to accumulate weekly departmental totals. Figure 151 is a sample summary sheet.

A combination of four weeks' (or thereabouts) summaries provide a monthly number of customers seen this month to input in this cell of the model.

6. Number of customers sold this month: Within the brackets, record the monthly departmental total of customers to whom at least one product was sold. These data can be captured manually with the production sheets in Figures 150 and 151. Personal bankers must count only those customers to whom they made a sale of

Personal Banking Departmental Summary

Week Ending: _____

Personal Banker	Total Customers Seen	Total Customers Sold at Least One Product	Total Products Sold
J. Smith			
T. Jones			
M. Stuart			
R. Edwards			
TOTAL			

at least one product. If multiple products were sold to the same customer, only one would be indicated on the production sheet. If no products were sold to the customer seen, no tally mark would be recorded. The total for this section should never exceed the "total customers seen" column.

7. Number of products sold this month: This is a grand total of all types of products sold. If several products are sold to a customer, they are accounted for here. These data are usually available from a mainframe report, because each new product sold requires some form of input to the system. Simply record the total for the month of the products sold. If this information is not available automatically, the production sheets (Figures 150 and 151) can capture the data. The total number of products sold may exceed the number of customers seen, as one customer sometimes buys multiple products.

8. Average total hours per FTE per day: Input the average total raw hours that an individual in this department is available, the standard work hours defined by bank policy. For example, if the starting time is 8:30 AM and closing time is 5:00 PM , the total

raw hours are 8.5 hours. Lunches and breaks are not excluded, as they are accounted for in the fixed activity section of the model.

9. Average number of retail accounts on file: For this required information, the month-end number of retail customers on file is sufficient. This is not a total of the number of DDA, savings, or money market accounts on file, but rather the number of customers who own these accounts. This relates directly to the maintenance activity—which customers, not individual accounts, are serviced.

Section A: Fixed Hours (per FTE)
10A–12. Percentage of total hours by position and fixed activity: In each bracketed cell in section A, input the percentage determined from the data-gathering analysis and surveys. At the end of each position section (personal banker, retail secretary, and retail support) in the data-gathering segment, a sample staffing model shows the actual percentages to input (Figures 120, 134, and 148). Each percentage must be entered as a decimal (e.g., input 25.2 percent as .252).

13A–13C. Percentage of total monthly hours (total): This automatic calculation, which requires no input, is a total of the percentages input for each fixed activity in each position.

Section B: Variable Hours
14A–16C. Standard hours required per items by position and variable activity: Section B requires the input of an hourly factor for the standard time required to perform the variable activity. This is determined from the data-gathering analysis for each personal banking position. Input the values from Figures 120, 134, and 148. Enter whole numbers carried out to two decimals as needed (e.g., enter .33 hours as .33).

Section C: Distribution of FTEs by Position
17A–22C. Full-time equivalents required, by position and activity: This entire section requires no manual input. Each cell has an automatic formula built in that calculates the FTE requirements, taking into account volume and fixed/variable standards

input. This is the goal of the staffing model. The FTE requirements indicate how many staff members are required per position, by activity.

23A–23C. Full-time equivalents required, total FTEs by position: Each cell is a summation of the optimum number of FTEs for the position of personal banker, retail secretary, or retail support clerk. Compared with the current number of FTEs, these numbers indicate whether the department is over- or understaffed.

24-30. Total FTEs, by activity, and grand total: These cells total the number of FTEs required in all positions to perform the given activity. Cell 30 shows a grand total FTE count for the entire personal banking division. This bottom-line result of the staffing analysis must be compared with the actual staff to determine whether staffing opportunities exist.

This completes the model development section of the personal banking chapter. The completed staffing model, using all standard information developed and hypothetical volumes, can be viewed in Figure 152. The next section outlines the analysis and benefits to be derived from using the model.

ANALYSIS, MEASUREMENT, AND USAGE

Once the model is developed and run, the final activity is to analyze and measure the data. This is crucial to determining how management will use the data and the course of action it will take as a result.

With the data obtained and calculated as in Figure 152, the analytical phase begins with a comparison of actual staff FTE to the FTE determined in the model. This is the primary goal of the staffing analysis. The information should be compared side by side, as in Figure 153.

The comparison is rather simple to perform and provides the information management is typically seeking. From the over/understaffed levels, determine the dollar opportunity by multiplying the overstaffed number of FTEs (if available) by the average annual salary for that position plus benefits. Of course, this dollar

F I G U R E   152

Completed Personal Banking Staffing Analysis

BANK:	[First National]	PERSONAL BANKING STAFFING MODEL	DATE: [June, 1991]
LOCATION:	[Center Street]		
BRANCH:	[Main]		

DATA REQUIRED

# CUST. SEEN THIS MONTH:	[500]	AVG. # TOTAL HOURS PER FTE PER DAY:	[8.5]
# CUST. SOLD THIS MONTH:	[420]	AVERAGE NUMBER OF RETAIL ACCOUNTS ON FILE:	[4000]
# PROD. SOLD THIS MONTH:	[750]		

A. FIXED HOURS (PER FTE):

	% OF TOTAL MONTHLY HOURS		
	PERSONAL BANKER	RETAIL SECRETARY	RETAIL SUPPORT
BUSINESS DEVELOPMENT:	[10.30%]	[ ]	[ ]
ADMINISTRATION:	[5.80%]	[11.20%]	[17.70%]
PERSONAL TIME:	[16.10%]	[16.10%]	[16.10%]
TOTAL:	32.20%	27.30%	33.80%

B. VARIABLE HOURS:

	STANDARD HOURS REQUIRED PER ITEM		
	PERSONAL BANKER	RETAIL SECRETARY	RETAIL SUPPORT
NEW PRODUCTS SOLD:	[0.33]	[0.40]	[0.47]
CUSTOMERS SEEN, NOT SOLD:	[0.25]	[ ]	[ ]
MAINTENANCE:	[0.33]	[0.10]	[0.05]

C. DISTRIBUTION OF FTEs BY POSITION:

	FULL-TIME EQUIVALENTS REQUIRED			
	PERSONAL BANKER	RETAIL SECRETARY	RETAIL SUPPORT	TOTAL FTE STAFF
NEW PRODUCTS SOLD:	1.46	1.76	2.07	5.29
CUSTOMERS SEEN, NOT SOLD:	0.12	0.00	0.00	0.12
MAINTENANCE:	7.76	2.35	1.18	11.29
BUSINESS DEVELOPMENT:	1.42	0.00	0.00	1.42
ADMINISTRATIVE:	0.80	0.36	0.31	1.47
PERSONAL:	2.37	0.60	0.36	3.33
TOTAL FTE:	13.92	5.08	3.93	22.93

F I G U R E 153

Actual Versus Calculated FTEs

Position	Current Actual FTE	Recommend FTE	Over (under) Staffed
Personal bankers	15.00	13.92	1.08
Retail secretaries	5.00	5.08	(.08)
Retail support	4.00	3.93	.07
Total FTE	24.00	22.93	1.07

opportunity is not achieved unless management actually reduces the staff or transfers the individuals to a department that is understaffed and would have needed to hire to fill the position.

Although this is a major benefit of the model, it is by no means the only one. Since personal banking, like commercial loans, is a sales division, it is very beneficial to management to understand how much time is actually devoted to sales and/or customer contact. This reflects the overall profile of a position within personal banking.

The personal banking profile is made up of six categories: business development, administrative activities, personal activities, new products sold, customers seen (not sold), and maintenance activities. Now that the model is completed, these activities can be ranked, by position, as a percentage of total FTEs or hours. Take each FTE determined, by activity, divide it into the total FTEs for that position, and multiply it by 100 to produce a percentage. Then rank the activities in descending order of percentages, as shown in Figure 154.

This ranking highlights for management where the personal banking staff is spending its time.

The six activity categories of the personal banking profile can be condensed further into the categories of sales (business development, new products sold, and customers seen, not sold), servicing (maintenance), and other (administrative and personal activities).

240

F I G U R E 154

Ranking of Activities by Position

Rank	Personal Banker		Retail Secretary		Retail Support	
1	Maintenance	55.8%	Maintenance	46.3%	New products	52.7%
2	Personal	16.8	New products	34.7	Maintenance	30.0
3	New products	10.5	Personal	11.9	Personal	9.4
4	Business development	10.2	Administrative	7.1	Administrative	7.9
5	Administrative	5.8		100.0%		100.0%
6	Customers seen, not sold	.9				
		100.0%				

F I G U R E 155

Ranking of Broad Categories by Position

Rank	Personal Banker		Retail Secretary		Retail Support	
1	Servicing	55.8%	Servicing	46.3%	Sales	52.7%
2	Other	22.6	Sales	34.7	Servicing	30.0
3	Sales	21.6	Other	19.0	Other	17.3
	TOTAL	100.0%		100.0%		100.0%

The percentages determined in Figure 154 can be totaled for each of the three broad categories to produce a new ranking, as shown in Figure 155.

This analysis is illustrated with greater impact by a pie chart, as shown in Figure 156. The pie chart enables management to see quickly where time is being spent.

From the rankings in Figure 155, a true analysis of the department can occur. Senior management can begin to evaluate whether this is the mix of activities they had planned or whether it is a surprise. For example, 55.8 percent of personal bankers' time is devoted to servicing existing customers, but only 21.6 percent of their time is spent on sales. A more desirable mix would be a 50/50 split between sales and servicing. Since the data-gathering phase produced the hourly factors used in the model, a re-analysis of these data is in order. Management may learn that personal bankers are handling too many phone calls or other nonsales-related

F I G U R E   156

Pie Chart of Personal Bankers' Activities

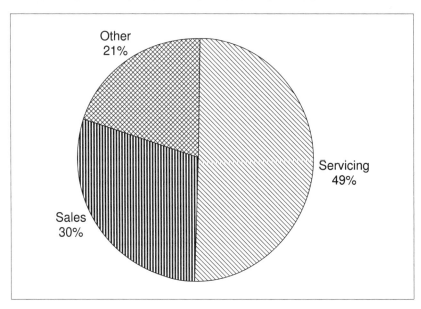

activities. These items could be rechanneled to either the retail secretaries or support clerks at a much lower unit cost than that incurred for personal bankers.

The mix of percentages shown in Figure 155 can affect the
amount of staff determined from the model. Management can
perform "what-if" analyses by altering the fixed percentages in
the model to increase the time devoted to sales and perhaps even
reduce the amount of staff required. Of course, any change in fixed
percentages in the model must be followed up with an actual
change in policy or procedure. For example, if breaks estimated
from personal bankers (15 minutes per day), were eliminated, the
current fixed percentage of 16.1 percent could be reduced to 12.8
percent of available time. This would decrease the total fixed time
committed and allow personal bankers to devote more time to the
variable activities (key volume indicators). Similarly, if the regular
weekly officers' meetings became quarterly, the percentage of
administrative time would be significantly reduced. In this type
of analysis, management may find that a lot of unproductive time
is taken up in meetings and various other activities. Acting on
some of these recommendations could easily save the cost of
hiring more people.

Although the fixed activities are probably the easiest to
evaluate and change, the variable hourly factors used in the model
can also be altered. Reducing an hourly factor from .33 to .20 hour,
for example, could reduce the amount of staff needed to perform
the task. The difficulty is finding what tasks can be eliminated or
sped up to reduce the overall time required. To do this, the user
should refer to the data-gathering section of the chapter and
analyze the specific tasks that went into calculating a particular
standard. Next, a flowchart should be developed for the steps
involved in the task.

The flowchart approach may help highlight areas that are
redundant or unimportant. If steps can be omitted, new time
estimates should be used to recalculate the factor. Unfortunately,
this is not as easy as it sounds. In most cases, reduction of an
hourly factor (standard) by a significant amount would probably
have to come as a result of automation. A classic example of this

is the time required to process a new product manually versus the time required using a platform automation system. The latter drives down the per-product time with considerable ease.

The analysis does not stop simply because the model has been run. The ongoing analytical process is important in using the model as an interpretive tool that can lead to significantly improved or streamlined processes for all positions in personal banking. Once management is comfortable with the standards used for the fixed and variable activities, the model can be used over and over as a guide to maintain staffing levels at consistent, cost-effective levels.

SUMMARY

The focus of this chapter has been on providing a methodology for evaluating and understanding the optimum staffing levels for the second major sales force in financial institutions, personal banking. The division is analyzed based upon the three positions that make up personal banking: personal bankers, retail secretaries, and retail support clerks. The chapter provides a detailed approach to determining optimum staffing levels for all these positions.

As with commercial loans and other departments, the starting point for all staffing analysis is the interview. The purpose of the interview is to understand the tasks performed, by position. What do these employees do? From the data gathered in the interview process, a profile—a set of fixed and variable activity categories that encompass all tasks performed—of the personal banking division can be determined.

The fixed activity categories do not depend on volume but occur as a result or by nature of the position. In personal banking, they are business development, administrative, and personal activities. In contrast, the time spent on these variable activities is directly proportional to volume. Variable activities can also be termed outcomes, outputs, and/or key volume indicators. In personal banking, they are new products sold, customers seen (not sold), and maintenance activities.

From the tasks determined in the interview process and profile, data must be gathered to develop the standards or factors used in the staffing model. Data are gathered through survey forms for each position, which are completed over a two-week period. Survey documents are used to determine average time estimates per task as well as volume, frequency, or occurrence of tasks. This information is calculated and charted to produce a specific factor for each profile activity. Fixed activities produce a percentage of available time; variable activities produce a time factor expressed as hours. Variable activity hourly factors are applied directly to volumes to produce the total time devoted to a particular activity and subsequently the amount of staff needed.

After all standards are developed, the staffing model must be constructed. The staffing model developed in this book uses Lotus 1, 2, 3, version 2.01. Instructions for developing the model and formulas are outlined in detail within the chapter. Volume information is necessary to run the model. If not available automatically from mainframe computer reports, it may be captured manually.

Once the model is run, an analysis should assess whether the department is over- or understaffed. The amount of time devoted to each activity should also be calculated as a percentage of total time and ranked in descending order. This will allow management to evaluate how time is spent and make adjustments if necessary. This may have a direct bearing on the amount of staff required in the division. The array of percentages is best illustrated by using a pie chart to reflect an entire day.

Finally, the model can be run as often as necessary, but quarterly or semiannually is recommended. Periodic use will provide for strict control of staff levels and assure management that resources are being utilized appropriately.

## CHAPTER 4

Human Resources Department Staffing Analysis

This chapter, although a bit of a deviation from analyzing the sales or customer contact department staff levels, provides the methodology for analyzing optimum staff levels for a purely staff-related department. This book provides an approach to scientifically analyzing both sales and staff departments in regard to how many employees are needed to perform the necessary tasks effectively.

For this chapter the human resources department was selected because it typifies a staff function within the organization—that is, it generally provides support and service to all departments within the financial institution. Staff functions of this nature are analyzed scientifically for staff levels, even more seldom than the sales areas. The reason given is similar to that voiced in the sales areas: it is too difficult due to the nature of the work. Human resource professionals do not often encode checks or handle customer transactions at a window or even make telemarketing calls. Their role is more support than it is the production or sale of a product. So why measure it? Why is knowing the appropriate staffing level important?

To answer this, one must understand the role human resources plays within a bank. One of its primary functions is to recruit new employees for the departments within the bank. This is a vital role for any organization that hopes to maintain a going concern and ultimately achieve its goals. If competent individuals are not attracted to the bank and hired, the bank cannot count on meeting specific sales goals, increasing market share, or even having a profitable year. It takes people to do this. If the human resource department is not suitably staffed to accommodate this important need or is too disorganized to staff itself efficiently, how can the other departments hope to have the necessary resources to attain their goals?

Often with staff-related functions such as human resources, if enough departments complain that their personnel needs are not being met some action may be taken. But it is not always clear how many people are required in human resources to provide the kind of support a financial institution needs. What indicators are available to tell bank management to what degree the department should grow? If an acquisition occurs, how does one determine the appropriate staff size of the human resources department? Should the two departments be combined, or are there economies of scale? Finally, how many people are needed to perform what function within the department?

These are not easy questions to answer. Some professionals would say they can be answered only by experience and judgment. Although those qualities are important, greater precision and objectivity in staffing can be attained through scientific measurement of the department's staff needs, based on the outputs produced and other indicators of performance. Staff departments (like sales departments) can be measured and staffed with the same precision as a back-office production department. Although the outcomes and key volume indicators may not be as obvious, the same basic approach used in production can be used in staff-related departments.

Human resources today, however, is changing. The advent of information technology is paving the way for more effective means of accessing services provided by the human resources function. Although technology is changing functions and access to service, it does not preclude the need for using staffing models.

Staffing models will always be needed as long as the department continues to employ people to perform various functions. One such area is interactive voice response systems (IVR), telephone technologies which enable a user to contact a number which will provide self-activated steps for obtaining the information that is sought. This technology is used very effectively in the customer service environment for external customers and serves to provide 24-hour coverage of service. This same technology can be put to use for human resources to field the questions and calls that are made to answer benefit and other types of typical calls that are channeled to the human resource department. Colleges also employ this device for registering students and providing access to the information required. This technology will change the factors used to account for handling inbound telephone calls. Again, this does not preclude the usage of the model, but rather serves to modify the variable factors that previously required human intervention and time to answer. Technologies such as IVR can and will help to make more efficient the reactive nature of the human resource job for providing information. This is an appropriate application of technology and one which should be considered for providing benefit information and other data to a growing employee base. Other opportunities include electronic-mail broadcasts and electronic rollup of information for hourly employees and other data requiring central databases. As banks migrate to managing internal and proprietary databases, even more information can be provided and controlled within the department. This will eliminate some human intervention but not all. Actually, there likely will be a change in the type and structure of the department to possibly include a database administrator in the future. In short, technology will be a welcome addition to this department and as such will help to improve the staffing compliments and their analysis as defined in this chapter.

Chapter 7 describes in detail the impact of a consolidating industry on staffing. Human resources will be continually challenged with the need to identify and quantify the staffing compliments necessary for newly combined entities. Because of this, the organization will be constantly challenged to determine the optimal levels and human resources needed to understand and maintain an appropriate staff compliment that can effectively manage these changes. Consolidations are pervasive, and the ability to assimilate organizations and merge and reduce staffs is a significant advantage. As such, the disciplines described in this chapter and Chapter 7 will aid the bank professional in preparing for and understanding the needs for a consolidating environment.

Human resources is a vital function within any bank. Management needs to understand the elements that are important to its, and subsequently the bank's, success. In this chapter, the human resource department is analyzed as the teller area, commercial lending, and personal banking were in the previous three chapters. The same concepts and principles are employed, with the goal of developing a working human resources department staffing model that can be used to predict and monitor optimum staffing levels. The approaches discussed in this chapter can be applied in other staff-related departments to achieve the same goals.

METHODOLOGY

The methodology in this chapter is the same basic approach used in the prior chapters—a five-step process of interviews, profile development, data gathering, model development, and running the model.

The concepts outlined in each of the five sections are standard in that they can be applied to any department in any organization. The only difference is that the detailed tasks and activities will vary by division.

Interviews

The starting point of any staffing analysis is the interview process, which outlines what is done in the particular department or division. To ensure that all tasks and activities are accounted for, all personnel in the human resources department must be interviewed.

The interviews are a fact-finding process. The interviewer seeks to find out the tasks, activities, and responsibilities of each employee in the department. The interviewer must be both a good listener, to make sure all information is covered, and a good director, to guide the employee to reveal overlooked tasks and assignments. During this phase, little analysis is done. It is more important to document as much information as possible; categorizing it will come later.

A typical interview session requires from 30 to 60 minutes of an employee's time. Throughout the process, the interviewer should become more and more knowledgeable about what the department does. This knowledge will help in categorizing tasks into the profile activities and associating them with key volume indicators. The actual profile will be developed from these data.

Profile Development

The employee profile essentially defines the activities within a given department. It is characterized by two major sections, fixed and variable activities. Fixed activities are those that by nature of the position are performed without regard to volume or primary output. Meetings, lunches, and breaks are typical fixed activities. During the development of the profile, fixed activities almost always fall into at least two categories, administrative and personal activities.

Variable activities, on the other hand, typically define the position and are its outputs. Every position is calculated to fulfill a specific purpose. For example, a commercial lender would not exist if there were no commercial loans to be made. In this case, the variable activities are the primary product produced by the position, the output that requires the majority of the individual's time and effort. They are variable because as the volume produced fluctuates, the amount of total time (and therefore the number of employees needed) will vary directly with that volume. These key volume indicators are the primary indicators upon which staff level is based.

Human resource personnel (and other staff-related positions) produce an output or product like any other position. For staff jobs, however, the output or key volume indicator may be more difficult to determine. In developing a profile for human resources personnel, the first question is, Why are they there? The duties of human resources professionals are principally recruitment, employee relations, and benefits administration. These are the primary elements; the actual activities fall into the six categories of recruitment/terminations, employee relations and development, benefits administration, compensation, general administration, and personal activities.

For human resources professionals, some activities can be both fixed and variable. In other words, some of the tasks performed within each category may directly depend on volume, while others are simply part of the job. To determine staffing levels accurately, both must be accounted for.

The human resources profile is then restated as follows:

1. Fixed activities:
   - Recruitment/terminations.
   - Employee relations and development.
   - Benefits administration.
   - General administration.
   - Personal.
2. Variable activities:
   - Recruitment.
   - Terminations.
   - Employee relations and development.
   - Compensation.
   - Benefits administration (general).
   - Benefits administration (new hires).
   - Benefits administration (terminations).

The original six core profile categories are accounted for in both the fixed and variable activities. Since the variable category is directly proportional to volume, its expansion of the profile to add terminations and new hires will increase the precision of the staffing model.

Based on industry study,[*] the most typical tasks related to the profile activities for most human resource departments are as follows:

1. Recruitment/terminations:
   - Interviewing/scheduling.
   - Recruiting.
   - New employee orientation.
   - College recruiting.
   - Applicant communications.
   - Exit interviews.
   - Outplacement.
   - Preretirement counseling.
   - Employee terminations.
   - Job postings/ad placement.
   - Job description development.
2. Employee relations and development:
   - Employee communications.
   - Promotion/transfer separation processing.
   - Newsletter.
   - Surveys.
   - Education/training.
   - Performance appraisals.
3. Compensation:
   - Payroll processing.
   - Incentive/bonus processing.
4. Benefits administration:
   - Insurance benefits claim processing.
   - Workers' compensation.
   - Pension/profit-sharing administration.
   - Unemployment compensation.
   - Affirmative action.
   - Recreational/social programs.
   - Health/wellness programs.

---

* Source: Bulletin to Management, *BNA Policy and Practice Series* (June 28, 1990), Bureau of National Affairs, Washington, DC 20037.

- Vacations/leaves of absence.
- Tuition/scholarships.
- Relocation services.
- In-house medical services.
- Flexible benefits plan administration.
- Child care.
- Occupational Safety and Health Administration (OSHA) compliance.

Since the general administration category involves the ongoing functioning of the department, the most common tasks might be as follows:

- Employee record-keeping (filing).
- Phone calls made/received.
- Messages taken.
- Phone calls transferred.
- Department billings.
- General filing.
- Miscellaneous reports.
- Meetings.

Each of these tasks can be split between fixed and variable activities as appropriate. The variable activities relate directly to volume, specifically the number of FTEs on staff, the number of new hires this month, the percentage of turnover, and the percentage of applicants hired.

These data must be captured and tracked for the model. This will be discussed in more detail later in this chapter.

Specific tasks associated with the profile categories are broken down between fixed and variable as follows:

I. Fixed activities/tasks
   A. Recruitment/terminations:
      1. College recruiting.
      2. General recruiting.
   B. Employee relations and development:
      1. Newsletters.

      2. Surveys.

      3. Education/training.

      4. Performance appraisals.

   C. Benefits administration:

      1. Pension/profit-sharing administration.

      2. Affirmative action.

      3. Recreational/social programs.

      4. Health/wellness programs.

      5. Flexible benefits plan administration.

      6. Safety/OSHA compliance.

   D. General administration:

      1. General filing.

      2. Telephone calls:

         External calls made/received.

         Phone calls redirected.

      3. Meetings:

         Departmental.

         Other.

      4. Miscellaneous reports.

      5. Departmental billings.

   E. Personal:

      1. Lunches.

      2. Breaks.

II. Variable activities/tasks

   A. Recruitment/terminations:

      1. Job description development.

      2. Job postings.

      3. Ad placement.

      4. Interview scheduling.

      5. Interviews.

      6. Pre-employment testing.

      7. Applicant communications.

      8. New employee orientation.

      9. Employee terminations (severance).

    10. Exit interviews.

    11. Preretirement counseling.

    12. Outplacement.

B. Employee relations and development:
    1. Employee communications:
        Internal calls from employees.
        External calls to employees.
        Meetings with employees.
    2. Promotion/transfer/separation processing.
C. Compensation:
    1. Payroll check processing.
    2. Incentive/bonus check processing.
D. Benefits administration:
    1. Insurance benefit claim processing.
    2. Workers' compensation claims.
    3. Unemployment claim compensation.
    4. Vacations/leaves of absence.
    5. Tuition reimbursement.
    6. Relocation handling.
    7. In-house medical services.
    8. Child care.
E. General administration:
    1. Employee record-keeping/filing.

The staff profile forms the foundation for the analysis. Each task performed will be associated with a profile item. In this way, one factor per profile activity can be used to assess the staffing levels needed while accounting for all tasks performed.

The next section of this chapter explains how the specific data are gathered and calculated to develop the standard factors used in the model.

Data Gathering

The data-gathering phase is vital to any staffing analysis. It involves obtaining data relative to volumes, frequency, and time estimates for the tasks performed. The tasks identified in the previous section are analyzed using a standard survey document (Appendix Exhibit I), which captures special information over a period of time. The survey is circulated to all members of the human resources department for completion over a two-week period.

Employees should be instructed to be as accurate as possible in providing time estimates for the completion of tasks. This approach is generally more realistic than a stopwatch time study. Any major differences (either overly conservative or overly liberal estimates) will even out once all estimates are averaged. The survey requires three basic types of information: time estimates, frequencies, and volumes.

Time estimates can usually be provided in one sitting if the employee devotes some care to thinking about them. The same is true with frequencies. If a particular task or activity occurs weekly, then its frequency is about four times per month.

Volume information, however, cannot be obtained in one sitting. Activity tally sheets attached to the survey are used to capture volume data. A tally mark is recorded for the particular activity as it occurs. This type of tallying should continue for two weeks, so each employee will submit 10 tally sheets with the survey. Actually, the longer tallying goes on, the greater precision in activity volumes will be obtained.

As will be demonstrated later in this section, the purpose of data gathering is to obtain the raw data unique to the financial institution that will be used in the calculations to determine the standard factor for each variable and fixed profile activity. These factors are the key variables for determining optimal staffing levels for the human resources department.

Only one survey is necessary for this department. Although specific positions can be identified in human resources, they often overlap and perform tasks associated with other profile activities. This will not hamper the analysis, for the staffing model will calculate and display optimum FTE staffing levels by each profile activity category. This not only will clarify needs by activity but also suggest how the activities should be divided among available positions. Each fixed and variable profile activity is outlined individually to illustrate the calculation or percentages and factors to be used in the model. A monthly total available hours per employee of 168.6 is used, for example, calculated in Figure 157. The user can vary this by supplementing elements of the formula as dictated by the individual bank's policy. This could then alter the amount of average working days per year. In Figure 157, 238

F I G U R E   157

Monthly Available Hours per Employee Calculation

	52	Weeks per year
×	5	Working days per week
	260	Working days per year
−	10	Holidays per year
−	2	Personal days per year
−	10	Average number of vacation days per year
=	238	Net working days per year
×	8.5	Total available hours per day
=	2,023	Total hours per year
÷	12	Months per year
=	168.6	Total monthly available hours

was used due to the amount of holidays, personal days, and vacation days allotted to employees in general. The actual working days could be 228 if 20 vacation days are allotted, or 240 if no personal days are granted. The important point is that the amount of working days per year can and will change based upon the policy of the bank.

Fixed Activities

All fixed activities for human resource personnel will be expressed as a percentage of available hours. Since fixed activities do not depend on the key volume indicators they occur on a very regular basis and require a specific percentage of an employee's available time at predictable intervals. Each of the fixed activities for human resource personnel is explained in the next section.

Recruitment/Terminations   Recruitment and terminations, as fixed activities, involve time devoted on a regular basis to attracting new personnel and talent to the organization. The specific activities related to this category center on college recruiting and general recruiting activities. From the survey data, the specific percentage of monthly available hours is calculated as in Figure

F I G U R E 158

Fixed: Recruitment/Termination

Activity	Total Min. Spent for All Employees/ Month		Min./ Hour		No. of Human Resources Employees		Avg. Hours/H.R. Employee/ Month
College recruiting	160	÷	60	÷	3	=	.89
General recruiting	80	÷	60	÷	3	=	.44
Total monthly hours per human resources employee						=	1.33
Monthly available hours per FTE						÷	168.6
Percentage of monthly available hours devoted to recruitment						=	.79%

158. The result, .79 percent, is an average per human resources employee. Although not every employee conducts recruiting sessions, this factor can be used in the staffing model to reveal the optimum number of FTEs required for this activity.

Employee Relations and Development Employee relations and development involves the generic duties associated with employee communications. These are not direct interactions with individual employees but rather global communications and relations. They would occur if there were one employee or one thousand. The specific tasks associated with employee relations as a fixed activity are employee/bank newsletters, employee surveys, education/training, and performance appraisal handling.

The human resources survey calls for an estimate of time devoted to such duties each month. The calculation is illustrated in Figure 159.

As indicated, the time estimate in minutes should be totaled for all employees before being averaged per employee.

Benefits Administration The administration of organization benefits involves the ongoing administration of company plans and programs. As a fixed activity this is nonspecific to individual

F I G U R E   159

Fixed: Employee Relations and Development

Activity	Total Min. Spent for All Employees/ Month		Min./ Hour	No. of Human Resources Employees		Avg. Hours/H.R. Employee/ Month
Employee newsletters	100	÷	60	÷ 3	=	.67
Employee surveys	30	÷	60	÷ 3	=	.17
Education/training	90	÷	60	÷ 3	=	.50
Performance appraisals	50	÷	60	÷ 3	=	.28
Total monthly hours per human resources employee					=	1.62
Monthly available hours per FTE					÷	168.6
Percentage of monthly available hours devoted to fixed employee relations					=	.96%

employees. A pension and profit-sharing plan involves regular maintenance regardless of how many employees are participants. As another example, an affirmative action plan may require regular attention to ensure compliance, but it does not relate specifically to any one employee or group of employees.

Fixed benefit administration activities could include pension and profit-sharing administration, affirmative action plans, recreational/social programs, health/wellness programs, flexible benefits plan administration, and safety/OSHA compliance.

Simply maintaining these plans and programs takes a regular amount of time. Using the data obtained from the survey, total the monthly time estimates for all employees and calculate the percentage of time available devoted to such tasks as shown in Figure 160.

General Administration   All departments have some general administrative tasks to perform. From a fixed activity standpoint these are generic tasks like filing, meetings, and phone calls that are nonspecific to the key volume indicators (employees). The specific tasks related to fixed general administrative tasks are

F I G U R E 160

Fixed: Benefits Administration

Activity	Total Min. Spent for All Employees/ Month		Min./ Hour		No. of Human Resources Employees		Avg. Hours/H.R. Employee/ Month
Pension/profit-sharing administration	1,200	÷	60	÷	3	=	6.67
Affirmative action	120	÷	60	÷	3	=	.67
Recreational/social programs	80	÷	60	÷	3	=	.44
Health/wellness programs	100	÷	60	÷	3	=	.56
Flexible benefits plan administration	50	÷	60	÷	3	=	.28
Safety/OSHA compliance	60	÷	60	÷	3	=	.33
Total monthly hours per human resources employee						=	8.95
Monthly available hours per FTE						÷	168.6
Percentage of monthly available hours devoted to fixed benefits administration						=	5.31%

general filing, departmental billings, telephone calls, miscellaneous reports, and meetings.

The raw data come from the employee survey. To determine the time factor devoted to these activities, three separate calculations are required. The first case, filing and billings, is similar to the other fixed activities in that a total time devoted to the function is determined, as shown in Figure 161.

In the second case, telephone calls, an average volume must be determined. This is accomplished by analyzing the human resources call tally, shown in Figure 162, which is submitted over a two-week period. Only external calls made/received, phone messages taken, and redirected calls are of concern for this category.

Miscellaneous reports must also be accounted for. Their volume can be determined from the human resources activity tally shown in Figure 163. Unlike the phone tally, the activity tally does not list days. If volume is not heavy, one can be used over

F I G U R E   161
Administrative: Filing/Billing

Activity	Total Min. Spent for All Employees/ Month		Min./ Hour		No. of Human Resources Employees		Avg. Hours/H.R. Employee/ Month
General filing	1,800	÷	60	÷	3	=	10.00
Department billings	300	÷	60	÷	3	=	1.67
Total monthly hours per employee						=	11.67

F I G U R E   162
Human Resources Call Tally

| Day | Employee Communications | | | | General | |
	Call from Employee	Call to Employee	Meeting with Employee	External Calls Made/ Received	Message Taken	Call Redirect
Monday						
Tuesday						
Wednesday						
Thursday						
Friday						
Saturday						
TOTAL						

F I G U R E 163

Human Resources Activity Tally

Activity	Tally	Total
Job posting		
Job description development		
Ad posting		
Applicant calls		
Exit interviews		
Preretirement counseling		
Outplacement processing		
Promotion/transfer processing		
Incentive/bonus check processing		
Insurance claims processing		
Workers' compensation claims		
Unemployment claims		
Vacation/leave of absence processing		
Tuition reimbursement		
Relocation handling		
Providing in-house medical service		
Providing child-care service		
Preparing miscellaneous reports		
Filing employee records		

Administrative: Phone Calls/Miscellaneous Reports

Activity	Total Dept. Vol.		Weeks to Annualize		Months/ Year		No. of H.R. Employees on Staff		Avg. Vol./H.R. Employee/ Month		Avg. Min./ Item		Min./ Hour		Avg. Hours/H.R. Employee/ Month
External calls made/ received	150	×	26	÷	12	÷	3	=	108.34	×	2.5	÷	60	=	4.52
Phone messages taken	200	×	26	÷	12	÷	3	=	144.5	×	.75	÷	60	=	1.81
Phone calls redirected	175	×	26	÷	12	÷	3	=	126.4	×	.25	÷	60	=	.53
Miscellaneous reports prepared	30	×	26	÷	12	÷	3	=	21.7	×	35	÷	60	=	12.66
Total hours per human resource employee per month														=	19.52

Administrative: Meeting Time Spent

Activity	Avg. Minutes/ Session		Avg. Freq./ Month		Min./ Hour		Avg. Hours/H.R. Employee/Month
Departmental meetings	60	×	1	÷	60	=	1.00
Training/seminars	90	×	.17	÷	60	=	.255
Total hours per employee per month						=	1.225

the two-week period. Otherwise, 10 must be completed. The analysis of phone calls and miscellaneous reports prepared is shown in Figure 164.

The last area, meetings, does not require the completion of a tally sheet. Both time estimates and frequency can be determined from the human resources survey. Only meetings that occur on a regular basis should be accounted for. These are usually departmental meetings and training seminars. Impromptu meetings need not be addressed, as they are not a standing commitment of time. The calculation of the time involved for meetings is illustrated in Figure 165. It is best to obtain an average of all respondent time estimates and frequencies per month.

Now that the three aspects of general administration have been quantified, the hours should be restated into a percentage of total available hours, as shown in Figure 166.

Personal   The last fixed category is personal activities, principally lunches and breaks, that take time away from that available for other fixed and/or variable activities. The time estimates for this are averaged from the human resources survey, as shown in Figure 167.

F I G U R E   166

General Administrative Summary

Activity	Average Monthly Hours per Human Resources Employee
Filing and billings	11.67
Phone calls/miscellaneous reports	19.52
Meetings	1.23
Total	32.42
Monthly average hours per FTE	÷ 168.6
Percentage of total available hours devoted to general administration per FTE	19.2%

F I G U R E 167

Fixed: Personal Activities

Activity	Avg. Min./ Occurrence		Days/ Month		Min./Hour		Avg. Hours/ Employee/ Month
Lunches	60	÷	21.7	÷	60	=	21.7
Breaks	15	÷	21.7	÷	60	=	5.4
Total monthly hours per FTE						=	27.12
Total monthly available hours per FTE						÷	168.6
Percentage of total monthly hours devoted to personal activities per FTE							16.1%

Recap: Fixed Activities This completes the analysis and determination of the factors for each fixed activity to be used in the staffing model. Figure 168 summarizes these percentages. Approximately 42.4 percent of the total monthly available hours are dedicated to fixed activities. This leaves about 57.5 percent of an individual's time for the key volume indicators associated with human resources. The actual percentages of times devoted to these activities

F I G U R E 168

Fixed Activities Summary

Activity	Percentage
Recruitment/terminations	.79%
Employee relations and development	.96
Benefits administration	5.31
General administration	19.2
Personal	16.1
Total	42.4%

may differ, but the approach will be the same. All tasks and categories must be accounted for to determine the appropriate factors for use in the staffing model.

Variable Activities

Variable activities for human resources are those tasks that occur as a result of and in direct proportion to the number of people on staff, new hires, terminations, and so forth. In other words, the amount of staff needed to handle these activities will depend directly on how often they occur. Unlike fixed activities, variable activities don't have to occur if there is no volume. However, if there were no volume there would be no need for the particular position.

The variable activities are similar to the fixed activities, but with some additions. The variable activity categories are recruitment, termination, employee relations and development, compensation, and benefits administration. Benefits administration is broken into subcategories of general, new hires, and terminations, so its latter two categories can be tied directly to volume. Terminations are now a separate category for the same reason.

The following sections outline each variable category, identifying the tasks that comprise it and showing the calculation of the monthly factor to be used in the model. For all variable activities, the factor is stated in hours rather than as a percentage of monthly available hours, so it can be applied directly to the volume incurred.

Recruitment   Recruitment is the process of screening, analyzing, and selecting new employees for the bank. As a variable activity, it refers to the volume of applicants generated from the initial need and the process they go through in order to be hired. The key volume indicator for the staffing model is the volume of applicants seen.

To calculate the hourly factor (time factor) per applicant, the analyst must understand the recruiting process. This will vary by financial institution, but a standard flow of steps would include:

- Prescreen applicants.
- Schedule first interview.
- Conduct first interview.
- Administer pre-employment test.
- Schedule second interview.
- Conduct second interview.
- Check references.
- Conduct new employee orientation.

For each of the eight levels of recruiting, the average survival rate must be determined, as a percentage. The starting point may be to determine what percentage of all applicants end up being hired. This type of information may already be tracked. If not, ask human resource personnel to estimate the percentage of applicants surviving at each level.

Ascertain what percentage of all applicants are typically hired and work backwards. This type of data is valuable and should be tracked regularly anyway for greater precision. A good tracking tool is a production or data sheet for each position being filed, as illustrated in Figure 169. This data sheet can then be stored and an average taken at each stage.

From the data in Figure 169, determine a portion of the recruitment factor by using the time estimates for these items in the human resources survey, averaging the time per employee and applying it to the volume of applicants. As Figure 170 illustrates, this is a more or less weighted average approach to determining a time factor that can be used for any applicant.

When the bank is comfortable with the survival percentages of applicants by activity level, the time factor will become most accurate.

This, however, does not complete the analysis. It is still necessary to account for other tasks: jobs posted, job descriptions developed, ads placed, and applicant communications.

Since these items are more all-encompassing, their average volume must be tracked over a two-week period. Using the human resources activity tally (Figure 163), each employee can tally the volume of these items taken over two weeks. Since the key

F I G U R E   169

Applicant Processing Data Sheet

Position being sought: _____
Date sought: _____
Number of applications obtained: _____

Activity	Number of Applicants Remaining	Percentage of Original Applicants Remaining
Prescreen applicants	300	100.0%
Schedule interviews	85	28.3%
Conduct interviews	85	28.3%
Administer pre-employment tests	45	15.0%
Schedule second interviews	25	8.3%
Conduct interviews	25	8.3%
Check references	25	8.3%
Conduct new employee orientation	15	5.0%

F I G U R E   170

Variable: Recruitment

Activity	Applicant Survivor Percentage		Avg. Min./ Activity		Min./ Hour		Total Hours/ Applicant
Prescreen applicants	100.0%	×	.75	÷	60	=	.02
Schedule interviews	28.0	×	10	÷	60	=	.05
Conduct interviews	28.0	×	25	÷	60	=	.12
Administer pre-employment tests	15.0	×	30	÷	60	=	.08
Schedule second interviews	8.3	×	10	÷	60	=	.02
Conduct interviews	8.3	×	25	÷	60	=	.04
Check references	8.3	×	17	÷	60	=	.03
Conduct new employee orientation	5.0	×	35	÷	60	=	.03
Total hours per applicant						=	.39

F I G U R E 171

Fixed: Recruitment

	Total Dept. Vol.		Weeks to Annualize		Months/ Year		No. of Applicants This Period		Multiple/ Applicant		Avg. Min./ Item		Min./ Hour		Avg. Hours/ Applicant
Jobs posted	10	×	26	÷	12	÷	300	=	.08	×	15	÷	60	=	.02
Job descriptions developed	8	×	26	÷	12	÷	300	=	.06	×	35	÷	60	=	.04
Ads placed	15	×	26	÷	12	÷	300	=	.11	×	15	÷	60	=	.03
Applicant communications	100	×	26	÷	12	÷	300	=	.73	×	1.5	÷	60	=	.02
Total average hours per applicant														=	.11

volume indicator is applicants, the volume of these items produced should be associated with the number of applicants received during that time.

The calculation of these factors from the survey and activity tally is shown in Figure 171. Add the result of .11 to the overall .39 (from Figure 170) to determine the total recruitment factor, .50 hour.

The number of applicants used in Figure 171 is an extrapolation, accurate and consistent with the formulas used in the model. Most human resource departments can provide the number of new hires. Figure 170 shows that, on average, 5 percent of all applicants reviewed are hired. So the number of applicants needed is 300, or 15 new hires divided by .05.

Employee Terminations Although not a separate part of the human resources profile, termination processing and analyzing are handled separately for ease of use in the model. Variable termination processing is directly related to the volume or number of staff that are leaving the bank as a result of voluntary or involuntary termination. Specific tasks are not performed unless a termination occurs. The specific tasks of human resources personnel are employee termination processing (severance, final pay, etc.), exit interviews, preretirement counseling, and outplacement. Benefits administration may also be involved from an insurance standpoint, but it will be discussed later in the chapter.

To determine the time factors required for this activity, average the time estimates provided in the human resources survey. Average only the time spent by staff members who actually perform these tasks. An analysis of the calculations required is illustrated in Figure 172.

As noted in Figure 172, one must know the mix of types of terminations to arrive at an hourly factor per termination. Employment terminations generally fall into two major categories, voluntary and involuntary. To be more precise, however, a third can be added for retirement. Voluntary terminations are resignations; involuntary may be dismissals for cause, reductions in force, or layoffs. If these data are not maintained in this particular order, the organization undoubtedly has the employee records to

F I G U R E   172

Variable: Employee Terminations

Termination Type	Total Occurrences/ Year	Percentage to Total	Minutes/ Termination		Minutes/ Hour		Weighted Avg. Time Factor/ Type
Voluntary	100	52.6%	×	75	÷	60	=	.66
Retirement	30	15.8	×	60	÷	60	=	.16
Involuntary	60	31.6	×	105	÷	60	=	.55
Total	190	100.0%					
Average hours per termination						=	1.37

Minutes per Termination

Activity	Voluntary	Retirement	Involuntary
Employee termination processing	30		30
Exit interview	45		45
Preretirement counseling		60	
Outplacement	—	—	30
Total time	75	60	105

reconstruct the reasons for someone ending employment. Obtain the number of terminations, by the three categories, over a period of six months to one year, if possible. Then determine a mix by percentage, from which a weighted average time factor can be determined that will yield a blended factor to be applied to any termination. The last element is the average time factor per activity for the department.

Figure 172's result of 1.37 hours per termination is the hourly factor that will be used in the staffing model.

Employee Relations and Development   Employee relations as a variable activity relates to those activities that can vary in volume based upon a specific key volume indicator. In this case, the key volume indicator is the number of employees on staff. As this

F I G U R E   173

Variable: Employee Relations and Development

Activity	Freq./ Employee/ Month		Avg. Min./ Item		Min./ Hour		Avg. Hours/ Employee/ Month
Communications							
Internal calls	.52	×	10	÷	60	=	.09
External calls	.26	×	8	÷	60	=	.04
Meetings	.16	×	20	÷	60	=	.05
Promotion/ Transfer/Separation	.05	×	25	÷	60	=	.02
Total hours per employee per month						=	.20

Activity	Total Dept. Vol.		Weeks to Annualize		Months/ Year		No. of Employees on File		Freq./ Employee/ Month
Communications									
Internal calls	100	×	26	÷	12	÷	418	=	.52
External calls	50	×	26	÷	12	÷	418	=	.26
Meetings	30	×	26	÷	12	÷	418	=	.16
Promotion/ transfer/ separation	10	×	26	÷	12	÷	418	=	.05

number changes, the volume of activities will also change proportionately.

Employee relations and development is made up of two major sections: employee communications and promotion/transfer/separation processing. Employee communications involve internal phone calls from employees, external phone calls to employees, and face-to-face meetings with employees. The reasons for these communications may be disciplinary problems, career planning, or general employee counseling.

Time estimates to perform each activity are taken, as an average for the department, from the human resources survey. The volume of items must be obtained from the human resources call tally (Figure 162) and activity tally (Figure 163). These data are totaled and analyzed as in Figure 173.

The total occurrence of each activity is associated with the total number of employees in existence, so the time factor per employee per month is representative of the average actual time taken. As the employee base increases or decreases, the total time required for employee relations will fluctuate in direct proportion. The result of .2 hour per employee means that approximately 12 minutes are devoted to each employee each month for career planning, disciplinary, or general counseling activities. This is an average; the reality is fewer employees who each require more time. The bottom line, however, is that this factor is associated with the key volume indicator of employees on staff (FTE).

Compensation   Another variable activity directly associated with the number of employees on staff is compensation, the processing of payroll and bonus/incentive checks. Payroll processing is usually a fairly labor-intensive process and is sometimes its own department. In any event, it is directly related to the size of the staff, so the time required to process the payroll must be associated with the total number of FTEs on staff to determine a per-FTE time factor. This is based on the survey's estimate of time devoted to processing payroll and other types of bonus/incentive checks each month. The calculation is illustrated in Figure 174. The bonus/incentives total is based on 48 hours annually and assumes a once-a-year occurrence.

The total time is associated with the key volume indicator, employees on staff, to develop a factor per employee. The total time, then, will fluctuate proportionately with increases or decreases to the total staff.

Benefits Administration   The last category of variable activities is benefits administration, the processing of benefit claims that are directly proportionate to occurrence, volume, and the number of employees on staff. The specific tasks under variable activities for this category are as follows:

Variable: Compensation

	Total Min./ Month		Avg. Min./Hour		No. of Employees on Staff		Avg. Hours/ Employee
Payroll	2,025	÷	60	÷	418	=	.08
Bonus/incentives	240	÷	60	÷	418	=	.0095
Total monthly hours per FTE							.0895

- Insurance benefit claims.
- Workers' compensation claims.
- Unemployment compensation claims.
- Vacation/leave of absence processing.
- Tuition reimbursement.
- Relocation handling.
- In-house medical services.
- Child care service.

Employees will require these services at different intervals and times, but they will require most of them at some point. For this reason the volume of occurrence for these hours is tracked (via the activity tally) and then associated directly to the amount of employees on staff. Although this tally contains only two weeks' worth of volumes, it will suffice for determining the hourly factor.

If more precision is desired, consider tracking these volumes by activity on an ongoing basis. Regular tracking will virtually guarantee complete accuracy in determining the hourly factor associated with benefits administration. In addition to volumes, the survey provides time estimates for handling each task. The time estimates and volumes are combined to complete the analysis as illustrated in Figure 175.

According to Figure 175, approximately .023 hour (or 1.38 minutes) is spent each month for each employee on benefits

F I G U R E 1 7 5

Variable: General Benefits Administration

Activity	Frequency/ Employee/Month		Average Minutes/Item		Minutes/ Hour		Average Hours/ Employee/Month
Insurance claims	.05	×	10	÷	60	=	.008
Workers' compensation	.01	×	20	÷	60	=	.003
Unemployment claims	.01	×	25	÷	60	=	.004
Vacation/leave of absence	.01	×	15	÷	60	=	.003
Tuition reimbursement	.015	×	20	÷	60	=	.005
Relocation	0	×	30	÷	60	=	0
Medical services	0	×	30	÷	60	=	0
Child care	0	×	30	÷	60	=	0
Total hours per employee per month						=	.023

Activity	Total Department Volume		Weeks to Annualize	Months/ Year		No. of Employees on File		Frequency/ Employee/ Month
Insurance claims	10	×	26	12	÷	418	=	.05
Workers' compensation	1	×	26	12	÷	418	=	.01
Unemployment claims	1	×	26	12	÷	418	=	.01
Vacation/leave of absence	1	×	26	12	÷	418	=	.01
Tuition reimbursement	2	×	26	12	÷	418	=	.015
Relocation	0	×	26	12	÷	418	=	0
Medical services	0	×	26	12	÷	418	=	0
Child care	0	×	26	12	÷	418	=	0

F I G U R E 176

Variable: Specific Benefits Administration

Activity	Average Minutes	Minutes per Hour	Average Hours per Activity
New hires	30	÷ 60	= .50
Terminations	30	÷ 60	= .50

administration, in general. The .023 factor will be used in the model.

In addition to general benefit administration, time is also spent with new hires and on terminating employees' benefits, particularly insurance. The key volume indicator for these is not total employees, as in general benefits administration. They are directly associated with the volumes of new hires and terminating employees. If there were none, no time would be spent in this area.

The accounting for this is relatively simple. Using the survey, average the estimates of time spent handling these activities. The minutes need only be restated as hours, as illustrated in Figure 176. In this example, a half hour is spent counseling employees on their various insurance benefits and issues as they join or leave the organization. Since these tasks are associated directly with different key volume indicators, they require separate input fields in the human resources staffing model, which appears at the end of this section (Figure 181).

Recap: Variable Activities   This completes the data gathering, calculations, and analysis of the information needed to develop the factors for the staffing model. Figure 177 summarizes the variable activity factors determined in the previous pages.

Summary/Analysis

As in the previous chapters, the data-gathering phase yields standards for each of the fixed and variable activities in the profile. However, these estimates may be distorted. To check this, analyze

F I G U R E   177
Variable Activities Summary

Activity	Hourly Factor
Recruitment (per applicant)	.50
Terminations	1.37
Employee relations and development	.20
Compensation	.0895
Benefits administration (general)	.023
Benefits administration (new hires)	.50
Benefits administration (terminations)	.50

the pool of existing hours and assign available hours to the actual work completed to determine the actual hours spent and/or a more accurate variable hourly factor. The comparison of the standard to the actual lends precision to the data contained in the staffing model.

It is assumed that the percentages of times devoted to fixed activities are accurate—a reasonable assumption, since the time devoted is clearly legitimate. Lunches and breaks are a good example, as are meetings. It is certain how much time will be spent on these per day.

The first part of the analysis is to calculate how many hours are available for other activities after the fixed activities are subtracted. This analysis is shown in Figure 178.

From the data obtained in Figure 178, the analysis can be completed to determine the actual hourly factors per variable activity. Simply divide the remaining hours available for variable activities among the variable activities to determine the factors. Since only a finite number of hours remains after the fixed activities, only so much time can be assigned to the variable tasks. This analysis is shown in Figure 179. The calculated hourly factor is from Figure 177 and the hours remaining from Figure 178.

Based on the previous calculations, the actual and standard variable factors can be compared.

F I G U R E   178

Total Departmental Fixed and Variable Hours

1. Total monthly hours available per human resources FTE		168.6
2. Total number of human resource FTEs		× 3
3. Total departmental hours available per month		505.8

Fixed Activity	Percentage of Time Devoted		Total Departmental Hours Available		Total Departmental Hours Committed
Recruitment/ terminations	.96	×	505.8	=	4.85
Employee relations and development	.79	×	505.8	=	.40
Benefits administration	5.31	×	505.8	=	26.86
General administration	19.3	×	505.8	=	97.62
Personal	16.1	×	505.8	=	81.43
Total fixed hours committed				=	214.76
Total hours available for variable activities (505.8 − 214.76 = 291.04)				=	291.04

Variable Activity	Standard Hours	Actual Hours	Difference
Recruitment	.50	.63	.13
Terminations	1.37	1.70	.33
Employee relations/ development	.20	.25	.05
Compensation	.08	.12	.04
Benefits administration:			
General	.023	.03	.007
New hires	.50	.63	.13
Terminations	.50	.62	.12

The difference between the actual and standard hours is slight, indicating that the standard factors determined in the data-gathering section are very accurate. The standard factors appear a bit more conservative, since more time is actually avail-

278

Actual Variable Activity Hourly Factors

Variable Activity	Average Monthly Volume		Calculated Hourly Factor		Total Hours Required	Percentage of Total Hours		Hours Remaining for Variable Activities		Average Monthly Volume		Actual Variable Activity Hourly Factor
Recruitment	125	×	.50	=	62.5	26.7	×	291.04	÷	125	=	.63
Terminations	16.3	×	1.37	=	22.3	9.5	×	291.04	÷	16.3	=	1.70
Employee relations/ development	418	×	.20	=	83.6	35.7	×	291.04	÷	418	=	.25
Compensation	418	×	.0895	=	37.42	16.0	×	291.04	÷	418	=	.12
Benefits administration												
General	418	×	.023	=	9.61	4.1	×	291.04	÷	418	=	.03
New hires	21	×	.50	=	10.5	4.5	×	291.04	÷	21	=	.63
Terminations	16.3	×	.50	=	8.15	3.5	×	291.04	÷	16.3	=	.63
					234.08	100.0%						

F I G U R E 180

Human Resources Profile Summary

1. Fixed activities	Percentage of Available Hours
Recruitment/terminations	.79%
Employee relations/ development	.96
Benefits administration	.5.31
General administration	19.3
Personal	16.1

2. Variable activities	Hourly Factors*
Recruitment	.57
Terminations	1.55
Employee relations/ development	.23
Compensation	.09
Benefits administration:	
General	.03
New hires	.57
Terminations	.57

*Average of standard and actual factors.

able to spend on the variable tasks. For greater accuracy, use the average of the actual and standard factors in the model.

Figure 180 summarizes the fixed and variable activity factors that will be used in the human resources staffing model. These items are then shown in an example of the staffing model itself, Figure 181. The model will be constructed in the next section.

Model Development and Reports

A staffing model has been developed to aid in predicting optimum staffing levels in the human resources department. The model provides management with an analytical tool to use in

F I G U R E   181

Human Resources Staffing Model

```
BANK:            [      ]    HUMAN RESOURCES STAFFING MODEL      DATE:    [        ]
LOCATION:        [      ]
BRANCH:          [      ]
```

```
DATA REQUIRED
    # NEW HIRES THIS MONTH:   [      ]  AVG. # TOTAL HOURS PER FTE PER DAY:    [        ]
    % TURNOVER:               [      ]  PERCENT OF APPLICANTS HIRED:           [        ]
    # FTE ON STAFF:           [      ]
```

A. FIXED HOURS (PER FTE):

	% OF TOTAL MONTHLY HOURS	ACTUAL MONTHLY HOURS USED
GENERAL ADMINISTRATION:	[19.30%]	0.00
EMPLOYEE RECRUITMENT:	[0.79%]	0.00
EMPLOYEE RELATIONS:	[0.96%]	0.00
BENEFITS ADMINISTRATION:	[5.31%]	0.00
PERSONAL:	[16.10%]	0.00
TOTAL:	42.46%	0.00%

B. VARIABLE HOURS:

	STANDARD HOURS REQUIRED PER ITEM	ACTUAL MONTHLY HOURS USED
EMPLOYEE RECRUITMENT:	[0.570]	0.00
EMPLOYEE TERMINATIONS:	[1.550]	0.00
EMPLOYEE RELATIONS/DEV.:	[0.230]	0.00
COMPENSATION:	[0.090]	0.00
BENEFITS ADMINISTRATION:	[0.030]	0.00
BENEFITS—NEW HIRES:	[0.570]	0.00
BENEFITS—TERMINATIONS:	[0.570]	0.00
TOTAL:		0.00

C. DISTRIBUTION OF MONTHLY HOURS REQUIRED, BY CATEGORY:

	TOTAL MONTHLY HOURS		TOTAL FTE REQUIRED
EMPLOYEE RECRUITMENT:	0.00	EMPLOYEE RECRUITMENT/TERM.:	0.00
EMPLOYEE RELATIONS/DEV.:	0.00	EMPLOYEE RELATIONS/DEV.:	0.00
COMPENSATION:	0.00	COMPENSATION:	0.00
BENEFITS VARIABLE:	0.00	BENEFITS ADMINISTRATION:	0.00
GENERAL ADMINISTRATION:	0.00	GENERAL ADMINISTRATION:	0.00
EMPLOYEE RECRUITMENT:	0.00	PERSONAL:	0.00
EMPLOYEE RELATIONS:	0.00		
BENEFITS ADMINISTRATION:	0.00		
PERSONAL:	0.00		
TOTAL MONTHLY HOURS:	0.00	TOTAL STAFF REQUIRED:	0.00

determining the appropriate staffing levels for the department based upon key volume indicators. The key volume indicators used in the model are as follows:

- Number of applicants.
- Number of new hires.
- Number of terminations.
- Number of total FTEs on staff (bank-wide).

This section of the chapter provides the specifics on how to create and use the staffing model. Detailed instructions allow anyone using this book to actually construct an organization staffing model for ongoing use. Essentially, the staffing model will tell management the optimum FTE staff needed to perform the functions in human resources, based on each profile activity and total. Pinpointing how many FTEs are required, for which activity, allows management to assign and utilize the staff properly. The model also calculates an overall total optimum FTE staff size.

Creating the Model

The staffing model was developed using Lotus 1, 2, 3, version 2.01. An exact duplicate of Figure 182 can be created in any bank using the Lotus spreadsheet software. Each cell is coded by a number. This section provides exact instructions for building the model, including formulas and number codes.

The individual responsible for creating the model should first develop its structure or format. This is the physical appearance—all headings, titles, brackets, and boundary lines. Figure 182 should be recreated so that it fits on an 8 1/2" × 11" sheet of paper. The spacing and positioning of headings, brackets, and so forth should copy the example as closely as possible.

The developer should then review the explanations corresponding to the code number in the model. In some cases, nothing needs to be added at this time; in other cases, a formula is provided. A narrative formula explains the components of the formula, and a formula in the language of Lotus 1, 2, 3 follows. Since

F I G U R E 182

Human Resources Staffing Model

BANK:	[1]	HUMAN RESOURCES STAFFING MODEL	DATE:	[4]
LOCATION:	[2]			
BRANCH:	[3]			

DATA REQUIRED

# NEW HIRES THIS MONTH:	[5]	AVG. # TOTAL HOURS PER FTE PER DAY:	[8]
% TURNOVER:	[6]	PERCENT OF APPLICANTS HIRED:	[9]
# FTE ON STAFF:	[7]		

A. FIXED HOURS (PER FTE):

	% OF TOTAL MONTHLY HOURS	ACTUAL MONTHLY HOURS USED
GENERAL ADMINISTRATION:	[10]	16
EMPLOYEE RECRUITMENT:	[11]	17
EMPLOYEE RELATIONS:	[12]	18
BENEFITS ADMINISTRATION:	[13]	19
PERSONAL:	[14]	20
TOTAL:	15	21

B. VARIABLE HOURS:

	STANDARD HOURS REQUIRED PER ITEM	ACTUAL MONTHLY HOURS USED
EMPLOYEE RECRUITMENT:	[22]	29
EMPLOYEE TERMINATIONS:	[23]	30
EMPLOYEE RELATIONS/DEV.:	[24]	31
COMPENSATION:	[25]	32
BENEFITS ADMINISTRATION:	[26]	33
BENEFITS—NEW HIRES:	[27]	34
BENEFITS—TERMINATIONS:	[28]	35
TOTAL:		36

C. DISTRIBUTION OF MONTHLY HOURS REQUIRED, BY CATEGORY:

	TOTAL MONTHLY HOURS		TOTAL FTE REQUIRED
EMPLOYEE RECRUITMENT:	37	EMPLOYEE RECRUITMENT/TERM.:	47
EMPLOYEE RELATIONS/DEV.:	38	EMPLOYEE RELATIONS/DEV.:	48
COMPENSATION:	39	COMPENSATION:	49
BENEFITS VARIABLE:	40	BENEFITS ADMINISTRATION:	50
GENERAL ADMINISTRATION:	41	GENERAL ADMINISTRATION:	51
EMPLOYEE RECRUITMENT:	42	PERSONAL:	52
EMPLOYEE RELATIONS:	43		
BENEFITS ADMINISTRATION:	44		
PERSONAL:	45		
TOTAL MONTHLY HOURS:	46	TOTAL STAFF REQUIRED:	53

the cell addresses are uncertain, the code numbers in Figure 182 will be used in their place. When the developer inputs the appropriate formula, he or she must translate the code number into the proper cell format on the spreadsheet.

1, 2, and 3. Bank, location, and branch: Space must be created to all for the input of the bank's name, address, and branch name (if applicable). The space must contain enough room to allow for at least 15 to 20 characters. Brackets are put outside the cell to indicate that this is a required input field.

4. Date: Space should be created to allow 15 to 20 characters to provide the month and year, enclosed by brackets.

5, 6, 7, 8, and 9. Data required: These cells all require an input and are therefore surrounded by brackets. In these fields, numbers rather than letters are required. Enough space should be allowed in each cell for at least six to eight characters. Each cell should be formatted to contain at least one decimal, since the averages used for this input may contain fractions.

The second data field, "percent of turnover," should be formatted to reflect a percentage.

Section A: Fixed Hours (per FTE)

10–14. Percentage of total monthly hours: This is the first profile activity item requiring input. Since the five fixed activities are stated as a percentage of variable hours, each will have a percentage input. Enough space should be allowed, in each cell, to allow for six characters to include the percent sign (100.0%). The cells should be bracketed and formatted to reflect percentages carried out to at least one decimal.

15. Total fixed hours as percentage of total monthly hours: This is the first of the automatically calculated fields, so no input and no brackets are required. In this cell, input a formula that will sum the fixed activity percentages. The narrative formula is:

$$\left(\begin{array}{l} \text{General} \\ \text{admin.} \\ \text{percentage} \end{array} + \begin{array}{l} \text{Employee} \\ \text{recruitment} \\ \text{percentage} \end{array} + \begin{array}{l} \text{Employee} \\ \text{relations} \\ \text{percentage} \end{array} + \begin{array}{l} \text{Benefit} \\ \text{admin.} \\ \text{percentage} \end{array} + \begin{array}{l} \text{Personal} \\ \text{percentage} \end{array} \right)$$

Lotus formula:

@sum(10..14)

16–20. Actual monthly hours used: Each cell contains an automatic formula to calculate the total monthly hours devoted to each fixed activity per FTE. The narrative formula is:

$$\left(\begin{array}{l} \text{Average} \\ \text{total hours} \\ \text{per FTE} \\ \text{per day} \end{array} \times \begin{array}{l} 238 \\ \text{working} \\ \text{days} \\ \text{per year} \end{array} \div \begin{array}{l} 12 \text{ months} \\ \text{per year} \end{array} \times \begin{array}{l} \text{Fixed} \\ \text{activity} \\ \text{percentage of} \\ \text{available} \\ \text{hours} \end{array} \right)$$

Lotus formulas:

16	((8*238)/1)*10
17	((8*238)/1)*11
18	((8*238)/1)*12
19	((8*238)/1)*13
20	((8*238)/1)*14

21. Total actual monthly hours used: This is an automatic formula field and requires no input. The formula will sum the actual monthly hours for items 16 through 20. The narrative formula is:

$$\left(\begin{array}{l} \text{General} \\ \text{administration} \\ \text{hours} \end{array} + \begin{array}{l} \text{Employee} \\ \text{recruitment} \\ \text{hours} \end{array} + \begin{array}{l} \text{Employee} \\ \text{relations} \\ \text{hours} \end{array} + \begin{array}{l} \text{Benefit} \\ \text{administration} \\ \text{hours} \end{array} + \begin{array}{l} \text{Personal} \\ \text{hours} \end{array} \right)$$

Lotus formula:

@sum(16..20)

Section B: Variable Hours

22–28. Standard hours required per item: In the variable activities of the human resources profile, each cell requires input and is therefore framed by brackets. Unlike the fixed activity percentages, these will be reflected as whole numbers. Allow enough space to carry them out to three decimals (12.082).

29–35. Actual monthly hours used: These are automatic formula fields and require no input. For each cell, build a formula to calculate the total monthly hours required to accommodate the volume. The key volume indicator data are contained in the "data required" section (items 5-9). Allow space for at least eight characters to two decimal places (e.g., xxxx.xx). The narrative formulas are:

29   ((Number of FTE on staff × percent of turnover) / percentage of applicants hired) × employee recruitment standard hours per item

30   (Number of FTE on staff × percent of turnover) × employee terminations standard hours per item

31   (Number of FTE on staff × employee relations / development standard hours per item)

32   (Number of FTE on staff × compensation standard hours per item)

33   (Number of FTE on staff × benefits administration standard hours per item)

34   (Number of new hires this month × benefits administration – new hires standard hours per item)

35   (Number of FTE on staff × percent of turnover) × benefits administration – terminations standard hours per item

Lotus formulas:

29   ((7*6)/9)*22
30   ((7*6)/9)*23
31   (7*24)
32   (7*25)
33   (7*26)
34   (5*27)
35   (7*6)*28

36. Total actual monthly hours used: This is a formula field and requires no brackets. The formula will sum the actual monthly hours used for each of the variable activities. The narrative formula is:

$$\left(\begin{array}{l} \text{Employee} \\ \text{recruitment} \\ \text{actual} \\ \text{hours} \end{array} + \begin{array}{l} \text{Employee} \\ \text{terminations} \\ \text{actual} \\ \text{hours} \end{array} + \begin{array}{l} \text{Employee} \\ \text{relations /} \\ \text{development} \\ \text{actual} \\ \text{hours} \end{array} + \begin{array}{l} \text{Compensation} \\ \text{actual} \\ \text{hours} \end{array} + \right.$$

$$\left. \begin{array}{l} \text{Benefits} \\ \text{administration} \\ \text{actual} \\ \text{hours} \end{array} + \text{Benefits} - \begin{array}{l} \text{New} \\ \text{hires} \\ \text{actual} \\ \text{hours} \end{array} + \text{Benefits} - \begin{array}{l} \text{Terminations} \\ \text{actual} \\ \text{hours} \end{array} \right)$$

Lotus formula:

@sum(29..35)

Section C: Distribution of Monthly Hours Required
37–45. Total monthly hours, by category: Section C is entirely formula driven; no input is required. This last section calculates the actual staffing total hours used, from which the optimum staffing level recommendations will be derived. The categories included (items 37-45) contain both fixed and variable activities. The narrative formula is:

37   (employee recruitment variable monthly hours + employee terminations variable monthly hours)
38   (employee relations/development variable monthly hours)
39   (compensation variable monthly hours)
40   (benefits administration variable monthly hours + benefits – new hires variable monthly hours + benefits - terminations variable monthly hours)
41   ((employee recruitment total monthly hours + employee relations/development total monthly hours + compensation total monthly hours + benefits variable total monthly hours) / (1 – total fixed hours percentage)) × general administration fixed percentage
42   ((employee recruitment total monthly hours + employee relations/ development total monthly

hours + compensation total monthly hours +
benefits variable total monthly hours) / (1 – total
fixed hours percentage)) × employee recruitment
fixed percentage

43   ((employee recruitment total monthly hours +
employee relations / development total monthly
hours + compensation total monthly hours +
benefits variable total monthly hours) / (1 – total
fixed hours percentage)) × employee relations
fixed percentage

44   ((employee recruitment total monthly hours +
employee relations / development total monthly
hours + compensation total monthly hours +
benefits variable total monthly hours) / (1 – total
fixed hours percentage)) × benefits administration
fixed percentage

45   ((employee recruitment total monthly hours +
employee relations / development total monthly
hours + compensation total monthly hours +
benefits variable total monthly hours) / (1 – total
fixed hours percentage)) × personal fixed percentage

Lotus formulas:

37   (#29+#30)
38   (#31)
39   (#32)
40   (#33+#34+#35)
41   ((#37+#38+#39+#40)/(1–#7))*#10
42   ((#37+#38+#39+#40)/(1–#7))*#11
43   ((#37+#38+#39+#40)/(1–#7))*#12
44   ((#37+#38+#39+#40)/(1–#7))*#13
45   ((#37+#38+#39+#40)/(1–#7))*#14

46. Grand total monthly hours: For this summation of the
individual total activity hours previously calculated, no input is
required. The result is automatically calculated by formula. The
narrative formula is:

$$\left(\begin{array}{l}\begin{array}{ccccc}\text{Employee} & \text{Employee} & & \\ \text{recruitment} & \text{relations} & \text{Compensation} & \text{Benefits} \\ \text{variable} + & \text{variable} + & \text{variable} + & \text{variable} + \\ \text{monthly} & \text{monthly} & \text{monthly} & \text{monthly} \\ \text{hours} & \text{hours} & \text{hours} & \text{hours} \end{array} \\ \begin{array}{ccccc} \text{General} & \text{Recruitment} & \text{Employee} & & \\ \text{administrative} & \text{fixed} & \text{relations} & \text{Benefits} & \text{Personal} \\ \text{fixed} + & \text{monthly} + & \text{fixed} + & \text{fixed} + & \text{fixed} \\ \text{monthly} & \text{hours} & \text{monthly} & \text{monthly} & \text{monthly} \\ \text{hours} & & \text{hours} & \text{hours} & \text{hours} \end{array}\end{array}\right)$$

Lotus formula:

@sum(#37..#46)

47–52. Total FTE required: This is the result of the staffing analysis. Each line in this section reveals the FTE requirements, by activity, based on the data input *and* fixed and variable standards. Management can compare these FTE requirements to actual FTE levels to determine whether opportunities exist. The FTEs are calculated based on the total monthly hours determined in items 37 through 45. The activities have been consolidated back to core profile items, as discussed early in this chapter. No input is required; automatic formulas are input. The narrative formulas are:

47 ((employee recruitment total variable hours +
    employee recruitment fixed total hours) / ((average
    total hours per FTE per day × working days per year) /
    12 months per year))

48 ((employee relations variable hours + employee
    relations fixed hours) / ((average total hours per
    FTE per day × working days per year) / 12 months
    per year))

49 ((compensation variable hours) / ((average total
    hours per FTE per day × working days per year) /
    12 months per year))

50 ((benefits variable hours + benefits fixed hours) /
    ((average total hours per FTE per day × working days
    per year) / 12 months per year))

51   ((general administration fixed hours) / ((average total hours per FTE per day × working days per year) / 12 months per year))

52   ((personal fixed hours) / ((average total hours per FTE per day × working days per year) / 12 months per year))

Lotus formulas:

47   ((#37+#42)/((#9*238)/12))
48   ((#38+#43)/((#9*238)/12))
49   ((#39)/((#9*238)/12))
50   ((#40+#44)/((#9*238)/12))
51   ((#41)/((#9*238)/12))
52   ((#45)/((#9*238)/12))

53. Total staff required: The last field also requires no input. It is a summation field calculated by formula. Allow enough space for at least six characters (xxx.xx). The narrative formula is:

$$\frac{\text{Employee recruitment / terminations}}{\text{total FTE}} + \frac{\text{Employee relations}}{\text{total FTE}} + \frac{\text{Compensation}}{\text{total FTE}} + \frac{\text{Benefits admin.}}{\text{total FTE}} + \frac{\text{General admin.}}{\text{total FTE}} + \frac{\text{Personal total}}{\text{FTE}}$$

Lotus formula:

@sum(#47..#52)

This completes the creation of the model. The next section discusses data input and analysis.

Running the Model

In order to run the model, the user must understand what data should be input. The following discussion of code numbers explains what information is required and its origin. Refer back to Figure 182.

1, 2, 3. Bank, location, and branch: Type in the name of the bank, its address, and location name (e.g., main office) as an identifier.

4. Date: Type in the date when the study is being conducted. This is usually the month and year (e.g., November 1991) or a quarter (e.g., 3rd Quarter 1991).

5. Number of new hires this month: This is the actual number of FTEs hired during the particular month. This type of data should be already accumulated in the human resources department. If not, a mechanism must be developed to track it.

6. Percent of turnover: This is the actual number of FTEs who leave the bank, whether due to voluntary or involuntary termination. This information should also be readily available. Calculate the percent of turnover by dividing the monthly terminations by the number of employees on staff in the organization. Input the turnover as a decimal. Since the cell is formatted as a percent, a percentage will appear.

7. Number of FTE on staff: This number should be readily attainable from human resources. It must be expressed as FTEs; That is, the total of all employees (full and part-time) must be totaled, then divided by the full-time equivalent weekly hours. For example, if a bank has 300 full-time and 150 part-time employees, the total head count is 450 employees. The full-time equivalent count, however, is 375 or (150 part-time employees × 20 hours per week = 3,000 hours) + (300 full-time employees × 40 hours per week = 12,000) = 15,000 total hours per week ÷ 40 hours per FTE.

8. Average total hours per FTE per day: Input the average total raw hours that an individual in this department is available as defined by bank policy.

For example, if the employee starts work at 8:30 AM and stops at 5:00 PM, the total raw hours are 8.5. Lunches and breaks are included here, they are accounted for in the fixed activity section of the model.

9. Percentage of applicants hired: This figure is also input as a decimal but expressed as a percentage. If not already tracked by human resources, it can be captured as in Figure 183. The running percentage of the cumulative hires and applications received is taken and input.

Section A: Fixed Hours (per FTE)
10–14. Percentage of monthly total hours: For each fixed activity, use the percentage determined from the analysis of fixed activities in the data-gathering section. Enter each percentage as

F I G U R E 183

Applicants to Hires Tracking Analysis

Month	Applications/Resumes Received	Actual Hires	Cumulative Percentage of Applicants Hired
January	325	10	3.08%
February	15	2	3.53%
March	50	6	4.62%
April	225	9	4.39%
May	400	22	4.83%
June	70	8	5.25%

a decimal, since the cell is formatted for percents. The data from the profile summary (Figure 180) can be used here.

15. Total percentage of monthly hours: This is an automatic calculation of the total of all fixed percentages, showing the total percentage per FTE.

16–20. Actual monthly hours used: These are automatically determined by formula upon input of the percentages. They indicate the actual monthly hours per FTE represented by the percentage in the first column.

21. Total actual monthly hours: This too is automatically determined by formulas. It is the sum of the actual monthly fixed hours volume per FTE.

Section B: Variable Hours

22–28. Standard hours required per item: Input the standard hourly factor, determined from the analysis in the data-gathering section. In most cases the input will be in the form of a decimal representing a portion of an hour. Take the standards from the data provided in Figure 180.

29–35. Actual monthly hours used: These cells are automatically calculated by formula. They represent the total hours required to complete the various fixed activities as determined by the standard factor input. This will suggest how much time is necessary to complete the variable activities, based on the key volume indicators: number of FTEs on staff, number of terminations, and number of new hires.

36. Total actual monthly hours used: Again, this is an automatic calculation by formula. It is the sum of the actual monthly hours needed for variable activities.

Section C: Distribution of Monthly Hours Required

37–45. Total monthly hours, by profile category: For each profile activity, a total number of hours is calculated, by formula, to indicate the total hours needed. The variable items are listed first and the fixed second. This accounts for the entire number of hours needed for the department, by activity.

46. Total monthly hours: Calculated by formula, it is the total of all hours needed for the department based upon the input and key volume indicators.

47–52. Total FTE required: This section is the primary product of the staffing model. It calculates, by the major profile categories, the amount of FTE needed. This may help management separate or combine functions. The results indicate the optimum number of FTEs the department should need, based on the "data required" input.

53. Total staff required: This is the grand total of the FTEs needed for the department. It should be compared with the existing FTE levels to determine whether any staffing opportunities exist.

This completes the human resources staffing model. It can be run as often as necessary; quarterly or semiannually is best. Figure 184 is an example of the completed staffing model, using the information developed and hypothetical volumes.

ANALYSIS, MEASUREMENT, AND USE

Once the model has been developed and run, the analytical phase begins. The model gives management an understanding of the optimum staffing levels for human resources given the input of the key volume indicators. This can identify staffing opportunities

F I G U R E 184

Completed Human Resources Staffing Model

```
BANK:          [First Bank   ]   HUMAN RESOURCES STAFFING MODEL        DATE:     [July 1991    ]
LOCATION:      [50 W. Main   ]
BRANCH:        [Main         ]

DATA REQUIRED
  # NEW HIRES THIS MONTH:   [      21 ] AVG. # TOTAL HOURS PER FTE PER DAY:     [     8.50  ]
  % TURNOVER:               [    3.90%] PERCENT OF APPLICANTS HIRED:           [    13.00%]
  # FTE ON STAFF:           [   418.00 ]
======================================================================================
A. FIXED HOURS (PER FTE):
```

	% OF TOTAL MONTHLY HOURS	ACTUAL MONTHLY HOURS USED
GENERAL ADMINISTRATION:	[19.30%]	32.54
EMPLOYEE RECRUITMENT:	[0.79%]	1.33
EMPLOYEE RELATIONS:	[0.96%]	1.62
BENEFITS ADMINISTRATION:	[5.31%]	8.95
PERSONAL:	[16.10%]	27.14
TOTAL:	42.46%	71.58%

```
======================================================================================
B. VARIABLE HOURS:
```

	STANDARD HOURS REQUIRED PER ITEM	ACTUAL MONTHLY HOURS USED
EMPLOYEE RECRUITMENT:	[0.57]	71.48
EMPLOYEE TERMINATIONS:	[1.55]	25.27
EMPLOYEE RELATIONS/DEV.:	[0.23]	96.14
COMPENSATION:	[0.09]	37.62
BENEFITS ADMINISTRATION:	[0.03]	12.54
BENEFITS—NEW HIRES:	[0.57]	11.97
BENEFITS—TERMINATIONS:	[0.57]	9.29
TOTAL:		264.31

```
======================================================================================
C. DISTRIBUTION OF MONTHLY
   HOURS REQUIRED, BY CATEGORY:
```

	TOTAL MONTHLY HOURS		TOTAL FTE REQUIRED
EMPLOYEE RECRUITMENT:	96.75	EMPLOYEE RECRUITMENT/TERM.:	0.60
EMPLOYEE RELATIONS/DEV.:	96.14	EMPLOYEE RELATIONS/DEV.:	0.60
COMPENSATION:	37.62	COMPENSATION:	0.22
BENEFITS VARIABLE:	33.80	BENEFITS ADMINISTRATION:	0.35
GENERAL ADMINISTRATION:	88.65	GENERAL ADMINISTRATION:	0.53
EMPLOYEE RECRUITMENT:	3.63	PERSONAL:	0.44
EMPLOYEE RELATIONS:	4.41		
BENEFITS ADMINISTRATION:	24.39		
PERSONAL:	73.95		
TOTAL MONTHLY HOURS:	459.35	TOTAL STAFF REQUIRED:	2.72

F I G U R E 185

Actual versus Calculated FTE Levels

Position	Current Actual FTE	Recommended FTE	Over (Under) Staffed
Recruitment/terminations	.75	.60	.15
Employee relations	.50	.60	(.10)
Compensation	.50	.22	.28
Benefits administration	1.00	.35	.65
General administration	1.00	.53	.47
Total	3.75	2.30	1.45

and reassure management that staff levels are within acceptable ranges, with resources fully utilized.

Upon completion of the model, compare its FTE levels with the current ones. This type of analysis, shown in Figure 185, can highlight staff overages or shortages by activity. Analyzing each activity to see if it is properly addressed from a staffing standpoint may assist management in organizing the department more effectively.

Analyzing the data as in Figure 185 may enable management to specialize the human resources department, gaining greater efficiencies in specific areas where certain individuals have more talent than in others. For example, an employee may be very good at recruiting people but not so talented in office administration work, such as benefits or compensation. A division between two broad areas could be made based on the activities that make up the profile. Recruitment/termination and employee relations could be assigned to the employee interaction area, and compensation, benefits, and general administration could all come under the umbrella of administration.

Separating the department into two major divisions could introduce greater efficiencies as well as control. This is somewhat like a sales department in which employee interaction is the sales or customer contact function and administration is back-office support. The staffing model provides a breakdown of recommended FTE levels per profile activity. Using Figure 184, the FTE requirements could be totaled to indicate the staff levels for the two broad areas. Employee interaction would require 1.42 FTEs (.60 for recruitment/termination plus .60 for employee relations plus half of the .44 for personal activities), and administration would require 1.32 FTEs (.22 plus .35 plus .53 plus half of .44).

A key analytical feature of the model is the ability to pinpoint where time is being or should be spent. This will dictate where management should begin to take corrective action. Once the model is run, it is desirable to break down the core profile activities by percentage of total available time. Which activities capitalize the most time? Does this conform to management's expectations and the needs of the bank?

Again using the data from Figure 184, array the resulting staffing requirements by activity in percentage order of total time devoted. In Figure 186, the recruitment of new employees and employee relations are at the top of the list. Pie charts are particularly useful for analyzing this kind of data because they quickly show, pictorially, how much time is devoted to each activity and how it relates to the total time available. Figure 187 is a pie chart based on the data from Figure 186.

F I G U R E 186

Hours Spent as Percentage of Total Time

Activity	Total FTE Required	Percentage of Total Time
Employee recruitment	.60	22.1%
Employee relations	.60	22.1
General administration	.53	19.5
Personal	.44	15.3
Benefits administration	.35	12.9
Compensation	.22	8.1
Total	2.72	100.0%

F I G U R E   187

Pie Chart of Time Spent by Activity

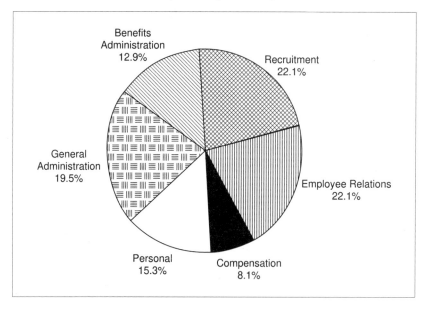

Breaking down the department into two major areas reveals that 51.85 percent of staff time is devoted to employee interaction and 48.15 percent to administration. This is almost a 50/50 split.

At this point, it is hard to tell whether this is a desirable distribution. Once the pie chart is drawn and activities are ranked by percentage, management may suggest that entirely too much time is spent on general administrative tasks. This category is third on the list, with a 19.5 percent time portion. If management is concerned that the human resources staff is too large, it can use the model to perform "what-if" analyses. If general administration is in fact too high at 19.5 percent, a new percentage—perhaps 12 or 15 percent—can be input in the model. This immediately reduces the level of staff needed, as shown in Figure 188. Lowering general administration to 15 percent would also lower this activity to fourth in time consumption, below personal.

F I G U R E   188

Modified Human Resources Staffing Model

```
BANK:          [First Bank   ]    HUMAN RESOURCES STAFFING MODEL        DATE:      [July 1991   ]
LOCATION:      [50 W. Main   ]
BRANCH:        [Main         ]
```

DATA REQUIRED
```
    # NEW HIRES THIS MONTH:    [      21  ] AVG. # TOTAL HOURS PER FTE PER DAY:        [   8.50  ]
    % TURNOVER:                [    3.90%] PERCENT OF APPLICANTS HIRED:               [  13.00%]
    # FTE ON STAFF:            [  418.00  ]
```

A. FIXED HOURS (PER FTE):

	% OF TOTAL MONTHLY HOURS	ACTUAL MONTHLY HOURS USED
GENERAL ADMINISTRATION:	[15.00%]	25.29
EMPLOYEE RECRUITMENT:	[0.79%]	1.33
EMPLOYEE RELATIONS:	[0.96%]	1.62
BENEFITS ADMINISTRATION:	[5.31%]	8.95
PERSONAL:	[16.10%]	27.14
TOTAL:	38.16%	64.33%

B. VARIABLE HOURS:

	STANDARD HOURS REQUIRED PER ITEM	ACTUAL MONTHLY HOURS USED
EMPLOYEE RECRUITMENT:	[0.557]	69.85
EMPLOYEE TERMINATIONS:	[1.550]	25.27
EMPLOYEE RELATIONS/DEV.:	[0.230]	96.14
COMPENSATION:	[0.090]	37.62
BENEFITS ADMINISTRATION:	[0.300]	12.54
BENEFITS—NEW HIRES:	[0.570]	11.97
BENEFITS—TERMINATIONS:	[0.570]	9.29
TOTAL:		262.48

C. DISTRIBUTION OF MONTHLY HOURS REQUIRED, BY CATEGORY:

	TOTAL MONTHLY HOURS		TOTAL FTE REQUIRED
EMPLOYEE RECRUITMENT:	95.12	EMPLOYEE RECRUITMENT/TERM.:	0.58
EMPLOYEE RELATIONS/DEV.:	96.14	EMPLOYEE RELATIONS/DEV.:	0.59
COMPENSATION:	37.62	COMPENSATION:	0.22
BENEFITS VARIABLE:	33.80	BENEFITS ADMINISTRATION:	0.33
GENERAL ADMINISTRATION:	63.72	GENERAL ADMINISTRATION:	0.38
EMPLOYEE RECRUITMENT:	3.36	PERSONAL:	0.41
EMPLOYEE RELATIONS:	4.08		
BENEFITS ADMINISTRATION:	22.56		
PERSONAL:	68.39		
TOTAL MONTHLY HOURS:	424.77	TOTAL STAFF REQUIRED:	2.52

Various "what-if" scenarios can be performed with instant results, but these results will not occur unless action is actually taken. In other words, if management does not review the activities that make up general administration and take action to eliminate some (for example, meetings) then the results cannot be attained. However, it is precisely for these reasons that the model is used. "What-if" scenarios will point management in a direction to act on specific tasks to achieve the desired staffing level.

When seeking to reduce staff, focus attention first on the fixed activities and percentages, which are by far the easiest to control. In most cases, some duties can be reduced or eliminated, reducing the percentage of time and thus the staff required.

Cutting back on variable activities is a bit harder, although not impossible. Perhaps analysis of the model and the subsequent ranking of activities by percentage suggests that too much time is devoted to benefits administration. To reduce the standard time required for it (or any variable activity), analyze the steps that make up the activity. These can be found in the employee survey, which is the result of the interview process. Some tasks may turn out to be redundant or entirely too manual. Eliminating or even streamlining these tasks reduces the standard determined for the variable activity. This translates into less time and therefore less staff involvement for that particular activity.

In general, the analytical process uses the staffing model as a tool to identify and highlight areas that merit attention. Although its primary purpose is to predict staffing levels, it also can provide enough detail about staffing requirements to enable management to control staffing based on the expectations and needs of the organization.

A further example of its use as an analytical and forecasting tool is in the budgeting process. If a specific growth rate is anticipated or an acquisition is targeted, the organization will likely increase in total staff. With more overall personnel, the human resources area may need to increase its staff. Inputting projected staff increases into the model will reveal the staff needed to accommodate organizational growth. As a forecasting tool, the model will lend much precision and logic to the staffing processing for determining future needs.

SUMMARY

This final chapter, although a deviation from the sales-oriented chapters, illustrates the complexities of evaluating a staff-related function. Human resources is truly a staff function in that it is not a direct line function in banking for customer contact and sales. This chapter explores the specific details for creating a staffing analysis and model for human resources and analyzes the methodology for accomplishing this. The primary goal is to develop a staffing model that will effectively and efficiently predict optimum staffing levels for this department.

The human resources staffing analysis begins with the interview process. This function is important to gain an understanding of what human resources personnel do. Although much detail on tasks can be learned in the process, the purpose is to hone the information down into an overall profile of a human resource employee—a set of key activities that define his or her position. These activities generally are referred to as outputs, outcomes, or products of the particular function. All tasks and time required to perform them will ultimately be related to these activities to develop the standard on which the staffing analysis can be performed.

Profile activities are always categorized into two areas, fixed and variable. Fixed activities are performed regardless of any volume produced. They occur on a regular basis, for the same duration, simply because they are part of the job. Examples of fixed activities are lunches, breaks, and meetings. Variable activities, on the other hand, relate directly to volumes. They are actually termed key volume indicators. The total time spent on these activities will fluctuate proportionately with volume. If no volume is received, no time is spent. The combination of these fixed and variable profile factors will ultimately predict optimum staffing levels for the bank.

For human resources, the key volumes related to variable activities are total FTEs on staff (bankwide), employee turnover, and new employees hired/applicants taken.

The profile for the human resource division includes recruitment/terminations, employee relations and development, compensation, benefits administration, general administration, and personal activities.

For the staffing model, the profile was broadened into the following fixed and variable categories:

1. Fixed activities:
   - Recruitment/terminations.
   - Employee relations/development.
   - Benefits administration.
   - General administration.
   - Personal.
2. Variable activities:
   - Recruitment.
   - Terminations.
   - Employee relations/development.
   - Compensation.
   - Benefits administration:
     - General.
     - New hires.
     - Terminations.

From the profile, standard time factors were determined based on information provided in the human resources survey during the data-gathering process. The information was gathered over a two-week period and used to calculate the standards for the model. During this process, the individual tasks performed (times) were determined major profile activities.

Once all standards are developed, the staffing model is created using Lotus 1, 2, 3, version 2.01, to develop an interactive staffing model on the spreadsheet. Instructions for developing the model and all formulas are outlined in this chapter.

At this point, key volume information is input into the model. The optimum staffing level is calculated from this key volume data. The model reveals the recommended staffing levels for human resources, in total and by activity.

The last step in the process is analysis of the data obtained. The staffing model is designed to be interactive. It can perform instant "what-if" scenarios that enable management to take direct, specific action to affect the level of staff deployed by the department, now and in the future. Current and recommended staff levels can be compared to determine if opportunities exist. Furthermore, the model breaks down information in detail by activity, potentially allowing management to reorganize the department and specialize.

The staffing model introduces many new capabilities and benefits. It can be used over and over again, as new data are input, to provide tremendous control and direction for the ongoing analysis of the most important resource of any department—people.

## CHAPTER 5

Staffing the Call Center

The call center is a growing phenomenon that has emerged in banking within the recent last few years. Previously, the call center was predominantly telephone customer service, but now has taken on a more strategic role. Call centers of today handle much more than the standard customer service call, although this remains a significant part of their function. Call centers are also involved in proactive outbound telemarketing, switchboard services, and other centralized call functions. In other words, the department can take on the role of a profit center through telemarketing and opening accounts over the telephone.

For the most part, however, the concept of reactive customer service, where customers call a centralized point for the bank still prevails as a major function. In this regard the bank is receiving and handling a large volume of telephone calls that are made to the bank for a variety of reasons. In most cases customers tend to call for balance inquiries or other general information regarding the status of checks or deposits. In other cases, however, calls concern problems, and the client is calling on the financial institution to perform some sort of research towards the resolution of the problem. These calls can require more time in order to determine the appropriate amount of information to initiate a research claim.

Every call received by the call center requires some amount of time to handle. Today, with the proliferation of interactive voice response (IVR) units, many of these calls can and will be handled without human intervention. IVR systems tend to handle the calls requiring information about customer accounts, such as balance inquiries, leaving the more difficult calls to the live customer service representative. Although call volumes can be affected by IVR units, this is not necessarily a reduction in live call volume. As bank customers become more comfortable with the utilization of IVRs, the amount and frequency of usage tends to increase, per user. When this occurs the large influx, although first going to the IVR, invariably will generate live calls. The dramatic increase in volume can result in more calls going to the live operator in the long run. As a result, the call center is once again challenged with providing the appropriate amount of staff to handle a growing volume of calls.

Customer service representatives are similar to tellers in that they are generally the first people, or in some cases the only people, the client interfaces with. Impressions of the bank are founded on the ability to provide knowledgeable, quality service to the customer. One of the most important aspects of this function is to ensure that customers do not wait for inordinate amounts of time, which is considered a poor level of service. In order to avoid this it is imperative that the function be properly staffed to ensure that quality is absolutely maintained.

Because these challenges are driven by volume of transactions (calls), the approach that can be employed to analyze optimum staffing levels is very similar to that of tellers, as outlined in Chapter 1 of this publication. Considering both the call center and tellers are confronted with the same basic issues of staff scheduling and staff size, the procedures and models outlined in this book will be applied to this function as well. The reasons for this is that the call center receives calls, throughout the day, at given volumes for each hour. These volumes will fluctuate by the hour and, in some cases, by the day of the week. In the same way customer transaction patterns for access to live tellers operates in the same fashion. As a result, teller managers are always faced with the question of how many tellers to staff, by hour, to ensure an optimum level that keeps costs at a minimum. The same holds true for the call center. A call center manager must understand the volumes of calls that typically occur, by hour, to determine the level of staff needed at that time and on a permanent basis.

The teller staffing model used in this book can provide the same information to the call center as that provided to the teller. Thus, this chapter defines how this model is developed and how it is to be used for managing and coordinating a call center function to provide quality service to customers.

METHODOLOGY

The analysis of call center employees, like that of any other area, involves a number of steps towards developing an effective model for utilization. The steps in the process include: interviews, profile development, data gathering, model development, and reporting.

Interviews

The first step is to understand what the call center does in the financial institution. Not all call centers perform the same functions at all financial institutions. On the contrary, some may carry out other outbound telemarketing duties, whereas others may be truly reactive. The bank may also include centralized attendant duties (i.e., switchboard), although this should be analyzed separately from the customer service aspect of the call center. During the initial interview process it must be determined what functions are performed by the call center. Today most call centers will perform one or more of the following functions:

1. Customer service.
2. Switchboard.
3. Telemarketing (outbound).
4. Account opening.

Since each of the above has an impact on time and customer patterns, it is necessary to understand the elements of each so that a profile of the call center representative can be developed for the purposes of analyzing staffing.

The reader should begin the process by interviewing the call center manager, who will have a good sense as to what functions are provided, overall, and can then direct the reader to the appropriate individual(s) for additional interviews if necessary. The interview process does not have to be extensive and can be conducted with one individual, such as the manager, if he or she is truly knowledgeable for all aspects of each of the functional areas. If this is not the case the reader should ask the manager to identify a representative or representatives that can provide the type of information necessary to develop the profile.

Once individuals are identified, contact should be made and the interview begun. The interview should be structured to ascertain, from the employee, what specific functions are performed within the broad categories listed above. Since most, if not all, of the call centers in operation handle inbound customer service calls and switchboard, the initial focus will be on these two areas. The purpose of the interview is to develop a specific list of the type of calls that typically come into the center on a day to day basis. This will include balance inquirers, check look ups, and other common calls. The same will be determined from the switchboard or attendant function. The idea is to develop a comprehensive list of the call types that occur regularly, as well as any other functions that are performed within the department. In some cases other, non-call center duties could be performed which are necessary to capture in order to develop a true staffing model.

Profile Development

The profile development phase is designed to take the information learned in the interview process and categorize it into broad outputs or outcomes. The outcomes relate directly to the function of a call center representative, or rather the key function that defines their position. In this particular case, the call center is predominantly defined by incoming telephone calls. This becomes the key volume indicator or outcome that defines the function. As with tellers, the important consideration is the function on which the representative spends the most time. In virtually all cases this should be taking inbound telephone calls, similar to transaction volumes for the teller.

Outputs are categorized into two areas, fixed and variable. Fixed outputs refer to those activities that will occur regularly and for predetermined lengths of time. This could include regular staff meetings, training, or other types of activities that normally occur. The three categories of fixed activities that are most analyzed are personal, administrative, and other activities. Generally there is one category for variable activities. This category relates directly to the key volume indicator or outcome of the call center job, taking inbound telephone calls. Figure 189 displays a listing of the activities which fall under both the fixed and variable categories. Additionally, Exhibit J, sections I through IV provides a worksheet for the development of such information.

Data Gathering

In the data-gathering phase the information that ultimately will be used in the development of the staffing model is captured. In the prior section, the call center profile, the goal is to capture 100 percent of the call center representative's time, not merely the time involved in handling calls alone. Where most models fail is their inability to capture everything that is involved in the call center representative's day. Beginning with variable transactions (i.e., call center volume) the following will outline the information to be gathered and how it is to be structured for usage, ultimately, in the model.

Call Center Volume
Call center volume involves inbound telephone calls that enter the call center queues and are answered by the representatives. In order to effectively capture this type of information it is necessary to perform several steps. Most PBX automatic call distribution (ACD) systems capture statistics in fine detail; unfortunately, they

F I G U R E 189

Call Center Profile

I. Fixed activities
  A. Personal
    1. Lunches
    2. Breaks
    3. Other
  B. Administrative
    1. Meetings (staff)
    2. Training
  C. Other activities
    1. Research
    2. Outbound telemarketing
II. Variable activities
  A. Inbound telephone calls
    1. Balance inquiries
    2. Check/deposit status
    3. Stop payments
    4. Account transfers
    5. Errors
    6. Statement questions
    7. General rate information
    8. Name/address changes
    9. Other

cannot capture the type of calls that are received, which is critical to the accurate determination of optimum staffing levels.

The first step is to determine the mix of call volume that is received, using the call center profile. This is accomplished by implementing the production tracking document that is contained in Appendix J, section V, and by performing the following:

1. From the most common types of information determined in the interview, a production document is developed for capturing inbound call volume. An example of this form is shown in Figure 190. From the call center profile a finite number of types of calls should be indicated on the standard production form as indicated in the example. No more than ten categories should be recorded, with the last item being "other." In this way 90 to 95 percent of all calls should fall into the defined nine categories with the remaining 5 to 10 percent lumped into the "other" category. The production form need not display time intervals because this data invariably is captured in ACD systems. If, however, this is not the case, time intervals (usually 60 minutes) should be defined.

2. Circulate the production form to all call center representatives. Ideally the production sheet should be capable of capturing a full week of data. In this scenario it is desirable to obtain two full weeks of data to be as completely accurate as possible.

3. All call center representatives must be instructed in the usage of the form. This includes clearly recording the name of the individual and the week that the information was recorded. Each representative should be instructed to record tally marks, next to the category type of the call, for each call received (as illustrated in Figure 190). It is extremely important that each representative capture every call received.

4. Have all call center representatives turn in the first week's form upon completion when they leave at the end of the week. Completed forms should then be passed on to whomever is developing the staffing model for accumulating data.

5. The analyst must them accumulate all call information and begin to analyze it for usage in the model.

The analysis of the production forms yields a weighted average time per call handled. Again, if the financial institution is using a sophisticated ACD system that captures the average time required per telephone call, the production sheet is less important. However, the production form can be used to understand call mix, which may be instrumental in actually lowering the amount of time required per call. For the purposes of the model the number obtained from the ACD is most accurate and should be used. If this does not exist, the analyst must determine the information

F I G U R E 190

Call Center Representative Production Form

Representative: _____
Week of: _____

Call Type	Tally Count	Total
Balance inquiries	₩ ₩ ₩ ⅠⅠⅠ	18
Check/deposits status	ⅠⅠⅠ	3
Stop payments	₩ ₩ ₩ ₩	20
Account transfers	ⅠⅠ	2
Errors	₩ ₩ ⅠⅠ	12
Statement questions	ⅠⅠⅠ	3
Rate information	ⅠⅠⅠⅠ	4
Name/address changes	₩ ⅠⅠⅠⅠ	9
Other	ⅠⅠ	2

through further interviewing and weighting the call time by developing a matrix that lists call type categories and seeks average times per type of call. This type of document is illustrated in Figure 191. The analyst must interview at least three call representatives and either time calls, by categories, or ask the representatives to estimate the time each category of calls requires.

Once this is completed, the analyst can prepare the *weighted average call time calculation* chart, shown in Figure 192. The purpose of this form is to determined a single weighted average time per call taken. Again, this is used if no automatic system can produce this information. The weighted average approach relies on the information initially captured in terms of the percentage or mix of total inbound call by category. From this the average times per call, also previously captured, is multiplied by these percentages to arrive at a single weighted average time per inbound call. This is the equivalent of what may be produced from an automatic call distribution system.

F I G U R E   191

Average Call Times (Minutes)

Call Type	Rep. #1	Rep. #2	Rep. #3	Rep. #4	Rep. #5	Rep. #6	Average
Balance inquiries	1.50	1.34	1.25	1.89	1.40	1.00	1.40
Check/deposits status	0.75	0.89	1.00	1.10	0.92	0.87	0.92
Stop payments	2.30	2.50	2.80	2.10	1.89	2.60	2.37
Account transfers	2.00	2.30	2.60	2.10	2.00	2.00	2.17
Errors	4.00	5.10	3.50	2.90	3.76	4.00	3.88
Statement questions	1.40	1.20	1.50	1.87	1.23	1.10	1.38
Rate information	0.23	0.45	0.34	0.29	0.25	0.36	0.32
Name/address changes	1.20	1.30	1.28	1.45	1.54	1.43	1.37
Other	3.45	2.78	3.78	4.21	2.98	3.21	3.40

F I G U R E   192

Weighted Average Call Time Calculation

Call Type	Total Volume Calls	Percent of Total Calls	Average Minutes per Call	Weight Factor
Balance inquiries	18	24.66%	1.40	0.35
Check/deposits status	3	4.11%	0.92	0.04
Stop payments	20	27.40%	2.37	0.65
Account transfers	2	2.74%	2.17	0.06
Errors	12	16.44%	3.88	0.64
Statement questions	3	4.11%	1.38	0.06
Rate information	4	5.48%	0.32	0.02
Name/address change	9	12.33%	1.37	0.17
Other	2	2.74%	3.40	0.09
Total	73	100.00%		2.07

As shown in Figure 192, the weighted average call time, for the example data, is 2.07 minutes per call. This indicates that any call received, on average, will require 2.07 minutes regardless of the type, since that was accounted for in the calculation. As stated previously, some call center tracking systems can produce this same number without the previous exercises, and it should be used if it is available as it is the most accurate. The 2.07 minutes becomes the variable activity call time which will be used in the model for determining optimum staffing levels.

Our attention next focuses on the other elements that account for the remainder amount of time of the call center representative.

Personal Activities

Personal activities are fixed activities that will occur regularly for the same amount of time. In almost all cases for staff employees this includes lunches and breaks. Fixed activities of this sort are those not devoted to the business at hand, handling calls, but rather which occur by nature of the position. Nevertheless, this time must be accounted for in order to accurately predict proper staffing levels.

Personal activity times are determined from the call center worksheet contained in Appendix J, section I. Although they will vary from bank to bank, lunches will usually fall within the range of 45 minutes. Sometimes breaks are permitted for 15 minutes, or a combined lunch and break of 60 minutes. In this regard the percentage of time devoted to personal time can be calculated as indicated in Figure 193.

For the purposes of the model all numbers in this category are stated as a percent of the total available time for the staff member for the month. In most cases, the average monthly hours worked, per employee, is approximately 168.6. This is calculated as illustrated in the hourly worksheet in Figure 193. Again, this may vary by institution, but by using the worksheet in Figure 194 the bank analyst can substitute other numbers that more accurately reflect the policies of the bank. Based upon the numbers indicated in the illustrations, the average amount of time spent, per representative, on personal activities is 11.7 percent of total

F I G U R E   193

Personal Time Calculation per Call Center Representative

	No. Days per Month		Minutes per Activity		Minutes per Hour		Average Hours per Rep. per Month
Lunches	19.8	×	45	÷	60	=	14.85
Breaks	19.8	×	15	÷	60	=	4.95
Total							19.80

F I G U R E   194

Monthly Work Hours per Representative Worksheet

1. Number of weeks per year	52	
2. Number of days per week	x 5	
Total working days per year		260
3. Less: Holidays per year	10	
Personal days per year	2	
Vacation days per year	10	
Days not worked per year		− 22
4. Number of total hours per day		× 8.5
Total actual working hours per year		= 2,023
5. Number of months per year		÷ 12
Total actual monthly working hours per representative		= 168.6

available monthly hours. (This number will be utilized in the staffing model later in the chapter.) The 11.7 percent is determined by dividing the total hours in the month by the 19.8 hours derived in Figure 193. This calculation will yield 11.7 percent and represents the percentage of available hours that are dedicated to nonproduction-related work. In short the employee begins with only approximately 88 percent of his or her time, or one full-time equivalent (FTE) before being applied to the production work. Most staffing calculations are suspect because they assume that one FTE is one FTE, which was just proven not to be the case.

Administrative Activities

The second set of fixed activities that must be accounted for is administrative activities. Similar to personal activities, administrative activities are fixed because they occur with regularity and for fixed amounts of time per occurrence. This will depend exclusively upon on the policies and procedures of the financial institution. For the purposes of illustration, however, the author has assumed that the call center participates in or conducts regular monthly staff meetings and has a policy that indicates that every call center representative participates in training on a quarterly basis. The time required for these activities must be accounted for. This is accomplished by following the same formula as previously accomplished with the personal activities. An example of how this is developed is indicated in Figure 195.

As shown, the average hours per month required for this activity is 1.5. This represents the amount of available monthly hours that must be accounted for since the administrative tasks will occur and take time away from productive hours. As with personal activities the 1.5 is divided by the total available hours in a month for one FTE to determine the percent of time this

F I G U R E 195

Administrative Activities Worksheet

	No. Times per Month		Minutes per Activity		Minutes per Hour		Average Hours per Rep. per Month
Meetings	1	×	60	÷	60	=	1.00
Training	.33	×	90	÷	60	=	.50
Total							1.50

represents. In this case this represents .89 percent of the total available time. Although not much, this percentage can vary by organization.

Other Activities/Duties

The last subcategory of fixed activities to be considered is other activities. Other activities are clerical, administrative, or "as assigned" duties that are performed regularly but are not part of the key volume indicator, or primary outcome of the department.

For the call center, the bulk of the time of the representative should be devoted to handling customer calls, or customer window transactions, as is the case with tellers. If the representatives are mired in other activities, or a significant percentage of their available hours are involved in other duties, then it is questionable whether they are truly call center representatives. This information will be provided later in the model, and is a key point to monitor when analyzing staffing levels.

During the interview process, utilizing the worksheet in Appendix J, the analyst must determine what other duties are performed by the staff. In most cases, based upon experience, call center representatives will almost exclusively be dedicated to handling inbound telephone calls. At the start of this chapter, however, it was indicated that call centers today may also handle switchboard calls as well as outbound telebanking calls. If the representative also makes calls, the time involved in this must be accounted for. To do this, as stated, the interview process and worksheet in Appendix J is used. In the case of other duties the amount of time is accounted for in a manner similar to that used for administrative and/or personal activities. Particularly in this case, the amount of time is controllable and can be fixed; hence, a fixed activity. For example, outbound telemarketing calls must be analyzed to determine the average length of time devoted to each. This can be accomplished by surveying call center representatives as with the inbound call, or by timing them. Either way, it is desirable to obtain an average time. Outbound calls can be more precisely controlled, as opposed to inbound calls, because they are initiated and therefore controlled by the representative. To

Other Activity Calculation Worksheet

Number of outbound telemarketing calls per representative per month:	100	
Average time (minutes) per call:	× 2	
Total minutes per representative per month	200	
Number of minutes per hour:	÷ 60	
Hours per month per representative		3.33
Number of minutes devoted to research per month:	600	
Number of minutes per hour:	÷ 60	
Hours per month per representative		10.00
Grand total "other activity" hours:		13.33

determine the percentage of time devoted to this and other duties, such as research, the analyst must determine the average amount of time devoted to these other duties per month. This is calculated as shown in Figure 196. The total hours shown of 13.33 per month are then divided by the total available hours per month (13.33/168.6) to yield 7.91 percent of the total available hours.

With this last calculation the analyst can now determine the total amount of fixed time devoted to activities other than the key outcome of the department. In the example this becomes 20.5 percent of the total available hours. This leaves 79.5 percent of the time to be devoted to the key volume indicator of calls handled. In short, we begin the staffing analysis at literally three-quarters of an FTE rather than one FTE.

This completes the information gathering necessary for the model to produce the optimum staffing levels. The next phase is to build the actual staffing model.

Model Development

Model development is the process by which the staffing mechanism is produced to analyze and track optimum staffing and/or scheduling of personnel to correspond with the volume of work (key volume indicator) received. The model itself is a microcomputer-based program designed to use Lotus 123. The purpose of the model is to provide the analyst with an automatic mechanism for not only producing staffing analyses but also to perform "what if" scenarios in order to plan staffing at varying volume scenarios. This is particularly useful when the financial institution is evaluating an acquisition or contemplating programs to promote fast growth. Chapter 8 discusses, in detail, the benefits and impacts of analyzing staff in this way, using the models in consolidation and other growth situations.

The model itself, pictured in Figure 197, is designed in the format of a report. That is, it is an 8 1/2" × 11" document that can be produced on paper, then stored and/or reported to other areas and managers throughout the organization.

Creating the Model

Anyone reasonably proficient in using Lotus 123 spreadsheet software can build the model relatively quickly. This book assumes that the analyst can copy the basic structure (headings, captions, input brackets, model borders, and cosmetics) as displayed in Figure 197. Beyond this, the actual calculations, formulas, and linkages necessary for the staffing analysis are provided.

Once the basic shell of the model is developed, the next step is to understand what information and/or formulas are to be contained in the various cells. Numbers 1 through 33, placed in various sections of the report, represent locations where either an input item (name or value) or a formula is required. The numbers in the following explanation correspond to the numbers in Figure 197.

Keep in mind that the Lotus equivalent formula must be input into the cell for each particular category. The item numbers here and in Figure 197 must be replaced with the *actual* cell numbers in a Lotus 123 spreadsheet. Lotus 123 cell numbers are typically stated as in the form of A1, B2, C3, D4, and so forth, and will be placed between the parentheses when building the form. The following steps are required to build the model.

1. Bank: Within the brackets the bank name will be recorded for identification. The analyst should leave enough space between the brackets for this purpose.

F I G U R E 197

Call Center Staffing Model Shell

```
BANK:        [  1  ]         CALL CENTER STAFFING MODEL        PERIOD:      [    5    ]
BRANCH:      [  2  ]
LOCATION:    [  3  ]
             [  4  ]
```

A. DATA REQUIRED

```
           1.  AVERAGE NUMBER TOTAL HOURS PER FTE, PER DAY:          [   6   ]
           2.  DESIRED CALL CTR. REP. UTILIZATION PERCENT:           [   7   ]
B.  INBOUND CALL VOLUME (monthly total, by day and hour):
```

	7–8	8–9	9–10	10–11	11–12	12–1	1–2	2–3	3–4	4–5	5–6	6–7	MONTHLY TOTAL
MONDAY	[8]	[ ]	[ ]	[ ]	[ ]	[ ]	[ ]	[ ]	[ ]	[ ]	[ ]	[ ]	8A
TUESDAY	[ ]	[ ]	[ ]	[ ]	[ ]	[ ]	[ ]	[ ]	[ ]	[ ]	[ ]	[ ]	
WEDNESDAY	[ ]	[ ]	[ ]	[ ]	[ ]	[ ]	[ ]	[ ]	[ ]	[ ]	[ ]	[ ]	
THURSDAY	[ ]	[ ]	[ ]	[ ]	[ ]	[ ]	[ ]	[ ]	[ ]	[ ]	[ ]	[ ]	
FRIDAY	[ ]	[ ]	[ ]	[ ]	[ ]	[ ]	[ ]	[ ]	[ ]	[ ]	[ ]	[ ]	
SATURDAY	[ ]	[ ]	[ ]	[ ]	[ ]	[ ]	[ ]	[ ]	[ ]	[ ]	[ ]	[ ]	
SUNDAY	[ ]	[ ]	[ ]	[ ]	[ ]	[ ]	[ ]	[ ]	[ ]	[ ]	[ ]	[ ]	
TOTAL	9	0	0	0	0	0	0	0	0	0	0	0	10

```
C.  FIXED ACTIVITY HOURS:           ||   D.  VARIABLE ACTIVITY HOURS (per item):
                                    ||
                                    ||                        WEIGHTED AVERAGE
                                    ||                        HOURS PER TRANSACTION
PERSONAL:           [  11  ]        ||
ADMINISTRATION:     [  12  ]        ||   CALLS HANDLED:              [   14              ]
OTHER DUTIES:       [  13  ]        ||
                    ----------      ||
TOTAL                 13A           ||
                    ======          ||
```

E. STAFF SCHEDULER (staff required to handle the volume, by day and hour):   AVERAGE STAFF REQUIRED

	7–8	8–9	9–10	10–11	11–12	12–1	1–2	2–3	3–4	4–5	5–6	6–7	PER DAY
MONDAY	15												16
TUESDAY													
WEDNESDAY													
THURSDAY													
FRIDAY													
SATURDAY													
SUNDAY													
AVERAGE	0	0	0	0	0	0	0	0	0	0	0	0	

F. STAFFING SUMMARY:

	MONTHLY HOURS REQUIRED	FTE REQUIRED	PERCENT TO TOTAL
INBOUND CALLS:	17	18	27
PERSONAL:	19	20	28
ADMINISTRATION:	21	22	29
OTHER DUTIES:	23	24	30
TOTAL	25	26	31

2. Branch: Within the brackets the name of the branch being evaluated is recorded.

3–4. Location: The exact address of the branch or facility being evaluated is recorded.

5. Period: This is the time period, typically a month, over which the analysis was conducted. It should define the dates covered for purposes of documentation and future reference. The actual display can be written as follows:

$$9/01/96 - 9/30/96$$

6. Average number of total hours per FTE, per day: This begins the "data required" section. Record the total number of hours in a typical working day for a call center representative— the raw hours, from the time the call center representative starts to the time he or she ends work. In other words, this is the bank's workday. Lunches and breaks are not excluded from this count. For example, 8:30 AM to 5:00 PM = 8.5 hours; 9:00 AM to 5:00 PM = 8.0 hours; and so forth.

7. Desired call center representative utilization percent: Within these brackets, record a percentage (1 to 100) to indicate how fully the bank wants each call center representative to be utilized at his or her station. The higher the percentage, the fewer the gaps in time between customer transactions. At 100 percent, it would be management's desire to have a continual stream of customers calling the call center representative one after another. In reality, of course, it is unknown how many transactions will occur in a given hour. If 100 percent is used, the total number of call center representatives required to handle a given volume will decrease because they will be fully utilized. A lesser percentage indicates that the bank desires to increase the time between the calls received so that more time can be spent with customers. This, of course, will require the financial institution to hire more call center representatives, in order to decrease call center utilization. This is beneficial and useful to do when call center representatives are needed to perform more research-related work, which may require time away from the phone. If however, the bank has a separate research unit, the utilization percentage should be high, typically 100 percent.

8. Inbound call volume (monthly total): Record the actual average monthly call volumes (as whole numbers). These are the number of calls taken monthly, during the period of time surveyed. Most telephone systems utilized by banks provide very detailed call volume information, readily accessible. This is by far the best system, since the data is very accurate. The call center manager should simply access this information and record it in the document. If however, the telephone system utilized does not provide this type of data then it must be captured manually. Although this is more time consuming, it will suffice for the purposes of predicting staff levels. To accomplish this, the call center manager can utilize a call volume production form as illustrated in Figure 198. (This document is recreated in Appendix J.) Tally marks can be recorded for every call taken, by hour and day. This form must be used to capture a full month of data. It is best to select a month that is representative of a typical month, not one that would be unusually high or low in call volume. The production forms should be turned in to the call center manager weekly.

9. Total call volume: This is the total monthly call volume by hour. It is merely the sum of the average call volume, by hour, for the combined working days in the week. This portion of the model does not contain brackets ([]) because it can be summed automatically via formula. When building the Lotus 123 model, for each hour in this section, input the "sum" formula:

$$@sum(cellxx..cellxx)$$

This standard Lotus 123 formula should be used for each hour of the day. For simplicity and clarity in reporting, it is a whole number, without decimals.

10. Monthly total: This represents the grand total call volume for all call center representatives, hours and days. The same formula is used for this section as in #9 in the last page.

11. Personal: This section of the model is a fixed item that requires the input of a number. This represents the percentage of time devoted to lunches, breaks, and any other nonwork-related activities. The average time from the call center survey is trans-

FIGURE 198

Call Center Production Form

DAY	7–8	8–9	9–10	10–11	11–12	12–1	1–2	2–3	3–4	4–5	5–6	6–7	Total
Monday													
Tuesday													
Wednesday													
Thursday													
Friday													
Saturday													
Sunday													
Total													

lated into a percentage of the total monthly hours available for work. This percentage is input and calculated as follows:

Frequency of Lunches/Breaks per Month	Average Minutes Per Occurrence	Average Hours per FTE per Month	Total Monthly Hours Available	Hours Devoted to Personal Activities
19.8 ×	60/60 =	19.8 ÷	168.6 =	11.7%

In this example, 11.7 percent would be input into the brackets. (Bracketed items can be changed at any time by the individual using the model.) Personal activity hours will vary if the bank's policies change with respect to lunches and breaks.

12. Administrative: Like personal activities, this line is variable. Administrative activities can change over time, depending on need or changes of management. Administrative duties are also translated into a percentage of monthly available hours based on the raw data supplied in the initial call center survey. From the information contained in the profile development section of this chapter, an overall percentage can be determined, as in Figure 195. In this example, 1.5 hours were calculated as the hours devoted to administrative hours per FTE per month. This results in the following percentage of available hours:

Average Hours per FTE per Month	Total Monthly Hours Available	Hours Devoted to Administrative Activities
1.5 ÷	168.6 =	.89%

In this example, .89 percent should be input into the brackets (#12), as in the model example from Figure 197.

13. Other duties: The last category under fixed activities is the final block of time regularly devoted to noncall-related activities. The total hours for other duties are determined as in Figure 196 and ultimately translated into a percentage of total monthly hours, as follows:

Average Hours per FTE per Month	Total Monthly Hours Available	Hours Devoted to Administrative Activities
13.33 ÷	168.6 =	7.91%

In this example, 7.91 percent would be recorded in the model, #13.

14. Calls handled: For call center representatives, only one activity is truly variable: receiving and handling inbound calls requires that a call center representative's time be based upon the volume of calls handled. This section calls for a factor that will be applied to the actual monthly volumes in section B of the model to determine the total queue time required, on average. (Figure 192 provides the format used to calculate a weighted average time per transaction, as determined from the call volume survey.) The formula for the weighted average based upon a weighted average minutes per call of 2.07 is as follows:

Weighted Average Minutes per Call		Number of Minutes per Hour		Weighted Average Hours per Call
2.07	÷	60	=	.0345

In this regard, the weighted average minutes per call are converted into hours. According to the previous formula, .0345 hours are required for each call handled. This number is then recorded in the model, between the brackets, in #14 as shown in Figure 197.

It is important to note that all the figures used through item 14 are subject to change. These figures are for illustrative purposes only and will vary by financial institution, based on the results of the call center survey. The remaining sections of the model (items 15 through 31) cannot change. They calculate and report values from the information entered into sections A, B, C, and D of the model. In section E, formulas are used to calculate and produce staffing analysis data for interpretation.

15. Staffing scheduler: This section parallels section B, the call center volume section, but translates the volumes into the number of FTE required per hour, per day, on average. These are the actual staffing requirements, based on the volume results of the organization. Items 15 and 16 outline FTE requirements for handling inbound calls only. Fixed activities (personal, administrative, and other duties) are factored into the total staffing requirements in items 17, 18, and 19. The staffing analysis (by day and hour) uses the weighted average hours per call handled (item #14) to produce the required FTE for handling calls. Thus, this section can also provide assistance in scheduling call center representatives.

Formulas must be built into the model to calculate this information. Although the formulas conform to the proper format in Lotus 123, the identifying numbers must be replaced by actual cell numbers. By hour, daily staffing requirements are calculated as follows:

$$\left(\begin{array}{c}\text{Monthly}\\ \text{transaction}\\ \text{volume}\end{array} \times \begin{array}{c}\text{12 months}\\ \text{per year}\end{array}\right) \div \begin{array}{c}\text{52 weeks}\\ \text{per year}\end{array} \times \begin{array}{c}\text{Weighted}\\ \text{average}\\ \text{hours}\\ \text{per call}\end{array}$$

$$\div \left(\begin{array}{c}\text{Time per}\\ \text{interval}\\ \text{usually}\\ \text{one hour}\end{array} \times \begin{array}{c}\text{Desired}\\ \text{utilization}\\ \text{percent}\end{array}\right) = \begin{array}{c}\text{FTE representatives}\\ \text{required on average}\\ \text{for that day}\\ \text{and interval}\end{array}$$

Or, from the model in Figure 197:

(#8 × 12 months) / 52 weeks per year × #14 / (1 hour × #7)

Input this formula in every cell under both day and hour in the staffing analysis section so that all spaces except for the "total" line are filled with formulas. The result will be an FTE requirement for every hour of every day throughout the week. This will indicate the number of call center representatives needed to staff the call center, on average, for each day.

An individual proficient in Lotus 123 can format each formula in a way that will allow ease of copying for the entire staffing analysis section.

16. Average staffing required per day: The average provides an arithmetic mean that indicates the daily average FTE needs for any given day of the week for each particular hour. This figure is a baseline for the number of call center representatives required to handle inbound calls. The formula is:

$$\left(\!\!\left(\!\!\left(\!\!\begin{array}{c} \text{Month total} \\ \text{volume for} \times \dfrac{12}{\text{months}} \\ \text{day} \end{array}\!\!\right) \div \dfrac{52}{\text{weeks}} \times \begin{array}{c} \text{Weighted} \\ \text{average hours} \\ \text{per call} \end{array}\!\!\right) \div \right.$$

$$\left.\left(\!\!\begin{array}{c} \text{Desired} \\ 1 \times \text{utilization} \\ \text{percent} \end{array}\!\!\right)\!\!\right) \div \begin{array}{c} 10 \text{ peak} \\ \text{time intervals} \end{array}$$

Or, from the model:

$$(((\#8A \times 12 \text{ mos.})/52 \text{ weeks} \times \#14)/(1 \times \#7))/10 \text{ peak intervals}$$

17. Monthly hours required: This begins the "staffing summary" section of the model. Section F recaps the monthly hours required for the branch by each category (calls handled, personal, administrative, and other duties). In addition, it provides a percentage breakdown (percent to total) to show the concentration of hours in one segment over another. Finally, the monthly hours are translated into full-time equivalents and totaled to show the optimal staffing level needed for the call center to handle inbound calls. Management should compare its current staffing level to this to determine if there is an opportunity to reduce or a need to increase staff.

This line, in the model, calls for a monthly total number of hours needed to handle inbound call volume. Multiply the monthly grand total call volume by the weighted average hours per call factor. This will provide the total raw hours required to handle inbound calls. The formula for calculating this amount is:

$$\left(\!\!\left(\!\!\begin{array}{c} \text{Grand total} \\ \text{monthly call} \end{array} \times \begin{array}{c} \text{Weighted average} \\ \text{hours per call} \end{array}\!\!\right) \div \left(\!1 \times \begin{array}{c} \text{Utilization} \\ \text{percent} \end{array}\!\!\right)\!\!\right)$$

Or, from the model:

$$((\#10 \times \#14)/(1 \times \#7))$$

18. Calls handled, FTE required: The monthly raw hours required can now be translated into full-time equivalents. The complement of staff required to handle the monthly volume of calls handled is determined by analyzing how many actual hours are available to accommodate variable call volume. First, learn how many hours per month are devoted to the fixed activities of personal, administrative, and other activities and thus unavailable for the handling of inbound calls. To calculate accurately the FTE required, use the following formula:

$$\begin{pmatrix} \text{Monthly call} \\ \text{volume hours} \div \\ \text{required} \end{pmatrix} \begin{pmatrix} \text{Average number} \\ \text{of hours per day} \times \\ \text{per FTE} \end{pmatrix} \begin{matrix} 238 \text{ working} \\ \text{days per} \\ \text{year} \end{matrix} \div \begin{matrix} 12 \text{ months} \\ \text{per year} \end{matrix} \end{pmatrix} \end{pmatrix}$$

Or, from the model:

$$(\#17 \, / \, (\#6 \times 238 \text{ days per year} \div 12 \text{ months}))$$

19. Personal activities, monthly hours required: The number of hours recorded in this section is also determined by an arithmetic formula that represents the total number of hours per month devoted to the personal activities previously defined. This amount must be extrapolated from the FTEs required for inbound calls, using the following formula:

$$\begin{pmatrix} \begin{pmatrix} \text{Grand total} \\ \text{monthly call} \times \\ \text{volume} \end{pmatrix} \begin{matrix} \text{Weighted} \\ \text{avg. hours} \div \\ \text{per call} \end{matrix} \begin{pmatrix} 1 \times \dfrac{\text{Utilization}}{\text{percent}} \end{pmatrix} \end{pmatrix} \div$$

$$\begin{pmatrix} \begin{pmatrix} \text{Average} \\ \text{hours} \\ \text{per FTE} \\ \text{per day} \end{pmatrix} \begin{matrix} 238 \\ \text{working} \\ \text{days per} \\ \text{year} \end{matrix} \div \begin{matrix} 12 \text{ months} \\ \text{per year} \end{matrix} \end{pmatrix} \begin{pmatrix} 1 - \begin{matrix} \text{Total} \\ \text{fixed account} \\ \text{percent} \end{matrix} \end{pmatrix} \end{pmatrix}$$

$$\begin{pmatrix} \begin{matrix} \text{Average hours} \\ \text{per FTE} \\ \text{per day} \end{matrix} \times \begin{matrix} 238 \text{ working} \\ \text{days per year} \end{matrix} \div \begin{matrix} 12 \text{ months} \\ \text{per year} \end{matrix} \end{pmatrix} \times \begin{matrix} \text{Personal} \\ \text{activity} \\ \text{percent} \end{matrix}$$

Or, from the model:

$$((\#10 \times \#14 \, / \, (1 \times \#7)) \, / \, ((\#6 \times 238 \, / \, 12) \times (1 - \#13\text{A}))) \times$$
$$(\#6 \times 238 \, / \, 12) \times \#11$$

Since only a percentage (60 to 75 percent) is usually devoted to inbound calls, the formula accounts for the other 25 to 40 percent.

20. Personal activities, FTE required: Simply translate the monthly hours into the number of full-time equivalents, using the formula:

$$\left(\begin{array}{c}\text{Personal} \\ \text{monthly} \\ \text{hours required}\end{array} \div \left(\begin{array}{c}\text{Average hours} \\ \text{per FTE} \\ \text{per year}\end{array} \times \frac{238 \text{ working}}{\text{days per year}} \div \frac{12 \text{ months}}{\text{per year}}\right)\right)$$

Or, from the model:

$$(\#19 \,/\, (\#6 \times 238 \,/\, 12))$$

21. Administrative monthly hours required: Similar to personal activities, this is determined by formula. The total monthly hours devoted to regular administrative assignments and functions are extrapolated from the original hours required for inbound calls, as in the following formula:

$$\left(\left(\begin{array}{c}\text{Grand total} \\ \text{monthly call} \\ \text{volume}\end{array} \times \frac{\text{Weighted avg.}}{\text{hours per call}} \div \left(1 \times \frac{\text{Utilization}}{\text{percent}}\right)\right) \div \right.$$

$$\left(\left(\begin{array}{ccc}\text{Average} & 238 & \\ \text{hours} & \text{working} & 12 \text{ months} \\ \text{per FTE} & \text{days} & \text{per year} \\ \text{per day} & \text{per year} & \end{array}\right) \times \left(1 - \begin{array}{c}\text{Total} \\ \text{fixed} \\ \text{activity} \\ \text{percent}\end{array}\right)\right)$$

$$\left(\begin{array}{ccc}\text{Average} & 238 & \\ \text{hours} & \text{working} & 12 \text{ months} \\ \text{per FTE} & \text{days per} & \text{per year} \\ \text{per day} & \text{year} & \end{array}\right) \times \begin{array}{c}\text{Admin.} \\ \text{activity} \\ \text{percent}\end{array}$$

Or, from the model:

$$((\#10 \times \#14 \,/\, (1 \times \#7)) \,/\, ((\#6 \times 238 \,/\, 12) \times (1 - \#13A))) \times$$
$$(\#6 \times 238 \,/\, 12) \times \#12$$

22. Administrative activities, FTE required: The total monthly administrative hours are translated into the number of FTE required via the following formula:

$$\left(\begin{array}{c}\text{Admin.}\\\text{monthly}\\\text{hours}\\\text{required}\end{array}\div\left(\begin{array}{c}\text{Average hours}\\\text{per FTE}\\\text{per year}\end{array}\times\begin{array}{c}238\\\text{working}\\\text{days per}\\\text{year}\end{array}\div\begin{array}{c}12\text{ months}\\\text{per year}\end{array}\right)\right)$$

Or, from the model:

$$(\#21 / (\#6 \times 238 / 12))$$

23. Other duties, monthly hours required: This category involves the regularly performed activities that do not relate directly to the main function of a call center representative, handling inbound calls. Other duties were determined as a fixed percentage of a call center representative's time, using the formula:

$$\left(\left(\begin{array}{c}\text{Grand total}\\\text{monthly call}\\\text{volume}\end{array}\times\begin{array}{c}\text{Weighted avg.}\\\text{hours per call}\end{array}\div\left(1\times\begin{array}{c}\text{Utilization}\\\text{percent}\end{array}\right)\right)\div\right.$$

$$\left.\left(\left(\begin{array}{c}\text{Average}\\\text{hours}\\\text{per FTE}\\\text{per day}\end{array}\times\begin{array}{c}238\\\text{working}\\\text{days per}\\\text{year}\end{array}\div\begin{array}{c}12\text{ months}\\\text{per year}\end{array}\right)\times\left(1-\begin{array}{c}\text{Total}\\\text{fixed}\\\text{activity}\\\text{percent}\end{array}\right)\right)\right)$$

$$\left(\begin{array}{c}\text{Average hours}\\\text{per FTE}\\\text{per day}\end{array}\times\begin{array}{c}238\text{ working}\\\text{days per year}\end{array}\div\begin{array}{c}12\text{ months}\\\text{per year}\end{array}\right)\times\begin{array}{c}\text{Other}\\\text{activity}\\\text{percent}\end{array}$$

Or, from the model:

$$((\#10 \times \#14 / (1 \times \#7)) / ((\#6 \times 238 / 12) \times (1 - \#13A))) \times$$
$$(\#6 \times 238 / 12) \times \#13$$

24. Other activity, FTE required: The total monthly other duties are translated into the number of FTE required, as in the following formula:

$$\left(\begin{array}{c}\text{Other}\\\text{monthly}\\\text{hours}\\\text{required}\end{array}\div\left(\begin{array}{c}\text{Average hours}\\\text{per FTE}\\\text{per year}\end{array}\times\begin{array}{c}238\text{ working}\\\text{days per year}\end{array}\div\begin{array}{c}12\text{ months}\\\text{per year}\end{array}\right)\right)$$

Or, from the model:

$$(\#23 \,/\, (\#6 \times 238 \,/\, 12))$$

25. Total monthly hours required: The monthly hours required for all four categories (inbound calls, personal, administrative, and other duties). The formula is:

(Sum of monthly hours required for: inbound calls, personal, administrative, and other activities)

Or, from the model:

$$(\#17 + \#19 + \#21 + \#23)$$

26. Total FTE required: This uses the same approach as total monthly hours required. It is the sum of the FTE requirements for each category of inbound calls, personal, administrative, and other activities, calculated in the following formula:

(Sum of FTE required for: inbound calls, personal, administrative, and other activities)

Or, from the model:

$$(\#18 + \#20 + \#22 + \#24)$$

27. Percentage to total hours: Using the monthly hours required from the model (items #17, 19, 21, and 23), determine a percentage of the total hours required for each category. The results for items 27 through 31 provide a quick analysis of the mix of activities and time spent. The formula for inbound calls is as follows:

$$\left(\begin{array}{ccc} \text{Monthly hours} & & \text{Grand total} \\ \text{required for} & \div & \text{monthly hours} \\ \text{inbound calls} & & \text{required} \end{array} \right)$$

Or, from the model:

$$(\#17 \,/\, \#25)$$

28. Percentage to total hours, personal activities formula:

$$\left(\begin{array}{ccc} \text{Monthly hours} & & \text{Grand total} \\ \text{required for} & \div & \text{monthly hours} \\ \text{personal activities} & & \text{required} \end{array} \right)$$

Or, from the model:

$$(\#19 / \#25)$$

29. Percentage to total hours, administrative activities formula:

$$\left(\begin{array}{ccc} \text{Monthly hours} & & \text{Grand total} \\ \text{required for} & \div & \text{monthly hours} \\ \text{admin. activities} & & \text{required} \end{array} \right)$$

Or, from the model:

$$(\#21 / \#25)$$

30. Percentage to total hours, other activities formula:

$$\left(\begin{array}{ccc} \text{Monthly hours} & & \text{Grand total} \\ \text{required for} & \div & \text{monthly hours} \\ \text{other activities} & & \text{required} \end{array} \right)$$

Or, from the model:

$$(\#23 / \#25)$$

31. Total percentage: The sum of the individual percentages calculated for items 27, 28, 29, and 30. The formula is as follows:

$$\left(\begin{array}{ccccccc} \text{Inbound call} & & \text{Personal} & & \text{Administrative} & & \text{Other} \\ \text{percent} & + & \text{activity} & + & \text{activity} & + & \text{activity} \\ \text{total} & & \text{percent} & & \text{percent} & & \text{percent} \\ & & \text{total} & & \text{total} & & \text{total} \end{array} \right) = 100\%$$

Or, from the model:

$$(\#27 + \#28 + \#29 + \#30)$$

At this point the creation of the call center staffing model is complete. Be sure to save the model and protect it well. Create a backup copy. Although the developer can customize the model as desired, it may be prudent to copy it as displayed in Figure 197, which is an exact representation of how it would be viewed on a PC or in a report format.

The next section discusses the actual running of the model and the procedures required to produce the desired analysis.

Running the Model

Once the model is complete, running it involves inputting the variable information unique to the organization (items 1 through 14 in Figure 197). For the most part, the information is supplied from the telephone system used by the call center or from manual survey forms obtained. To recap, the following section explains the information that must be supplied in the model.

Headings

Brackets are provided to supply the bank name, branch, and location for identification purposes. The period of time covered should also be documented in the appropriate space.

Data Required

The first two items relate to general questions not found in the call center representative survey. The remaining volume data are determined from the telephone system software used or from call center production forms.

1. Average number total hours per FTE, per day: This refers to the call center representative's actual daily hours, including lunches and breaks. It is the standard number of hours required for the bank's policy. For example, if the call center representative's hours are from 8:30 AM to 5:00 PM, the total hours are 8.5.

2. Desired utilization percentage: The utilization percentage (1 through 100 percent) indicates the level at which call center representatives are solely devoted to handling inbound calls. At 100 percent, call center representatives are handling customers one after another, with no gaps in the flow of calls. The lower the percentage, the more time exists between customers and, therefore, the more call center representatives are available and not fully utilized. Care must be taken when selecting an actual percentage. On one hand, 100 percent is not desirable, as this may cause overwork, backups in queue, and possibly poor service. On the other hand, targeting the utilization percentage at too low a rate would be an inefficient use of personnel. The optimum selection is one that is challenging yet allows enough gap time so that customers are serviced on a timely basis. Record a value of 1 to 100 percent in this section.

   3. Inbound call volume: These are the actual, total (aggregate) inbound calls taken over the past month (four weeks approximately). All call volumes are combined for each hour interval and day of the week. The information is taken from the call center software (telephone system) and / or production forms. A specific value must be input in each bracket in this section of the model.

Fixed Hours

The fixed hours are designated percentages that correspond to the three areas of regularly occurring activities. These activities do not relate to the key volume indicator (inbound calls), but rather to the other demands on time for the average call center representative.

   1. Personal: Lunches, breaks, and other miscellaneous personal time spent away from the job are accounted for in this category. The information is determined from the call center representative survey and calculated using the format in the data-gathering section of this chapter. The model calls for a percentage to be input into the designated section.

   2. Administrative: This represents the fixed time devoted to meetings, handling phone calls, and other administrative tasks. Again, input a percentage.

   3. Other duties: This set of activities involves all other functions that are performed regularly by the call center representative—for example, outbound telemarketing or detailed research which is performed regularly. This is also a percentage.

Variable Hours

The last area requiring input is the most important. Input the number of hours required to handle a single inbound telephone call, determined from a weighted average. The appropriate response for this space will likely be a decimal. For example, a factor of 2 minutes would equal .034 hours, and a full hour would be 1.00. Translate the data into hours so that the model can run properly.

Once all these fields are input, the model is complete and the actual analysis/result is performed instantly. Figure 199 is an example of the completed model, using fictitious data for discussion.

ANALYSIS, MEASUREMENT, AND USE

The previous sections defined the elements of the model and the process of determining the appropriate data to use. This last section discusses the usage and benefits of the staffing analysis and approach.

Whenever the model is run, some form of analysis must follow to draw conclusions from the data presented. This begins with an understanding of the current call center staffing level. A comparison made between the actual level and the staffing level determined in the model reveals whether the location is under-, over-, or appropriately staffed. Using the data in Figure 199, the analysis is best outlined in a report similar to Figure 200. From this report, further data can be determined that will indicate the financial impact of the result on the organization.

In Figure 200, it appears an opportunity exists; that is, an overstaffed situation of 1.32 FTE call center representatives has been determined. Reducing the staff by the number indicated would translate into a monetary benefit correspondent to the salary plus benefits paid to call center representatives who would be eliminated. This is a fairly obvious conclusion to draw from the data presented. If data gathering and model building are done properly, the results will be reliable.

When performing this type of analysis, round any fraction FTE totals down to the nearest whole number. In Figure 200, the 1.32 FTE staff overage would actually round to 1.0 FTE. This is a more realistic opportunity than attempting to trim to part-time hours to account for the fraction.

F·I G U R E 199

Completed Call Center Staffing Model

BANK: [First National] CALL CENTER STAFFING MODEL   PERIOD: [June 20 through July 31, 1996]
BRANCH: [Main   ]
LOCATION: [Anytown, USA]
             [   ]

A. DATA REQUIRED

        1. AVERAGE NUMBER TOTAL HOURS PER FTE, PER DAY: [8.5]
        2. DESIRED CALL CTR. REP. UTILIZATION PERCENT: [100.0%]
B. INBOUND CALL VOLUME (monthly total, by day and hour):

	7–8	8–9	9–10	10–11	11–12	12–1	1–2	2–3	3–4	4–5	5–6	6–7	MONTHLY TOTAL
MONDAY	[ ]	[275]	[275]	[274]	[267]	[256]	[207]	[300]	[222]	[300]	[300]	[ ]	2,676
TUESDAY	[ ]	[215]	[215]	[201]	[192]	[229]	[196]	[226]	[236]	[298]	[333]	[ ]	2,341
WEDNESDAY	[ ]	[167]	[167]	[184]	[257]	[219]	[186]	[259]	[258]	[310]	[256]	[ ]	2,263
THURSDAY	[ ]	[198]	[198]	[205]	[219]	[223]	[181]	[285]	[222]	[278]	[258]	[ ]	2,267
FRIDAY	[ ]	[258]	[258]	[260]	[237]	[226]	[239]	[241]	[222]	[259]	[274]	[ ]	2,474
SATURDAY	[ ]	[203]	[203]	[270]	[225]	[236]	[240]	[256]	[210]	[222]	[214]	[ ]	2,279
SUNDAY	[ ]	[ ]	[ ]	[ ]	[ ]	[ ]	[ ]	[ ]	[ ]	[ ]	[ ]	[ ]	0
TOTAL	0	1,316	1,316	1,394	1,397	1,389	1,249	1,567	1,370	1,667	1,635	0	14,300

===

C. FIXED ACTIVITY HOURS: ‖   D. VARIABLE ACTIVITY HOURS (per item):
                                   ‖   WEIGHTED AVERAGE
                                   ‖   HOURS PER CALL
PERSONAL: [11.7%]   ‖
ADMINISTRATION: [2.0%]   ‖   CALLS HANDLED: [0.034]
OTHER DUTIES: [8.0%]   ‖
                 ─────────   ‖
TOTAL   21.7%   ‖
                 =====   ‖

===

E. STAFF SCHEDULER (staff required to handle the volume, by day and hour):   AVERAGE STAFF REQUIRED

	7–8	8–9	9–10	10–11	11–12	12–1	1–2	2–3	3–4	4–5	5–6	6–7	PER DAY
MONDAY	0.00	0.45	0.45	0.45	0.44	0.42	0.34	0.49	0.36	0.49	0.49	0.00	0.44
TUESDAY	0.00	0.35	0.35	0.33	0.31	0.37	0.32	0.37	0.39	0.49	0.54	0.00	0.38
WEDNESDAY	0.00	0.27	0.27	0.30	0.42	0.36	0.30	0.42	0.42	0.51	0.42	0.00	0.37
THURSDAY	0.00	0.32	0.32	0.33	0.36	0.36	0.30	0.47	0.36	0.45	0.42	0.00	0.37
FRIDAY	0.00	0.42	0.42	0.42	0.39	0.37	0.39	0.39	0.36	0.42	0.45	0.00	0.40
SATURDAY	0.00	0.33	0.33	0.44	0.37	0.39	0.39	0.42	0.34	0.36	0.35	0.00	0.37
SUNDAY	0.00	0.00	0.00	0.00	0.00	0.00	0.00	0.00	0.00	0.00	0.00	0.00	0.00
AVERAGE	0	0.31	0.31	0.33	0.33	0.32	0.29	0.37	0.32	0.39	0.38	0.00	0.39

===

F. STAFFING SUMMARY:

	MONTHLY HOURS REQUIRED	FTE REQUIRED	PERCENT TO TOTAL
INBOUND CALLS:	486.20	2.88	78.3%
PERSONAL:	72.65	0.43	11.7%
ADMINISTRATION:	12.42	0.07	2.0%
OTHER DUTIES:	49.68	0.29	8.0%
TOTAL	620.95	3.68	100.0%

F I G U R E   200

Call Center Representative Staffing Comparison

As of date:_____

Department	Actual Staff Level	Required Staff Level	Over/Under-Staffed
Call center	5.0	3.68	1.32

What would happen if the analysis revealed that the locations were understaffed? In this entirely likely event the answer lies in a detailed analysis of the elements in the model relative to the call center representative profile.

If the call center is shown to be understaffed, most bankers would not immediately go out and hire people on the spot. Budgets must be considered, requisitions approved, and managers convinced that increasing staff is fully justified. If this approach is followed, the model itself should be justification enough and can be accepted at face value. Still, the decision to add staff is always a difficult one. The likely result of this scenario is that further questions will be posed, focusing on what can be done to avoid hiring additional people. It is difficult to provide appropriate answers without a detailed staffing model. With the model, however, very specific ideas for maintaining efficiency without adding to staff can be tested, with tangible results.

To accomplish this, the call center manager should display the model on a PC, including all data previously input. The next step is to evaluate each of the fixed and variable call center profile categories. Since the values contained on these lines have a great impact on the staffing levels determined by the model, adjustment of these values would produce a different result. In other words, if personal activities were reduced from 11.7 percent of a call center representative's day to 5 percent, the immediate result would be less staff required than the original numbers indicated (see Figure 201). The benefit of using the staffing model on-line is that the banker can perform various "what-if" scenarios with immediate feedback, which will help the individual determine the best approach to take.

In Figure 201, if personal activity were reduced to 5 percent, we might find that the location is no longer understaffed and no additional call center representatives need be hired. But can this be done? The action required would be to virtually eliminate lunches, which is not a feasible solution to the problem. This leaves administrative, other duties, and inbound call time, all of which are appropriate candidates for analysis.

If either the administrative or other duties percentage were reduced, no additional personnel would be required. For example, to reduce administrative activities, refer to the initial call center survey form (Appendix J). This document shows exactly how much time is spent on various administrative activities (meetings, phone calls, etc.). From this, determine what activities might be eliminated or redirected. If too much time is being spent in staff meetings every week, control it. The manager can simply reduce the frequency of meetings and/or reduce the length of each meeting.

The first step, then, in using the model is to set up hypothetical situations by adjusting the fixed activity percentages. If this provides the desired FTE staff level, the manager knows what areas (activities) to focus on. When various activities and tasks are eliminated, the hypothetical percentages become the standard for future measurement.

The weighted average time required to handle each transaction should not be overlooked. Although this factor is produced from call center estimates, volumes, and the weighted average calculation approach used earlier in the chapter, several methodologies can be used to improve it. Begin with a review of the call center survey form. The call center manager can evaluate the types of inbound calls and the frequency with which they occur. In many cases a particular type of call occurs more frequently than others. If this is the case, focusing on the cause of the calls may provide the answer in terms of resolving it. Once this is known, it is necessary to brainstorm what can be done to either streamline

F I G U R E 201

Modified Call Center Staffing Model

```
BANK:        [First National ] CALL CENTER STAFFING MODEL      PERIOD:      [June 20 through July 31, 1996]
BRANCH:      [Main        ]
LOCATION:    [Anytown, USA ]
             [            ]
```

A. DATA REQUIRED

```
            1. AVERAGE NUMBER TOTAL HOURS PER FTE, PER DAY:        [  8.5  ]
            2. DESIRED CALL CTR. REP. UTILIZATION PERCENT:         [100.0%]
```
B. INBOUND CALL VOLUME (monthly total, by day and hour):

	7–8	8–9	9–10	10–11	11–12	12–1	1–2	2–3	3–4	4–5	5–6	6–7	MONTHLY TOTAL
MONDAY	[　]	[275]	[275]	[274]	[267]	[256]	[207]	[300]	[222]	[300]	[300]	[　]	2,676
TUESDAY	[　]	[215]	[215]	[201]	[192]	[229]	[196]	[226]	[236]	[298]	[333]	[　]	2,341
WEDNESDAY	[　]	[167]	[167]	[184]	[257]	[219]	[186]	[259]	[258]	[310]	[256]	[　]	2,263
THURSDAY	[　]	[198]	[198]	[205]	[219]	[223]	[181]	[285]	[222]	[278]	[258]	[　]	2,267
FRIDAY	[　]	[258]	[258]	[260]	[237]	[226]	[239]	[241]	[222]	[259]	[274]	[　]	2,474
SATURDAY	[　]	[203]	[203]	[270]	[225]	[236]	[240]	[256]	[210]	[222]	[214]	[　]	2,279
SUNDAY	[　]	[　]	[　]	[　]	[　]	[　]	[　]	[　]	[　]	[　]	[　]	[　]	0
TOTAL	0	1,316	1,316	1,394	1,397	1,389	1,249	1,567	1,370	1,667	1,635	0	14,300

```
C. FIXED ACTIVITY HOURS:          ||  D. VARIABLE ACTIVITY HOURS (per item):
                                  ||                           WEIGHTED AVERAGE
                                  ||                           HOURS PER CALL
PERSONAL:          [   5.0%]      ||
ADMINISTRATION:    [   2.0%]      ||     CALLS HANDLED:          [   0.034  ]
OTHER DUTIES:      [   8.0%]      ||
                   ---------      ||
TOTAL               15.0%         ||
```

E. STAFF SCHEDULER (staff required to handle the volume, by day and hour):

	7–8	8–9	9–10	10–11	11–12	12–1	1–2	2–3	3–4	4–5	5–6	6–7	AVERAGE STAFF REQUIRED PER DAY
MONDAY	0.00	0.45	0.45	0.45	0.44	0.42	0.34	0.49	0.36	0.49	0.49	0.00	0.44
TUESDAY	0.00	0.35	0.35	0.33	0.31	0.37	0.32	0.37	0.39	0.49	0.54	0.00	0.38
WEDNESDAY	0.00	0.27	0.27	0.30	0.42	0.36	0.30	0.42	0.42	0.51	0.42	0.00	0.37
THURSDAY	0.00	0.32	0.32	0.33	0.36	0.36	0.30	0.47	0.36	0.45	0.42	0.00	0.37
FRIDAY	0.00	0.42	0.42	0.42	0.39	0.37	0.39	0.39	0.36	0.42	0.45	0.00	0.40
SATURDAY	0.00	0.33	0.33	0.44	0.37	0.39	0.39	0.42	0.34	0.36	0.35	0.00	0.37
SUNDAY	0.00	0.00	0.00	0.00	0.00	0.00	0.00	0.00	0.00	0.00	0.00	0.00	0.00
AVERAGE	0	0.31	0.31	0.33	0.33	0.32	0.29	0.37	0.32	0.39	0.38	0.00	0.39

F. STAFFING SUMMARY:

	MONTHLY HOURS REQUIRED	FTE REQUIRED	PERCENT TO TOTAL
INBOUND CALLS:	486.20	2.88	85.0%
PERSONAL:	28.60	0.17	5.0%
ADMINISTRATION:	11.44	0.07	2.0%
OTHER DUTIES	45.76	0.27	8.0%
TOTAL	572.00	3.39	100.0%

the average time it takes to handle the call or reduce/eliminate the type of call. In the former case the call center manager should scientifically analyze the issues surrounding the type of call. If the call is typically to determine the status of outstanding checks, several things can be done. First, the manager may want to look at the system which provides the information. Is it slow? Is it adequate to deliver the information the individual is seeking? If the answers to both of these questions is no, then time spent with a system analyst or programmer may help to identify ways to provide the information more efficiently, which in turn could reduce the total time to handle the call. If this type of call represents a large percentage of the total calls, any adjustments to improve the system will result in considerable savings in time and, subsequently, the need for less staff to handle the volume—a true opportunity realized.

In the case of reducing or eliminating the volume altogether, further possibilities exist. Once the reason for the majority of calls is known, the manager and staff should analyze what can be done or provided to customers to give them enough information to preclude them from making such calls. This could mean launching a communication campaign to encourage users to use the bank's interactive voice response (IVR) system to answer their questions. Other possibilities exist in terms of alternate delivery mechanisms, such as home banking, or other means of providing the data other than through a phone call. In this scenario any reduction in call volume reduces workload and subsequently the staff required to handle it. In either case there is an element of control; it need only be analyzed. Scientific analysis requires the manager to look at the steps performed, in detail, and the reasons for calls. This type of analysis allows the manager to make changes that will have an impact either on the time required for each call and/or ways to eliminate calls from occurring in the first place.

One topic not yet discussed is training. The concept of reducing the average time required to handle each call can be improved simply through training. Call center representatives need training to teach them how effectively to handle calls. Training conducted to teach call center representatives how to control conversations, ask questions, obtain information, and close the conversation can be instrumental in driving down the time required to handle each call.

These are but a few of the opportunities for reducing the overall average time per call or call volume. The model can help managers determine scientifically the optimum staffing level for the bank and the best ways to achieve it. The result is the development of standards for fixed and variable activities, which should be used to assess the average level of staffing for the call center.

This book provides a uniform methodology for assessing teller staffing levels, but it does not mandate actual times that go into making up the standards. The major drawback of many approaches is that they generalize too much. Some banks rely on a ratio of number of accounts to number of call center representatives based upon national or regional averages. Such estimates will always be suspect because they do not take into account the different systems used by banks, different procedures, different policies, and different mixes of calls. For this reason, the model approach offered in this book tailors the results to the individual bank, leading to far greater accuracy than the broad generalizations made from other methods.

Finally, once the analysis has been completed and the bank is comfortable with the results, the fixed and variable activity items should become the standard for the bank. They should be used for evaluating staffing levels periodically. Running the model every six months or so will provide management with a level of comfort throughout the year and an opportunity to make adjustments should staff levels begin to grow.

SUMMARY

The focus of this chapter has been on staffing the call center. The approach developed uses a staffing model for predicting and scheduling call center staff. Call centers, similar to teller areas, are governed by a common denominator unique to each function. For tellers this is transaction volume; for call centers it is inbound calls.

This is not to say, however, that other duties are neglected. On the contrary, call centers today perform a variety of functions. In some cases not only are inbound, reactive, calls received, but outbound telebanking calls might also occur. Although these would be included in "other activities" there is opportunity to do more than simply answer calls. Another duty is handling research claims. This calls for analysis and thus pulls the representative from the phone for a specified period of time. In any case, one must use caution to ensure that "other duties" do not come to overwhelm the primary reason for the existence of the call center—handling inbound calls.

The model development and usage has been outlined in great detail to provide the reader with enough information to literally build the model from scratch, as defined. In this way the user can gain a true understanding of the dynamics of staffing analysis and achieve solid results.

As always, models are only as good as the data input and the analysis of the results. If the user does not spend time to properly understand the call center and determine personal, administrative, and other activity hours, or to assess the time required to handle each call properly, then the results can only be skewed. On the other hand, if great care is taken in obtaining this information (by using the call center survey from Appendix J), then the results can be invaluable to the manager. Analysis of the model is critical in the process because it takes the information obtained and returns a staffing decision based upon it. When this occurs the manager can and should take some form of action. This may be analyzing more fully the steps involved in work processes or simply controlling the volume of inbound calls. In any event the analytical stage requires the manager to act and thus achieve the benefits he or she originally sought.

The model should be run at six-month intervals. This will provide appropriate checkpoints, preventing staff overruns by allowing timely analysis for action.

## CHAPTER 6

Staffing the Collection Department

The collection department of a commercial bank is made up of telephone collectors staffed to call delinquent loan customers. In most cases a collection department exists for this function for at least installment credit. In some cases the financial institution may also have a credit card portfolio and must perform debt collection on these accounts as well. The collection of delinquent accounts, in either case, involves making telephone calls to customers in an effort to prompt the required payment. Without the actual telephone call and follow up, the financial institution would run the risk of increasingly higher charge-offs and losses to the bank.

Managing the collection department requires both good information and good feedback so as to determine the level of success. As in other operating areas, the collection effort is labor intensive; that is, the number of collectors required is a function of the amount of delinquent accounts that exist on a regular basis, by level of delinquency. The primary output of the collection process is *dollars collected*. In this regard, the more money collected the less likely the account will be written off or become a loss to the bank. Although it is impossible to assume that all accounts will be fully collected, the proper management of collections can result in significantly decreased losses and, indirectly, can positively impact the earnings of the bank.

Staffing the collection department is therefore critical to the bottom-line success of the department's ability to collect money at appropriate levels. The goal is to staff the optimum number of collectors to ensure that delinquencies are managed effectively, while at the same time not overstaffing the area such that dollars collected are eroded by the dollars required to collect the money.

This chapter defines the requirements for developing an effective collection department staffing model, which can be used to predict optimum staffing levels or simply to analyze and ensure that existing levels are appropriately sized. The approach to collection department staffing is scientific in that it requires an analysis of the steps leading towards the development of an effective model.

METHODOLOGY

The analysis of collection department employees, as in any other area, involves a number of steps towards developing an effective model for utilization: interviews, profile development, data gathering, model development, and reporting.

Interviews

The first step is to understand the collector's role in the financial institution. In general, this is self-explanatory; however, some collectors may perform other duties in conjunction with their primary role, and this must be documented and understood in order to develop an effective model. Furthermore, collectors are sometimes organized by level of delinquency. In other words, there may be one or more collectors devoted solely to collecting accounts that are 30 days delinquent. Others may collect accounts at the 60- or 90-day level. Some financial institutions prefer that the collector work all delinquencies within a particular cycle, but the author does not favor this approach and has structured the model to take into account the specialization of the collector by level of delinquency, the reason being that specialization by delinquency stage aids collectors in their ability to excel at the tasks required at each stage and become most efficient in their execution. In conjunction with this collectors should perform tasks associated with the process of collection, such as skip tracing, a process by which debtors are located by the collector when their addresses are no longer valid. This type of work requires investigation, research, and patience and may draw the collector away from the telephone until a valid number or address is located. Collectors also send letters and notices when phone numbers or phones are unavailable. Although most systems are automated, there sometimes is a need to devote time to organize and execute the production of these letters and notices.

Each of the above has an impact on time, so it is necessary to understand the elements of each so that a profile of the collector can be developed for the purposes of analyzing staffing.

Begin the process by interviewing the collection manager, who will have a good sense as to what functions are provided, overall, and can then direct the reader to the appropriate individual(s) if necessary for additional interviews. The interview process does not have to be extensive; it can be conducted with one individual, such as the manager, if he or she is truly knowledgeable about all aspects of each of the functional areas. If this is not the case, the reader should ask the manager to identify a collector (or collectors) who can provide the type of information necessary to develop the profile.

Once individuals are identified contact should be made and the interview begun. The interview should be structured to ascertain the specific functions the employee performs within the broad categories of telephone collections and skip tracing. The purpose of the interview is to develop an understanding and documentation of all of the regular, daily functions of the collector, including telephone collections, skip tracing, and other maintenance-related duties for the collector portfolio.

Profile Development

The profile development phase is designed to categorize the information learned in the interview process into broad outputs or outcomes. The outcomes relate directly to the key function that defines the collector's position. In this particular case, the collector is predominantly defined by the delinquent accounts existing and the calls which must be made. This becomes the key volume indicator or outcome that defines the function. As with tellers, call center representatives, personal bankers, and others the important consideration is the function on which the collector spends the most time. In virtually all cases this should be making outbound collection calls, like transaction volumes for tellers or calls for call center representatives.

Outputs are categorized into two areas, fixed and variable. *Fixed outputs* refer to those activities that will occur regularly and for predetermined lengths of time. This could include regular staff meetings, training, or other types of activities that normally occur. Three categories of fixed activities are analyzed most often—personal, administrative, and other activities. Generally there is one category for variable activities, which relates directly to the key volume indicator or outcome of the collector's job, making outbound telephone calls. Figure 202 displays a listing of the activities which fall under both the fixed and variable categories. Additionally, Exhibit K, sections I through IV provides a worksheet for the development of such information.

Data Gathering

The data-gathering phase captures the information that ultimately will be used in the development of the staffing model. In the prior section, the collector profile, the goal was to capture 100 percent of the collector's time, not merely the time involved in making calls alone. Most models fail in their inability to capture everything involved in the collector's day. Beginning with variable tasks (i.e., outbound collection calls), the following outlines the information to be gathered and how it is to be structured for use, ultimately, in the model.

Outbound Call Volume

Outbound call volume involves calls made directly by collectors to delinquent customers. In order to effectively capture this type

F I G U R E 202

Collector Profile

I. Fixed activities
  A. Personal
    1. Lunches
    2. Breaks
    3. Other
  B. Administrative
    1. Meetings (staff)
    2. Training
  C. Other activities
    1. Payment distribution
    2. Report distribution
II. Variable activities
  A. Outbound telephone calls
    1. 30 days delinquent
    2. 60 days delinquent
    3. 90 days delinquent
    4. 120+ days delinquent

of information it is necessary to perform several steps. Because many collection systems today are fully automated, the volume of delinquent customers can easily be obtained from the host system. Seldom will it be necessary to gather this type of information manually. The data, however, should be captured, for the purposes of the staffing model, by four categories of delinquencies: 30, 60, 90, and 120+ days delinquent. Ideally, this should be done on a month-by-month basis to determine the average volume of delinquent accounts.

Personal Activities
Personal activities are fixed activities; that is, they occur regularly for the same amount of time. In almost all cases for staff employees this will account for lunches and breaks. Fixed activities of this

sort are not devoted to the business at hand—collecting accounts—but rather are inherent in the nature of the position. Nevertheless, the time spent on them must be accounted for in order to accurately predict proper staffing levels.

Personal activity times are determined from the collection department worksheet contained in appendix K, section I. Although this will vary from bank to bank, lunches will usually fall within the range of 45 minutes. Sometimes breaks are permitted at 15 minutes or a combined lunch of 60 minutes. In this regard the percentage of time devoted to personal time can be calculated as indicated in Figure 203.

For the purposes of the model all numbers in this category are stated as a percent of the total available time for the staff member for the month. In most cases, the average monthly hours worked, per employee, is approximately 168.6. This is calculated as illustrated in the hourly worksheet in Figure 204. Again this may vary by institution, but by using the worksheet in Figure 204 the bank analyst can substitute other numbers that more accurately reflect the policies of the bank. Based upon the average numbers indicated in the illustrations the average amount of time spent, per collector, on personal activities is 11.7 percent of total available monthly hours, determined by dividing the total hours in the month by the 19.8 hours determined in Figure 203. This percent will be utilized in the staffing model later in the chapter. This represents the percentage of available hours dedicated to nonproduction-related work. In short, the employee begins with

F I G U R E 203

Personal Time Calculation per Collector

	No. Days per Month		Minutes per Activity		Minutes per Hour		Avg. Hours per Rep. per Month
Lunches	19.8	×	45	÷	60	=	14.85
Breaks	19.8	×	15	÷	60	=	4.95
Total							19.80

F I G U R E 204

Monthly Work Hours per Collector Worksheet

1. Number of weeks per year	52	
2. Number of days per week	× 5	
Total working days per year		260
3. Less: Holidays per year	10	
Personal days per year	2	
Vacation days per year	10	
Days not worked per year	−	22
4. Number of total hours per day	×	8.5
Total actual working hours per year	=	2,023
5. Number of months per year	÷	12
Total actual monthly working hours per collector	=	168.6

only approximately 88 percent of his or her time or of one full-time equivalent (FTE) before being applied to the production work. Most staffing calculations are suspect because they assume that one FTE is one FTE, which was just proven not to be the case.

Administrative Activities

The second set of fixed activities that must be accounted for is administrative activities. Similar to personal activities, administrative activities are fixed because they occur with regularity and for fixed amounts of time per occurrence, and they will depend exclusively upon on the policies and procedures of the financial institution. For the purposes of illustration, however, the author has assumed that the collector participates in or conducts monthly staff meetings and has a policy that every collector will participate in training on a quarterly basis. The time taken out for these activities must be accounted for. This is accomplished by following the same basic approach as with personal activities, as illustrated in Figure 205.

Administrative Activities Worksheet

	No. Times per Month		Minutes per Activity		Minutes per Hour		Avg. Hours per Rep. per Month
Meetings	1	×	60	÷	60	=	1.00
Training	.33	×	90	÷	60	=	.50
Total							1.50

As shown, the average hours per month required for this activity are 1.5. This represents the amount of available monthly hours that must be accounted for by the administrative tasks that take time away from productive hours. The 1.5 hours are divided by the total available hours in a month for one FTE to determine the percent of the total available time this represents—in this case, .89 percent. Although this is not much this percentage can vary by organization.

Other Activities/Duties

The last subcategory of fixed activities to be considered is other activities. These are any other clerical, administrative, or "as assigned" duties which are performed regularly but are not part of the key volume indicator or primary outcome of the department.

The bulk of the collector's time should be devoted to working delinquent accounts, predominantly making outbound collection calls. If the collectors are mired in other activities, or a significant percentage of their available hours are consumed by other duties, then it is questionable whether they are truly collectors. (This information will be provided later in the model, and is a key point to monitor when analyzing staffing levels.)

During the interview process, utilizing the worksheet in appendix K, the analyst must determine what other duties are performed by the staff. In most cases, based upon experience,

collectors will almost exclusively be dedicated to working delinquent accounts. If the collector performs other noncollection duties, the time involved in them must be accounted for. To accomplish this, as stated, the interview process and worksheet in
appendix K are used. In the case of other duties the amount of
time is accounted for in a manner similar to that of administrative
and/or personal activities. Particularly with other duties, the
amount of time is controllable and can be fixed—hence, a fixed
activity. In this case, the distribution of applications, credit bureau
reports, and other materials needed by collectors may be considered other duties. Surveying collectors will reveal the functions
they perform with regularity in the department. It is then necessary to determine the percentage of time devoted to these duties.
The analyst must determine the average amount of time devoted
to these other duties per month for use in the model. This is
calculated as shown in Figure 206. The total hours, 15.00 per
month, are then divided by the total available hours per month
(15.00/168.6), yielding 8.89 percent of the total available hours.

The analyst can now determine the total amount of fixed time
devoted to activities other than the key outcome of the department—in this case, 21.48 percent of the total available hours. This

F I G U R E 206

Other Activity Calculation Worksheet

Number of minutes of distribution and retrieval work per collector per month:	600	
Total minutes per collector per month:	600	
Number of minutes per hour:	÷ 60	
Hours per month per collector		10.00
Number of minutes devoted to other tasks per month:	300	
Number of minutes per hour:	÷ 60	
Hours per month per collector		5.00
Grand total "other activity" hours:		15.00

leaves 78.52 percent of the time to be devoted to the key volume indicator of collection accounts worked. In short, we begin the staffing analysis at literally three-quarters of an FTE rather than one FTE.

This completes the information necessary for the model to produce the optimum staffing levels. The next phase is to build the actual staffing model.

Accounts Worked

The accounts worked section calls for a value for the amount of time required per account worked. This is a very important section and differs from the previous one in that it is variable rather than fixed. The accounts worked category *is* the key volume indicator or output of the collection effort, the function that gives meaning to the collector's position. It is variable because the volume of accounts in the delinquency categories varies every month, even though the time required for working each account is fixed.

In past chapters, this factor has been usually determined by the bank's particular procedures and policies. In the case of collectors, however, the factors that will be used are previously defined, in this section, based upon what typically is required for each stage of delinquency. The derivation of these factors emanates from experience and is recommended for usage in order to ultimately determine optimum staffing levels for the collection department. Of course, the reader may have other considerations and is free to refine these factors as deemed appropriate. For these reasons the detail for each factor is clearly identified.

Delinquent accounts typically fall into four categories of work: 30, 60, 90, and 120+ days delinquent. Although credit card accounts can reach the stage of 180 days delinquent before they are written off the books, the collection work or effort necessary at the 120-day stage is equivalent to that at the 150- and 180-day stage, however different from the earlier stages. Therefore, in order to determine the factors that will be used for input into the model, it is necessary to determine the average amount of work time required, for each account, by the stage of delinquency in which it exists. This factor will result in the number of *minutes* per account and will be a combination of all the following tasks or behaviors, which must be performed to these accounts:

1. Actual discussion with the debtor, on the phone.
2. Noncontact call attempt, resulting in a "left message to call," a "no answer," a "busy," "disconnected" or other such nondebtor contact. This will include second passes as well.
3. A record of the results of the account worked, on paper or on-line.
4. Ordering or executing a notice or letter to the debtor.
5. Ordering other materials for phone numbers, such as applications, credit bureau reports, and other listings.
6. Skip tracing efforts by calling other numbers or leads which may produce a contact.
7. Preparation time between accounts worked.

In addition to the above seven standard behaviors, a specific number of accounts at each stage of delinquency should be worked per collector, per day. Imposing this system allows the collector quality time with each account, with the ultimate goal of collecting money. This quality time actually increases as the delinquency stage increases, simply because as the debt persists the collector will need to expend increasingly more effort to collect the debt or, in some cases, actually locate the debtor. Figure 207 outlines the number of accounts and the contact percentage recommended to be worked by each collector daily. Again, these are derived from experience and will dramatically increase the odds of successful collection.

These contact percentages generally require effort and can't necessarily be guaranteed. However, the number of accounts worked per day can be. The reason for limiting the number of accounts worked per day to a specified amount is to enable the collector to call some accounts again, when someone may be home, or seek other ways to reach the individual. In other words, by capping the number of accounts worked per day, the

F I G U R E 207

Volume of Accounts/Percent Contact Goals per Collector

Delinquency Stage	Number of Accounts	Percent Contacted
30 days	125 accounts per day	40%
60 days	100 accounts per day	35%
90 days	75 accounts per day	30%
120+ days	50 accounts per day	25%

collector is forced to become more creative and attempt to achieve the contact percentage. In the long run, if the contact percentage is attained regularly, the collection attempt will succeed, assuming the collector is well versed in handling a collection conversation.

The tasks that are involved in achieving the goals indicated in Figure 207 must be specifically defined. Each task or behavior requires a specified amount of time, resulting in an average amount of time required, per account, at each stage. Ultimately, this average amount of time per account will be used in the staffing model and forms the basis for the variable portion of the activities, which relates directly to the key volume indicator or output of collection, the working of delinquent accounts. The recommended tasks/behaviors and the time associated with them are identified below (and recreated in appendix K).

A. 30-day delinquency stage (125 accounts per day/40% contact)
  1. Data:
    a. Production standard per day: 125 accounts
    b. Contacts per day: 50 (40%)
    c. Noncontacts (left message, no answer, busy, etc.):   75
    d. Return calls (10% of noncontacts: 8
  2. Analysis:

Category	Minutes per Item	Total Time Required
Talk time	2	116
Noncontact	1	75
Notation	.75	93
Letter/notice	.50	62
Order reports	N/A	N/A
Skip trace	N/A	N/A
Preparation	.50	63
Total		409 minutes
÷ production standard accounts:		÷ 125
= minutes per account:		3.27

B. 60-day delinquency stage (100 accounts per day/35% contact)

   1. Data:

      a. Production standard per day: 100 accounts

      b. Contacts per day: 35 (35%)

      c. Noncontacts (left message, no answer, busy, etc.):   65

      d. Return calls (10% of noncontacts):   7

   2. Analysis:

Category	Minutes per Item	Total Time Required
Talk time	2	84
Noncontact	1	65
Notation	.75	75
Letter/notice	.50	50
Order reports	1	65
Skip trace	N/A	N/A
Preparation	.50	50
Total		389 minutes
÷ production standard accounts:		÷ 100
= minutes per account:		3.89

C. 90-day delinquency stage (75 accounts per day/30% contact)

1. Data:
   a. Production standard per day: 75 accounts
   b. Contacts per day: 23 (30%)
   c. Noncontacts (left message,
      no answer, busy, etc.):   52
   d. Return calls (10% of noncontacts):   5
2. Analysis:

Category	Minutes per Item	Total Time Required
Talk time	2	56
Noncontact	1	52
Notation	.75	56
Letter/notice	.50	38
Order reports	1	52
Skip trace	3	156
Preparation	.50	50
Total		460 minutes
÷ production standard accounts:		÷ 75
= minutes per account:		6.134

D. 120+ day delinquency stage (50 accounts per day/25% contact)

1. Data:
   a. Production standard per day: 50 accounts
   b. Contacts per day: 13 (25%)
   c. Noncontacts (left message,
      no answer, busy, etc.):   37
   d. Return calls (10% of noncontacts):   4
2. Analysis:

Category	Minutes per Item	Total Time Required
Talk time	2	34
Noncontact	1	37
Notation	.75	38
Letter/notice	.50	25
Order reports	1	N/A
Skip trace	5	185

Volume of Accounts/Percent Contact/Minutes per
Account/Targets per Collector

Delinquency Stage	Number of Accounts	Percent Contacted	Minutes
30 days	125 accounts per day	40%	3.27
60 days	100 accounts per day	35%	3.89
90 days	75 accounts per day	30%	6.13
120+ days	50 accounts per day	25%	9.38

Category	Minutes per Item	Total Time Required
Preparation	3	150
Total		469 minutes
÷ production standard accounts:		÷ 50
= minutes per account:		9.38

To recap, each stage has an average amount of time allotted
per account that should be spent in strategizing and attempting
to gain an actual contact for the number of accounts worked.
Following the tasks/behaviors described above will lead to success. Figure 208 recaps the volumes, contact percentages, and
minutes per account targets from the previous analysis.

Again, although there may be some slight variation in the
above, in most cases the numbers identified should be applied
directly to the staffing model to determine the optimal staffing
levels.

Model Development

Model development is the process by which a mechanism is
produced to analyze and track optimal staffing and/or scheduling of personnel to correspond with the volume of work (key
volume indicator) received. The model itself is a microcomputer-

based program designed using Lotus 1-2-3. The purpose of the model is to provide the analyst with an automatic mechanism for not only producing staffing analyses but also to perform "what if" scenarios in order to plan staffing at varying volume scenarios. This is particularly useful when the financial institution is evaluating an acquisition or contemplating programs to promote fast growth. Chapter 7 discusses, in detail, the benefits and impacts of analyzing staff using the models in consolidation and other growth situations.

The model itself, pictured in Figure 209, is designed in the format of a report. That is, it is an 8 1/2" × 11" document that can be produced in paper form and stored and / or distributed to other areas and managers throughout the organization.

Creating the Model

Anyone reasonably proficient in using Lotus 123 spreadsheet software can build the model relatively quickly. This book assumes that the analyst can copy the basic structure (headings, captions, input brackets, model borders, and cosmetics) as displayed in Figure 209. Beyond this, the actual calculations, formulas, and linkages necessary for the staffing analysis are provided.

Once the basic shell of the model is developed, the next step is to understand the information and / or formulas to be contained in the various cells. Numbers 1 through 44, placed in various sections of the report, represent locations where either an input item (name or value) or a formula is required. The numbers in the following explanation correspond to Figure 209.

Keep in mind that the Lotus equivalent formula must be input into the cell for each particular category. The item numbers here and in Figure 209 must be replaced with the *actual* cell numbers in a Lotus 123 spreadsheet. Lotus 1-2-3 cell numbers are typically stated as in the form of A1, B2, C3, D4, and so forth, and will be placed between the parentheses when building the form. The following steps are required to build the model.

1. Bank: Within the brackets the bank name will be recorded for identification. The analyst should leave enough space between the brackets for this purpose.

F I G U R E 209

Collection Department Staffing Model Shell

```
BANK:        [ 1 ]      COLLECTION DEPARTMENT STAFFING MODEL        PERIOD:  [    4    ]
BRANCH:      [ 2 ]
LOCATION:    [ 3 ]
             [   ]
```

A. DATA REQUIRED

```
              1.  AVERAGE NUMBER TOTAL HOURS PER FTE, PER DAY:        [   5   ]
              2.  DESIRED COLLECTOR UTILIZATION PERCENT:              [   6   ]
```

B. DELINQUENT ACCOUNT VOLUME (by month volume):

	JAN	FEB	MAR	APR	MAY	JUN	JUL	AUG	SEP	OCT	NOV	DEC	MONTHLY AVERAGE
1. 30 day:	[7]	[ ]	[ ]	[ ]	[ ]	[ ]	[ ]	[ ]	[ ]	[ ]	[ ]	[ ]	8
2. 60 day:	[ ]	[ ]	[ ]	[ ]	[ ]	[ ]	[ ]	[ ]	[ ]	[ ]	[ ]	[ ]	9
3. 90 day:	[ ]	[ ]	[ ]	[ ]	[ ]	[ ]	[ ]	[ ]	[ ]	[ ]	[ ]	[ ]	10
4. 120+ day:	[ ]	[ ]	[ ]	[ ]	[ ]	[ ]	[ ]	[ ]	[ ]	[ ]	[ ]	[ ]	11

TOTAL	12	0	0	0	0	0	0	0	0	0	0	0	0
	====	====	====	====	====	====	====	====	====	====	====	====	====

```
=================================================================================
C.  FIXED ACTIVITY HOURS:      ||  D.  VARIABLE ACTIVITY HOURS (per delinquent account):
                               ||                              WEIGHTED AVERAGE
                               ||                              HOURS PER ACCOUNT
PERSONAL:          [ 13 ]      ||
ADMINISTRATION:    [ 14 ]      ||     COLLECTION CALLS:
OTHER DUTIES:      [ 15 ]      ||      —30 day delinquent:        [   17 ]
                   ------      ||      —60 day delinquent:        [   18 ]
TOTAL                16        ||      —90 day delinquent:        [   19 ]
                   ======      ||      —120+ day delinquent:      [   20 ]
```

```
=================================================================================
E.  STAFFING SUMMARY:
```

	MONTHLY HOURS REQUIRED	FTE REQUIRED	PERCENT TO TOTAL
COLLECTION TASKS:			
—00 day delinquent:	21	22	37
—60 day delinquent:	23	24	38
—90 day delinquent:	25	26	39
—120+ day delinquent:	27	28	40
PERSONAL:	29	30	41
ADMINISTRATION:	31	32	42
OTHER DUTIES:	33	34	43
TOTAL:	35	36	44
	====	====	====

```
=================================================================================
```

2. Branch: Within the brackets the name of the branch being evaluated is recorded.

3. Location: The exact address of the branch or facility being evaluated is recorded.

4. Period: This is the time period over which the analysis was conducted. Typically a year, it should define the dates covered for purposes of documentation and future reference. The actual display can be written as 1/96–12/96.

5. Average number of total hours per FTE, per day: This begins the "data required" section. Record the total number of hours in a typical working day for a collector from the time the collector starts to the time the collector ends work. In other words, this is the bank's workday. Lunches and breaks are not excluded from this count. For example, 8:30 AM to 5:00 PM = 8.5 hours; 9:00 AM to 5:00 PM = 8.0 hours; and so forth.

6. Desired collector utilization percent: Within these brackets, record a percentage (1 to 100) to indicate how fully the bank wants each call center representative to be utilized at his or her station. The higher the percentage, the fewer the gaps in time between customer transactions. At 100 percent, it would be management's desire to have a continual stream of customers calling the representatives one after another. In reality, of course, it is unknown how many transactions will occur in a given hour. If 100 percent is used, the total number of call center representatives required to handle a given volume will decrease because they will be fully utilized. A lesser percentage indicates that the bank desires to increase the time between accounts worked so that more time can be spent on other issues. This, of course, will require the financial institution to hire more collectors, so that collection department utilization will be decreased. Generally, this is not something that would be done unless other work is required which necessitates more gap time between working accounts. Today, with the advent of auto dialers, the gap time between accounts will be minimal anyway. Generally speaking this percentage should always be in the high 90s or 100 percent all the time.

7. Delinquency account volume: This is the monthly delinquent account volume that occurs by delinquency stage. This information is taken directly form the bank's mainframe computer for each month of the year. Accounts will be input in accordance with their level of delinquency. At the stage of 120 days all accounts beyond this stage of delinquency, but not yet charged off, are combined in this category.

8. 30-day monthly average accounts: This is an average of the 12 months of 30-day delinquent accounts.

9. 60-day monthly average accounts: This is an average of the twelve months of 60-day delinquent accounts.

10. 90-day monthly average accounts: This is an average of the 12 months of 90-day delinquent accounts.

11. 120+ days monthly average accounts: This is an average of the 12 months of accounts 120 days or more delinquent but not as yet charged off.

12. Total average monthly delinquent accounts: This is the total monthly average of all delinquent accounts (all stages of delinquency) for any given month, as an average.

13. Personal: This section of the model is a fixed item that requires the input of a number. It represents the percentage of time devoted to lunches, breaks, and any other nonwork-related activities. The average time from the collection department survey is translated into a percentage of the total monthly hours available for work, calculated as follows:

Frequency of Lunches/Breaks per Month	Average Minutes per Occurrence	Average Hours per FTE per Month	Total Monthly Hours Available	Hours Devoted to Personal Activities
19.8	× 60/60 =	19.8	÷ 168.6 =	11.7%

In this example, 11.7 percent would be input into the brackets. Bracketed items can be changed at any time by the individual using the model. Personal activity hours will vary if the bank's policies change with respect to lunches and breaks.

14. Administrative: Like personal activities, this line is variable. Administrative activities can change over time, depending on need or changes of management. Administrative duties are also translated into a percentage of monthly available hours, based on the raw data supplied in the initial collection department survey. From the information contained in the profile development section of this chapter, an overall percentage can be determined as in Figure 205. In this example, 1.5 hours were calculated as the hours devoted to administrative hours per FTE per month. This results in the following percentage of available hours:

Average Hours per FTE per Month		Total Monthly Hours Available		Hours Devoted to Administrative Activities
1.5	÷	168.6	=	.89%

Thus, .89 percent should be input into the brackets (#14) in the model example from Figure 210.

15. Other duties: The last category under fixed activities is the final block of time regularly devoted to non-collection related activities. The total hours for other duties are determined as in Figure 206 and ultimately translated into a percentage of total monthly hours, as follows:

Average Hours per FTE per Month		Total Monthly Hours Available		Hours Devoted to Administrative Activities
15.00	÷	168.6	=	8.90%

In this example, 8.90 percent would be recorded in the model, #15.

16. Total fixed hours percent: The total fixed hours percent is calculated based upon the percentages contained in personal, administrative, and other activities. The total of these percents yields the total fixed activity percentage. This is an automatically calculated formula and nothing need be input:

$$\left(\begin{array}{ccc} \text{Personal} & \text{Administrative} & \text{Other} \\ \text{activity} + & \text{activity} & + \text{activity} \\ \text{percent} & \text{percent} & \text{percent} \end{array}\right)$$

Or, from the model:

(#13+#14+#15)

17. 30-days factor: This begins the variable activity section of the model. This section requires a number to be input expressed in terms of hours. This number is taken from the recommended minutes per account calculation contained in Figure 208. The conversion to hours yields .055 hours calculated as follows:

(3.27 minutes per account / 60 minutes per hour)

18. 60-days factor: This section requires a number to be input expressed in terms of hours. This number is taken from the recommended minutes per account calculation contained in Figure 208. The conversion to hours yields .065 hours, calculated as follows:

(3.89 minutes per account / 60 minutes per hour)

19. 90-days factor: This section requires a number to be input expressed in terms of hours. This number is taken from the recommended minutes per account calculation contained in Figure 208. The conversion to hours yields .103 hours calculated as follows:

(6.13 minutes per account / 60 minutes per hour)

20. 120+ days factor: This section requires a number to be input expressed in terms of hours. This number is taken from the recommended minutes per account calculation contained in Figure 208. The conversion to hours yields .157 hours, calculated as follows:

(9.38 minutes per account / 60 minutes per hour)

21. Monthly hours required, 30 days delinquent: This begins the staffing summary section of the model and indicates the total hours required for working delinquent accounts at this stage only, and is calculated based upon the variable hours per account from line #17 in the model. This is an automatically calculated value, with the following formula included in the model:

$$\left(\left(\left(\begin{array}{cc} 30\text{-day} & 4 \text{ passes} \\ \text{monthly} \times & \text{per account} \\ \text{average} & \text{per month} \end{array}\right) \times \begin{array}{c} 30\text{-day} \\ \text{hours} \\ \text{per call} \end{array}\right) \div \begin{array}{c} \text{Utilization} \\ \text{percent} \end{array}\right)$$

Or, from the model:

$$(((\#8 \times 4 \text{ passes}) \times \#17)/\#6)$$

The reader will note that four (4) passes are indicated in the formula, indicating that each delinquent account should be worked no less than four times per month, or once per week at the very least, to affect collections.

22. FTE required, 30 days delinquent: This field represents the actual number of FTE required to work 30-day delinquent accounts. The formula for this calculation is as follows:

(30-day monthly hours required ÷ (average hours per FTE × 238/12))

Or, from the model: $(\#21/(\#5 \times 238/12))$

23. Monthly hours required, 60 days delinquent: This line begins the staffing summary section of the model and indicates the total hours required for working delinquent accounts at this stage only, calculated based upon the variable hours per account from line #18 in the model. This is an automatically calculated value, with the following formula included in the model:

$$\left(\left(\left(\begin{array}{cc} 60\text{-day} & 4 \text{ passes} \\ \text{monthly} \times & \text{per account} \\ \text{average} & \text{per month} \end{array}\right) \times \begin{array}{c} 60\text{-day} \\ \text{hours} \\ \text{per call} \end{array}\right) \div \begin{array}{c} \text{Utilization} \\ \text{percent} \end{array}\right)$$

Or, from the model:

$$(((\#9 \times 4) \times \#18)/\#6)$$

24. FTE required, 60 days delinquent: This field represents the actual number of FTE required to work 60-day delinquent accounts. The formula for this calculation is:

(60-day monthly hours required/(average hours per FTE × 238/12))

Or, from the model:

$$(\#23 / (\#5 \times 238 / 12))$$

25. Monthly hours required, 90 days delinquent: This line begins the staffing summary section of the model and indicates the total hours required for working delinquent accounts at this stage only, calculated based upon the variable hours per account from line #19 in the model. This is an automatically calculated value, with the following formula included in the model:

$$\left(\left(\left(\begin{array}{c} \text{90-day} \\ \text{monthly} \\ \text{average} \end{array} \times \begin{array}{c} \text{4 passes} \\ \text{per account} \\ \text{per month} \end{array} \right) \times \begin{array}{c} \text{90-day} \\ \text{hours} \\ \text{per call} \end{array} \right) \div \begin{array}{c} \text{Utilization} \\ \text{percent} \end{array} \right)$$

Or, from the model:

$$(((\#10 \times 4) \times \#19) / \#6)$$

26. FTE required, 90 days delinquent: This field represents the actual number of FTE required to work 90-day delinquent accounts. The formula for this calculation is as follows:

$$(\text{90-day monthly hours required} / (\text{average hours} \\ \text{per FTE} \times 238 / 12))$$

Or, from the model:

$$(\#25 / (\#5 \times 238 / 12))$$

27. Monthly hours required, 120+ days delinquent: This line begins the staffing summary section of the model and indicates the total hours required for working delinquent accounts at this stage only, and is calculated based upon the variable hours per account from line #20 in the model. This is an automatically calculated value, with the following formula included in the model:

$$\left(\left(\left(\begin{array}{c} \text{120+ day} \\ \text{monthly} \\ \text{average} \end{array} \times \begin{array}{c} \text{4 passes} \\ \text{per account} \\ \text{per month} \end{array} \right) \times \begin{array}{c} \text{120+ day} \\ \text{hours} \\ \text{per call} \end{array} \right) \div \begin{array}{c} \text{Utilization} \\ \text{percent} \end{array} \right)$$

Or, from the model:

$$(((\#11 \times 4) \times \#20) / \#6)$$

28. FTE required, 120+ days delinquent: This field represents the actual number of FTE required to work 120+ day delinquent accounts. The formula for this calculation is as follows:

$$(120+ \text{ day monthly hours required} / (\text{average hours per FTE} \times 238/12))$$

Or, from the model:

$$(\#27 / (\#5 \times 238/12))$$

29. Personal activities hours required: The number of hours recorded in this section is also determined by an arithmetic formula. It represents the total number of hours per month devoted to the personal activities previously defined. This amount must be extrapolated from the FTEs required for handling collection accounts, using the following formula:

$$\frac{\left(\left(\begin{array}{c}30\text{-day}\\\text{monthly}\\\text{hours}\end{array} + \begin{array}{c}60\text{-day}\\\text{monthly}\\\text{hours}\end{array} + \begin{array}{c}90\text{-day}\\\text{monthly}\\\text{hours}\end{array} + \begin{array}{c}120+\text{ day}\\\text{monthly}\\\text{hours}\end{array}\right) \div \left(\left(\begin{array}{c}\text{Average}\\\text{hours}\\\text{per FTE}\end{array} \times \frac{238\text{ days}}{\text{per year}} \div \frac{12}{\text{months}}\right) \times \left(1 - \begin{array}{c}\text{Total fixed}\\\text{activity}\\\text{percent}\end{array}\right)\right)\right)}{\left(\begin{array}{c}\text{Average}\\\text{hours}\\\text{per FTE}\end{array} \times \frac{238\text{ days}}{\text{per year}} \div \frac{12}{\text{months}}\right) \times \begin{array}{c}\text{Personal}\\\text{activity}\\\text{percent}\end{array}}$$

Or, from the model:

$$((\#21+\#23+\#25+\#27) / ((\#5\times238/12)\times(1-\#16)))\times$$
$$(\#5\times238/12)\times5\,\#13$$

30. Personal activities, FTE required: Simply translate the monthly hours into the number of full-time equivalents, using the formula:

$$
\left(
\begin{array}{l}
\text{Personal} \\
\text{monthly} \\
\text{hours} \\
\text{required}
\end{array}
\div
\left(
\begin{array}{l}
\text{Average} \\
\text{hours} \\
\text{per FTE} \\
\text{per year}
\end{array}
\times
\begin{array}{l}
238 \\
\text{working} \\
\text{days} \\
\text{per year}
\end{array}
\div
\begin{array}{l}
12 \text{ months} \\
\text{per year}
\end{array}
\right)
\right)
$$

Or, from the model:

$$(\#29 / (\#5 \times 238 / 12))$$

31. Administrative activities hours required: The number of hours recorded in this section is also determined by an arithmetic formula. It represents the total number of hours per month devoted to the administrative activities previously defined. This amount must be extrapolated from the FTEs required for working collection accounts, using the following formula:

$$
\left[
\left(
\begin{array}{l}
\text{30-day} \\
\text{monthly} \\
\text{hours}
\end{array}
+
\begin{array}{l}
\text{60-day} \\
\text{monthly} \\
\text{hours}
\end{array}
+
\begin{array}{l}
\text{90-day} \\
\text{monthly} \\
\text{hours}
\end{array}
+
\begin{array}{l}
\text{120+ day} \\
\text{monthly} \\
\text{hours}
\end{array}
\right)
\div
\right.
$$

$$
\left.
\left(
\begin{array}{l}
\text{Average} \\
\text{hours} \\
\text{per FTE}
\end{array}
\times
\frac{238 \text{ days}}{\text{per year}}
\div
\frac{12}{\text{months}}
\right)
\times
\left(
1 -
\begin{array}{l}
\text{Total fixed} \\
\text{activity} \\
\text{percent}
\end{array}
\right)
\right]
$$

$$
\left(
\begin{array}{l}
\text{Average} \\
\text{hours} \\
\text{per FTE}
\end{array}
\times
\frac{238 \text{ days}}{\text{per year}}
\div
\frac{12}{\text{months}}
\right)
\times
\begin{array}{l}
\text{Administrative} \\
\text{activity} \\
\text{percent}
\end{array}
$$

Or, from the model:

$$((\#21+\#23+\#25+\#27) / ((\#5 \times 238 / 12) \times (1 - \#16))) \times$$
$$(\#5 \times 238 / 12) \times 5 \# 14$$

32. Administrative activities, FTE required: Simply translate the monthly hours into the number of full-time equivalents, using the formula:

$$
\left(
\begin{array}{l}
\text{Administrative} \\
\text{monthly} \\
\text{hours} \\
\text{required}
\end{array}
\div
\left(
\begin{array}{l}
\text{Average} \\
\text{hours} \\
\text{per FTE} \\
\text{per year}
\end{array}
\times
\begin{array}{l}
238 \\
\text{working} \\
\text{days} \\
\text{per year}
\end{array}
\div
\begin{array}{l}
12 \text{ months} \\
\text{per year}
\end{array}
\right)
\right)
$$

Or, from the model:

$$(\#31 / (\#5 \times 238 / 12))$$

33. Other activities hours required: The number of hours recorded in this section is also determined by an arithmetic formula. It represents the total number of hours per month devoted to other activities previously defined. This amount must be extrapolated from the FTEs required for working collection accounts, using the following formula:

$$\left(\left(\begin{array}{c} \text{30-day} \\ \text{monthly} \\ \text{hours} \end{array} + \begin{array}{c} \text{60-day} \\ \text{monthly} \\ \text{hours} \end{array} + \begin{array}{c} \text{90-day} \\ \text{monthly} \\ \text{hours} \end{array} + \begin{array}{c} \text{120+ day} \\ \text{monthly} \\ \text{hours} \end{array}\right) \div \right.$$
$$\left.\left(\left(\begin{array}{c} \text{Average} \\ \text{hours} \\ \text{per FTE} \end{array} \times \frac{238\,\text{days}}{\text{per year}} \div \frac{12}{\text{months}}\right) \times \left(1 - \begin{array}{c} \text{Total fixed} \\ \text{activity} \\ \text{percent} \end{array}\right)\right)\right)$$
$$\left(\begin{array}{c} \text{Average} \\ \text{hours} \\ \text{per FTE} \end{array} \times \frac{238\,\text{days}}{\text{per year}} \div \frac{12}{\text{months}}\right) \begin{array}{c} \text{Other} \\ \times \text{activity} \\ \text{percent} \end{array}$$

Or, from the model:

$$((\#21+\#23+\#25+\#27) / ((\#5\text{x}238 / 12)\text{x}(1-\#16)))\text{x}(\#5\text{x}238 / 12)\text{x}\#15$$

34. Other activities, FTE required: Simply translate the monthly hours into the number of full-time equivalents, using the formula:

$$\left(\begin{array}{c} \text{Other} \\ \text{monthly} \\ \text{hours} \\ \text{required} \end{array} \div \left(\begin{array}{c} \text{Average} \\ \text{hours} \\ \text{per FTE} \\ \text{per year} \end{array} \times \begin{array}{c} 238 \\ \text{working} \\ \text{days} \\ \text{per year} \end{array} \div \begin{array}{c} 12\,\text{months} \\ \text{per year} \end{array}\right)\right)$$

Or, from the model:

$$(\#33 / (\#5 \times 238 / 12))$$

35. Total monthly hours required: This line is the total monthly hours required for all four categories (telephone collection, personal, administrative, and other duties). The formula is as follows:

(30-day delinquent hours + 60-day delinquent hours + 90-day delinquent hours + 120+ day delinquent hours + personal hours + administrative hours + other activity hours)

Or, from the model:

(#21+#23+#25+#27+#29+#31+#33)

36. Total FTE required: Use the same approach as for total monthly hours required. This is the sum of the FTE requirements for each category of telephone collection calls, personal, administrative, and other activities, calculated in the following formula:

(30-day FTE + 60-day FTE + 90-day FTE + 120+ day FTE + personal FTE + administrative FTE + other activity FTE)

Or, from the model:

(#22+#24+#26+#28+#30+#32+#34)

37. Percentage to total hours—30-day collection: Using the monthly hours required from the model (items #21, 23, 25, 27, 29, 31, and 33), determine a percentage of the total hours required for each category. The results for items 37 through 44 provide a quick analysis of the mix of activities and time spent. The formula for 30-day collection is as follows:

(30-day monthly hours / total monthly hours required)

Or, from the model:

(#21 / #35)

38. Percentage to total hours—60-day collection:

(60-day monthly hours required / total monthly hours required)

Or, from the model:

(#23 / #35)

39. Percentage to total hours—90-day collection:

(90-day monthly hours required / total monthly hours required)

Or, from the model:

(#25 / #35)

40. Percentage to total hours—120+ day collection:

(120+ day monthly hours required / total monthly
hours required)

Or, from the model:

(#27 / #35)

41. Percentage to total hours—personal activities:

(Personal activities monthly hours required / total monthly
hours required)

Or, from the model:

(#29 / #35)

42. Percentage to total hours—administrative activities:

(Administrative activities monthly hours required / total
monthly hours required)

Or, from the model:

(#31 / #35)

43. Percentage to total hours—other activities:

(Other activities monthly hours required / total monthly
hours required)

Or, from the model:

(#33 / #35)

44. Total percentage: This is the sum of the individual percentages calculated for items # 37, 38, 39, 40, 41, 42 and 43. The formula is as follows:

(30-day percent + 60-day percent + 90-day percent 120+ day
percent + personal activity percent + administrative activity
percent + other activity percent)

Or, from the model:

(#37+#38+#39+#40+#41+#42+#43)

At this point the creation of the call center staffing model is complete. Be sure to save the model and protect it well. Create a backup copy. Although the developer can customize the model as desired, it may be prudent to copy it as displayed in Figure 209, an exact representation of how it would be viewed on a PC or as a report.

The next section discusses the actual running of the model and the procedures required to produce the desired analysis.

Running the Model

Once the model is complete, running it involves inputting the required information unique to the organizations (items 1 through 20 in Figure 209). For the most part, the information supplied is taken from host reports and data that the collection system used produces.

To recap, the following section explains the information that must be supplied in the model.

Headings
Brackets are provided to supply the bank name, branch, and location for identification purposes. The period of time covered should also be documented in the appropriate space.

Data Required
The first two items relate to general questions not found in the collection department survey. The remaining volume data are determined from the host collection system.

1. Average number total hours per FTE, per day: This refers to the actual hours from start to end of the collector's day, including lunches and breaks. It is the standard number of hours required for the bank's policy. For example, if the collector's hours are from 8:30 AM to 5:00 PM, the total hours are 8.5.

2. Desired utilization percentage: The utilization percentage (1 through 100 percent) indicates the level at which the collector

is devoted to handling collection accounts. At 100 percent, collectors are handling accounts one after another, with no gaps in the flow of work or outbound calls. The lower the percentage, the more time exists between accounts and, therefore, the collectors are not fully utilized. Care must be taken when selecting an actual percentage. On one hand, exceeding 100 percent may be detrimental, causing overwork and backups in queue. On the other hand, targeting a utilization percentage that is too low would be an inefficient use of personnel. The optimal percentage is one that is challenging yet allows enough gap time so accounts are properly handled.

Delinquent Account Volume

1. Account volume: The actual number of delinquent accounts categorized by stage of delinquency for the indicated month. Input the actual value in the brackets for each month by the stages of 30, 60, 90, and 120+ days delinquent.

Fixed Hours

The fixed hours are designated percentages that correspond to the three areas of regularly occurring activities. These activities do not relate to the key volume indicator (handling collection accounts), but rather to the other demands on time for the average collector.

1. Personal: Lunches, breaks, and other miscellaneous personal time spent away from the job are accounted for in this category. The information is determined from the call center representative survey and calculated using the format in the data-gathering section of this chapter. The model calls for a percentage to be input into the designated section.

2. Administrative: This represents the fixed time devoted to meetings, training, and other administrative tasks. Again, input a percentage.

3. Other duties: This set of activities involves all other functions that are performed regularly by the collector—for example, report distribution, account maintenance, or other activities, if applicable. This is also a percentage.

Variable Hours

The last area requiring input is the most important: the number of hours required to handle a single collection account by the four stages of delinquency. The appropriate response for this space will be a decimal. For example, a factor of 2 minutes would equal .034 hours, and a full hour would be 1.00. Translate the data into hours so that the model can run properly. This information should be taken directly from Figure 208. Although it is possible to change these numbers based upon the criteria used, the factors contained in Figure 208 can and should be used as accurate representations of the collection time per account.

Once all fields are input, the model is complete and the actual analysis/result is performed instantly. Figure 210 is a completed example of the model.

ANALYSIS, MEASUREMENT, AND USE

The previous sections defined the elements of the model and the process of determining the appropriate data to use. This last section discusses the usage and benefits of the staffing analysis and approach.

Whenever the model is run, some form of analysis must follow to draw conclusions from the data presented. This begins with an understanding of the current collection department. A comparison is made between the actual level and the staffing level determined in the model to reveal whether or not the location is under-, over-, or appropriately staffed. Using the data in Figure 210, the analysis is best outlined in a report similar to Figure 211. From this report, further data can be determined that will indicate the financial impact the result has on the organization.

In Figure 211, it appears that an understaffed situation of .78 FTE collectors has been determined. Increasing the staff by the number indicated is necessary based upon the volume of delinquent accounts. This is a fairly obvious conclusion to draw from the data presented. If data gathering and model building were done properly, the results are reliable.

F I G U R E 210

Completed Collection Department Staffing Model

BANK: [First National] COLLECTION DEPARTMENT STAFFING MODEL   PERIOD: [1/96–12/96]
BRANCH: [Main   ]
LOCATION: [Anytown, USA]
             [   ]

A. DATA REQUIRED

    1. AVERAGE NUMBER TOTAL HOURS PER FTE, PER DAY: [8.5   ]
    2. DESIRED COLLECTOR UTILIZATION PERCENT: [100.0%]

B. DELINQUENT ACCOUNT VOLUME (by month volume):

	JAN	FEB	MAR	APR	MAY	JUN	JUL	AUG	SEP	OCT	NOV	DEC	MONTHLY AVERAGE
1. 30 day:	[925]	[901]	[1,074]	[1,074]	[1,074]	[1,074]	[1,074]	[1,215]	[1,119]	[1,069]	[822]	[979]	1,038
2. 60 day:	[256]	[194]	[250]	[250]	[250]	[250]	[250]	[211]	[412]	[294]	[293]	[241]	263
3. 90 day:	[142]	[137]	[150]	[150]	[150]	[150]	[150]	[204]	[187]	[200]	[121]	[173]	160
4. 120+ day:	[100]	[99]	[95]	[86]	[95]	[100]	[110]	[110]	[115]	[120]	[120]	[120]	106
TOTAL	1,423	1,331	1,569	1,560	1,569	1,574	1,584	1,740	1,833	1,683	1,416	1,513	1,566

C. FIXED ACTIVITY HOURS: ‖ D. VARIABLE ACTIVITY HOURS (per delinquent account):
                                   ‖   WEIGHTED AVERAGE
                                   ‖   HOURS PER ACCOUNT
PERSONAL: [11.7%]   ‖
ADMINISTRATION: [2.0%]   ‖   COLLECTION CALLS:
OTHER DUTIES: [5.0%]   ‖   —30 day delinquent: [0.055]
                   ————————   ‖   —60 day delinquent: [0.065]
TOTAL   18.7%   ‖   —90 day delinquent: [0.103]
                   =====   ‖   —120+ day delinquent: [0.157]

E. STAFFING SUMMARY:

	MONTHLY HOURS REQUIRED	FTE REQUIRED	PERCENT TO TOTAL
COLLECTION TASKS:			
—30 day delinquent:	228	1.36	48.1%
—60 day delinquent:	68	0.40	14.4%
—90 day delinquent:	66	0.39	13.8%
—120+ day delinquent:	66	0.39	14.0%
PERSONAL:	29	0.17	6.1%
ADMINISTRATION:	5	0.03	1.0%
OTHER DUTIES:	12	0.07	2.6%
TOTAL:	475	2.82	100.0%

F I G U R E 211

Collector Staffing Comparison

As of date:_____			
Department	**Actual Staff Level**	**Required Staff Level**	**Over/Under-Staffed**
Collection	2.82	3.60	(.78)

When performing this type of analysis, round any fraction FTE totals down to the nearest whole number. In Figure 211, the .78 FTE staff shortage would actually round to 1.0 FTE. This is a more realistic approach than attempting to trim to part-time hours to account for the fraction.

If the collection department is shown to be understaffed, most bankers will not immediately go out and hire someone on the spot. Budgets must be considered, requisitions approved, and managers convinced that increasing the staff is fully justified. If this approach is followed, the model itself should be justification enough and can be accepted at face value. Still, the decision to add to staff is always a difficult one. The likely result of this scenario is that further questions will be posed, focusing on what can be done to avoid hiring additional people. Without a detailed staffing model, it is difficult to provide appropriate answers. With the model, however, very specific ideas for maintaining efficiency without adding to staff can be tested, with tangible results.

To accomplish this, the collection manager should display the model on a PC, including all data previously input. The next step is to evaluate each of the fixed and variable collection profile categories. The values contained on these lines have a great impact on the staffing levels determined by the model, and adjusting them would produce a different result. In other words, if administrative and other activities were reduced to 0 percent of a collector's day, the immediate result would be less staff required; however, if the utilization percent were also reduced to 75 percent then an increase in staff would be required (see Figure 212). The benefit of using the staffing model on-line is that the banker can perform various "what-if" scenarios with immediate feedback. This will guide the individual to determine the best approach.

In Figure 212, if administrative and other activities were reduced to zero, with utilization changing to 75 percent we might find that the department is understaffed and additional collectors are needed. But can this be done? The action required would be to virtually eliminate lunches, which is not a feasible solution to the problem. This leaves administrative, other duties, and collection account handling time, all of which are appropriate candidates for analysis.

If either the administrative or other duties percentage were reduced, no additional personnel would be required. For example, to reduce administrative activities, refer to the initial collection department survey form (Appendix K). This document shows exactly how much time is spent on various administrative activities (meetings, phone calls, etc.) From this, determine what activities might be eliminated or redirected. If too much time is being spent in staff meetings every week, control it by reducing their frequency and / or their length of each meeting.

The first step, then, in using the model is to set up hypothetical situations by adjusting the fixed activity percentages. If this provides the desired FTE staff level, the manager knows what areas (or activities) to focus on. When various activities and tasks are eliminated, the hypothetical percentages become the standard for future measurement.

The time required to handle each collection account should not be overlooked. Although this factor is produced from actual experience, it can still be changed. Several methodologies can be employed to improve this figure. Evaluating these opportunities begins with a review of the collector survey form. The collection manager can evaluate the types of calls made and the results obtained (busy, left message, no answer, etc.) and the frequency with which they occur. In many cases a particular type of result occurs more frequently than others. When this is known the collection manager can brainstorm to determine other methods of

F I G U R E 212

Modified Collection Department Staffing Model

```
BANK:          [First National ] COLLECTION DEPARTMENT STAFFING MODEL          PERIOD:  [  1/96–12/96  ]
BRANCH:        [Main          ]
LOCATION:      [Anytown, USA ]
               [              ]
```

A. DATA REQUIRED

    1. AVERAGE NUMBER TOTAL HOURS PER FTE, PER DAY: [8.5]
    2. DESIRED COLLECTOR UTILIZATION PERCENT: [75.0%]

B. DELINQUENT ACCOUNT VOLUME (by month volume):

	JAN	FEB	MAR	APR	MAY	JUN	JUL	AUG	SEP	OCT	NOV	DEC	MONTHLY AVERAGE
1. 30 day:	[.925]	[901]	[1,074]	[1,074]	[1,074]	[1,074]	[1,074]	[1,215]	[1,119]	[1,069]	[822]	[979]	1,038
2. 60 day:	[256]	[194]	[250]	[250]	[250]	[250]	[250]	[211]	[412]	[294]	[293]	[241]	253
3. 90 day:	[142]	[137]	[150]	[150]	[150]	[150]	[150]	[204]	[187]	[200]	[121]	[173]	160
4. 120+ day:	[100]	[99]	[95]	[86]	[95]	[100]	[110]	[110]	[115]	[120]	[120]	[120]	106
TOTAL	1,423	1,331	1,569	1,560	1,569	1,574	1,584	1,740	1,833	1,683	1,416	1,513	1,566

C. FIXED ACTIVITY HOURS: || D. VARIABLE ACTIVITY HOURS (per delinquent account):
                         || WEIGHTED AVERAGE
                         || HOURS PER ACCOUNT

```
PERSONAL:        [  11.7%  ]    ||
ADMINISTRATION:  [   0.0%  ]    ||   COLLECTION CALLS:
OTHER DUTIES:    [   0.0%  ]    ||     —30 day delinquent:       [  0.055 ]
                 ─────────      ||     —60 day delinquent:       [  0.065 ]
TOTAL               11.7%       ||     —90 day delinquent:       [  0.103 ]
                                ||     —120+ day delinquent:     [  0.157 ]
```

E. STAFFING SUMMARY:

	MONTHLY HOURS REQUIRED	FTE REQUIRED	PERCENT TO TOTAL
COLLECTION TASKS:			
—30 day delinquent:	305	1.81	50.2%
—60 day delinquent:	91	0.54	15.0%
—90 day delinquent:	88	0.52	14.4%
—120+ day delinquent:	89	0.53	14.6%
PERSONAL:	35	0.21	5.8%
ADMINISTRATION:	0	0.00	0.0%
OTHER DUTIES:	0	0.00	0.0%
TOTAL:	607	3.60	100.0%

obtaining numbers or increasing the likelihood of an actual contact, which is the goal. By breaking down the actual results it will become very clear where the manager needs to spend his time and attention. When too many left messages occur the manager may wish to shift the hours of work such that collectors are calling at times when they are more likely to contact the debtor. This will increase the odds of collection. This type of analysis is imperative to scientifically understand how to manage and improve productivity and efficiency. This will not occur on its own. The model is used to highlight and to point the collection manager in a direction for areas which may be controllable.

One topic not discussed is training. Although the model defines the steps and the amount of time required per delinquent account, and if the collector is successful in contacting people but does not collect money, something is wrong. Collection will not occur effectively if the collector is not able or well trained on controlling conversations and knowing how to ask for money in a way that will ensure success. The model itself guides the manager to utilize specific steps which are necessary for collection to occur. If the collection staff does this, yet does not collect money, the answer to this problem then is the collector's ability to talk with people over the phone. This is an area where only through training will progress occur. In this way the model can be used as a means of ruling out areas which are not at the root of the problem. The model will ultimately point at a direction to aid the manager. Furthermore, with "what if" analysis the manager can pinpoint areas that he or she can control and change to reduce staff and save money. This interactive staffing analysis feature is most beneficial when used in this manner.

These are but a few of the opportunities for analysis and improvement of efficiency. The model can help managers determine scientifically the optimal staffing level for the bank and the best ways to achieve it. The result is the development of standards for fixed and variable activities, which should be used to assess the average level of staffing for the collection department.

This book provides a uniform methodology for assessing collector staffing levels, but it does not mandate actual times that go into making up the standards. The major drawback of many approaches is that they generalize too much. Some banks rely on a ratio of collection accounts to the number of collectors based upon national or regional averages. The estimates produced from these will always be suspect because they do not take into account the different systems used by banks, different procedures, different policies, and different mixes of delinquency. For this reason, the model approach offered in this book tailors the results to the individual bank, leading to greater accuracy than the broad generalizations made from other methods.

Finally, once the analysis has been completed and the bank is comfortable with the results, the fixed and variable activity items should become the standard for the bank. They should be used for evaluating staffing levels periodically as time goes on. Running the model every six months or so will provide management with a level of comfort throughout the year and an opportunity to make adjustments should staff levels begin to grow.

SUMMARY

The focus of this chapter has been on staffing the collection department. The approach used in this chapter is similar to that found in all the others in this book. In this regard, the development of the staffing model and the elements which comprise the staffing analysis are defined in detail. The model itself is developed using Lotus 123, and each formula is outlined in the chapter so that it can be recreated by the reader at his or her leisure. Regardless of whether the model is actually developed or not, the chapter defines the elements that are important to consider when analyzing staffing for the collection function. Using the information contained in the chapter and the survey form, contained in appendix K, the reader can build a database of information from which a deeper understanding of the collection function and how it relates to staffing can be achieved.

What is different from other chapters, however, is that the variable activity time required for handling collection accounts is recommended rather than empirically derived. This is because the effective collection is standard—that is the tasks and steps are relatively clearly defined and are universal. Furthermore, experience dictates that following the procedures and times as defined will ensure that collection occurs with the appropriate level of delinquency resulting. In this regard the model requires very little input data, short of the volume of accounts and breakdown of fixed activities.

Finally, in other chapters the analysis section is most important. It is from this analytical mode that positive results occur in terms of improved productivity or efficiency. This represents the bottom line and thus the purpose for embarking on a campaign of analyzing staffing levels in key departments. With the advent of auto dialers and improved automation, the collection of delinquent accounts will become more and more efficient. This does not preclude the need for a staffing model. On the contrary, regardless of automation, the staffing model can and should be used as a means to constantly check progress and evaluate the current status of staffing levels.

## CHAPTER 7

Financial Institution Staffing, Consolidations, and Technology

Over the last 10 years (1985–95) the number of commercial banks in this country have dwindled by a startling 31 percent. By the turn of the century, this is expected to decline even further. If the current trend continues, there could be fewer than 8,000 commercial banks in the USA or less, a reduction of almost 50 percent from the 14,500 banks that existed in 1985. This is a monumental change and indicates that acquisitions and consolidations will become a normal occurrence in the next several years. The challenge this creates is the ability to assimilate a large, current labor force of financial institutions into a much smaller number of remaining banks.

These dramatic figures are not portents of doom but rather management challenges that require skill and precision to address effectively. Financial institutions have yet to move fully to automation. As a result, consolidating the staff of two or more organizations is not a simple matter of drawing straws but a complex process of understanding the size of the staff that is required in the combined entity. Care must be taken to understand newly combined workload volumes and predict staffing levels accurately and precisely.

Organizations that are acquisition oriented, or rather plan growth based upon acquisitions, must be prepared to accurately understand the optimum levels of staff required for several reasons. One major reason is to quickly and accurately determine the cost to run the consolidated bank. This will aid greatly in determining the appropriate price and financially determine the value of obtaining the entity. Additionally, of course, one must know what the staff compliment is so that the financial institution can be effectively managed.

For these reasons the need for scientifically derived staffing models is an absolute must. Given the preponderance of consolidations on the horizon, banks must act quickly to take advantage of acquisition opportunities which emerge on the market. Staffing models, as outlined in this book, emphasize areas of labor intensity within most technical institutions and, as such, can be effectively employed to predict and monitor ongoing staff levels.

ORGANIZATION AND METHODS FOR STAFF REDUCTIONS

Consolidating entities in the financial arena leads to some areas of duplication that require analysis. When consolidations occur, an organized plan for analyzing staffing levels must exist so that models can be applied to perform the actual prediction. In order to accomplish this effectively several steps are required, as follows:

1. Identify a consolidation coordinator.
2. Analyze areas of duplication and functional areas requiring staffing analysis.
3. Develop a planning template.
4. Run the staffing models.
5. Calculate the opportunities.

The next several pages will explain each of the above in detail.

Identify a Consolidation Coordinator

Analyzing staff compliments in a consolidation environment requires attention. The process begins early on, well before the
consolidation actually occurs. The consolidation coordinator is
responsible for initially developing a plan and analyzing the staff
compliments of the entity to be consolidated. Selection of the
consolidation coordinator should occur as soon as possible when
an entity is being considered for acquisition. Identifying this
individual early in the process will facilitate much of the due
diligence or preparatory work required for the initial planning of
the acquisition.

The consolidation coordinator should be well versed in acquisition and mergers and have broad familiarity with all aspects
of banking. This is important, as planning and assimilating the
acquired entity will require knowledge of many areas in order to
assess and plan for staffing needs. In this regard the coordinator
will, in all probability, be a member of senior management. The
role of the conversion coordinator, among other things, is to plan
for the human resource compliment both pre- and postacquisi-
tion. Pre-acquisition staffing assessments are necessary to establish a budget of staff size to be used in planning the acquisition
price, because incorrect figures can result in cost overruns detrimental to the combined entity.

Such coordination does not stop at external acquisitions
alone. Internal mergers, as well, require the same level of attention
and precision both pre- and postmerger. In short the coordinator
role is vital to the whole process.

ANALYZE AREAS OF DUPLICATION
AND FUNCTIONAL AREAS REQUIRING
STAFFING ANALYSIS

One of the first responsibilities of the conversion coordinator will
be to understand areas of overlap or duplication between the two
entities. Obviously, if a merger and consolidation is to occur there
will be a duplication of some departments. In these departments

it is absolutely vital to understand what the current staff compliment is and what it should be once a consolidation occurs. As previously stated, not all departments will be duplicated. In some cases an entity may have specialized functions requiring a separate department that doesn't exist at the acquiring bank, or vice versa. A decision usually must be made whether to continue to provide these services or functions in the new arrangement.

For the most part, however, the areas which likely will be duplicated will be as follows:

1. Deposit operations
2. Loan operations
3. Accounting
4. Bookkeeping
5. Customer service
6. Collections
7. Human resources
8. Proof
9. Information systems
10. Credit

In each of these areas, economies of scale can and should be attained as a result of the combination. This means that two plus two doesn't necessarily mean four. Usually there is enough capacity within each separate entity such that when the two organizations come together the full time equivalent (FTE) staffing will not equal the total of the two. In all of the above cases this should be true. Thus do organizations that come together achieve a savings in staff.

This is not to say, however, that economies cannot be achieved elsewhere. The newly consolidated entity should evaluate also the compliment of customers/clients that the bank is now serving, evaluating it against the size of the sales staff to support and maintain these clients effectively while at the same time determining the requirements for maintaining an adequate sales-force. One of the main purposes of this book is to enable the reader to quickly ascertain standard bank compliments through modeling, including analysis of the sales area. The purpose of identifying duplicate departments is to compare staffing compliments and determine what it should be, postconsolidation, as well as to understand the impact from a negotiation standpoint. The staffing models contained in this book are designed to provide consistency and be easily applied for quick analysis. The acquiring financial institution will always require an understanding of staff compliment for the very fact of its considerable impact on the bottom line and the success of the consolidation. Understanding areas of duplication and the dynamics of staffing will aid the institution in its ability to functional efficiently in the consolidated environment.

DEVELOP A PLANNING TEMPLATE

The planning template is a worksheet that identifies the areas of focus and the current and proposed arrangement of staff. If the financial institution is serious about optimizing staff in the pre- and postconsolidation environment, it is necessary to organize how this will occur. A template of sorts will provide the bank with a reservoir for capturing, organizing, and reporting information to the appropriate parties. It also serves as a working paper for easy reference to check progress or verify that projections have been attained. Figure 213 illustrates an example of a planning template.

The importance of this document becomes clear when action is taken to achieve or manage to the numbers contained on the document. Information should be as accurate as possible—major decisions will be made based upon it! Care should be taken in capturing the data that will be included in this document. This information is obtained during the due diligence which occurs prior to the consolidation of the new entity. The document contains categories for the acquiring entity and consolidated entity both. As shown in the example, full-time equivalents (FTE) are captured and recorded for each type, by department. The last columns contain the staffing numbers, determined from the staffing models and based upon the key volume indicators, required

F I G U R E 213

Consolidation Planning Template

Functional Department	Current FTE		Combined FTE	Key Volume Indicator	Combined Volume for Key Volume Indicators	Optimum Staffing Level	Net FTE Savings/ Opportunity
	Acquiring Bank	Acquisition Bank					
1. Deposit operations				DDA/Savings accts.			
2. Loan operations				Commercial/installment notes			
3. Accounting				Detail accounts			
4. Bookkeeping				Statements			
5. Customer service				Calls			
6. Collections				Delinquent accounts			
7. Human resources				FTE			
8. Proof				Encoded items			
9. Information systems				PCs/hardware			
10. Credit				Applications			
11. Tellers				Transactions			
12. Retail sales				Customers seen/ products sold			
13. Commercial sales				Loans made/renewed			

to run the staffing models. The final column compares the current staffing levels of the two entities: preconsolidation, determined from the due diligence; and postconsolidation determined from the staffing models. The difference between the two becomes the benefits gained from economies of scale. This is the bottom line, which becomes the objective in the consolidation process, from which cost estimates for running the combined entity are developed, and which are instrumental for developing the appropriate price to offer for the new entity.

Run the Staffing Models

Once the planning template is partially completed it is necessary to run the staffing models contained in this book to ascertain the levels estimated for the combined entity. Obviously, staffing model development requires other information, as identified in this book. Key volume indicators (i.e., the primary result or outcome of the particular department) are of vital importance in developing staffing models for usage. Examples of key volume indicators for the departments listed previously are contained in Figure 214.

A number of staffing models are contained in this book for this purpose. In some cases, however, a model may not exist for the department being evaluated. In this case the reader should still continue to capture current staffing level numbers, while at the same time obtaining actual volumes, which would be the key volume indicator. Staff level ratios should be assessed for the current organization as to the number of items in the key volume indicators to the FTE. The same ratio then can be applied to the combined entity to determine the optimum staffing level. This column is contained in the planning template and should be applied for all areas.

Calculate the Opportunity

The final step is to calculate the opportunity that should be associated with the consolidation. This is the primary reason for

F I G U R E 214

Key Volume Indicators

Department	Key Volume Indicator
1. Deposit operations	■ DDA, savings accounts
2. Loan operations	■ Commercial/installment notes
3. Accounting	■ Detail accounts (chart accounts by department)
4. Bookkeeping	■ Statements
5. Customer service	■ Calls
6. Collections	■ Delinquent accounts (by stage)
7. Human resources	■ Employees (FTE)
8. Proof	■ Encoded items
9. Information systems	■ PCs, hardware devices
10. Credit	■ Applications
11. Tellers	■ Transactions
12. Retail sales	■ Customers seen/products sold
13. Commercial sales	■ Loans made/renewed

proceeding with this exercise. During this process it is important to assess departments or areas of the bank that are not considered duplicate departments. Previously in this chapter, we discussed analyzing departments that would be duplicated in a consolidated environment. This is a must, because staff reduction will definitely occur in these areas due to economies of scale. However, one must not forget other areas of the bank that are not typically considered duplications. These too should be analyzed. Examples include the sales functions, both retail and commercial. The reason for this is that the procedures and systems of the acquiring bank may represent improvements over the financial institution being acquired, due to a platform automation system or other internal policies, standards, or goals. When the staffing model is run according to the steps outlined in this book for these two areas, the reader will most definitely be capturing specific data unique to the acquiring financial institution. When optimum staff levels are to be determined for sales, as in the planning template, the staffing model defined for the acquiring institution should be used when running it for the combined entity. In this way the parameters used in the model are unique to the financial institution acquiring the new entity. It is precisely the difference between the ways the entities perform their jobs, in terms of policies, procedures, and systems, that will create additional opportunities which should not be overlooked.

Action should be taken on the differences determined from this analysis. Obviously a financial opportunity should exist which results from the differences between the two groups. The dollar amount can be used in the pricing negotiation for the acquisition and will be instrumental in its financial success. The planning template should be readily accessible and used as a goal chart for comparing the actual results once action begins to be taken.

Growth of Technology in Banking

As mentioned earlier in the chapter, staffing should always be recalculated in terms of optimum levels because of the differences in procedures and work flows that necessarily exist between the entities. Many times these differences result from the systems deployed. In short, technology can play a significant role in minimizing and/or optimizing staffing levels.

During the decade of the 70s, when the microcomputer was born, futurists began to speculate upon the possibilities resulting from its power, such as a shorter work week and considerably improved efficiencies. In some cases these have been achieved; in others they have not. In any event, the nature and growth of technology promise tremendous innovations. In today's consolidating banking environment, the reduction of banks without erosion of access to product and services can only be achieved through technology. Organizations may be acquired in locations that are not near the home bank, to capitalize on a market area, and technology must be utilized to link branches and facilities to take advantage of such strategic sales opportunities.

As organizations consolidate, the challenge of effectively managing the staff remaining to man the bank grows. The continual focus must be on the efficiency ratio of the bank, major elements of which include both staff and premises. Technology must be challenged and applied to minimize the costs of both. One such method used today is telecommuting. Telecommuting involves the ability to work from home, accessing electronically all information required, as if the individual were in the office. IBM has effectively applied this strategy with their salesforce in recent efforts to rebound from financial challenges. Given the growing cost of physical space and premises, maximizing the utilization of space for the most cost-effective functions is a true necessity. Other applications of technology which have considerable impact on staffing levels consist of document imaging, video conferencing, and client server technologies. In all of these cases opportunities abound for cost savings as well as staff optimization.

Unfortunately, the real challenge for bankers in the 1990s and into the 21st century remains the effective utilization and application of new technologies in order to achieve the efficiencies they are designed to create. As previously mentioned, the power of the computer has not been realized as originally envisioned. Why? Is this a result of inadequately designed technology or application? In most cases it is likely the latter. We have yet to train and educate our managers on how to manage technology to achieve breakthrough benefits and apply it to achieve efficiencies. Once technology is provided, managers today seldom dramatically change the work processes to take advantage of its power. Particularly in banking we have not capitalized on this power. Managers typically justify the cost on a given set of savings, yet when the system is installed the procedures seldom change. When this occurs, the costs do not decrease but rather increase, with the net result of an eroding efficiency ratio. Therefore, the focus should be on developing programs to teach managers how to manage technology and to change behaviors and work processes to capitalize on it. Courses on how to use or navigate the technology exist, but not on how to manage the changes and opportunities created thereby.

Staffing opportunities, the focus of this chapter and book, can be dramatically improved through proper application of information technology and should not be overlooked. However, the requirements for a focus on optimizing staffing levels necessitate that managers understand that work processes can and must change to use technology. This creative effort must look at traditional work processes and be willing to alter them.

As consumers become more and more computer literate, and as more information becomes available to them, demand for products and services will continue to grow at startling rates. Traditional means of managing work processes will not work—indeed, they can literally put some banks out of business. Managers must focus on this change and reconsider the use and deployment of staff in order to keep up with highly intensive demand. The staffing models displayed and discussed in this book will become more and more important as we proceed. The key volume indicators in general will not change for the departments. What will change, however, is the time frames required to deliver the product or service as a result of technology. As this occurs, and hopefully it will, the new time frames required should be amended in the models and re-run. The resulting information will be reduced staff requirements. Therefore, staffing analysis and models should be used hand-in-hand with the proper application of information technology to both predict and manage to optimum staffing.

The Virtual Bank

Staffing today cannot be discussed without some reference to the virtual bank. The virtual bank has been a much discussed phenomenon of the current decade. Virtual banking cannot be accomplished without the application and utilization of information technology. As we proceed towards the end of this millennium it is very clear that things must change if we are to remain competitive, particularly given the speed with which technological advances are proceeding. Already the information superhighway is becoming a standard mode of communication for many organizations. In short, efforts must be made immediately in order to stay abreast of these changes.

Affecting consolidations in an acquisition mode which will create overnight growth will be effective only through the proper application of information technology and the optimization of costly staff. Management must have a scientifically derived model or formula for ascertaining the staff level to run a branch. The elements of this model will change when information technology is utilized. When consolidations occur today, many organizations seek entree into a particular market area which can add to their client base. Often times, however, the acquiring organization already possesses an operations center or other data center from which the support and back-office functions are performed. The newly acquired facilities are most often stripped of their functions and staff in lieu of the central operations. When this occurs, the surviving bank must be able to support and provide all of the features of a full-service bank to the location from a distant location or centralized operations center. This requires a wide area network and other electronic mechanisms for providing the needed information to a small, remote site, while simultaneously creating the ability to offer everything that a financial institution many times larger can offer but to a smaller site.

The virtual concept is important for banking in the future. If understood and used properly, staff compliments at remote facilities can be optimized, but at the same time they can be empowered or armed with the capability and information that previously required multiple, on-site support staff. In this regard effective consolidations can occur which will minimize costs without sacrificing quality or the amount of services and products offered.

Unfortunately, the virtual concept is only as effective as the financial institution's ability to provide this type of information and capability to the branch and, equally as important, its ability to understand the proper compliment of people required at the site. One might think this is simple. In reality, the most effective organizations in a consolidating world will determine the staffing compliment scientifically, not ad hoc. Scientifically derived staffing models or processes will not and should not be eliminated because of technology but rather be incorporated into the systems used. For example, teller systems are not microcomputer-based. Most systems easily capture and array transaction volumes entered into the systems. Since this is a primary ingredient of staffing models (certainly it is for the model outline in Chapter 1), a staffing model can be incorporated into the software to perform "what if" analysis with captured transaction data. The model can and should be used to calculate and present scheduling of tellers as well as determine optimal staff size. In short, models of this sort will only become more important and can become easier to use by incorporating them into the software used to perform the function. The models, elements, and concepts suggested for the sales staff can also be incorporated into platform systems for the personal bankers and commercial sales staff. Again, since platform systems are used to perform on-line, real-time transactions, information is already being captured and stored for use in a model, as suggested in Chapters 2 and 3.

In consolidations, the concept of scientific staffing analysis is incorporated into the systems currently in use. In other words it should become an integral part of the process of executing the functions. The data that is thus captured is true information, not impressions derived from tally sheets and observation. Although these latter two work effectively in a manual environment, the goal is to get the *most accurate data* possible on which to base decisions. Staffing is not simply a periodic exercise; it is almost a daily occurrence. The information is readily available anytime someone needs it, and it is integrated so that the daily or weekly reports incorporate an accurate assessment of the staff compliment.

SUMMARY

The one absolute that bankers can count on in the next several years is more change. As suggested at the start of this chapter, the world of independent banking is rapidly dwindling. This is a global phenomenon. Already there is foreign ownership of financial institutions in America. Information technology has created many opportunities for consolidations to occur at an unprecedented rate. As a result of this global downsizing, the concept of staff analysis and optimization becomes more and more important. Emerging technology creates tremendous opportunities every day, which affect work processes and the access to information. As this trend develops, its impact on staffing becomes an ever larger issue. Self-activated technologies, like automatic loan machines (ALMs), interactive ATMs, home banking (both direct and Internet), voice response systems, and wide variety of others are growing considerably. As time goes on, bank facilities may become self-activated financial centers that permit customers to perform banking services electronically, on their own, without live interaction. This will dramatically reduce the staff requirements at physical facilities. This scenario is yet to unfold; currently, bank clients still see physical facilities as important parts of who they bank with.

This chapter's purpose is to create an awareness of the changes afoot and provide a structure for developing plans for consolidations and managing staffing levels in a consolidating world. In order to effectively understand and apply the principles of staffing analysis one must have an approach. This chapter outlined the steps necessary for developing an organized campaign for assessing staff requirements for potential or existing consolidation scenarios. Given the changes occurring, this approach to staffing is necessary to ensure that the right price is offered, and once obtained, the acquired facilities are properly manned to ensure that costs are most prudently applied. An important element in this approach is to develop a template. The template serves as a guide both pre- and postconsolidation; its important purpose is to compare the requirements that were determined with actual results. Opportunity seldom happens independently. In most cases action must be taken to make the opportunity a reality. A scientifically derived staffing model can tell the banker what should be, but it cannot make this occur. The interpretation of this analysis requires organization on behalf of the manager, and for this reason the organization outlined was suggested.

The technology of virtual banking was also discussed. Financial institutions that capitalize on this power and integrate it into their business will reap significant rewards. Staffing models continue to play a key role, but must now be integrated into the microcomputer-based systems that are in current use. With the ratio of personal computers to employees in this country, for financial institutions, heading for the one-to-one level, the integration of staffing logic and intelligence into these systems will provide management with a wealth of accurate, timely data from which to monitor and assess staffing levels regularly, with little effort.

In short, the number of independent financial institutions is dwindling and will continue to do so. Correspondingly, the need for optimizing staff size will grow in importance to ensure effective utilization of human resources in conjunction with technical resources. The marriage of the two will be an important ingredient for success in this consolidating, changing environment.

A P P E N D I X   A

TELLER SURVEY DOCUMENT

Teller name: _____

Period (time): From: _____

To: _____

Bank: _____

Locations: _____

		Average Minutes per	
I.	**Personal**	**Occurrence**	**Frequency**
	A. Lunches	_____	_____
	B. Breaks	_____	_____
	C. Other	_____	_____

		Average Minutes per	No. of Occurrences
II.	**Administrative**	**Occurrence**	**per Month**
	A. Meetings	_____	_____
	B. Telephone calls:		
	Inbound	_____	_____
	Outbound	_____	_____
	Call transfer	_____	_____

		Average Minutes per	No. of Occurrences
III.	**Other duties**	**Occurrence**	**per Week**
	A. Drawer setup	_____	_____
	B. Drawer closing/balancing	_____	_____
	C. Count coin/currency	_____	_____
	D. Receptionist	_____	_____
	E. Filing	_____	_____
	F. _____	_____	_____
	G. _____	_____	_____
	H. _____	_____	_____
	I. _____	_____	_____
	J. _____	_____	_____

		Average Minutes per
IV.	**Window transactions**	**Transaction**
	A. Cashing checks	_____
	B. Depositing checks	_____
	C. Savings withdrawal	_____
	D. Loan payments	_____
	E. Traveler's checks	_____
	F. Money orders/cashier's checks	_____
	G. Savings cashback withdrawal	_____
	H. Utility payment	_____
	I. _____	_____
	J. _____	_____
	K. _____	_____
	L. _____	_____
	M. _____	_____

VI. Teller daily telephone call volume sheet

Day	Inbound	Outbound	Transfer
Monday			
Tuesday			
Wednesday			
Thursday			
Friday			
Saturday			
Total			
Monday			
Tuesday			
Wednesday			
Thursday			
Friday			
Saturday			
Total			

APPENDIX B

COMMERCIAL LOAN SURVEY QUESTIONNAIRE FOR COMMERCIAL LENDERS

Name: _____

Position: _____

Bank: _____

Division: _____

Location: _____

Date completed: _____

I. New and Renewed Loans

	Average Minutes/Loan	
A. Review and evaluation	**New Loan/New Customer**	**Renewed Loan/ Existing Customer**
1. Initial interview/analysis of request		
2. Review of business history		
3. Review of banking relationships		
B. Financial statement analysis		
1. Review and analysis		
C. Credit analysis		
1. Review of borrower's strengths/ weaknesses and character		
2. Collateral evaluation		
3. Review of management		
D. Loan structuring		
1. Pricing the loan		
2. Repayment terms		
3. Collateral adequacy review		
E. Approval		
1. Loan committee write up		
2. Presentation-supervisor		
3. Renegotiation and agreement		
4. Commitment letter		
F. Loan administration		
1. Documentation preparation and printing		
2. Note booking		
3. Note/document filing and safekeeping		
4. Collateral file development and safekeeping		
5. Credit file development and filing		
6. Funds disbursement		

II. Maintenance and Monitoring

	Minutes per Loan	Frequency per Year
A. Customer communication and relations		
1. Outside call to customer location (to include call report development)	_____	_____
2. Meeting with the customer in bank	_____	_____
3. Inbound call received from customer (problem, research, question, cross-sell)	_____	_____
4. Outbound phone call made to customer	_____	_____
5. Written correspondence to customer	_____	_____

	Minutes per Loan	Frequency per Month
B. Loan administration		
1. Overdraft report handled	_____	_____

		Frequency per Customer per Year
C. Monitoring		
1. Field audits	_____	_____
2. Financial statement analysis	_____	_____
3. Review/monitor compliance to loan agreement	_____	_____
4. Periodic review of loan documentation	_____	_____
5. Review of customer account balances	_____	_____
6. Collateral control review	_____	_____

III. Past Dues and Delinquencies

	Average Minute per Call	Average No. of Calls per Customer per Month
A. Phone calls to customers		
1. 15–30 days	_____	_____
2. 30–60 days	_____	_____
3. 60–90 days	_____	_____
4. 90+ days/workout	_____	_____

IV. Business Development

A. Potential customer contact	Average Minutes Required
1. Call received	_____
2. Call made	_____
3. Outside call to customer location	_____
4. Potential customer visit to bank	_____
5. Correspondence and follow up	_____

B. Strategy and planning	Average Time Spent per Week
1. Customer relationship report	_____
2. Potential market development	_____

C. Referral base development	Average Time Spent per Week	After Hours (Yes/No)
1. Community activities	_____	_____
2. Entertainment	_____	_____

V. Administration

A. Meetings	Average Minutes	No. of Times Held per Month
1. Sales meetings	_____	_____
2. Officer meetings	_____	_____
3. Training/seminars	_____	_____

B. Internal calls received/made	Average Time Minutes per Call
1. Internal call made	_____
2. Internal call received	_____

C. Special projects (if applicable)	Average Time Minutes per Month
1. Bank related	_____
2. Holding company related	_____

VI. Personal

A. Time away from job	Average Minutes per Occurrence
1. Lunches	_____
2. Breaks	_____
3. Other	_____

Commercial Loan Tally Sheet

Week of: _____

Name: _____

Please place a tally mark for each call as directed on the sheet below. This should be separated between maintenance-related and new business-related contacts. This should be completed for two (2) weeks, or two sheets.

Day	Internal Calls Received/ Made	Category	In-Person Meeting with Client		Telephone Calls		Corre- spon- dence (letters)
			At customer location	In bank	In- bound	Out- bound	
Monday		Existing customer					
		Potential customer					
Tuesday		Existing customer					
		Potential customer					
Wednesday		Existing customer					
		Potential customer					
Thursday		Existing customer					
		Potential customer					
Friday		Existing customer					
		Potential customer					
Saturday		Existing customer					
		Potential customer					
Total		Existing customer					
		Potential customer					

COMMERCIAL LOAN SURVEY QUESTIONNAIRE FOR SECRETARIES/ADMINISTRATIVE ASSISTANTS

Name: _____

Position: _____

Bank: _____

Location: _____

Date completed:_____

A. Administrative
**Average Minutes
Required/Item**

1. Typing
   - Internal memos _____
   - Miscellaneous reports _____
2. Telephone calls
   - Internal call made/received _____
   - Call routed to another _____
   - Message taken _____
3. General Administrative
   - Appointment scheduled _____
   - Meeting scheduled _____
   - Other _____

B. Personal

1. Lunches _____
2. Breaks _____

C. New/Renewed Loans
**Average Minutes
Required/Loan**

	New	**Renewed**
1. Typing		
■ Loan committee write-up	_____	_____
■ Commitment letters	_____	_____
■ Financial statement/credit analysis	_____	_____
■ Notes/documents	_____	_____
2. Loan Administration		
■ Credit file built and filed	_____	_____

D. Maintenance
Average Minutes/Item

1. Typing
   - Customer correspondence _____
   - Call reports _____
2. Telephone
   - Inbound phone call from customer _____
   - Outbound phone call to customer _____
3. Loan administration
   - Correspondence/call report filing _____
   - Payment handling _____
   - Advances/draws handled _____
   - Statements handled _____
   - Miscellaneous items filed in credit file _____
   - Other _____

Activity Tally Sheet

Volume Category	Tally	Total
Customer correspondence		
Call reports		
Internal memos		
Miscellaneous reports		
Items filed in credit file		
Payments handled		
Correspondence/call reports filed		
Advances/draws handled		
Statements handled		
Appointments scheduled		
Meetings scheduled		
Other _____		
Other _____		

Secretary/Administrative Assistant Tally Sheet

Week of: _____

Name: _____

Please place a tally mark for each call as directed on the sheet below. This should be completed for two (2) week, or two sheets.

Day	Inbound Calls Received from Customers	Outbound Calls Made to Customers	Internal Calls Made/ Received	Calls Taken and Rerouted	Messages Taken
Monday					
Tuesday					
Wednesday					
Thursday					
Friday					
Saturday					
Total					

COMMERCIAL LOAN SURVEY QUESTIONNAIRE
FOR LOAN OPERATIONS AND SUPPORT

Name: _____

Position: _____

Bank: _____

Location: _____

Date completed:_____

I. **Administrative**   **Average Minutes Required per Item**

  A. **Telephone call handling**
    1. Internal calls made/received   _____
    2. Calls rerouted   _____
    3. Messages taken   _____

	Frequency per Month	**Average Minutes**
B. **Meetings**		
1. Departmental	_____	_____
2. Other _____	_____	_____
C. **General administrative**		
1. Reports developed	_____	_____
2. Reports distributed	_____	_____
3. Other _____	_____	_____
4. _____	_____	_____
5. _____	_____	_____
6. _____	_____	_____

II. **Personal**

A. **Lunches**	_____	_____
B. **Breaks**	_____	_____

III. **New and renewed loans**   **Minutes per Item**

A. **Loan administration**	**New**	**Renewed**
1. Documentation	_____	_____
2. Notes booked	_____	_____
3. Note/documents filed	_____	_____
4. Collateral file developed	_____	_____
5. Credit file opened	_____	_____
6. Funds disbursed	_____	_____
7. Credit reports produced	_____	_____

IV. **Maintenance**   **Average Minutes per Item**

  A. **Customer communications**
    1. Inbound call received from customer   _____
    2. Outbound phone call made to customer   _____
    3. In-person meeting with customer   _____

B. Loan Administration

1. Loan closing/releases _____
2. Payment handling _____
3. Payoff handling _____
4. Document receipt and filing _____
5. Advances/draws handling _____
6. Statement handling _____
7. Filing customer correspondence and
   call reports _____
8. Overdraft report handling _____

C. Monitoring

1. Loan documentation review _____
2. Collateral review _____
3. Review/monitor compliance to loan
   agreement _____
4. Review of customer balances

Loan Operations/Support Tally Sheet

Day: _____

Name: _____

Please place a tally mark for each call as directed on the sheet below. This should be completed for two (2) weeks or two sheets.

Volume Category	Tally	Total
Documents prepared/printed		
Notes filed		
Documents filed		
Collateral files developed		
Credit files opened		
Funds disbursed (checks issued)		
Credit reports produced		
Loan closings/releases		
Payments handled		
Payoffs/paydowns handled		
Advances/draws handled		
Statements handled		
Correspondence, call reports, etc.		
Overdraft reports handled		
Documentation, collateral		
No. of times reports disbursed		
No. of reports developed		
Other _____		

Loan Operations/Support Tally Sheet

Week of: _____

Name: _____

Please place a tally mark for each call as directed on the sheet below. This should be completed for two (2) weeks or two sheets.

Day	Inbound Calls Received from Customers	Outbound Calls Made to Customers	Internal Calls Made/ Received	Calls Taken and Rerouted	Messages Taken
Monday					
Tuesday					
Wednesday					
Thursday					
Friday					
Saturday					
Total					

CREDIT ANALYST SURVEY QUESTIONNAIRE FOR CREDIT ANALYSTS

Name: _____

Position: _____

Bank: _____

Location: _____

Date completed:_____

Please record, in your experience, the amount of time, in minutes, it takes you to perform the indicated task/function for one loan. In your analysis of this, assume that the loan being made is a standard commercial term loan (equipment).

Record only the time you spend on this loan, not the time that other support personnel may spend on this.

I. New and Renewed Loans

	Average Minutes/Loan	
	New Loan	Renewed Loan

A. Financial Statement Analysis
1. Financial statement spread _____ _____
2. Ratio analysis _____ _____

B. Credit Analysis
1. Analysis of economic and local conditions _____ _____
2. Industry analysis _____ _____
3. Form of organization evaluation _____ _____
4. Review credit reports and strengths/weaknesses _____ _____
5. Financial statement/cash flow report development (as needed) _____ _____

C. Approval
1. Loan committee write-up _____ _____

II. Maintenance/Monitoring

A. Customer Communications — Minutes/Customer
1. Outside call to customer location _____
2. Call report development _____

B. Monitoring — Minutes/Customer — Freq./Customer/Year
1. Financial statement spread _____ _____

III. Business Development

A. Potential Customer Contact — Avg. Minutes Req.
1. Outside call to customer location _____
2. Phone call to customer _____

B. Strategy and Planning

Avg. Time
Spent/Month

   1. Customer relationship report   _____

   2. Potential market development   _____

IV. Administrative

	Avg. Minutes/ Session	No. of Times Held/Month
A. Meetings		
1. Sales meetings	_____	_____
2. Officer meetings	_____	_____
3. Loan committee meeting	_____	_____
4. Departmental meeting	_____	_____
5. Training/seminars	_____	_____

Avg. Time
Spent/Month
(Hours)

B. Special Projects/Analyses

   1. Special projects   _____

Avg. Minutes/
Call

C. Communications

   1. Internal calls received/made   _____

V. Personal

Avg. Minutes/
Occurrence

A. Time Away from Job

   1. Lunches   _____

   2. Breaks   _____

   3. Other   _____

Credit Analyst Tally Sheet

Week of: _____

Name: _____

Please place a tally mark for each call as directed on the sheet below. This should be separated between maintenance-related and new business-related contacts. This should be completed for two (2) weeks, or two sheets.

| Day | Internal Calls Received/ Made | Category | In-Person Meeting with Client | | Telephone Calls | | Call Reports |
			At customer location	In bank	In-bound	Out-bound	
Monday		Existing customer					
		Potential customer					
Tuesday		Existing customer					
		Potential customer					
Wednesday		Existing customer					
		Potential customer					
Thursday		Existing customer					
		Potential customer					
Friday		Existing customer					
		Potential customer					
Saturday		Existing customer					
		Potential customer					
Total		Existing customer					
		Potential customer					

PERSONAL BANKING SURVEY QUESTIONNAIRE
FOR PERSONAL BANKERS

Name: _____

Position: _____

Bank: _____

Location: _____

Date completed:_____

I. Business development

   A. Potential customer communications   **Avg. Minutes/Item**
      1. Phone call received
      2. Phone call made
      3. Telemarketing calls
      4. Outside call (visit)
      5. Correspondence/follow-up

   B. Strategy and planning   **Avg. Time Spent/Week**
      1. Market Development

II. Administrative

	Avg. Min./ Session	No. of Times/Month
A. Meetings		
1. Sales meetings		
2. Officer meetings		
3. Training/seminars		

   B. Telephone contact   **Avg. Minutes/Call**
      1. Internal (within bank) call made
      2. Internal call received

                                      Avg. Minutes/Month
   C. Miscellaneous duties

III. Personal

   A. Time away from job   **Avg. Minutes/Occurrence**
      1. Lunches
      2. Breaks
      3. Other

IV. New products sold

                           Average Minutes Required
   A. Loans   **(interview - approval)**
      1. Installment loan
      2. Home equity
      3. Overdraft line of credit
      4. Home improvement
      5. Student loan

B. Deposits

1. Demand   _____
2. Money market   _____
3. NOW account   _____
4. Savings   _____
5. Certificate of deposit   _____
6. Individual retirement account   _____

C. Non-deposit

1. ATM cards   _____
2. Safe deposit   _____
3. Credit cards   _____
4. Other   _____

V. Customers seen—not sold

A. Average interview/discussion time per customer not sold

_____

VI. Maintenance

A. Customer communication and relations   **Minutes per Item**

1. Outbound phone call to customer   _____
2. Inbound phone call received from customer   _____
3. Written correspondence to customer   _____
4. Outside call to customer location   _____
5. Meeting with existing customer in bank   _____

B. Servicing

1. Balancing/reconciling accounts   _____
2. Stop payment handling   _____
3. Wire transfer   _____
4. Loan payoffs   _____
5. Bank errors handled   _____
6. Other   _____

Personal Banking Tally Sheet

Week of: _____

Name: _____

Please place a tally mark for each call as directed on the sheet below. This should be separated between Maintenance related and New Business related contacts. This should be completed for two (2) weeks, or two sheets.

| Day | Internal Calls Received/ Made | Category | In-Person Meeting with Client | | Telephone Calls | | Tele-mar-keting Calls | Corre-spon-dence (letters) |
			At customer location	In bank	In-bound	Out-bound		
Monday		Existing customer						
		Potential customer						
Tuesday		Existing customer						
		Potential customer						
Wednesday		Existing customer						
		Potential customer						
Thursday		Existing customer						
		Potential customer						
Friday		Existing customer						
		Potential customer						
Saturday		Existing customer						
		Potential customer						
Total		Existing customer						
		Potential customer						

Personal Banker Services Volume Tally Sheet

Volume Category	Tally	Total
Beginning/Reconciling		
Stop Payments		
Wire Transfer		
Loan Payoffs		
Bank Errors Handled		
Other		

APPENDIX G

RETAIL SECRETARY SURVEY QUESTIONNAIRE

Name: _____

Position: _____

Bank: _____

Location: _____

Date completed: _____

I. Administrative

A. Typing

Average Minutes
Required/Item

1. Internal memos _____

2. Miscellaneous reports _____

B. Telephone calls

1. Internal calls made/received _____

2. Calls routed to another _____

3. Messages taken _____

C. General administrative

1. Appointments scheduled _____

2. Meetings scheduled _____

Average Minutes/Week

3. General filing _____

II. Personal

A. Lunches _____

B. Breaks _____

III. New products sold

A. Typing

1. Documents typed _____

2. Commitment letters typed _____

3. Other _____ _____

B. Account setup

1. Account file development _____

2. Documents, notes applications filed _____

3. Credit reports run _____

4. Other_____ _____

IV. Maintenance

A. Typing

1. Customer correspondence _____

2. Call reports _____

B. Telephone

    1. Inbound call from customer   _____

    2. Outbound call to customer   _____

C. Account administration

    1. Correspondence/call report filing   _____

    2. Payment handling   _____

    3. Statements handled   _____

    4. Stop payments/releases handled   _____

    5. Loan payoffs   _____

    6. Bank error resolution   _____

    7. Other _____   _____

Secretary Call Tally Document

Week of: _____

Name: _____

Please place a tally mark for each call as directed on the sheet below. This should be separated between Maintenance related and New Business related contacts. This should be completed for two (2) weeks, or two sheets.

Day	Internal Calls Received/ Made	Calls Routed to Another	Customer Calls		Total
			Inbound	Outbound	
Monday					
Tuesday					
Wednesday					
Thursday					
Friday					
Saturday					
Total					

Secretary Activity Tally

Volume Category	Tally	Total
Internal Memos Typed		
Miscellaneous Reports Typed		
Appointments Scheduled		
Meetings Scheduled		
General Filing		
Documents Typed		
Commitment Letters Typed		
Account Files Developed		
Documents, Notes, Applications Filed		
Customer Correspondence Typed		
Call Reports Typed		
Correspondence/Call Reports Typed		
Payments Handled		
Statements Handled		
Stop Payments/Releases Handled		
Loan Payoffs Handled		
Bank Errors Resolved		
Other		

RETAIL SUPPORT SURVEY QUESTIONNAIRE

Name: _____

Position: _____

Bank: _____

Location: _____

Date completed: _____

I. Administrative

A. Telephone Calls — **Average Minutes Required /Item**
1. Internal calls made/received
2. Calls routed to another
3. Messages taken

B. Meetings — **Freq./Month** — **Avg. Minutes**
1. Departmental
2. Training/seminars
3. Other ____

C. General administrative — **Avg. Minutes/Item**
1. Reports developed
2. Reports distributed

Avg. Minutes/Week
3. Miscellaneous filing

II. Personal

A. Lunches
B. Breaks

III. New products sold

A. Account setup
1. Documents development
2. Account/note input
3. Account file developed
4. Notes/documents filed
5. Funds disbursed
6. Credit reports produced

IV. Maintenance

A. Customer communications
1. Inbound call from customer
2. Outbound call to customer
3. In person meeting with customer

B. Account administration

1. Payment handling   _____

2. Loan/account closing   _____

3. Payoff handling   _____

4. Document receipt/filing   _____

5. Customer correspondence filing   _____

6. Other _____   _____

7. Other _____   _____

Retail Support Call Tally Document

Week of: _____

Name: _____

Please place a tally mark for each call as directed on the sheet below. This should be separated between Maintenance related and New Business related contacts. This should be completed for two (2) weeks, or two sheets.

Day	Internal Calls Received/ Made	Calls Routed to Another	Messages Taken	Customer Calls			Total
				In-bound	Out-bound	In-Person Visit	
Monday							
Tuesday							
Wednesday							
Thursday							
Friday							
Saturday							
Total							

RETAIL SUPPORT ACTIVITY TALLY

Volume Category	Tally	Total
Reports Developed		
Reports Distributed		
Documents Developed		
Account/Note Input		
Account File Developed		
Notes/Documents Filed		
Funds Disbursed		
Credit Reports Produced		
Payments Handled		
Loan/Account Closings		
Payoff Handling		
Document Receipt/Filings		
Customer Correspondence Filing		
Other		

HUMAN RESOURCES SURVEY QUESTIONNAIRE

Name: _____

Position: _____

Bank: _____

Location: _____

Date completed:_____

I. Recruitment/terminations   **Average Time (Minutes)**
                                                         Devoted/Month

   1. College recruiting
   2. General recruiting

                                       Average Minutes/Item

   3. Job posted
   4. Job description developed
   5. Ad placed
   6. Pre-screen application
   7. Interview scheduled
   8. Applicant interview conducted
   9. Pre-employment test administered
  10. Applicant communications (calls)
  11. Second interview scheduled
  12. Reference checking
  13. New employee orientation
  14. Employee termination
  15. Exit interview
  16. Pre-retirement counseling
  17. Outplacement processing

II. Employee relations and development   **Average Time (Minutes)**
                                                         Devoted/Month

   1. Employee newsletter
   2. Surveys
   3. Education/training
   4. Performance appraisals

                                         Average Minutes/Item

   5. Employee communications
      a. Internal call from employee
      b. External call to employee
      c. Meeting with employee
   6. Promotion/transfer/separation processing

III. Compensation

                                         Average Time/Month

   1. Payroll checks processed
   2. Incentive/banks/check processed

IV. Benefits Administration   **Average Time (Minutes)**
                                                        Devoted/Month

   1. Pension/profit sharing administration   _____

   2. Affirmative action   _____

   3. Recreational/social programs   _____

   4. Health/wellness programs   _____

   5. Flexible benefits plan administration   _____

   6. Safety/OSHA compliance   _____

**Avg. Minutes/
Item Processed**

   7. Insurance benefit claims

   8. Workmen's compensation claims

   9. Unemployment claim compensation

  10. Vacation/leave of absence processing

  11. Tuition reimbursement

  12. Relocation handling

  13. In-house medical services

  14. Childcare service

  15. New hires

  16. Terminations

V. General administration

**Avg. Time (Minutes)
Devoted/Month**

   1. General filing

   2. Departmental billings

Avg. Minutes/Item

   3. Telephone calls:

      a. External call made/received

      b. Phone message taken

      c. Phone call redirected

   4. Miscellaneous report

   5. Employee record filing

**Avg. Min./
Meeting**   **Freq./Month**

   6. Meetings:

      a. Departmental

      b. Training/seminars

VI. Personal

		Avg. Min.	Freq./Day
1.	Lunches	_____	_____
2.	Breaks	_____	_____

Human Resources Activity Tally

Date: _____

Employee: _____

Activity	Tally	Total
Job posted		
Job description developed		
Ad posted		
Applicant calls		
Pre-retirement counseling		
Outplacement processing		
Promotion/transfer processed		
Incentive/bonus checks processed		
Insurance claims processed		
Workmen's compensation claim		
Unemployment claims		
Vacation/leave of absence processed		
Tuition reimbursement		
Relocation handled		
In-house medical service provided		
Childcare service processing		
Miscellaneous report prepared		
Employee record filed		

Human Resources Call Tally

Day	Employee Communications				General	
	Call from Employee	Call to Employee	Meeting with Employee	External Calls Made/ Received	Message Taken	Call Redirect
Monday						
Tuesday						
Wednesday						
Thursday						
Friday						
Saturday						
Total						

CALL CENTER SURVEY DOCUMENT

Call center
representative name: _____

Period (time):   From: _____

                      To: _____

                    Bank: _____

               Locations: _____

		Average Minutes per Occurrence	**Frequency**
I.	**Personal**		
	A. Lunches	_____	_____
	B. Breaks	_____	_____
	C. Other	_____	_____

		Average Minutes per Occurrence	**No. of Occurrences per Month**
II.	**Administrative**		
	A. Meetings	_____	_____
	B. Training	_____	_____
	C. Other:	_____	_____
	_____	_____	_____
	_____	_____	_____

		Average Minutes per Occurrence	**No. of Occurrences per Week**
III.	**Other duties**		
	A. Telebanking (outbound)	_____	_____
	B. Research	_____	_____
	C. Switchboard	_____	_____
	D. Other:	_____	_____
	E. _____	_____	_____
	F. _____	_____	_____
	G. _____	_____	_____
	H. _____	_____	_____
	I. _____	_____	_____
	J. _____	_____	_____

		Average Minutes per Call
IV.	**Inbound Calls**	
	A. Balance inquiries	_____
	B. Check/deposits status	_____
	C. Stop payments	_____
	D. Account transfers	_____
	E. Errors	_____
	F. Statement questions	_____
	G. Rate information	_____
	H. Name/address changes	_____
	I. Other:	_____
	J. _____	_____
	K. _____	_____
	L. _____	_____
	M. _____	_____

V. Call center production form

Day	7–8	8–9	9–10	10–11	11–12	12–1	1–2	2–3	3–4	4–5	5–6	6–7	TOTAL
Monday													
Tuesday													
Wednesday													
Thursday													
Friday													
Saturday													
Sunday													
Total													

COLLECTION DEPARTMENT SURVEY DOCUMENT

Collector name: _____

Period (time):   From: _____

　　　　　　　　　　 To: _____

　　　　　　　　　　Bank: _____

　　　　　　　　Locations: _____

I. Personal	**Average Minutes per Occurrence**	**Frequency**
A. Lunches		
B. Breaks		
C. Other		

II. Administrative	**Average Minutes per Occurrence**	**No. of Occurrences per Month**
A. Meetings		
B. Training		
C. Other		

III. Other duties	**Average Minutes per Occurrence**	**No. of Occurrences per Week**
A. Report distribution		
B. Account maintenance		
C. Other:		
D. _____		
E. _____		
F. _____		
G. _____		
H. _____		
I. _____		
J.		

IV. Delinquent account handling

A. Production standards

	30	60	90	120+
1. Accounts worked per day per collector	125	100	75	50
2. Contacts per day	50	35	23	13
3. Noncontacts per day	75	65	52	37
4. Return calls	8	7	5	4

B. Activity time (minutes)

    1.   Talk time per contact   _____ _____ _____ _____

    2.   Noncontact time (times
        2 for second attempt)   _____ _____ _____ _____

    3.   Letter/notice time
        (per each account worked)   _____ _____ _____ _____

    4.   Order applications/bureaus
        per noncontact account   N/A   _____ _____   N/A

    5.   Skip tracing per noncontact
        account   N/A   N/A   _____ _____

    6.   Preparation of account per
        account worked   _____ _____ _____ _____

    7.   Notation time   _____ _____ _____ _____

C. Total time per activity (minutes per activity times production standard)

    1.   Talk time per contact   _____ _____ _____ _____

    2.   Noncontact time (times
        2 for second attempt)   _____ _____ _____ _____

    3.   Letter/notice time
        (per each account worked)   _____ _____ _____ _____

    4.   Order applications/bureaus
        per noncontact account   N/A   _____ _____   N/A

    5.   Skip tracing per noncontact
        account   N/A   N/A   _____ _____

    6.   Preparation of account per
        account worked   _____ _____ _____ _____

    7.   Notation time   _____ _____ _____ _____

    Total Minutes   _____ _____ _____ _____

÷   Accounts worked per day   125   100   75   50

=   Average minutes per account   _____ _____ _____ _____

÷   Minutes per hour   60   60   60   60

=   Average hours per account factor
    (input in model)   _____ _____ _____ _____

V. Collector production sheet

Collector: _____

Day/Date: _____

Type	7–8	8–9	9–10	10–11	11–12	12–1	1–2	2–3	3–4	4–5	5–6	TOTAL
Contacts												
Left message												
No answer												
Busy												
Disconnect												
Return call												
Total												

INDEX

Kent S. Belasco is currently Executive Vice President and Chief Information Officer for First Midwest Bank, N.A. based in Itasca, Illinois. He is responsible for all facets of information technology for First Midwest, including the application of technology and the attainment of benefits resulting from improved efficiency and productivity.

He received a B.A. degree from Lake Forest College and an M.B.A. degree from Lake Forest Graduate School of Management. He holds a C.P.A. certificate from the State of Illinois and C.F.P. certificate in Financial Planning. Currently, he is a doctoral candidate at Northern Illinois University finalizing the degree requirements for the Ed.D. degree in Business Education and MIS.

Before joining First Midwest Bank, he was employed by Deloitte Haskins & Sells as a manager in the financial institutions consulting practice. Prior to that, Mr. Belasco was with Exchange National Bank in Chicago, as vice president of productivity.

Kent Belasco is the author of other bank publications, including: *Bank Productivity, Managing Bank Conversion, Bank Systems Management,* and *Earnings Enhancement Handbook for Financial Institutions.*